Third Edition

Explorations

Conducting Empirical Research in Canadian Political Science

Loleen Berdahl & Keith Archer

OXFORD
UNIVERSITY PRESS

OXFORD
UNIVERSITY PRESS

Oxford University Press is a department of the University of Oxford.
It furthers the University's objective of excellence in research, scholarship,
and education by publishing worldwide. Oxford is a registered trade mark of
Oxford University Press in the UK and in certain other countries.

Published in Canada by
Oxford University Press
8 Sampson Mews, Suite 204,
Don Mills, Ontario M3C 0H5 Canada

www.oupcanada.com

First Edition published in 1998 by ITP Nelson Canada
Second Edition published in 2011 by Oxford University Press Canada

Library and Archives Canada Cataloguing in Publication

Archer, Keith, 1955–, author
Explorations : conducting empirical research in Canadian political science / Loleen Berdahl & Keith Archer. — Third edition.

Revision of: Archer, Keith, 1955-. Explorations.
Includes bibliographical references and index.
ISBN 978-0-19-900898-8 (pbk.)

1. Political science—Research—Textbooks. 2. Political statistics—Textbooks. I. Berdahl, Loleen, 1970-, author II. Title.

JA71.5.A72 2015 320.072 C2014-907617-7

Cover image: © iStock/yewkeo

Oxford University Press is committed to our environment.
Wherever possible, our books are printed on paper which comes
from responsible sources.

Printed and bound in the United States of America

1 2 3 4 — 18 17 16 15

Contents

Preface

Many students in political science, and in the social sciences generally, try to avoid research methods courses because they dislike or even fear math. Some resent being confronted with the very thing that they had designed their undergraduate program to avoid. Others are simply anxious about their ability: "Will this be the course that kills my GPA?"

To paraphrase former American president F.D. Roosevelt, you have nothing to fear but fear itself. If you can add, subtract, multiply, divide, and plug numbers into simple equations, you are as ready as you need to be. The content of this text is primarily conceptual. Our goal is to give you the tools required to think clearly about research issues in political science, to understand both the power and limitations of quantitative data. The math is there, but it is there as a form of conceptual understanding more than as a form of calculation.

Some contemporary research methods books shy away from mathematical computations altogether, recognizing that most students will be working with computer-based statistical packages that will effortlessly do the calculations for them. However, it is our belief that some hands-on familiarity helps students to acquire greater conceptual confidence. Statistical tests and measures can be difficult to understand in the abstract; thus, we will provide simple illustrations to allow you to work through the basic formulas. Furthermore, online video tutorials (indicated by ▶) will guide you through such topics as variables, IBM® SPSS® Statistics software ("SPSS"), and measures of association. We do not expect that you will abandon computer-based programs in favour of pencil and paper but that you will have some first-hand experience with the statistical terminology you will encounter in your own reading and research. You will be more comfortable with this terminology if you have had this opportunity.

In the chapters to come, we will take you through the steps involved in empirical research. How should you conceptualize a research problem? What evidence, or data, should you bring to bear on the problem? How do you measure the concepts you wish to address? How do you describe the research findings? What statistical tests might be used? Under what ethical guidelines should you operate? We will also engage you in the text material via "Apply Your Understanding" boxes, which allow you to test your own thinking and comprehension. These activities are not meant to be formal exercises with right and wrong answers but to invite you to think about the material and to apply it in familiar situations. The same objectives guide the discussion and study questions at the end of each chapter.

Throughout the text, we will bring real data into play through "Expand Your Knowledge" boxes. These sections are real-life illustrations frequently drawn from the kinds of surveys and reports that you encounter daily in newspapers and on television. Others, and perhaps the more important, come from the political science and social science literature. Our objective in both cases is the same: to illustrate how empirical research methods can be used to enrich and expand our understanding of the political world and, in some cases, to illustrate how mistakes can be made.

There is, then, an applied character to the text. But this approach should not imply an avoidance of normative issues. We recognize that an interest in the shoulds and oughts of politics is what draws many students into political science. We also recognize that normative questions cannot be reduced to empirical questions; knowing how the world *is* does not tell us how it *should be*. At the same time, a great deal of normative debate in politics and political science employs empirical evidence and understanding. Should there be seat-belt laws? Prohibition of smoking in public places? Controls on violence in television programming? Limitations on campaign spending in federal or provincial elections? Our answers to such questions partially depend on assumptions about empirical effects. Thus, a nuanced empirical understanding of the political world is a means to a richer normative debate and not a way of avoiding such discussion.

While this text emphasizes the benefits of using the scientific method in understanding and evaluating the empirical—or observable—world, it is also important to remain mindful of the method's limitations, particularly as they relate to the social sciences. Although the scientific method purports to be a way of understanding the world on the basis of observable facts, we will show that, at times, these facts are a matter of dispute. There are many possible reasons to explain different perceptions of reality, and these will be introduced and explored throughout the text.

Underlying this assumption about the importance of empirical understanding is the reality that research skills are essential in the contemporary labour market. An ability to design, conduct, and, more commonly, assess empirical research is no longer a frill; it is rapidly becoming a necessity. Research literacy is as essential to today's job market as literacy was to the job market of earlier generations. We are convinced that, of all the courses you take, research methods courses are the most immediately relevant to getting and keeping a job.

Finally, we would like to emphasize the thematic intent of the book's title, *Explorations*. It is not our intent to give the last word on empirical research methodology, for the field is rich, vast, and complex. We hope to open some doors, to provide you with a rough understanding of empirical research in political science. Our aim is to equip you with both the basic skills you need to handle research material and an appreciation of the strengths and weaknesses of empirical research. The text, then, is no more than a preliminary exploration. The destinations identified for each chapter are not final but are way stations on what, for many readers, will undoubtedly become a much longer journey. For others, we trust that you will find the exploration interesting and helpful as you continue to run up against political issues and debates throughout your life.

A number of people assisted in the writing of this new edition. We thank the anonymous reviewers and the following who took time to comment on the manuscript: Kelly Blidook, Memorial University of Newfoundland; Elizabeth Bloodgood, Concordia University; Jason Roy, Wilfrid Laurier University; and Ruben Zaiotti, Dalhousie University.

We thank Roger Gibbins for his work as co-author on the first edition and for supporting our revision of the text. We also extend our appreciation to Martin Gaal (University of Saskatchewan), Erick Lachapelle (Université de Montréal) Alexandre Morin-Chassé (Université de Montréal), Natasja Treiberg (Athabasca University), Linda Trimble (University of Alberta), and Jared Wesley (University of Alberta and University of Manitoba) for their contributions to the third edition. Finally, we thank our respective families for their support during the revision process: Troy, Katie, and Zoë Berdahl; Lisa Hurst-Archer and Justin, Alison, Ben, Will, and Isaiah Archer; and Caitlin, Jeff, and Kaia Montgomery.

PART I

Conducting Political Science Research

Many of you will be enrolled in your first course in political science research methods. Some of you might even be coming to this course, and this book, with a sense of trepidation about the math involved in political science research. Many of the students we've taught have expressed such concerns. So, let's be frank about this matter at the outset. This book introduces a number of techniques that can be used to assess the strength of relationships between variables, and we often represent these relationships by using quantitative data. This approach means that we will be counting and grouping people's responses to assess how strongly one characteristic is related to another. To help summarize these relationships, a number of statistical techniques—based on mathematical formulas—are introduced.

This book, therefore, includes some math. However, political science research involves much more than conducting tests of the relationships between variables. We begin with a broader discussion of the use of the scientific approach in studying politics. Many of you are enrolled in a course in a department of political science. Although a couple of generations ago such a department might have been called political economy or simply politics, today it is more common to refer to the discipline and the university or college department as political science. Chapter 1 considers what such a label implies for the ways people in this academic discipline gain knowledge and understanding of their subject matter. In Chapter 2 we differentiate between quantitative and qualitative approaches to politics, which are both valid and useful. We emphasize the quantitative approach but expressly consider qualitative approaches in several chapters.

The discussion then turns to applying the scientific method to the study of politics. In Chapter 3, we ponder the role that theory plays in our empirical models and examine the degree to which we can use quantitative methods to identify causal relationships in politics. This chapter also introduces the idea of testing hypotheses as a way of conducting empirical research and identifies a number of alternative models for such hypothesis-testing.

Chapters 4 and 5 raise the question of how political scientists define concepts in the research and how such concepts are "operationalized" as variables that can be measured. The language used in political science research must be precise so that, when a term is used to describe a phenomenon, there is as little confusion or disagreement as possible regarding the meaning of that term. As we'll see, achieving this goal is more difficult than it might seem.

This part concludes with Chapter 6, a discussion of ethics as it relates to conducting research on human beings. Such research requires that subjects be treated with respect and dignity and that a number of safeguards be in place to ensure compliance with such an expectation.

These chapters set the stage for the more detailed discussions in Part II, concerning research design and data collection, and Part III, focused on data analysis. The goal is to ensure that you understand each stage of the research process and, by following the steps outlined throughout the text, become more informed consumers of political science research. You will begin to develop tools to conduct your own projects as well.

CHAPTER 1

The Scientific Approach to Politics

Destination

By the end of this chapter, you should be able to

- state the distinction between normative and empirical analysis;
- explain the idea of science in political science;
- outline the basic postulates of science;
- describe the general methodology of science as applied to the more specific study of politics; and
- discuss some of the limitations and critiques of the scientific method.

One of the goals of an undergraduate education, and particularly of a course in research methods in the social sciences, is to help students think critically, by which we mean to reject arguments unless they are accompanied by sufficiently compelling evidence. Critical thought involves weighing and evaluating the merits of evidence marshalled in support of an argument. Researchers ask whether they understand the evidence and interpret its implications in the same way that others do. If the evidence is found wanting, either because it fails to provide sufficiently strong support or because it does not bear directly on the argument, the argument can be rejected. Thus, the ways in which we perceive and interpret evidence are two key aspects of critical thought.

An aim of the **scientific approach to politics** is to use critical thought as a guide to our perceptions of the political world. Boldly stated, the scientific study of politics attempts to provide a method whereby observations of the political world can be relatively independent of the observer. Stated more cautiously, it can help in determining when and why political perceptions differ.

Not surprisingly, this book takes the view that pursuing the goals of **scientific analysis** is worthwhile. Yet we accept the premise that most political research falls far short of the goal of providing similar observations and interpretations of political reality. A good deal of our attention will be focused on understanding why political scientists so often disagree about so many of the most fundamental questions of politics. This discord does not mean that our understanding of politics has not progressed. On the contrary, much knowledge has been gained. In some areas of political science, including the study of voting, elections, and political belief systems, the scientific approach has so transformed both political practice and research that they are unrecognizable from earlier generations. Nonetheless, the scientific approach to politics is not a simple template that can be applied holus-bolus to any political problem or research question. Its application requires detailed and careful attention from students and researchers alike.

An example of a divisive issue may help illustrate the role of the scientific approach. One of the most common features of political life in advanced industrial democracies is the persistence of female underrepresentation in legislative assemblies. In the 2011 Canadian general election only 76 of the 308 people (24.7 per cent) elected to the House of Commons were women. Hence, the fact that women are underrepresented in legislatures can scarcely be disputed. Far more controversial are the explanations that account for this finding. Some argue that women are underrepresented out of choice, that they are less inclined than men to seek elective public office. This explanation can be broken down into the following propositions: (1) women and men are socialized to have different preferences and/or (2) women and men have different responsibilities throughout the life cycle that, for instance, place a greater onus on women for child-rearing and thereby allow men to engage in other activities, including participating in political parties and seeking election. Another possible explanation is the systematic bias against strong women candidates that may exist in political parties. That is to say, the parties may present barriers that make it difficult for female candidates to win nominations for office, particularly in highly competitive ridings.

Which of these three explanations for the underrepresentation of women in legislatures is the most accurate and informative?[1] The answer is important because it can have profound implications for public policy. If female underrepresentation is caused mainly by the parties systematically excluding women, the solution (assuming one believes, as we do, that this is a problem) may be quite different than if it stems largely from gender-specific differences in either the life cycle or socialization. (Each of these explanations may contain a partial truth about the causes of differences in political representation.) The key feature of the scientific approach to politics is that it requires the formulation of testable hypotheses (see p. 59–60) and the marshalling of empirical data that can confirm or fail to confirm the hypotheses. It provides a way of applying empirical data to normative questions and public policy debates.

Normative and Empirical Analysis

The goal of all political analysis is to advance our knowledge and understanding of the political world. There are two dominant forms of political analysis: normative and empirical. **Normative analysis**, the realm of political theory and philosophy, is prescriptive in nature and addresses how society and political life should be. Because it entails the discussion of ideals, this form of political analysis is infused with value judgments and preferences. Normative discussions invoke convictions and feelings, things that are terribly important but difficult to measure and observe empirically in day-to-day life. In addition, people bring different values, priorities, and moral perspectives to their observations, which creates disagreements about the "truth" of normative statements. For example, both sides of the capital punishment debate are presented as fact in statements such as "It is wrong to kill anyone, even murderers" and "It is wrong to allow those who take life to continue life." The position that one sees as true depends upon one's own values and beliefs; the distinction is normative, not factual. We can identify normative analysis by the use of value-laden terms such as *good, bad, right, wrong, should, must,* and *ought.* Many political debates concern normative issues because people often disagree about what ends should be sought and the best means for reaching them.

The second branch of political analysis is **empirical research**. Empirical political analysis is descriptive in nature; the goal is to describe and to explain the political world as it is rather than as it should be. Whereas normative analysis is self-consciously value based, empirical research purports to be more fact based. Factual evidence is gathered from the physical and social worlds; unless a phenomenon can be observed (experienced through the senses), it cannot be considered admissible evidence (Singleton et al. 1988, 31). Knowledge obtained from methods other than observation—such as faith, intuition, or common sense—is not considered empirical knowledge. This statement is not meant to discredit other ways of knowing but to emphasize the distinction between empirical and non-empirical knowledge.

Empiricism requires observation and therefore measurement. Empirical facts must be independently observed and agreed upon by many people. This quality is known as **intersubjectivity**. How one observes an event is ultimately subjective—as those who have witnessed a car accident can attest, there are often two, three, or even six sides to every story. By requiring that more than one person observe and give a similar account of the event, we are able to increase objectivity. Intersubjectivity also requires that more than one observation occur; in the scientific process this practice is known as **replication**. Researchers seek out evidence that confirms the findings of other researchers, thus checking the latter's observations. The more people who observe a phenomenon and the more times it is observed, the more willing we are to accept it as fact. An empirical statement does not indicate preferences or values but presents observable facts.

A key issue for empirically based research is the degree to which facts exist independently of the observer. Witnesses to an accident quite literally perceive things very differently. With the attendant legal and financial implications of an event such as a traffic accident, it may be

Expand Your Knowledge

Normative and Empirical Approaches to Democracy: Robert Dahl

An interesting example of the difference between the normative and empirical approaches to political analysis is seen in the work of Robert Dahl, who devoted much of his long academic career to the study of democracy. Initially, he worked as an empiricist, seeking to explain how democracy works. In *Who Governs?* (1961), Dahl explored the distribution of power in New Haven, Connecticut. He found that, although power appears to be concentrated in political elites, interest groups have great influence on the decisions elites make, leaving government to act more as a referee between conflicting interests than as a powerful decision-maker with interests of its own. Dahl assumed that all relevant social interests could form groups to lobby the government and that all groups have political weight. From these assumptions, he concluded that democratic politics is not elite dominated.

The idea that democracy is a contest among numerous groups and "potential" groups is asserted by the pluralist school, which has been challenged empirically on many fronts. Critics include public choice theorists, who argue that not all interests are equally likely to form lobby groups, and neo-Marxists, who argue that powerful corporate interests have greater status than non-economic elites in the battle between interests.

Two decades later, the normative component of Dahl's writing emerged more clearly. In *Democracy and Its Critics* (1989), Dahl distinguishes between the ideal and practice of democracy. He defines political orders based on democratic practices—such as free elections, inclusive suffrage, freedom of expression, and representative government—as polyarchies rather than as democracies. Polyarchy can be empirically observed: if a country has democratic institutions, it is a polyarchy. Dahl reserves the word *democracy* for the ideal toward which all polyarchies strive, the system under which liberty and self-development flourish. He writes (1989, 322):

> In my view, neither political equality nor the democratic process is justified as intrinsically good. Rather, they are justified as the most reliable means for protecting and advancing the good and interests of all persons subject to collective decisions. . . . [Political equality is] an essential means to a just distribution of freedom and to fair opportunities for self-development.

Thus, Dahl's later work clearly makes normative judgments: liberty is good and, given that democracy is the best means to liberty, democracy should be pursued.

in the interest of those concerned to observe things differently: neither driver wishes to be charged with a traffic offence nor have his or her insurance premiums rise. There may be an incentive, either conscious or unconscious, for perceptions of reality to be distorted.

Some researchers regard this particular example of "fact" filtering as generalizable in perceptions of the social and political world. In this view, facts are not completely objective, but perceptions of fact are influenced or mediated by the social and political context of the observer. To the extent that this statement is true, it may be difficult to fully separate facts and values or the empirical and normative aspects of the study of politics.

There are other ways in which normative and empirical analysis overlap in the study of politics. Empirical research is used to question the conclusions of normative analysis, and normative analysis often employs empirical facts in its arguments. Consider environmental debates. Environmentalists state empirical facts—changing climate conditions, endangered species—before stating normative positions: we should reduce emissions, clean up the oceans, and so on. Similarly, opposition to the environmental movement's normative positions contains appeals to empirical fact. Julian Simon (1995, 11) strongly asserts, "Every measure of material and environmental welfare in the United States and in the world has improved rather than deteriorated . . . there is every scientific reason to be joyful about the trends in the conditions of the Earth." Some of the most contentious environmental debates occur when there is no concrete, agreed-upon empirical evidence. For instance, do harp seals really deplete cod stocks? Is the global temperature increasing, or are we just witnessing short-term fluctuations around a constant norm? Is it safer to transport bitumen from the Alberta oil sands to the west coast of British Columbia by rail or by a dedicated oil pipeline? While this text is concerned with empirical research, you should note how frequently empiricism is used in normative debates.

APPLY YOUR UNDERSTANDING

Normative and Empirical Statements

Identify the following statements as either normative or empirical:

1. Seat belt usage decreases automobile-related fatalities.
2. Seat belt usage ought to be mandatory.
3. Democracy is the best system of government available.
4. Democratic systems, on average, have better human rights records.
5. In terms of demographic weight, women are severely underrepresented in legislatures.
6. The electoral system should be changed to ensure a more representative legislature.

In assessing these statements, note the impact that specific words can make. In the fifth statement, does the addition of the adverb *severely* affect your categorization of the statement as normative or empirical? Can *better* in statement four be evaluated in empirical terms, or is it inherently normative?

What Is Science?

At its root, **science** is a set of rules that help us understand the world around us. The rules describe *how* we know, not *what* we know. Science is a method for acquiring knowledge rather than the knowledge itself. We would call something science not because of the subject that was being studied but because of the way in which it was being studied. If a study is done according to the rules of science, it is science. The scientific method consists of formulating hypotheses about the causal relationship between **variables** and empirically testing the hypotheses. The goal is to ensure that many observers, acting independently, will make similar observations and draw similar conclusions about the cause-and-effect relationship.

Natural and Social Sciences

By understanding science as a method of gaining knowledge, we can extend the application of the scientific method beyond the natural sciences of physics, chemistry, and the like to include the social science areas of human interactions in social relations. This expansion has given rise to the development of social scientific research in the areas of anthropology, archaeology, economics, political science, sociology, and others. (Whether psychology is a natural or social science depends upon the branch of the discipline.) As we will see, applying the scientific method to social relations brings with it a number of attendant problems, some related to science generally and others more specific to studying people. While researchers need to be aware of these limitations, they usually find that the advantages of the scientific approach far outweigh its disadvantages.

One significant difference between much of the research in the natural versus social sciences is the amount of control that the researcher has over the research setting. The laboratory, a site for highly controlled experiments, remains a mainstay of much research in the natural sciences. As a result, researchers have a high degree of success in isolating the few variables selected for study. In the social sciences, by contrast, the laboratory is replaced for the most part by field research, whether through survey research, participant observation, focus group analysis, or other methods. These methods, which we will discuss in later chapters, provide a variety of ways to attempt to control for extraneous factors, but in general they are less efficient in doing so than are controlled laboratory experiments. The result is that alternative **independent variables** may **confound** the analysis. However, as we discuss in Chapter 11, there is a growing interest within political science in the use of experimental approaches. In this field, experimental **treatments** are sometimes isolated.

A second difference between the natural and social sciences is the level of agreement within the scientific communities about the meaning and measurement of concepts. For example, physicists share a common understanding of such terms as *mass*, *density*, *heat*, and *speed*. According to Thomas Kuhn (1962) in *The Structure of Scientific Revolutions*, such agreement characterizes mature sciences, enabling the progression from one **paradigm** (a framework for understanding) to another. By contrast, the social sciences are characterized by considerable disagreement over the definition and measurement of key terms. Disagreement persists—and perhaps always will—over the definition of terms such as *democracy*, *effective representation*, and *social class* (a topic explored in more detail in Chapters 4 and 5).

A third difference between the two branches of science is the degree of determinacy of the results. In the natural sciences, the goal is to derive laws of behaviour. In the social sciences, the presence of human agency—free choice—means that outcomes are never completely determined. Instead of deriving laws of behaviour, the social sciences use probability in stating the generalized form of causal relationships. The discipline tends to use probabilistic statements such as "Young people are less likely than the middle-aged to participate in politics" rather than deterministic phrases such as "Young people participate less in politics than do the middle-aged."

Despite these differences, the scientific method has a number of features that make it an attractive **epistemology**, or approach to knowledge. One strength is that it attempts to remove, or at least to minimize, the effect of the observer on the observed. Two people working independently of each other to explore a given topic and using the same methodology under similar conditions should perceive the same result. In this respect, the scientific method begins with the assumption that no single observer is uniquely suited to perceive the real world in ways that are denied to all others. Because of the independence of results from observers, no observer is inherently better able to acquire scientific knowledge. This principle points to the central place that replication has in science. If the results of a scientific study cannot be independently verified, they are not accepted as an addition to that area's body of knowledge. Therefore, it is essential that results of scientific research are reported in ways that enable others to verify them through repeated testing of the empirical relationships.

A second strength of the scientific approach results from its orientation toward cause and effect. In all scientific research, there is some outcome or set of outcomes that one wishes to explain. This outcome, or effect, must be clearly stated and defined. There must also be at least a minimal amount of **variance** to be explained. In other words, there must be some change over time or across space or differences in outcome patterns across cases in the **sample**. We could not explain, for example, why people voted (voter turnout) in an election if everyone voted because there is no variance in electoral participation to explain. The causes of voting (or non-voting) could be examined only if a comparative referent was introduced by including a set of non-voters in the database.

The task of the research then becomes one of finding which characteristics cause people (or cases) to vary in outcome. Research will usually involve testing the strength of alternative causes of an outcome. Continuing with the example of the likelihood of voting, we could speculate that education may be a factor that affects turnout: people with a higher level of education are more likely to vote than those with lower education. This idea is called a research **hypothesis**. We are proposing (hypothesizing) that increased education leads to an increased tendency to vote. At the outset of the research we do not know whether or not this hypothesis is true. But for a variety of reasons (other research that we have read, our personal experience, our intuition), we believe that it may be. However, there will be other probable or at least possible causes of voting turnout that we wish to examine. An alternative hypothesis here is that people with higher incomes are more likely to vote than people with lower incomes. Still another is that people who are more interested in politics are more likely to vote than those who have no such interest.

Each of these hypothesized causes of voting focuses on the characteristics of individuals. If we were using cross-national data, different characteristics of the political system could be used to explain differences in turnout. We might hypothesize that voting is more likely in those systems that minimize the costs of voting, such as those that register voters automatically. In addition, the perceived closeness of the race, the frequency of elections, and the differences between political parties or between governing coalitions could lead to differences in turnout rates. By highlighting the importance of the cause-and-effect structure of research hypotheses, the scientific approach ensures that research remains targeted at evaluating alternative causes of phenomena and rejecting those that are less powerful.

A third strength of the scientific approach is that it can be used to explain and predict events or outcomes. The approach assumes that there is an order and a structure to the real world and that, through a careful application of the methods of science, the order can be known and understood. This assumption of patterned behaviour, based on relationships of cause and effect, implies that we can gain knowledge of the present and, through that knowledge, predict future behaviours or events. Both the explanations of present events and the predictions about the future are themselves subject to further empirical verification.

Finally, the scientific approach tries to draw lawlike generalizations about the real world. Our understanding of specific events or outcomes, although useful in its own right, is of greater value to the extent that it reveals a more enduring quality about relationships among phenomena. It may be highly useful to know what effect, if any, the mortgage-lending practices of Canada's banks had on the country's housing market stability during the 2008 economic downturn, but it is even more useful to know the general effect of lending practices on housing market health. Does the effect of Canada's bank mortgage lending practices in 2008 hold across time? Across countries and different economic systems? This impulse to generalize is a core feature of the scientific project. The lawlike generalizations are formulated as **theories**; we will explore theory development in Chapter 3.

The scientific method is often referred to as **positivism**. The principles underlying the positivist approach in social science can be traced back to eighteenth-century sociologist Auguste Comte (Neuman 1994, 58). Positivism is based on empiricism and determinism: it is believed that almost everything can be objectively measured (empiricism) and that every event has an explanation or a cause (**determinism**). From a positivist perspective, the goal of research is to separate the researcher from the world being examined, to gather measurable evidence with which to test hypotheses, and to build theories on the basis of the observed empirical tests. Furthermore, the expectation is that other researchers, observing the world independently, can arrive at the same conclusion. The postulates of science (discussed in the next section) are extrapolations of these positivist principles.

Positivism is sometimes contrasted with **interpretivism**. The fundamental principle of interpretivism is that it is not possible, and may not even be desirable, to try to separate the observer from his or her observations. This perspective holds that human beings infuse the world with meaning; therefore, it is not reasonable to expect that independent observers would perceive events in an identical manner. In contemporary social science research, the different perspectives brought through the positivist and interpretivist approaches can be seen in the differences between the quantitative and qualitative approaches. These methods are discussed in more detail in Chapter 2.

Summary: Strengths of the Scientific Method

1. It attempts to minimize the effect of the observer on the observed.
2. It directs our attention to the dynamics of cause and effect.
3. It can be used both to explain and to predict.
4. It seeks lawlike generalizations that can be applied to the political world across time and space.

Expand Your Knowledge

Postmodernism

The assertion that the effects of the observer on the observed can be minimized is hotly contested by the proponents of **postmodernism**. The underlying premise of postmodernism is that reality is socially constructed and that the observer cannot be separated from what he or she purports to see. Furthermore, not only will one construction of the world differ from another, but there is also no method (and certainly no scientific method) that enables us to determine which perspective is accurate or correct. Indeed, postmodernism calls into question such notions as "accurate" or "correct"; the perspective that prevails will be the one backed by those with power. In this sense, power defines the nature of reality.

Postmodernism has had a dramatic impact on the arts, cultural studies, the humanities, and the social sciences. Although the tenets of postmodernism are hotly contested, they should be taken into account by anyone hoping to be conversant with contemporary political and cultural dialogue. For an excellent conceptual introduction, see Pauline Marie Rosenau's *Post-Modernism and the Social Sciences: Insights, Inroads, and Intrusions* (Princeton: Princeton University Press, 1992).

Postulates of Science

The scientific method asserts that knowledge can best be acquired by following certain rules or sets of rules that can lead to the formulation of lawlike generalizations about the social and political world. This methodology is predicated on certain beliefs (**postulates**) about nature and how nature can be known. If we do not accept these beliefs, the scientific method becomes less compelling. In an ironic twist, the method cannot be used to test these postulates. Although this foundational paradox has led some to reject the scientific method's validity, others are prepared to accept, or at least to turn a blind eye to, this incongruity and to judge the usefulness of scientific research by its output.

We find that all empirical research is premised on the following six postulates (see Nachmias and Nachmias 1987, 6–9):

1. *Nature is orderly.* Earlier we discussed the characteristic feature of scientific research as centring on cause-and-effect relationships. Such an orientation has meaning only when one accepts the belief that natural phenomena are ordered in causal sequences. The belief that everything has a cause, that nothing is random, is known as determinism, a term introduced in the previous section. In some aspects of our lives, a belief in the ordered sequencing of events is non-controversial. For example, in baseball we know that a home run ball results from the force of its impact with a baseball bat, which causes the ball to travel over the fence. The scientific method can be used when nature is ordered in such a way, and applying the method to social and political reality implies a belief in a similar type of ordering. It suggests that people do not protest at random and that revolutions do not occur by chance alone. In short, political attitudes, beliefs, and behaviours are not random occurrences.

This postulate does not imply that all people respond identically when faced with similar situations, for we know that this is not the case. (One of the reasons for variation may be that people experience similar situations in dissimilar ways; thus, one could say that the situations differ.) Nonetheless, use of the scientific method in political science implies a belief in the causal ordering of social and political reality, even if our understanding of that ordering is extremely limited at this time.

2. *We can know nature.* The belief that nature is orderly is devoid of empirical implications if the order cannot be revealed to us. Consequently, science postulates that, through a rigorous application of the scientific method, the pattern of natural phenomena can be revealed. This belief implies that no one has a privileged position in the search for knowledge. An awareness of the pattern assumed by a causal relationship does not spring from one's special gifts of perception nor is the structure of reality divinely revealed. Instead, knowledge about nature is available in equal measure to everyone. Furthermore, such knowledge results from an application of the scientific method, not from the observer's personal characteristics. Some may use that method with greater precision, insight, or creativity than others, but it is ultimately the method itself that reveals the patterned structures of natural and social phenomena.

3. *Knowledge is superior to ignorance.* This third postulate of science is based on the assumption that our awareness of the world around us can be one of two types: we can be ignorant about that reality or about the underlying causes of that reality, or we can understand them correctly and have knowledge of them. Ignorance of reality is a recipe for superstition about cause and effect and an invitation to paralysis in the face of social problems. Science's position is that it is always preferable to have a correct understanding of nature than to misunderstand it. Part of the reason for this stance is that, if one wishes to alter the present or future reality, one must at a minimum understand how that might be achieved. A political strategist could increase her party's standing in the electorate only if she correctly understands why people support one party over another.

A further reason for the superiority of knowledge over ignorance is the belief that knowledge and understanding can be ends in themselves. Knowledge is important because it is instrumental in helping us solve problems and because we believe that knowledge is desirable in and of itself. A greater understanding of our world and environment, be it social, political, physical, intellectual, or otherwise, is believed to be part of being human.

4. *Natural phenomena have natural causes.* Another way of describing the fourth postulate is to say that those aspects of social and political reality that we can perceive can be explained by other things that we can perceive. The postulate holds that attitudes and behaviour in the natural world are not produced by supernatural, or spiritual, forces. Once again, all observers can equally observe the natural world as well as the causal influences within it. As Agent Scully, from the 1990s television series *The X-Files*, observed: "Nothing happens in contradiction to nature, only in contradiction to what we know of it" (Carter, 1996).

If it is true that all natural phenomena have natural causes, one might ask, "Why have we not been able to isolate these causes more completely and strengthen our lawlike generalizations?" The reasons for the limited success in this area are complex and will be discussed at many places throughout this book. It should only be noted at this point that one of the most important reasons concerns problems of measurement and measurement error. There are some aspects of the natural world that cannot be measured very accurately or reliably; thus, their linkage to social and political behaviour remains highly underdeveloped. In other cases, our knowledge is simply too incomplete. DNA's importance in the inheritance of physical characteristics is well known. But we do not know the degree to which one's attitudinal and behavioural characteristics are transmitted through DNA. Is there a genetic link in the development of political ideologies, participatory strategies, or aggressive behaviour? We do not know because essential research has not yet been completed, although it has begun. Political scientist James Fowler (2006) and his team are researching genetics and voting behaviour. As *Scientific American* (2007) reports, "Their analysis of voting histories for 326 identical and 196 fraternal twins suggests that genetics was responsible for 60 percent of differences in voting turnout between twin types, with the rest coming from environmental or other factors."

A second question that arises from the postulate of natural phenomena having natural causes is the role of spirituality in the uncovering of nature. Does one have to be an atheist to use the scientific method? The answer is no. Although it is possible to interpret the scientific method, and in particular this fourth postulate of science, as a denial of God, one could understand the divine presence as providing the limits of the scientific method. This latter view sees divine presence as part of the residual category in scientific research. A **residual** is everything outside the explanatory factors in a model. Spiritual factors are included along with other influences that cannot be identified, isolated, and measured as causal influences. To identify the impact of spiritual or divine phenomena, we would need to use a research method other than the scientific method. At this time, the residual element in our understanding of the social and political worlds is immense and provides ample room for spirituality to be brought into play.

5. *Nothing is self-evident.* This postulate affirms that knowledge is not derived a priori or by intuition. Everything is subject to empirical testing through the scientific method. This idea was captured eloquently by René Descartes, a sixteenth-century philosopher and one of the founders of the scientific method. Descartes began his inquiry by denying the existence of everything and then accepting only those propositions that could be proven to be true. He went so far as to deny his own existence until it could be proven otherwise. Descartes's proof of his existence was expressed in his famous assertion, "I think, therefore I am." That is to say, "Because I am doing human things, like thinking, I am human and my existence is confirmed."

Another way to think about this postulate is to assume that nothing is beyond scientific investigation. There are no aspects of the natural world, including the social and political realm, that are outside the domain of science. Nothing is off limits. Whether the area of inquiry relates to the causes of war, the development of political ideologies, the stability of government, or the determinants of political participation, the scientific method can be used in uncovering the natural order. Furthermore, science challenges other ways of knowing, such as knowledge gained through communication with supernatural forces, as invalid. If knowledge is not subject to the rules of science, which in turn make it available to all who apply those rules, it is rejected.

6. *Knowledge is derived from the acquisition of experience.* The last postulate of science is that knowledge is acquired through a continuous application of the scientific method. Knowledge stems from repeated observation, careful testing, and a replication of the results under varying conditions. This postulate would seem to imply that scientific knowledge is cumulative, each step building upon preceding steps. But there are several alternative views about the advancement of knowledge. One is that the development of scientific thought is paradigmatic, that it comes by leaps and bounds rather than by gradual, incremental change. Some suggest that advances in science come about as monumental shifts in paradigms; one worldview is replaced by another when incremental gains in new knowledge gradually erode existing paradigms to the point of collapse. Paradigm shifts often entail a considerable amount of struggle against an established orthodoxy until a new view ultimately prevails.[2] This situation suggests that there is always a prevailing view within the scientific community and that individuals either subscribe to that view and conduct

"normal science" or fight to replace that view, while struggling against the institutional strength of the orthodox paradigm. (Postmodernists, for example, would see themselves as struggling against the positivist paradigm embedded in this text.)

A second argument is that scientific advances tend to be random occurrences and that science is more often characterized by disorder than by order. Nonetheless, whether scientific advances occur through cumulative incremental change, through paradigm shifts, or at random, there is general agreement that the critical factor is the accumulated experience that accompanies the continual application of the scientific method.

Summary: Basic Postulates of Science

1. Nature is orderly.
2. We can know nature.
3. Knowledge is superior to ignorance.
4. Natural phenomena have natural causes.
5. Nothing is self-evident.
6. Knowledge is derived from the acquisition of experience.

Expand Your Knowledge

Thomas Kuhn and *The Structure of Scientific Revolutions*

Thomas Kuhn's *The Structure of Scientific Revolutions*, first published in 1960 and republished in 1970, had a profound and far-reaching impact on our understanding of the social dynamics of knowledge in both the natural and social sciences. Kuhn argued that, while science routinely progressed through incremental, piecemeal increases in knowledge—what he calls normal science—incrementalism does not account for major paradigm shifts such as that from an Earth-centred to a Sun-centred solar system and from Newtonian physics to quantum mechanics. These paradigm shifts, which were indeed revolutionary, could be understood only by looking at the sociology of knowledge. Knowledge, in other words, is socially constructed; we see the world through our instruments and through paradigms that are the products of complex social, cultural, and political interactions.

Paradigm shifts do not emerge effortlessly from incremental change but are the consequence of power struggles between competing paradigms and the proponents of such paradigms. Kuhn (1970, 7) writes: "A new theory, however special its range of application, is seldom or never just an increment to what is already known. Its assimilation requires the reconstruction of prior theory and the re-evaluation of prior fact, an intrinsically revolutionary process that is seldom completed by a single man and never overnight."

Kuhn's work changed how we see science and thus constitutes a paradigm shift of far-reaching proportions.

The Methodology of Science

So far in our discussion, we have insisted on the need to use the scientific method to acquire knowledge about nature, including that of social and political life. This empirical approach can be used to gain knowledge about things as they are, that is, knowledge of social and political reality. Such empirical knowledge can be contrasted with normative knowledge, or knowledge about things as they ought to be or as we would wish them to be. This contrast in the study of politics is usually reflected in the differences between political philosophy and empirical political science.

Political philosophy typically focuses on normative questions: What is the good life? What is the meaning of justice? What is the most desirable social order? It also often concentrates on questions of what is right and wrong, good and bad. Empirical political science, in contrast, is generally more concerned with discovering why things are as they are. Why are some countries more stable or more successful at managing their national economies than others? Why do people vote as they do? Although values may underlie some questions of empirical research (i.e., the researcher might prefer political stability to instability or lower unemployment to lower inflation), the research cannot and does not claim to provide insight into normative issues. Empirical research cannot be used to conclude that increased inflation is superior to increased unemployment, although it could draw out some of the implications of either event or reveal who has the power to impose their preferred policy options. We can use the results of empirical research to pursue preferred policy outcomes, but the preferences for outcomes are not empirically derived.

As will be discussed in Chapter 3, we can use empirical research to both build and test theories. The methodology of science presents a set of sequential steps that guide the theory testing enterprise. Because all scientific theory testing research uses these essential steps, any particular research project is linked by the scientific method to the larger research enterprise. In beginning a project, it is useful to think of yourself as part of a broader research community, with your research building on previous research in a particular area and representing a continuation of investigations into that topic. Likewise, the research that you produce is subject to further replication, and subsequent research may either reject or accept the conclusions drawn in your study but cannot prove your conclusions.

Steps in the Scientific Theory Testing Method

1. *Identify the problem.* All scientific research begins with a problem, which involves variation on some outcome or event. Why do some people support economic development through extraction of non-renewable resources while others are opposed? Why do people support some parties rather than others? Why do some people calculate their income tax honestly and others cheat? When does conflict escalate into war? The "problem," or the outcome, in social scientific research is called the dependent event and is measured by the **dependent variable**. It is the thing we are trying to explain or understand.

The dependent event has a number of important features. First, it must contain sufficient variation that can be explained. If all people or governments thought or behaved alike, there would be little for social science to explain. Fortunately, human attitudes and behaviour are full of inconsistencies and variability, making social and political relations fertile ground for scientific research. Nonetheless, you must cast the problem in such a way that highlights the variation you wish to explain. Second, the dependent event must be susceptible to a clear definition and be measurable. These topics and the problems associated with them are discussed in detail in Chapters 4 and 5. For the moment, it should be recognized that empirical research requires that the dependent event be defined with enough precision and specificity that it can be linked to previous research. Likewise, the dependent variable must be measured in such a way that other researchers are able to replicate your study. As we will see, the issues of concept definition and operational measurement can create serious difficulties in empirical research, making close attention to these issues an essential component of useful and generalizable findings.

2. *Hypothesize the cause of the problem.* The goal of empirical research is to explain variation with respect to the dependent event. One can begin to explain the dependent event by proposing causes of the observed variation across cases or time. Hypothesized causes are called independent concepts and are measured by independent variables. The word *independent* implies that the variation in this concept is independent of, or not caused by, variation in the dependent event. The relationship between these two types of variables is hypothesized to be a causal sequence from the independent to the dependent variable and not vice versa. A hypothesis is an expected or proposed relationship of the type "A causes B."

For example, it has often been observed that older people are more likely than younger people to hold conservative political views. Thus, there is a relationship, or **correlation**, between age and political thinking. Since empirical research is concerned with identifying causal relationships, it is necessary to ask which of these factors is the independent variable and which is the dependent. In this case, it seems fairly obvious that political ideology cannot affect chronological age. One does not become older if one becomes more conservative. To the extent that there is a causal relationship between age and ideology, age must be the independent variable and ideology the dependent variable. Right? Not necessarily. Social and political phenomena are often bound together in highly complex relationships.

To continue with this example, some research has shown that affluence is negatively related to mortality rates (more affluent people live longer) and to ideology (they are more conservative). Age and ideology may be related but not according to the simple "aging" hypothesis offered. It may be that mortality rates are different for groups that fall predominantly into left-wing and right-wing camps (affluent versus non-affluent). Those to the right tend to outlive those to the left, although this does not mean that you can extend your lifespan by changing your political beliefs. There are more conservative elderly people, not because they have changed their ideology, but because of the presence of a third variable: mortality rates.

An important component of proposing a causal hypothesis is to identify the theory that underlies the independent concept's effect on the dependent event. When we speak of "theory" in this sense, we refer to generalized statements about the causes of attitudes or behaviour. Suppose we want to explain why people voted Conservative, Liberal, New Democrat, Green, or something else (including abstainers) in the last federal election. How do we explain variation on voting preference? One of the first things we must do is decide which theory of political choice will guide our research. One such theory is that voting in Canada is determined mostly by short-term factors and is therefore very unstable. An alternative theory is that people hold relatively firm political allegiances and that voting is characterized more by stability than by change. It is possible to design a research project that tests both theories. Nonetheless, it should be obvious that the selection of independent variables will depend heavily upon which theory is tested.

3. *Provide clear definitions of the concepts.* **Concepts** are abstractions used to describe the characteristics of a group or an individual case according to a given criterion or quality. Empirical research begins and ends at the abstract, conceptual level in which generalizations are made about social and political life. Some of the concepts that traditionally interest political scientists include political participation, social class, political stability, ideology, conflict, and political culture. To conduct research on any of these topics, they must be prepared to define precisely the characteristics or features of that abstraction. As we mentioned earlier, there can be considerable disagreement within the scholarly community about the meaning of many concepts.

For an idea of the difficulties that can arise when trying to get researchers to agree on the meaning of concepts, let's look at political participation. Several questions emerge when we attempt to define this important concept. Is political participation one thing, or is it a bundle of quite different activities? Do participatory activities differ in degree or in kind? That is, should participatory activities be thought of as being more or less participation or as different types or modes of activities? How far does the domain of the term *political* extend? Is political participation limited to electoral participation, or does it include other activities that can influence political decision-making? Does it include volunteer work for a community association or women's shelter? What about strikes and work stoppages? Are activities directed in the first instance at private market-oriented actors included as political participation? What about strikes among public sector workers or among those employed by Crown corporations or mixed enterprises? What about contacting one's member of Parliament (MP), taking part in a protest or demonstration, or discussing political issues over social media? Are these to be included in a measure of political participation and, if so, in what way? Is participating in a protest equivalent to voting in an election? Is there a difference between legal and illegal forms of political participation?

Empirical political scientists, together with Canadians more generally, may disagree in their answers to these questions. For researchers, those differences are likely to be reflected in different definitions of the concepts under study. Social science research has the added complexity that the language used in debate and analysis can sometimes be politicized to bring value judgments to the definition of terms. For example, the heavy oil deposits in northern Alberta are often called oil sands by those supporting their development and tar sands by those opposing it.

The general problem for social science research is that it is difficult to advance our knowledge and understanding of a concept when researchers are working with different definitions. At the same time, it is not possible to "require" that researchers agree on common definitions. Part of the research enterprise is to provide the intellectual freedom for researchers to pursue their work in a manner that they define as suitable and appropriate. The requirement to publicize research results in independent, peer-reviewed journals and books ensures to a degree that researchers are held accountable for their decisions. It also re-emphasizes the importance of a scholarly community conducting a common research enterprise.

4. *Operationalize the concepts.* An empirical research project moves from the general or conceptual level to the specific and concrete. This movement from concepts to variables is called **operationalization**. It involves obtaining a specific measurement of the concepts with respect to the data that have been collected. More specifically, for quantitative research it involves assigning a numerical score on a variable to each case in the data set. For some concepts the process is straightforward and non-controversial. The concept of sex is a good example of a simple concept for most research. Typically, the researcher thinks of sex as a dichotomous variable, and respondents are scored as male or female. This standard view assumes that people are differentiated into either of two distinct categories.

However, this dichotomy may be too simplistic. For example, it is well known that all humans possess both masculine (testosterone) and feminine (estrogen and progesterone) hormones. Although, in general, men have more masculine hormones and women have more feminine hormones, some men have more masculine hormones than other men and some women have more feminine hormones than other women. When one considers sex in these more biological terms, it becomes a continuous variable with everyone having a specific mixture of masculine and feminine aspects. If we turn from sex to gender, the measurement situation becomes considerably more complex. Gender is a more socially constructed concept than sex is and, consequently, defies simple dichotomization.

Other concepts may be even more intractable in operationalizing because of their multidimensionality. The concept may be a combination of attributes on several different criteria. Political participation appears to be a multidimensional concept because of the distinct ways that one can participate in politics. Social class would have a strong claim on multidimensionality because of the different components of the social hierarchy and the variation that may exist across those components, complexities discussed more fully in Chapters 4 and 5. At this stage, the key thing to remember is that a variable should reflect the abstract concept that it represents as closely as possible. Recall that research begins and ends at the conceptual level; the conclusions will relate to the abstract concept and not to the particular variable that was used in this single study. To the extent that the variable does not accurately reflect the concept, the conclusions derived from the research will be distorted.

5. *Gather empirical data.* All theory testing research includes a test of a hypothesis. This test requires that data be collected on both the independent and dependent variables and on intervening variables or those that cause a spurious relationship (the latter two types are discussed more fully in Chapter 3). There are many different types of data and **research design** strategies that can be used in the data collection phase. In Chapters 7 through 12, the methodologies involving survey research, population data, content analysis, experimental design, interviews, and other data collection strategies are discussed at length. There is no single right or wrong approach to data-gathering; each method has its advantages and disadvantages. The key consideration for any researcher is to gather data that best suit the purposes of the specific research questions. Faculty members and students alike often find it expedient and cost-effective to conduct secondary analysis on data that have already been gathered by other researchers. In view of the wealth of such data today, as well as their ready accessibility through data libraries and archives, this strategy is becoming increasingly attractive to all researchers.

6. *Test the hypothesis or hypotheses.* One of the defining characteristics of scientific research is that hypotheses are **falsifiable**. It must be possible, through both the logic of analysis and the design of the research, to demonstrate the absence of a causal relationship between the concepts being examined. If it is not possible to disprove the hypothesized relationship, the research cannot claim to have been conducted scientifically. Although the emphasis during the research design portion of a research project is on developing and justifying hypotheses about the causal relationship between concepts, the emphasis shifts during the empirical part of the project.

Empirical testing requires that the research hypothesis is inverted, or is replaced by its opposite, called the **null hypothesis**. The null hypothesis states that the two concepts or variables are independent of each other and are not causally related. While researchers typically expect the null hypothesis to be false and the research hypothesis to be true, the empirical test is conducted on the null hypothesis for an important reason. The research hypothesis can never be proven to be true; although data can and often do support the research hypothesis, they never prove it unequivocally because another experiment or empirical test could provide a context in which the hypothesis is disproved. Thus, research hypotheses can be disproved by a single test, whereas they cannot be proven even with a large number of repeated tests. The null hypothesis, on the other hand, is either accepted or rejected. The null hypothesis that there is no causal relationship between two variables is accepted if an empirical test shows that they are independent and is rejected if the test reveals that the variables are related to each other. Therefore, testing hypotheses involves deciding whether to accept or reject the null hypothesis, a matter discussed at greater length in Chapter 3.

Recall at this point that the researcher is conducting a single empirical test on a hypothesized relationship between two variables. The research is important but not so much for what it reveals about the particular variables in the time and place at which the data were gathered. Instead, it is significant to the degree to which the variables represent more general concepts in a more generalized temporal and spatial dimension. We can think about the generalized setting as representing the true relationship between concepts. The empirical test is taken as a measure or proxy of that true relationship.

7. *Reflect back on theory.* When drawing conclusions about the research, researchers return to the conceptual level. Variables are recast in their generalized form and conclusions are drawn about the nature of the causal relationships. At this stage, the researcher is able to evaluate the theoretical aspects of the research in light of the empirical evidence. Were the hypotheses confirmed? Which hypotheses and in what ways? What are the implications for the theoretical underpinnings of the study? Does the theory need revision in light of the research? What generalizations can be drawn from the study? Are there policy implications from the results of the research? In what direction should future research in this area be pursued? Remember that one of the chief goals of empirical research is to draw lawlike generalizations about social and political phenomena. These generalized statements find reflection in the theories developed to understand and explain politics. The later stages of empirical research require that we step back from the specific empirical findings and reflect upon the more general patterns of interaction and causality. The continual process of testing, refining, and adjusting theoretical statements of causality forms an essential step in the ongoing research enterprise.

8. *Publicize the results.* The old saying "publish or perish" holds an amount of truth. The weight of one's scholarly publications is the key indicator of academic performance at many universities, and a full curriculum vitae is often richly rewarded. Although publication certainly fulfills an important institutional function, it serves the more important purpose of enabling the scholarly community to engage in an ongoing research dialogue. Indeed, one of the responsibilities of researchers is to engage in this discourse. It is necessary not only to maintain an active research agenda but also to place the results of those efforts into the public domain for debate, discussion, challenge, and verification.

All levels of scholarly inquiry have outlets for such dialogue. For undergraduate students it typically occurs between student and course instructor. Part of the learning process at universities is to accept criticisms of your work, and part of the responsibility of instructors is to provide such criticism in a way that strengthens and improves research. For graduate students, the feedback from course instructors is supplemented with responses from their supervisory committees on independent or quasi-independent research projects in the form of master's theses or doctoral dissertations. For research scholars, including professors, the outlets for publicizing the results of research include scholarly journals, research institute monographs, public lectures or displays, and books. Typically, it is expected that the prepublication stage includes some form of blind **peer evaluation process**.

9. *Replicate the results.* The final step in the process of empirical research is replication, to repeat the study by using either the same data or data gathered at a different time or in a different setting. Since the goal of empirical research is to draw lawlike generalizations, research results are valuable to the extent that they can be generalized. If similar empirical tests conducted at other times and places fail to produce the same result, one is not able to generalize from the initial test. The importance of replication reinforces and highlights the need for researchers to systematically and completely describe each stage of the analysis, from designing the study to defining concepts, gathering data, operationalizing **measures**, testing the relationships, and drawing conclusions. Only then can the research be replicated and each stage of the research opened to critical examination.

Summary: Steps in the Scientific Theory Testing Method

1. Identify the problem.
2. Hypothesize the cause of the problem.
3. Provide clear definitions of the concepts.
4. Operationalize the concepts.
5. Gather empirical data.
6. Test the hypothesis or hypotheses.
7. Reflect back on theory.
8. Publicize the results.
9. Replicate the results.

APPLY YOUR UNDERSTANDING

Youth and Political Participation

Imagine that you are a researcher looking at the question, "Do young people participate politically at levels lower than the rest of the population?" What concepts need to be defined before you begin your study? How would you define them? If you do find that young people participate less, what reasons might explain this difference?

Expand Your Knowledge

Federal Theory and Empirical Research

Alan Cairns (2001) and other Canadian scholars of federalism have argued that the passage of the 1982 Charter of Rights and Freedoms had a pervasive and even profound impact on the Canadian political culture. The effect has been to heighten the political identities and influence of those groups able to claim constitutional status through their recognition within the Charter. Some claim that these "Charter Canadians" have changed the nature of constitutional discourse, disrupted executive federalism, and enhanced the role of the courts in the definition and application of public policy.

Others have argued that, while these changes may indeed have occurred, it is a mistake to attribute them to the introduction of the Charter. Drawing upon the **postmaterialism** theorizing of Ronald Inglehart, it is suggested that these changes in Canadian politics reflect broad patterns of social and ideological change that have swept across all Western democracies since the end of World War II. Those individuals coming of age in the era of postwar affluence, Inglehart (1977) argues, are less concerned about material well-being and success and are more concerned with aesthetic values and self-expression. The idiosyncratic effects of the Charter, therefore, pale beside the impact of these broader currents of postmaterial change. (Note that postmaterialism is not the same as postmodernism.)

This challenge to the Charter thesis was put to an empirical test by Ian Brodie and Neil Nevitte (1993). Employing data from the 1981 and 1990 World Values Surveys, they found that their "new politics theory" outperformed Cairns's "citizens' constitution theory" when it came to explaining such things as confidence in political and legal institutions. Their article and the rejoinder by Cairns (1993) provide a useful illustration of the dynamic interplay of theory and empirical data.

Criticisms and Limitations of the Scientific Approach to Politics

We stated earlier that the scientific approach is also known as positivism, which assumes that reality can be measured empirically, that measurements can be made objectively, and that nature is orderly. Furthermore, every effect has a cause and every event is determined by a prior event. Some people argue that empiricism, objectivity, and determinism—and therefore the scientific approach—have limited utility for the study of society and politics and recommend alternative approaches to replace positivism. Fortunately, such criticism has been largely constructive; by pointing out the weaknesses of the scientific model, the critics encouraged positivist researchers to refine and adapt their methods.

Many people have difficulty applying the idea of determinism to human behaviour, and for good reason. Determinism suggests that no choice exists, while most of us know that humans have free will. A pencil has no choice but to submit to the force of gravity; we, on the other hand, have control over our thoughts, feelings, attitudes, and behaviour. We cannot with certainty predict the actions or reactions of an individual. However, when we look at groups we can often make generalizations. Social scientists have been able to see patterns in human behaviour, patterns that are linked to outside phenomena. For example, we may find that most people whose parents are liberal are liberal too; thus, parental ideological views influence those of the child. At the same time, there are always some people who do not fit the pattern: some children of liberals are conservative. Having a liberal parent will increase one's probability of being liberal but does not determine liberalism.

Another critique is that not all aspects of reality can be empirically measured. How does one measure beliefs, thoughts, and attitudes? We cannot get inside people's heads and see exactly what is going on; we must rely on the information people give us, either through their words or actions. Even when we can access information about beliefs, there are difficulties in quantifying and comparing it across individuals. Did Bob and Sue mean the same thing when they each classified themselves as "highly religious"? Are our subjects being honest with us—and with themselves—when they respond to controversial questions? There are many practical difficulties in measuring reality, and we continually need to ask ourselves if we are in fact measuring what we believe we are measuring. These difficulties, moreover, go well beyond measurement error to include disagreements about the meaning of such terms as *full employment*, *unemployment*, *pay equity*, and *democratic government*. This issue is known as **measurement validity** and will be explored further in Chapter 5. The challenge to researchers is to select indicators that most closely tap the concept they wish to measure. In some cases, this task can be difficult.

Some critics question the objectivity of the scientific method, arguing that true neutrality is impossible and that there is no value-free system of study. These critics state that the observer's beliefs and values will always play a role in the interpretation of the facts; research will always contain a degree of subjectivity. Such subjectivity can be positive, as it allows the researcher to be sensitive to the context within which political action (or inaction) occurs, but it can also be the source of inadvertent bias. This criticism is particularly noteworthy for researchers who study a variety of cultures and societies. Political scientists who wish to evaluate the role of context for their subject often address the critique by using qualitative approaches to their studies.

Other assessments are more ideological in character. Some feminist, postmodern, and class theorists argue that "positivism defends the status quo because it assumes an unchanging order instead of seeing current society as a particular stage in an ongoing process" (Neuman 1994, 66). Attempts to objectively describe and explain the status quo are seen by some as a defence because there is often an implicit assumption that the identified reality is natural and immune to change. Such criticisms vividly demonstrate the fact that political science (and social science in general) lacks a single paradigm to which all can appeal. There is no common overriding view of how the social world is or of how to best measure that world. Even if we can agree on the principle of causality, there is confusion over what the important social determinants are. Some political economists point to the class system or the structure of the international political economy, feminists point to the gendered nature of social and political institutions, and so on. This inconsistency poses a serious limitation to the advancement of science: if knowledge is to be cumulative, it requires some degree of paradigm agreement (Baxter-Moore, Carroll, and Church 1994, 88). On the other hand, it can be argued that the variety of approaches to the study of politics is an advantage because it ensures that a diverse set of perspectives and interpretations of the social world is considered.

In conclusion, we would argue that, despite the criticisms, the scientific approach to politics is the best means by which we can work to understand the incredibly complex social world around us. Admittedly, political science has far to go; the discipline is just over a hundred years old. Attempts to compare such a "young" science to "older" ones such as biology and physics are perhaps unfair—think of how little was known about the human body when the study of anatomy was in its infancy stages. The goal of our journey is to advance our comprehension of politics and society. Although the final destination, "truth," may seem far away and beyond our reach, we must keep in mind that we have only really just begun the voyage.

APPLY YOUR UNDERSTANDING

Science and Politics

List the pros and cons of using the scientific method in the study of politics. How do the methods and principles of the scientific method fit with your own conception of politics? In what situations would the scientific method be particularly appropriate? Particularly inappropriate? How does the study of political and social life differ from the study of the natural world?

Working as a Team

1. Some people argue that the study of politics, and society in general, can never be considered a "true" science. They suggest, furthermore, that "political studies" is a more appropriate label than "political science." Do you feel the terms are misleading? Can the study of humans in aggregate be a science? (Give reasons to support your answers.) What are the pros and cons of political science as the name for our discipline? What might be a better or more appropriate name?
2. Discuss the advantages and disadvantages of applying the scientific method to the volatile public policy question, "Should Canadians support capital punishment?"

Discuss whether there are limits to the application of empirical approaches or if almost all questions benefit from empirical study. What questions do you see as beyond the reach of the scientific method?

Self-Study

1. How might the concept of socialism be approached in normative political analysis? What types of questions might be asked? How might it be approached in empirical political analysis? Again, what questions might be asked? Is either approach superior for increasing our understanding of socialism? Why or why not? What are the strengths and limitations of each? If you were asked to write a term paper on socialism in the contemporary world, would you adopt a normative approach, an empirical approach, or some blend of the two? How would you justify your choice?
2. What hypotheses would you suggest to explain current levels of electoral support for the federal government? What competing hypotheses can you offer? Do these hypotheses emerge from your readings, political science classes, political instincts, favourite political blogger, editorials in *The Globe and Mail*, or another source? If you had to rank your hypotheses in order of plausibility, which would strike you as the most compelling? The least compelling? What evidence would you need to test these hypotheses and to choose among them?

Notes

1. The three explanations discussed do not exhaust the range of possible explanations.
2. In the time of Nicolaus Copernicus (1473–1543), challenging the Earth-centred paradigm of contemporary physics could be quite literally a matter of life and death.

CHAPTER 2

Observing the Political World
Quantitative and Qualitative Approaches

Jared Wesley, University of Alberta and University of Manitoba[1]

Destination

By the end of this chapter, you should be able to

- identify the parallels between the casual ways in which we all view the political world and the more systematic methods used by social scientists;
- describe the epistemological and methodological distinctions between quantitative and qualitative research; and
- explain what trustworthiness is and what steps researchers can take to increase it.

Whether studying voter turnout and voting behaviour, laws and institutions, cultures and ideas, or any other topic, all political scientists confront the same set of fundamental questions when designing their research: Does my study seek to uncover broad generalizations about the political world or am I seeking a narrower, more in-depth understanding of a particular phenomenon? Will my examination involve a large number of individuals, groups, or countries or will I focus on a smaller number of cases? Do I have a pre-defined set of hypotheses I wish to test or is my study more **exploratory** in nature? Answers to these questions determine the most effective methodological approach to pursue. In particular, they establish whether the research should proceed in the **quantitative** or **qualitative tradition**—whether the study should involve a more deductive process of counting and statistical analysis (using a set of premises to draw conclusions) or a more inductive method of non-numerical interpretation (forming conclusions from empirical evidence).

Previous generations of political scientists viewed these two traditions as incommensurable. Many in the discipline believed in a hard-and-fast connection between quantitative methods and the tenets of positivism, on one hand, and qualitative methods and interpretivism, on the other. According to this perspective, quantitative positivists believed in the principles of inherency and verifiability, which put them at odds with the idea among qualitative relativists that all reality was socially constructed. In this environment, researchers toiled in opposing camps—either pursuing knowledge in a parallel but separate manner or actively seeking to undermine each other.

Until recently, heated debates between quantitative and qualitative researchers constituted one of the deepest divisions in the political science community. The chasm was broadest during the so-called **behavioural revolution**, a period consuming the second half of the twentieth century. With the advent of the computer and the development of mass survey techniques, quantitative approaches came to dominate the discipline. Qualitative methods were overshadowed, their decline the product of researchers' preferences, trends in post-secondary education, and—to a more limited degree—persecution at the hands of some positivist puritans.

Today's discipline is not entirely immune to these tensions.[2] As Manheim, Rich, and Willnat (2002, 318) describe, "Some quantitatively oriented scholars regard at least some qualitative work as so dependent on the perceptions of the individual researcher and so focused on specific cases as to be unverifiable and essentially useless. In contrast, some qualitatively oriented scholars judge quantitative methods to be so incomplete in their representation of reality as to be empirically misleading." Fortunately, though many empirical researchers continue to work under one tradition or the other, most have come to appreciate the value of the other approach and to recognize an important element of interdependence between the two. Brady, Collier, and Seawright (2004, 10) write:

> *In the social sciences, qualitative research is hard to do well. Quantitative research is also hard to do well. Each tradition can and should learn from the other.* One version of conventional wisdom holds that achieving analytic rigor is more difficult in qualitative than in quantitative research. Yet in quantitative research, making valid inferences about complex political processes on the basis of observational data is likewise extremely difficult. There are no quick and easy recipes for either qualitative or quantitative analysis. In the face of these shared challenges, the two traditions have developed distinctive and complementary tools. (Emphasis in original.)

Instead of struggling for methodological supremacy, most political scientists seek to "refine and develop the battery of techniques on offer, and above all to be as explicit as possible about the implications of the methodologies we employ" (Laver 2001, 9). Most researchers strive to develop strengths, or at least awareness, in a variety of different methodological techniques.

APPLY YOUR UNDERSTANDING

Evidence in Political Science Research

Think for a moment about the types of "evidence" we consider as political researchers. When measuring the level of tension between two countries, what type of data could we collect? We could use objective indicators, such as the number of vitriolic speeches aimed at one another or the prevalence of troop exercises along their borders. Alternatively, we could use subjective indicators, gleaned from interviews, surveys, or focus groups.

What would these various types of evidence look like? Would the data consist of numbers and statistics (such as the increase in troop movements or the frequency of speeches)? Or would the data take a non-numerical form, as in the words of the respondents or the tone of these speeches? How would the analysis differ, depending on whether the data was collected quantitatively or qualitatively? How would this choice affect the research process or the nature of its findings?

Quantitative and Qualitative Approaches to Empirical Research

Empirical research is based on observation and interpretation and includes two distinct traditions. The first, which typically comes to mind when one thinks of empirical research, is the **quantitative** approach. As the root of the word suggests, this approach seeks to understand political life through the study of a large quantity, or number, of cases. A **case** is a single unit, which could be individuals, legislatures, organizations, nation-states, court decisions, or whatever the unit of interest may be. Due to time and financial constraints, one can rarely conduct an in-depth study of large numbers of cases. Thus, quantitative research tends to have greater breadth than depth. The research is usually quite structured; a survey researcher will ask the questions listed on his or her polling sheet and nothing more.

The second approach is **qualitative research**. The emphasis here is on quality, or detail. Qualitative researchers attempt to learn about politics through a more thorough study of a small number of cases. In this way, qualitative research complements quantitative research, emphasizing depth over breadth. Qualitative research is as equally rigorous as quantitative but less structured, which allows the researcher to explore the subtleties of individual beliefs or group dynamics. For example, an interviewer may be intrigued by something his or her subject mentions and may choose to follow this point with a spontaneous line of questioning.

Three common misconceptions surround the relationship between these two modes of research. First, despite common impressions, no research topic is inherently qualitative or quantitative. Researchers can study any subject—from political participation to military intervention—using either approach. Certain topics have been approached more quantitatively (voting and elections come to mind); others have fallen largely under the purview of qualitative scholarship (including Indigenous politics and gender studies). Yet the subject matter itself does not determine which tradition should be employed. Second, specific methodologies do not belong solely to one tradition or the other. Surveys can be quantitative or qualitative, as can interviews, focus groups, textual analysis, observation research, or any other mode of inquiry. Third, although analysts are likely to develop certain preferences and skill sets, it is becoming increasingly uncommon (and unpopular) to refer to individuals as being purely quantitative or qualitative researchers. Instead of specializing in only one methodology, political scientists are expected to approach their research with entire "tool boxes" at their disposal, often through the use of research teams. Doing so means learning different methods, both qualitative and quantitative, depending on the task at hand.

Indeed, the choice between the two approaches depends upon the specific research question guiding the study. As Laver (2001, 9) suggests, "different theoretical problems will always demand different types of data." Quantitative research involves numbers, frequencies, intensities, and other measurements of degree; therefore, it is particularly well-suited to questions of "how much?", "how often?", and "how many?" By contrast, qualitative research deals best with questions involving conditions, norms, and values (Tashakkori and Teddlie 2003, 317). King, Keohane, and Verba (1993, 4–5) write: "Trends in social, political, or economic behavior are more readily addressed by quantitative analysis than is the flow of ideas among people or the difference made by exceptional individual leadership." In other words, all questions in political science involve some sort of comparison, but quantitative research is best equipped for "judgments of which phenomena are 'more' or 'less' alike *in degree*," whereas qualitative research is best suited to examine differences "*in kind*" (Ibid., 5; emphasis in original).

APPLY YOUR UNDERSTANDING

Quantitative and Qualitative Methods

Consider the question, "What is the Government of Canada's number one priority?" One set of evidence may be found in the government's Speech from the Throne (a semi-annual public statement of its agenda) or its Budget Speech (a detailed annual statement of how it intends to spend and raise revenue). The Poltext Project (poltext.org) has been compiling these speeches, dating back to the 1960s. The natural tendency may be to assume that Throne Speeches are best-suited for qualitative research, given their rhetorical character. How might you study them qualitatively? By the same token, some might view budgets as more quantitative in nature because they deal with dollars and cents. How might you study budget speeches using a qualitative approach?

Epistemological Differences

Even though most political scientists have accepted the value of, and have even tried to bridge the divide between, the two approaches, certain core differences between quantitative and qualitative research remain. There are important epistemological and methodological distinctions. In Chapter 1, we introduced the positivist approach to science and discussed its application in the social sciences. We also noted that positivism is not without its critics and that alternate approaches take more of an interpretative position (sometimes referred to as post-positivism). Quantitative approaches are often associated with positivism and qualitative with interpretivism, but in practice the lines are not always so clearly defined. As we have stated, most scholars do not sit solely in one "camp" or the other. Some will employ quantitative methods in one study and qualitative tools in another; some will combine both traditions in a single analysis. Despite the tendency to associate quantitative research with the positivist approach to political life and qualitative analysis with the interpretivist, most political science research fits somewhere between these two extremes (Bryman 2004, 442). Although the following descriptions of the epistemological differences refer to two ends of a continuum, keep in mind that most social scientists occupy the middle ground (see Table 2.1).

Primary Intent

The primary purpose of most quantitative analysis is to test hypotheses. Researchers employing this approach enter the data collection, processing, and analysis stages with pre-defined postulates, which they actively seek to disconfirm. Conversely, most qualitative scholarship approaches the investigation with broader research questions in mind. Specific expectations are both developed and assessed during the process of observation and analysis (Neuman and Robson 2007, 336). To be sure, quantitative analysis proceeds from research questions, just as some qualitative research seeks to test hypotheses. The difference in intent is more a matter of degree than kind. In general, researchers applying the quantitative method address the process with answers they seek to verify or disprove, whereas those pursuing a qualitative route approach the process with problems they seek to understand or address (Altheide 1996, 15).

Ultimate Objective

The ultimate objective of most quantitative analyses is to produce widely applicable results; however, most qualitative studies aim to shed intense light on a specific context. The

Table 2.1 Epistemological Differences between the Two Traditions

Element of Research	Quantitative Tradition	Qualitative Tradition
Primary intent	Test hypotheses	Address questions
Ultimate objective	Generalizability	Specificity
Approach to reality	Manipulative	Organic
Position of researcher	Distanced	Instrumental
Theory development	Primarily deductive	Primarily inductive

former often produce generalizable findings based on a wide range of cases. Proponents refer to this as a broad, **large-*N*** approach (*N* refers to the number of cases under study), but critics call it shallow. By conducting **small-*n* studies**, qualitative research designs produce more detailed understandings of specific cases. (Small-*n* studies are discussed at length in Chapter 7.) Some deem this analysis to be deeper and others narrower than quantitative research. Again, it is important to realize that quantitative analysis enables researchers to examine a large number of cases, yet not all quantitative studies involve a large-*N*. The same is true of qualitative analyses; they may require more resources, but some involve the examination of many cases.

Approach to Reality

Most quantitative scholarship treats "reality" as something that can be both measured and configured. Real-world observations are converted into numerical form, then manipulated statistically to produce findings. Qualitative research tends to take a less synthetic, more organic approach, adapting analytical techniques to the environment rather than vice versa (Guba and Lincoln 1985). To put it crudely, nature submits to the method in quantitative research, but the method is more likely to submit to nature in qualitative research.

For these reasons, quantitative research is often described as being harder than qualitative research. This difference does not lie in the level of difficulty or complexity associated with the former (although some may portray it as such). Instead, quantitative research is commonly viewed as nearer to the physical ("hard") sciences than to the ("soft") arts- or humanities-focused brand of qualitative research (see Brady et al. 2004, 10–11; Guba and Lincoln 1994, 105–06).

Position of Researcher

Most quantitative analysis aims to limit the researcher's personal imprint on the findings. Often recognized and acknowledged, researcher biases are actively minimized during the investigation, as they are seen as contaminants of objective inquiry. Such prejudices are deemed more benign (or, at least, less malignant) in most brands of qualitative research. There, researcher biases are more likely to be perceived as unavoidable elements of interpretive inquiry than as pollutants. Researchers are typically the instruments of qualitative study; they are the agents of quantitative research (Merriam 2002b, 5).

Theory Development

Chapter 3 will explain the distinction between deductive and inductive research. For now, simply note that the quantitative and qualitative traditions combine deduction and induction to differing degrees in their analyses (Punch 2005, 196–7; Neuman and Robson 2007, 111). Quantitative analyses tend to apply existing theories to the data at hand in order to deduce patterns among pre-defined variables. The qualitative method is more conducive to an inductive process whereby themes and explanations emerge from the data. All told, and

Expand Your Knowledge

The Availability of Existing Research

Our choice of traditions is often constrained by the amount of existing theory or data on a particular topic. Quantitative analysis frequently depends on a great deal of this background research; qualitative research may be more exploratory in nature. Consider trying to research the immediate impact of a new free trade deal between Canada and India. Without any statistics or theories based on the economic relationship between advanced and emerging markets, it may be simpler to design an inductive, qualitative study. The results of that analysis, in turn, could be used to build theories and hypotheses for testing once quantitative data becomes available.

as mentioned earlier, quantitative research is more closely connected to the positivist school of social science, wherein theory precedes observation. In qualitative research, theory tends to emerge from observation—a notion closer to the interpretivist approach to social science (Creswell 2003, 182; see also Strauss and Corbin 1994, 194; Ryan and Bernard 2003, 278–80; Babbie and Benaquisto 2002, 378–9; Punch 2005, 209).

Methodological Differences

The broader epistemological divisions influence the narrower, methodological differences between quantitative and qualitative analyses (see Table 2.2). To reiterate, the following discussion treats the two traditions as poles on a spectrum; however, most political science research is conducted in the middle ground between these two extremes.

Table 2.2 Methodological Differences between the Two Traditions

Element of Data	Quantitative Tradition	Qualitative Tradition
Data format	Numerical (frequency, amount, salience, intensity)	Non-numerical (words, images)
Data reduction	Variables (operationalized a priori)	Themes (emergent)
Substance of data	Meaning is inherent	Meaning is contingent
Data recording	Standardized instrument	Variable instrument
Data processing	Mathematical	Conceptual
Data reporting	Statistical, graphical	Verbal
Standards of evidence	Probability	Plausibility

Data Format

Quantitative analysis deals in numbers and qualitative research does not. By definition, this method requires the "quantification" of political phenomena. Behaviours, ideas, and other observations must be converted into numbers by means of counting or scoring. Qualitative scholarship approaches political life differently, treating phenomena in terms of words, images, symbols, and other non-numerical forms.

Data Reduction

The desired format of the data leads those employing quantitative and qualitative methods to pursue different means of reducing their "raw materials" into manageable portions. In quantitative analysis, data reduction involves categorizing observations according to a series of pre-defined criteria. Phenomena are counted or ranked based on the means by, and extent to, which they vary in terms of certain attributes. In other words, observations are filtered through a set of variables, with specific values assigned to them. As outlined in Chapter 5, this variation may be expressed in nominal, ordinal, or interval form. Crucially, these categories are determined prior to the data reduction process, such that the resulting data set is the product of how each variable was defined and which variables were studied.

Scholars employing qualitative methods make sense of their observations through the identification of themes. This process may be achieved through a wide range of techniques, with various researchers referring to the process as one of soaking, chunking, puzzle-solving, or concept-mapping. Regardless of the terminology, all qualitative researchers search for patterns in their data as they group different observations according to certain non-numerical relationships. Such organization may involve linking similar ideas or respondents under given schools of thought or combining related concepts into distinct pillars of understanding.

In this sense, regardless of the method they apply, all researchers impose orderliness on their data. They simply approach this data reduction process from different perspectives and use different tools. As one group of methodologists explains, "Quantitative researchers conceptualize and refine variables in a process that comes before data collection or analysis. By contrast, qualitative researchers form new concepts or refine concepts that are grounded in the data" (Neuman and Robson 2007, 336–7).

Substance of Data

A guiding, if unstated, premise of quantitative analysis holds that meaning is intrinsic to the data itself. Given the **operational definition** established a priori, the nature of an observation is inherent, intersubjective, static, and **univocal**. This idea differs from the qualitative approach, whose practitioners insist that meaning is more contingent, or subject to, the unique perspectives of the observer and the diverse qualities of the observed. As such, most qualitative social scientists view observations as necessarily subjective, dynamic, and—ultimately—**equivocal**.

Data Recording

Based on these perspectives, data collection is pursued quite differently in the quantitative and qualitative traditions. For the former, meaning is inherent in the data, which allows analysts to use a standardized recording instrument (e.g. a closed questionnaire or code sheet). The latter is more "flexible" in terms of recording data (Babbie and Benaquisto 2002, 381; Neuman and Robson 2007, 111). In this tradition, meaning varies from observation to observation and from observer to observer. A more inclusive form of data collection is necessary to allow for these variations. Hence, qualitative analyses employ open-ended questionnaires, interviews, and coding techniques, in which full, directly quoted phrases are used instead of being filtered through pre-defined variables. (Open-ended questions will be discussed further in later chapters.)

Data Processing

Quantitative research applies proven statistical formulas, correlation coefficients, regression analyses, tests of significance, and other mathematical procedures in an effort to reveal the regularities of political life. Conversely, qualitative approaches provide a "softer" approach of "extracting" distinct themes and motifs. The data reduction, processing, and analysis stages are distinct and sequential in quantitative analyses and are subsumed under the qualitative coding process (see Chapter 13).

Data Reporting

Findings in quantitative analyses are depicted largely in numerical terms, in the form of graphs, tables, charts, and other figures. Analysts working in the qualitative tradition use words, not numbers or statistics, to express their findings. Again, these statements are generalizations. Nearly every qualitative analysis invokes numbers or speaks in terms of frequency or intensity, just as almost all quantitative scholarship "qualifies" its findings with reference to quotations or other non-numeric evidence. Suffice it to say, that quantitative research formats, reduces, and manipulates data and reports findings in numerical terms, while qualitative analysis informs through words and concepts.

Standards of Evidence

A final distinction between the quantitative and qualitative traditions lies in their differing definitions of *proof* or *evidence*. According to the tenets of interpretivism, social scientists need not—indeed cannot—establish their conclusions with absolute certainty. Rather, their aim is to approximate "truth," limiting the scope of their findings by applying certain disciplinary standards. Grounded in numbers and mathematics, quantitative research relies on statements of statistical significance and other measures of **probability** to establish the boundaries of its conclusions. Conversely, qualitative research reports the **plausibility** of its findings, based not on statistical odds but on the results' conceivability and fitness to the real world; rather than conduct mathematical tests, analysts marshal evidence and logic to establish the soundness of their findings (Neuman and Robson 2007, 336; Manheim et al. 2002, 317). Although closely related, *probability* and *plausibility* are by no means synonymous.

APPLY YOUR UNDERSTANDING

The World of Word Clouds

Social scientists are finding new (even fun) ways to challenge the boundaries between the qualitative and quantitative traditions. Consider the development of word clouds as a means of depicting research findings. Word clouds measure the frequency of word use in a particular document (a quantitative approach) but illustrate this measurement qualitatively (by creating "clouds" consisting of words of different sizes, shapes, and colours). Any document can be fed into a word cloud generator, including student essays and even this textbook. Here is a word cloud depicting the contents of this chapter:

To see how this process works, search online for full-text versions of the United Nations Declaration of Human Rights and the Canadian Charter of Rights and Freedoms. Then visit Wordle.net, which provides free web-based word cloud software. Simply follow the on-screen instructions to copy and paste the text from the UN Charter into the Wordle generator. Save the resulting cloud, do the same for the Canadian Charter, and compare the results. Identify the key differences between the two clouds and explain whether the analysis is quantitative or qualitative.

Summary

Each tradition has its benefits and limitations. One advantage of the quantitative approach is that the large size of the group studied allows us to make generalizations from the sample to a larger unit, such as society as a whole. This ability is more limited in qualitative research, due to the small size of the group being studied.

In addition, quantitative research is often seen as more objective than qualitative research. The research methods employed in the latter require a greater degree of interpretation on the part of the researcher and are therefore more subjective. However, qualitative research allows for a richer understanding of the political phenomena being studied. Political research often concerns individual beliefs, attitudes, and behaviours, topics that cannot be completely explored by quantitative research. One of the most insightful studies of ideological belief systems in the United States (Lane 1962) was based on in-depth interviews with only 15 male respondents in New Haven, Connecticut. Although the researcher was unable to make empirical generalizations to the American population at large, he was able to provide vivid insights into how "the American Common Man" (defined, at that time, in very narrow terms) tries to make sense out of a complex political world.

As noted earlier, choosing between the two approaches depends upon the research question and objectives of the study. If one wishes to develop generalizations that are broad in scope, the quantitative approach may be more appropriate. If one desires a greater understanding of the phenomena in question, with less concern for generalizability, the qualitative approach is better. Of course, in political science we often wish to achieve both

Expand Your Knowledge

The Quantitative/Qualitative Balance in Canada

Since the behavioural revolution, much has been made of political science favouring the quantitative tradition over the qualitative when it comes to publication. This imbalance has created deeper divisions in the United States than elsewhere, with entire associations and journals emerging to cater to each "side" of the discipline (Sigelman 2006).

The divide is less stark in Canada, and the balance between qualitative and quantitative scholarship actually favours the former. In their 2008 study, Montpetit, Blais, and Foucault found that political scientists in Canada were far more likely to publish articles based on qualitative research than on quantitative analysis. They examined all major journal articles published by Canadian political scientists between 1985 and 2005, finding that a full 85 per cent (or 1,574) were qualitative in nature compared to just 15 per cent (or 286) that were quantitative. The growth in the proportion of quantitative studies has been slower in Canada than in the United States, yet Canadian quantitative studies were nonetheless more likely to be cited than qualitative ones. (The average journal article produced by a Canadian political scientist was cited three times; the average quantitative article was cited five times.) These data suggest that, though Canadian political scientists were more likely to produce qualitative research, those that did publish quantitative articles likely had a larger and more receptive audience. This result, in turn, is likely due to the prevalence of the quantitative tradition in other countries.

ends. The solution, then, is to combine the two research strategies, allowing the strengths of one to complement those of the other. A researcher might combine a large-*N* quantitative telephone survey with a series of in-depth, qualitative interviews with a small subset of respondents. The survey allows him or her to ask an identical set of questions to a large sample, and the interviews allow him or her to explore the issues in depth with a smaller group of individuals. Combining research approaches, known as mixed methods, is discussed later in this chapter.

Trustworthy Research

Having established the core differences between quantitative and qualitative scholarship, our focus now turns to the common ground between them. Although they may use different terminology, both traditions rely on similar standards to judge the respectability of their research.

The core question at the heart of all political research, both qualitative and quantitative, is, "How do we ensure that the knowledge generated through political science is legitimate?" For most scholars employing quantitative methods, the answer is relatively straightforward. Their research must achieve three standards of accuracy: validity, reliability, and objectivity. Many purely qualitative researchers, particularly postmodernists and other relativists, reject these notions entirely. For them, all explanations of social life are constructed and subjective; thus, no universal standards of "proof" or "truthfulness" can be applied. Today's political scientists have found a middle ground by agreeing that the two approaches—which attach slightly different labels and impose unique measurement requirements—share a common set of expectations regarding scholarly research. This view is best captured by Guba and Lincoln's (1985) concept of **trustworthiness**. Building on these authors' seminal account, the following discussion outlines the four essential elements of all legitimate social science research: authenticity, portability, precision, and impartiality (see Table 2.3).

Authenticity

At its basic level, **authenticity** connotes a correspondence between the observation and the observed. To what extent is the recorded data a genuine reflection of reality? In this matter, "the goal is to demonstrate that the inquiry was conducted in such a manner as to ensure

Table 2.3 Criteria for Trustworthiness

Criteria	Quantitative Tradition[1]	Qualitative Tradition[2]
Authenticity	Measurement validity	Credibility
Portability	External validity	Transferability
Precision	Reliability	Dependability
Impartiality	Objectivity	Confirmability

1, 2 Adapted from Guba and Lincoln (1985).

that the subject was accurately identified and described" (Marshall and Rossman 1989, 145). In quantitative research, this notion is known as measurement validity, "the degree to which the measurement of a concept truly reflects that concept" (Bryman 2004, 541). As they harbour more reservations about the intersubjectivity of "accuracy," many scholars toiling in the qualitative tradition generally prefer the term ***credibility*** to *validity*. To have integrity or authenticity, a qualitative account must provide a tenable, believable depiction of the subject under study. In other words, the observation and data must "fit" the world being described—an evaluation that depends less on the true nature of reality than on the judgment of the reader (Krippendorff 2004, 314).

Portability

A second important criterion for assessing the trustworthiness of a social scientific study is its **portability**. Most researchers acknowledge that, to make a substantive and substantial contribution to knowledge, studies must move beyond the explanation of a small number of cases. The results ought to connect to broader questions about social life; they ought to be "portable," or applicable to other environments in some way. Researchers working in the quantitative tradition refer to this as **external validity**, the degree to which "the results of a study can be generalized beyond the specific research context in which it was conducted" (Bryman 2004, 539). This validity is often established through the specification of operationalized variables, causal models, and regression models, which may be repeated in other contexts. Many researchers employing qualitative methods prefer the term ***transferability***, reflecting the view that a study's findings must be transposed in order to establish their portability. In this sense, "the burden of demonstrating the applicability of one set of findings to another context rests more with the investigator who would make that transfer than with the original investigator" (Lewis and Ritchie 2006, 145). Merriam (2002a, 28–9) suggests,

> The most common way generalizability has been conceptualized in qualitative research is as reader or user generalizability. In this view, readers themselves determine the extent to which findings from a study can be applied to their context. Called case-to-case transfer by Firestone (1993), "It is the reader who has to ask, what is there in this study that I can apply to my own situation, and what clearly does not apply?"

Precision

The inability of researchers conducting qualitative research to replicate their results constitutes the most crucial point of contention among followers of the two traditions. **Replicability** is a fundamental component of the positivist approach to social science. To confirm its **reliability**—"that quality of measurement method that suggests the same data would have been collected each time in repeated observations of the same phenomenon" (Babbie and Benaquisto 2002, 497)—any finding in quantitative research must be repeatable.

Expand Your Knowledge

Internal and External Validity

When conducting positivist, quantitative research, the researcher must always ask, "How valid is my research design?" **Validity**, in this instance, refers to how useful our design is in advancing the knowledge we are trying to obtain. There are two broad forms of validity that we need to be concerned with when considering research design: internal validity and external validity. **Internal validity** concerns the validity within the study: Are we measuring what we believe we are measuring (measurement validity)? Are our conclusions supported by the facts of our study? Have we ruled out alternative explanations and spurious relationships? Internal validity can vary with the degree to which we can control our study. If we are able to hold conditions constant, we can rule out alternative factors, and our conclusions are more likely to be supported. In such a case, we have high internal validity. If, on the other hand, there are many factors that we cannot control and therefore many alternative explanations that may compete with our conclusions, we have low internal validity. In a nutshell, low internal validity means that we have less confidence in our conclusions about the study, whereas high internal validity means that we have a strong degree of confidence.

Note that, with internal validity, we are concerned with the validity of the study itself. Questions of external validity focus on the legitimacy of generalizations made from the study. Was the study representative, or was it a "rogue" or "fluke" study, a one-in-a-million occurrence? Can our study allow us to make generalizations about the real world or are the conclusions applicable only to the single study? When conducting theory-oriented research, we desire high external validity, since we wish to use the studies to make generalizations about the larger political world. Quite often there are trade-offs between internal and external validity. The more "realistic" one's study is, the greater the external validity. However, as realism increases, the researcher's level of control over the study decreases, reducing internal validity. How the researcher addresses such dilemmas depends on his or her research objectives.

As the process of qualitative research is more fluid and dependent upon the researcher's role as an instrument in the process, findings cannot be reproduced in the same sense as quantitative ones (Lewis and Ritchie 2006, 270). This is not to say that qualitative research ignores the value of **precision**. Rather, the focus shifts from the more intersubjective notion of reliability to the standard of **dependability**. According to Merriam (2002a, 27),

> Replication of a qualitative study will not yield the same results, but this does not discredit the results of any particular study; there can be numerous interpretations of the same data. The more important question for qualitative researchers is *whether the results are consistent with the data collected* . . . That is, rather than insisting that others get the same results as the original researcher, reliability lies in

others' concurring that given the data collected, the results make sense—they are consistent and dependable (emphasis in original).

Provided that the research process is clearly specified and transparent, readers may assess its precision by asking the question, "Is it reasonable to assume that, given the opportunity to repeat the exercise under the same conditions, a researcher would have reported the same results from the same observations?" If yes, the qualitative study is verifiable and dependable in the same way that a quantitative analysis is replicable and reliable.

Impartiality

Lastly, but certainly not in terms of importance, most social scientists agree that research should convey **impartial** knowledge about the world as opposed to normative opinions or value-laden wisdom. As Marshall and Rossman (1989, 147) put it, "How can we be sure that the findings are reflective of the subjects and the inquiry itself rather than the product of the researcher's biases or prejudices?" In attempting to minimize their own biases, researchers employing quantitative methods aim to protect a study's **objectivity**—a term clearly at odds with the interpretive principles of qualitative scholarship. Researchers using qualitative methods are more likely to acknowledge (even embrace or test) their personal biases as unavoidable elements of the research process (Merriam 2002b, 5; King et al. 1993, 14–15). As a result, all qualitative inquiry contains some element of subjectivity. When striving for trustworthy results, the qualitative tradition demands that readers ask, "Can these findings be *confirmed* by another individual, independent of the original researcher's predispositions?" This question is the essence of **confirmability**.

Summary

Neither of the two traditions is beyond reproach when it comes to producing trustworthy results. Preserving validity is the greatest challenge for students employing quantitative methods. For example, coding platforms and speeches has the potential to reduce complex, living texts to a series of simpler, colder numbers. The opposite issue confronts analysts in the qualitative tradition. By delving into the deeper meaning of these documents, relying upon more "intuitive, soft, and relativistic" modes of interpretation, they risk compromising the dependability, transferability, and confirmability of their findings (Creswell 1998, 142; see also Manheim et al. 2002, 315). Hence, on their own, neither the quantitative nor qualitative tradition stakes claim to being a superior method. Both have their own advantages and drawbacks. Fortunately, their weaknesses are offset by their complementary strengths, and common tools are available to maintain the trustworthiness of their research.

Ensuring Trustworthiness

There are numerous ways for political scientists to bolster the authenticity, portability, precision, and impartiality of their research.[3] Many of these tools are available to quantitative and qualitative scholars, regardless of tradition or method. Leading methodologist John

Creswell (1998, 203) recommends adopting at least two legitimacy checks, but you would be wise to incorporate as many of the following practices as possible to ensure the trustworthiness of your analyses (see Table 2.4). You can also use these criteria to assess the trustworthiness of the research studies that you read.

Triangulation

By selecting a research approach, we choose to see the world in a particular way. Kathleen Driscoll and Joan McFarland (1989, 185–6) write: "Techniques of data collection and analysis are not neutral. . . . Each technique's usefulness and its limitations are structured by its underlying assumptions. Adopting a research technique means adopting its underlying conceptual framework." Each research design privileges some forms of information over others. Perhaps the best analogy is a line of sight (Berg 1989, 4). If we stand in front of an object, we get one impression of it; standing behind, above, or below the same object can lead to different observations. To best understand the object and to get the most complete picture, we should take in as many perspectives as possible.

The same holds true for understanding political and social phenomena: comprehension grows as we approach data collection in various ways. The combination of multiple research strategies in social research—known as **triangulation**—maximizes the variety of data collected. As the image of the triangle suggests, triangulation implies the use of three

Table 2.4 Ensuring Trustworthiness in Political Science

Checks	Authenticity	Portability	Precision	Impartiality
Triangulation	•	•	•	•
Detailed findings	•	•	•	
Established techniques	•	•		
Report method	•		•	
Discrepant evidence	•		•	•
Publish data	•		•	•
Member checks	•			•
Intense exposure	•			
Research teams		•	•	•
Computerized coding			•	•
Intracoder testing			•	
Intercoder assessment			•	
Pilot studies and training			•	
Report biases				•
Peer assessment	•	•	•	•

different methods of data-gathering, although a researcher may choose to use only two or more than three.

Triangulation is the foremost means of protecting the legitimacy of political research, although the definition of the term is somewhat ambiguous.[4] Some view triangulation as the concurrent use of a number of different methods in a single research study. This approach may involve combining content analysis with, for example, interviews or direct observation. To others, combination may take place through separate studies, either consecutively or in tandem (Boyatzis 1998, xiii). Still others believe that triangulation can be achieved by using existing literature to provide "supplemental validation" of research findings (Creswell 1998).

Moreover, the complementary strengths of qualitative and quantitative research have pushed many dualists to develop "hybrid" approaches as a "third way" of conducting social science research (Tashakkori and Teddlie 2003, x). Whether to compensate for the weaknesses of a single approach or to address a particularly complex topic, an increasing number of social scientists are adopting a broader perspective on research (Creswell and Clark 2007). Some refer to this stance as **mixed methods research**—"the use of both qualitative and quantitative method in one study or sequentially in two or more studies" (Hesse-Biber and Leavy 2006, 316). For qualitative researchers, this approach may mean "**quantizing**" their verbal analyses by buttressing their findings with reference to frequencies and other quantitative measures (Ibid., 326–30; see also Gerring 1998). By the same token, quantitative researchers may "**qualitize**" their data, contextualizing their findings with direct quotations from various documents or sources (Hesse-Biber and Leavy 2006, 330–3; see also Neuman and Robson 2007, Chapter 16).

APPLY YOUR UNDERSTANDING

Mixed Methods Research

As social science (indeed, academia in general) becomes more interdisciplinary, there is increasing pressure on analysts to combine methodological approaches in the course of their research. Whether in the design of their research or grant proposals or in the course of the peer-review process, researchers are now being challenged on their use of a single methodology. This movement has encouraged many to pursue mixed method research, either by conducting quantitative and qualitative research on their own or by assembling a research team to approach their subject from different angles.

Imagine that you are preparing a conference paper for presentation at a multidisciplinary conference. Your research project analyzes the effect of neo-liberalism on Canadian foreign policy, particularly its approach to building trade relationships with emerging markets in the Middle East. What sort of evidence (or data) would you compile? How would you ensure that your analysis is viewed as trustworthy by reviewers on either side of the traditional qualitative/quantitative divide?

Whatever the definition, the purpose of triangulation is clear: by invoking multiple data sources to support their findings, researchers may substantiate the overall trustworthiness of their work.

Detailed Findings

Only by providing a meticulous account of their results can researchers offer readers the information necessary to draw their own conclusions about the authenticity, portability, and precision of the findings. Qualitative researchers must provide "thick description" of their cases; this is often accomplished through the inclusion of direct quotations and copious footnoting. In addition to statistical tables and data appendices, quantitative analyses must involve "colour" or "substance" in their reporting as well. Doing so provides the meaning behind the numbers presented.

Established Techniques

Where possible, political scientists should seek to build upon established techniques. In quantitative research, this task may mean drawing upon existing surveys, interview scripts, or coding manuals. Students using qualitative methods may rely on general methodological guidelines, including the widely accepted three-stage process of open, axial, and selective coding (see Chapters 12 and 13). Employing these guidelines does not mean the abandonment of methodological innovation—far from it. Great strides have been made by testing, challenging, expanding, adapting, and improving popular research designs. But building on tested techniques allows researchers to elude many pitfalls encountered during earlier studies and to avoid a state of methodological anarchism (Budge and Bara 2001).

Report Method

To provide readers with the opportunity to assess a study's authenticity and precision, researchers must report the exact process through which they achieved their results. In quantitative analysis, reporting is most efficiently accomplished through the publication of the research instrument (questionnaire, coding manual, or other guides). With no standardized instrument, analysts conducting qualitative studies must provide their readers with an **audit trail**—a detailed account of the coding "protocol," including how conclusions were reached (Altheide 1996, 25–33). Holliday (2007, 7) suggests that all research "needs to be accompanied by accounts of how it was really done . . . [Analysts must] reveal how they negotiated complex procedures to deal with the 'messy' reality of the scenarios being studied."

Discrepant Evidence

Most practitioners readily acknowledge the limitations of political science when it comes to representing and explaining reality. Rather than absolute "proof" or "truth," most analysts aim to establish the persuasiveness of their accounts relative to alternative explanations.

Many researchers employing quantitative methods turn to the statistics of probability, just as those following the qualitative tradition depend on "plausibility arguments" to buttress their claims (Richerson and Boyd 2004, 410–11). In both traditions, researchers are encouraged to seek out and report discrepant evidence to place reasonable boundaries on their conclusions. Becker (1998), Esterberg (2002, 175), and Berg (2004, 184) refer to this practice as the "null hypothesis trick": analysts ought to approach the data by assuming that no patterns exist and then by providing clear evidence, using concrete examples, to establish their presence. George (2006, 155) explains that the seasoned researcher

> considers not just one inferential hypothesis when reading and rereading the original . . . material, but also many alternatives to it. He systematically weighs the evidence available for and against each of these alternative inferences. Thus, the results of his analysis, if fully explicated, state not merely (1) the favored inference and the content "evidence" for it, but also (2) alternative explanations of that content "evidence," (3) other content "evidence" which may support alternative inferences, and (4) reasons for considering one inferential hypothesis more plausible than others.

Without these qualifications and justifications, the analysis may lack validity or credibility (Holliday 2007, 167–81).

Publish Data

To guard against criticisms of inauthenticity, imprecision, and partiality, political scientists should provide reasonable access to both their data and raw materials, whether qualitative or quantitative. In qualitative research, coding databases and memos (and the original documents) should be made available for private or public verification. In an electronic age, sharing this information has never been easier, and there are few legitimate excuses (beyond important privacy concerns) to withhold access to such material.

Member Checks

Most researchers seasoned in the qualitative tradition are familiar with the notion of **member checks**—a process through which their inferences are verified by the subjects of their analysis. Field observations may be referred to some of the participants; surveys may be followed by in-depth interviews of the respondents; or focus group data may be shared with members of the study. In textual analysis, such checks require consulting the authors of the source documents. Sometimes this step is not desirable or even possible. (Some documents have too many authors to consult, or no willing, surviving, or identifiable authors.) When completed, however, member checks may alert researchers to inauthentic claims or biased interpretations.

Intense Exposure

Extended, intense contact with source materials is more likely to produce valid or credible interpretations of their contents. To produce authentic results, both qualitative and quantitative researchers must read and re-read these materials, much the same way that field researchers spend prolonged periods with their subjects or interviewers in close contact with their respondents. Various researchers refer to this process as one of immersing, marinating, or soaking oneself in the data in order to "absorb" their meanings. Although no disciplinary standard exists in terms of how long researchers ought to spend with their raw materials, as a general rule analysts should remain immersed in the data until they are "saturated"—that is, until no new meanings or interpretations appear evident.

Research Teams

Political analysis is no longer conducted solely by independent researchers toiling by lamplight. The academic community has long since embraced the value of collaboration, be it intra- or interdisciplinary in scope. **Investigator triangulation** refers to the use of research teams, rather than individuals, to study and interpret events or phenomena. The material benefits are obvious: a large group of researchers can collect and process a wider range of materials, generate more data, and produce more analyses than a single individual can. Furthermore, a larger working group can help to ensure the precision of the data and impartiality of the analyses. More eyes mean more perspectives, and more minds mean more debate. As we all know, three people observing the same event will have differing reports and interpretations of what actually occurred. Increasing the number of observers helps increase our confidence in the interpretations.

Whether due to their ontological predispositions or lack of experience with collaboration, many qualitative analysts have been less eager or equipped than their quantitative counterparts when it comes to adopting the team-based approach. Doing so may lead to an improved sense of dependability and confirmability in their analyses.

Training and Pilot Studies

Conducting a **pilot study** is another important means of improving the precision of political science research. Pretesting allows analysts to hone their research techniques and tools while submitting their results to critical internal and external review. To be accurate, every scientist requires properly calibrated instruments. In qualitative political analysis—in which the researcher is an important instrument in the process—each analyst must be well trained prior to engaging his or her raw materials (Morse and Richards 2002). Options include attending coding workshops held at many universities and conferences, collaborating with experienced researchers as a means of apprenticeship, or intensely studying a variety of methods guidebooks. Above all, practice is the best means of attaining experience and publication the best means of attaining credentials. Both help enhance the reliability or dependability of one's work.

Report Biases

To convince readers that a body of research offers an impartial view of the world, analysts ought to recognize, acknowledge, and minimize the amount of personal bias that enters the study. Critical self-reflection and open admission of bias is a key component of qualitative research, particularly for those who engage in field studies and participant observation (Creswell 2003, 182).

Peer Assessment

Ultimately, the trustworthiness of research is judged by its legitimacy in the eyes of the scientific community (Kuhn 1962). Peer assessment is critical to such judgments, whether it takes place near the beginning of the research process or in its final stages. Where possible, it is wise to have a diverse group of peers assessing one's work, including experts with the methodology, experts in the subject matter, and outsiders. In the interests of interdisciplinarity, it may be suitable to invite input from peers outside one's home academic community. Doing so often sets high standards of trustworthiness, but there is no better way to test the research's authenticity, portability, precision, and impartiality. As Merriam (2002a, 26) contends,

> In one sense, all graduate students have a peer review process built into their thesis or dissertation committee—as each member reads and comments on the findings. Peer review or peer examination can be conducted by a colleague either familiar with the research or one new to the topic. There are advantages to both, but either way, a thorough peer examination would involve asking a colleague to assess whether the findings are plausible based on the data.

APPLY YOUR KNOWLEDGE

Evaluating Secondary Sources for Trustworthiness

The tools and techniques discussed in this chapter are useful for both producing and consuming political science research. In the Information Age, it can be challenging to distinguish trustworthy from untrustworthy studies. To ensure you are using the best evidence to support your research, your sources should

- combine more than one research technique or method,
- provide an adequate description of the methodology they employed,
- employ a tried-and-tested research design,
- include any evidence uncovered that conflicts their central findings,
- allow researchers access to their raw data,
- consult with their research participants for feedback on their findings, and
- subject their findings to rigorous testing by their colleagues.

Even with the inclusion of these various checks, political scientists are still vulnerable to charges that they have been selective in incorporating data to suit their purposes. That is, they may have purposefully misrepresented, omitted, or downplayed evidence in order to bolster their arguments. The qualitative student of rhetoric is not unlike the quantitative survey researcher in this regard; all face the temptation to massage data or falsify results (King et al. 1993). In this vein, beyond assurances of academic integrity, both qualitative and quantitative analysts must make every effort to be as transparent as possible to allow for the verification of their method, data, and findings.

Conclusion

A lot has been made of the differences between quantitative and qualitative research, both in this chapter and, historically, within the political science discipline. Indeed, previous generations of political scientists would have perceived a deep divide between those working in the quantitative tradition and those employing qualitative methods. Scholars would have spent their entire careers in one "camp" or the other. They would have learned and applied one set of methodological tools, with little regard (and, in some cases, respect) for researchers in the other tradition. Though the core epistemological and methodological distinctions between quantitative and qualitative research remain, times have changed in that more political scientists see value in approaching politics from a variety of different empirical perspectives.

This approach need not mean a "watering down" of disciplinary standards. To move beyond cold number-crunching and armchair musings, analysts employing both quantitative and qualitative methods must take numerous steps to ensure the trustworthiness of their research. From triangulation, audit trails, and member checks to computerized coding, intercoder reliability tests, and peer review, a host of tools exist to protect the authenticity, portability, precision, and impartiality of their work. These four standards may be given different names in each tradition, and researchers pursuing either quantitative or qualitative analysis must approach them in slightly different ways. Nonetheless, as criteria for trustworthiness, scholars in both methodological traditions must pay heed to their principles. A methodological middle ground exists between the statistical and interpretive approaches, helping practitioners of both camps to work together in furthering our understanding of the political world.

In an age when social scientists must carry complete "tool boxes" when approaching their research problems, the willingness, ability, and desire to combine various methodological techniques are definite assets. By appreciating the credibility, transferability, dependability, and confirmability of the qualitative method and the validity, reliability, and objectivity of the quantitative approach, political scientists may gain the best of both worlds and get the most out of their research.

Working as a Team

1. Discuss the main similarities and differences between the qualitative and quantitative approaches to politics. Identify a research question that is of interest to the group and discuss whether one can explore it with both qualitative and quantitative approaches.
2. Elaborate on the type of data collection strategy that would be used for either approach to your team's question.

Self-Study

1. This chapter shows that, although qualitative and quantitative approaches can be viewed as mutually exclusive and competing perspectives, they can (and should) be viewed as complementary. What do you think? Make an argument that these approaches are either contradictory or complementary.
2. Justify your argument from the previous exercise by using an example.

Notes

1. Material in this chapter previously appeared in Jared J. Wesley, "Building Bridges in Content Analysis: Quantitative and Qualitative Traditions." Paper presented at the Annual Meeting of the Canadian Political Science Association, Carleton University, Ottawa, May 2009.
2. Divisions within the American political science community run particularly deep, as evidenced by the recent Perestroika movement. For more information, see Monroe (2005).
3. This discussion draws upon a wide range of sources. See Marshall and Rossman (1989, 144–9); Krippendorff (2004, 212–16, 313–21); Creswell (1998, 197–209); Creswell (2003, 196); Hodder (1994, 401); Lewis and Ritchie (2006, 275–6); Bryman (2001, 272–6); Holliday (2007, 167–81); Merriam (2002a, 24–31); King et al. (1993); Platt (2006, 112–13); George (2006, 155–7).
4. Some qualitative scholars disagree with this view, arguing that "triangulation is not a tool or strategy of validation, but an alternative to validation" (Denzin and Lincoln 1994, 2).

CHAPTER 3

Theory-Oriented Research and the Issue of Causality

Destination

By the end of this chapter, you should be able to

- explain the role that theory plays in empirical political research;
- outline the distinctions between basic and applied research and between inductive and deductive research; and
- detail how theories are developed and applied in empirical research and how causal explanations can be both advanced and confused.

When we think of research, most of us picture a laboratory with men and women in white coats examining test tubes and seeking the cure for cancer, or at least for the common cold. As Chapter 1 argued, the scientific approach can be extended beyond the natural sciences and the laboratory to include the social sciences and to advance knowledge in the broader social world. This chapter explores the different research approaches that political scientists use to augment our understanding of politics and society. In particular, the role of theory in political science research will be explored; within this context, we will see why cause-and-effect relationships are difficult to establish in the political realm.

Basic and Applied Research

Empirical researchers differ in their reasons for conducting studies. Some research is directed at answering specific questions or solving immediate problems: What is the best way to implement a new home-care program? What are the costs and benefits of an employee-training program? How effective has a teenage anti-smoking campaign been? How can a particular political party strengthen its appeal among young voters? Research directed at finding answers to specific problems, with immediate practical usage, is known as **applied research**. Examples include cost–benefit analyses, social impact assessments, needs assessments, and evaluations of existing programs or policies, all of which provide job opportunities for social science graduates. Applied research is frequently used by governments, businesses, marketing agencies, political campaign organizers, hospitals, and educational facilities to help fine-tune their programs, products, and strategies. Given that such agencies have to work with limited resources, their money and time must be put to the most effective and efficient usage. Applied research, then, is used to maximize effectiveness and efficiency in the short term.[1]

The federal granting councils (the Social Sciences and Humanities Research Council, the Natural Sciences and Engineering Research Council, and the Canadian Institutes of Health Research—collectively known as Canada's Tri-Council Agencies), together with the federal and provincial governments and universities and colleges, have increasingly advocated for the societal mobilization of research conducted in Canada's publicly funded post-secondary institutions. Whether referred to as knowledge mobilization, knowledge transfer, or knowledge translation, the goal of such advocacy is to increase the salience of applied research for the benefit of Canadians.

A limitation of applied research is that it is usually descriptive in nature; it indicates how things are but does not explain why they are that way. Applied research often addresses a single question in an extremely narrow manner and may fail to advance our knowledge of the larger political and social world. However, this narrow scope may be viewed as an advantage. Since applied research is outcome-oriented, the question posed in an applied research project may be how a general process applies in a particular setting. Consider a project whose purpose is to reduce gang membership in metropolitan Vancouver. The researchers may begin with the general idea that greater social interaction in a safe and supportive environment decreases the incidence of gang membership among "at-risk" youth (e.g. 15- to 24-year-old males). They may then identify and apply various kinds of opportunities for social interaction among at-risk youth in the area and assess the effectiveness of each. The solutions found in this community in Vancouver may not be effective among similar groups in Calgary, Toronto, Montreal, or Halifax, but the finding that they work among the target group in Vancouver is sufficient. Therefore, the relative limited application of the results in this applied research project would be enough to justify the research.

Basic research, on the other hand, aims to broaden our understanding of political life. Seeking to advance general knowledge, basic researchers (usually academics) examine theories about politics and attempt to formulate explanations and generalizations by empirically testing hypotheses. Basic research might address why there are so few women in elected public office and, from this research, develop a number of explanations and theories. These explanations are not immediately translated into policies to address the problem, but they add to our foundational understanding of the impact of gender in the political realm. Basic research is theory-oriented research, and much academic research falls into this camp.

In basic research, then, knowledge is pursued for its own sake and to expand our knowledge base. This is not to say that this type of investigation lacks practical implications. The ideas that emerge from basic research are frequently utilized in applied research, although the importance of basic research may not immediately be seen. We must remember that knowledge is cumulative and continually advancing. Over time, "irrelevant" research findings can have a great impact on our lives. As W. Lawrence Neuman (1994, 21) writes, "Today's computers could not exist without the pure research in mathematics conducted over a century ago, for which there was no known practical application at the time."

Some of the biggest research projects in the history of Canadian social sciences have combined applied and basic research. The Royal Commission on Aboriginal Peoples, which reported in late 1996, provides an example. Its research reports constitute a massive amount of applied and basic knowledge with respect to Aboriginal peoples. A second example is the Royal Commission on the Future of Health Care (the Romanow Commission, 2002), which was informed by research papers, public opinion analyses, discussion papers, and a series of consultations. A third example is the Metropolis Project, a collaboration between Citizenship and Immigration Canada (a federal department) and the Social Sciences and Humanities Research Council that operated from 2000 to 2012. This project involved an international network of academics and public servants studying migration, diversity, and immigrant integration in cities in Canada and elsewhere. In all three cases, the marriage of applied and basic research was complementary and mutually reinforcing.

APPLY YOUR UNDERSTANDING

Basic and Applied Research

Imagine that you are gathering documentary evidence in a study of Canada's "national identity." What questions would you ask if you were conducting basic research? Applied research?

Theory: Relationships between Concepts

As academic researchers, our primary goal is to advance theory. Before discussing how we develop a political theory, we should first think about what exactly a theory is and what it contains. As stated in Chapter 1, a theory is an integrated set of explanations of the political and social worlds. In other words, we attempt to understand the complex political world by simplifying reality into theories. A theory identifies a general pattern of behaviour, from which we can both make predictions and empirically test relevant hypotheses. We might theorize that support for ideological conservatism varies with socioeconomic status. From this idea, we can predict that two individuals with differing socioeconomic status will show dissimilar support for a conservative party, and we can test the theory with empirical data by seeing if the generalizations fit with our observations. As Jarol B. Manheim and Richard C. Rich (1981, 17) note, "[t]heories are simply intellectual tools . . . theories are neither true nor false in any absolute sense, but only more or less useful." Basic research is continually testing hypotheses based on theories to maximize their explanatory power.

Hypotheses are statements of the relationships between concepts or, more specifically, are proposed explanations for an observable phenomenon. One can hypothesize that an increase in political interest leads to an increase in political participation. A **proposition** states that, if the hypothesis is true, the following predicate of a subject is either true or false. (It can be useful to think of a proposition as an "if–then" statement.) Continuing with our example, the following proposition can be stated: *if* an increase in political interest leads to an increase in political participation, *then* Canadians with a high level of political interest will display relatively high levels of political participation (that is, relative to Canadians as a whole). The proposition follows from the hypothesis. Whether the hypothesis is true or false will be known only after empirical analysis is conducted.

Expand Your Knowledge

Action Research

When applied research is conducted for social purposes defined a priori, it may fall outside our definitions of scientific research. This **action**, or **advocacy**, **research** often begins with a premise that one group is socially or economically disadvantaged and proceeds to draw the implications of that disadvantage or to assume its causes. For feminist action research, the cause of disadvantage could be the male hegemonic power structure. For Aboriginal action research, it could be the Eurocentric, materialistic power structure. For labour action research, it could be the corporate power structure.

Action research need not be based on only the support of the socially disadvantaged. Instead, it could be conducted in reaction to the perception of a group receiving too much support. Conservative (re)action research could begin from the premise that the government (through the legislature, the courts, or the administration) acts in support of the disadvantaged. Thus, the governmental/interest group power structure may be the source of the problem. Whether such research stems from the ideological left or right, it is inconsistent with the scientific method to the extent that it violates the idea that nothing is self-evident (the fifth postulate of science; see Chapter 1). If something is taken as an empirical fact, it must be demonstrably true. Put another way, a demonstration of the sources of power must be a part of the overall research enterprise.

A concept is a defined term that enables us to organize and classify phenomena. The terms *politician*, *region*, *discrimination*, *power*, *income*, and *sexism* are all examples of concepts. A concept can be either concrete or abstract, which means that some require more elaborate definitions than others if they are to be measured. For example, age is a simple concept; a person's age is equal to the present year less the year they were born. Equality, on the other hand, is a very complex idea, and political scientists differ in how they define it.

In addition to allowing us to classify phenomena, concepts enable us to make comparisons through categorization. Categories designate the variation that occurs within a concept. Income can be classified as high, medium, or low; religion can be classified as Protestant, Catholic, Jewish, Muslim, Hindu, Buddhist, etc. All concepts contain a degree of variation; hence, when we measure concepts empirically, we refer to them as variables. We are able to see variation in a concept by identifying the different values, or categories, that exist.

The simplest way to classify concepts with discrete values is to identify the significant points where variation occurs. An example of this treatment is seen in Max Weber's theory of authority. Weber argued that three types of authority exist: charismatic, traditional, and legal. Charismatic authority is derived from an individual leader's unique qualities. Traditional authority derives from established patterns (i.e. doing things in a certain way because they have always been done that way). Legal authority derives from the legal specification of duties (Albrow 1970, 37–40).

When classifying variables that can be ordered or ranked, we often use a **continuum**. (As will be explained in Chapter 5, such variables are known as ordinal variables.) We order a concept's values along a dimension, ranging from low to high or from less to more. In his classic work, *An Economic Theory of Democracy*, Anthony Downs (1957) arranged political ideologies along a single-dimension continuum. This "left–right spectrum" organizes political ideologies in terms of positions toward the desired role of the state in the economy. Socialism is located to the left; liberalism is positioned in the centre; and conservatism is to the right. Downs argued that both political parties and individuals can be located on

Expand Your Knowledge

The Conventional Left-Right Spectrum

Left - - - - - - - - - - **Centre** - - - - - - - - - - **Right**

Left	Right
Full government ownership of the means of production	No government ownership of the means of production
Extensive government regulation	No government regulation
Extensive redistribution of income	No redistribution of income

the spectrum; in fact, a party's location depends on where voters are located. Parties seek to maximize the number of votes they receive and, accordingly, position themselves at the point where the greatest number of voters is located.

The **ideal type** and **typology** are other means of classifying concepts. In the former approach, a non-existent ideal is outlined and observed cases are then compared with this ideal. An example is Weber's ideal type bureaucracy, organized hierarchically with all rules, procedures, and responsibilities defined impartially (Albrow 1970, 37–40). Although Weber does not suggest that the ideal type bureaucracy exists in reality, it does serve as a model against which to compare existing organizational systems. In a typology, the relationship between two or more concepts is expressed in a way that leads to the creation of new concepts. One well-known typology in political science is Aristotle's typology of regimes, which divides political systems along two dimensions: the number of rulers and the beneficiaries. Note that each concept has categories of its own: number of rulers takes three values (one, few, many), while beneficiaries has two (citizens and rulers). The resultant categories—monarchy, tyranny, aristocracy, oligarchy, polity, and democracy—are the different values of the concept of regime.

Along with concepts, a theory requires relationships, or correlations, between concepts. Furthermore, a theory requires a statement of **causality** between the principal concepts. It is important to distinguish between a correlation and a causal relation. Two concepts are correlated if a change in one occurs when there is a change in the other. There is a causal relation when the change in one of the variables leads to or produces a change in the other. We will first discuss the character of correlation and turn to causality later in the chapter.

To provide an example, age and voting turnout are correlated if people of different ages tend to vote in different numbers. Variations occur simultaneously within each concept; the two are said to covary. However, a theory does not only state that concepts are correlated but also indicates the direction of the correlation. A **positive correlation** occurs when an increase in value in one concept is accompanied by an increase in value in the other concept. Similarly, a decrease in the value in one concept is accompanied by a decrease in value in the other. The direction of change is the same for each variable. If voter turnout increases when age increases, there is a positive correlation.

A **negative correlation** does not mean that there is no relationship between the two variables but that the direction of change is inverse. A negative correlation between voting turnout and age would occur if an increase in age accompanied a decrease in voting. In order for a relationship to have direction, it must be possible to order the values of the concepts involved. When either of the concepts in a relationship cannot be ordered (as will be explained in Chapter 5, such variables are known as nominal variables), the correlation cannot have direction. In such cases, we simply note that the concepts are correlated.

Overall, a hypothesis will state the relationships between concepts by providing a statement of the proposed cause of an observable phenomenon, and the underlying theory will attempt to explain why these relationships exist. A proposition is then a statement of fact that follows from the accuracy of the hypothesis, such that, if the hypothesis is true, the following condition will prevail. Propositions are combined to create theories. Some theories are quite broad in scope, making sweeping generalizations about social and political life. Other theories are less ambitious and seek, for example, to explain events in a single country rather than all countries.

APPLY YOUR UNDERSTANDING

Examples of Theory

For each of the following political science theories, identify the key concepts and the key propositions (relationships between the concepts). Which has a broader scope?

Michels' Iron Law of Oligarchy

Robert Michels, a loyal socialist, studied the inner dynamics of the German Social Democratic Party. Although the party was committed to participatory decision-making, Michels (1962) found that a leadership elite emerged within the party. He reasoned that this result was due to the need for organization: for a political party to operate efficiently, an elite must emerge to take charge and keep the party on track. Michels discovered that the leadership elite often pursued its own interests rather than those of the party as a whole. In other words, an oligarchy had emerged. Given that a revolutionary democratic party was the last place Michels expected to find self-interested leadership, he concluded that any need for organization will be met by the creation of oligarchies, despite contrary claims of democracy: "the government, or . . . the state, cannot be anything other than the organization of a minority . . . and can never be truly representative of the majority. The majority is thus permanently incapable of self-government" (1962, 351). He summarizes the process in the statement "Who says organization says oligarchy." This broad assertion is known as the iron law of oligarchy.

Brodie and Jenson's "Defining the Political" Theory

There are a number of different approaches to the study of political party development. In the mobilization approach, parties "are strategic actors engaged in defining the issues of importance in political conflict and in mobilizing voters behind their issue positions" (Archer et al. 1995, 417). This theory is put forward by Janine Brodie and Jane Jenson (1980), who argue that Canadian political parties have effectively written social class out of the political realm. Political parties are able to control what social cleavages are seen as "important" through the issues they champion. By refusing to focus on issues of social class, Canadian parties—including the Co-operative Commonwealth Federation (CCF) and New Democratic Party (NDP)—keep such matters from becoming politically relevant. It is in this way that political parties "define the political."

Developing and Testing Theories

How does one develop a theory? There are two approaches: inductive and deductive. Inductive approaches move from data to theory—we begin by observing the world and develop generalizations and conclusions from our observations. If we observe that members of the Canadian Union of Public Employees (CUPE) are more likely than non-members to support the NDP, we might generalize that union membership is correlated with ideological position. (The validity of such generalizations may depend upon the specific union to which members belong; members of the Canadian Auto Workers may be different from CUPE members.) Induction, then, involves the progression from empirical evidence to generalization. Inductive research is also often exploratory: we begin with an open mind and look for patterns in behaviour.

A classic example of inductive theorizing is Alexis de Tocqueville's (1863) *Democracy in America*. Tocqueville visited the United States to assess the desirability of the republican system of government for France. He found that America was characterized by social equality (a lack of aristocracy) and political equality. Yet the high levels of parity were correlated with mediocre leadership: the popularly elected representatives were not the best or the brightest men in the country. He feared that the love for equality and majority rule would lead to the "tyranny of the majority," in which majority interests are pursued at the expense of minority liberties. He concluded by theorizing that increased levels of political equality lead to decreased leadership quality and that democracy threatens the rights and liberties of minorities. Tocqueville began with an observation and used it to generalize about the nature of democracy.

Deductive theorizing moves the other way, from the general to the specific. We engage in deductive research when we begin with specific assumptions, or hypotheses, and set out to test them in the real world. We might assume that union members will support left-wing parties because of common policy agendas. To see if our theory holds, we might survey union members and ask their ideological position or test the degree to which supporters of left-wing parties are sympathetic to concerns of union members, such as the right to collective bargaining. If the evidence confirms our hypothesis, our theory is supported. Deductive research is often referred to as **hypothesis-testing**, discussed in more detail later in the next section.

Deductive research requires that we have a source for our assumptions. Sometimes our source is merely logic: the theory makes sense. Other times, our source is pre-existing research or theorizing: the literature suggests that a relationship or pattern exists, and we seek empirical evidence to test it. Take Tocqueville's theory that democracy is correlated with mediocre leadership. We could test this theory by looking at the quality of leadership in a single country or across countries and time. Is Canada governed by intellectual or economic elites or by "ordinary people"? And, if the latter, is a reduction in the quality of leadership an inevitable result?

One way to distinguish between inductive and deductive reasoning is to consider the analogy of a wheel. Think of the wheel's centre as its most specific or particular point and of the wheel's extremity as the more general point. Outward movement along the spokes is a movement from the particular to the general, and inward movement is from the general to the particular. Using this analogy, inductive reasoning moves outward, from the specific to the general, and deductive reasoning moves inward, from the general to the specific.

Inductive and deductive research play off each other (see Figure 3.1). We might notice a pattern in society and make the broad generalizations necessary to develop a theory based on our observation (inductive research). Then we might seek to test hypotheses derived from the theory more directly by gathering data from different sources (deductive research). This process of data collection may lead us to note new or different patterns, from which we might generalize into different theories (inductive research). We would develop hypotheses based on the new theories, then test them empirically (deductive research), and so on. Overall, inductive research tends to be broader in scope, whereas deductive research tends to be more directed and narrower in scope.

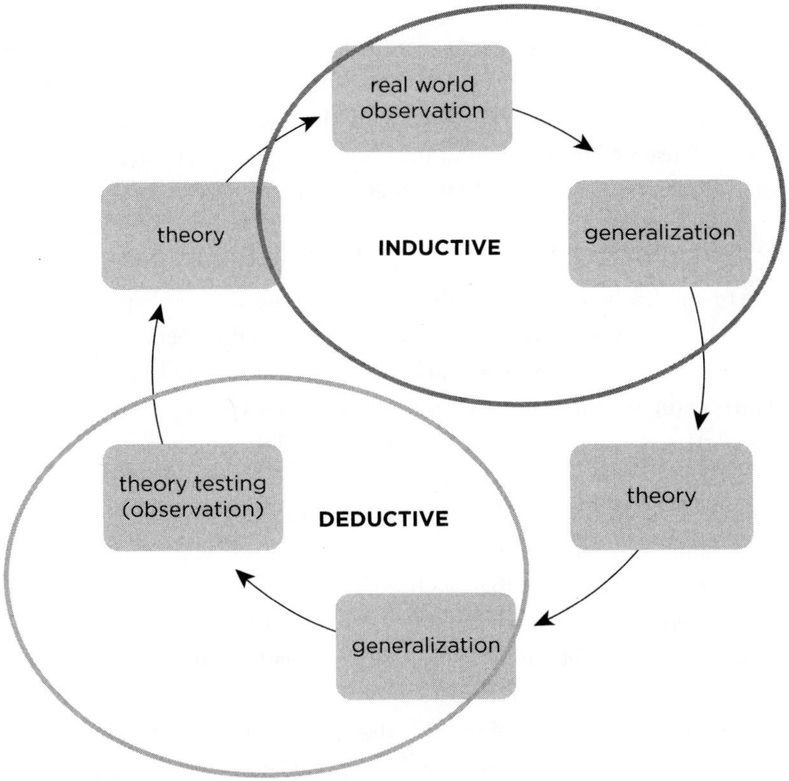

Figure 3.1 Relationship between Inductive and Deductive Research

APPLY YOUR UNDERSTANDING

Inductive and Deductive Research

How would you examine the relationship between age and political conservatism inductively? What are the observations you have made, and what theories can you develop? How would you examine the relationship deductively? What hypotheses could you test? How did you develop these hypotheses? How might you test them?

Hypothesis-Testing

With deductive research, we seek to test our hypotheses empirically. Recall that a hypothesis states a relationship between two concepts. When we empirically test theories, concepts are defined more specifically as variables. Simply stated, then, a hypothesis is a testable statement of relationship between two variables. It is a statement, not a question. Usually, a hypothesis will state a direction (positive or negative) and will contain a comparison. Take the hypothesis "High-income earners are more likely to support conservatism than low-income earners." A relationship is stated between two variables: income and support for conservatism. The direction of the relationship is positive; as income increases, support for conservatism increases. And the hypothesis includes a comparison between high-income and low-income earners. Is the hypothesis empirically testable? Yes, we could measure attitudes toward conservatism among the general population and see if there are differing levels of support among different income groups.

When we formulate hypotheses, we must ensure that they are empirically testable, which means that we do not use normative statements. A hypothesis does not state preferences or judgments. Often, we have to reformulate our ideas to make them empirically testable. This can be done by making our assumptions more explicit and by ensuring that all the elements of a hypothesis—relationship, comparison, direction, testability—are present. If we start with the normative statement "democratic regimes are better than authoritarian regimes" (a comparison), we need to evaluate what we mean by "better." What is regime type being related to? Perhaps we are interested in human rights and believe that democratic regimes have better human rights records than authoritarian regimes do. Now we have included a relationship (between human rights and regime type) and a direction (as democracy increases, human rights records improve). This idea is now a testable hypothesis.

In political analysis, our goal is to test our hypotheses or, more specifically, to see if and to what extent those hypotheses are supported by empirical data. We gather empirical data to see if the evidence agrees with or contradicts our hypotheses. As support grows for a particular hypothesis, we gain more confidence in it and are more inclined to see it as "true." However, we never state that we have "proven" a hypothesis. The reason is that skepticism is important in the scientific method. Recall that science avoids any notions of certainty: if we are certain, we assume perfect knowledge, something scientists are reluctant to claim. There is always the chance that further knowledge will develop or that new information will be discovered, information that may question our "truths." This has happened many times in the history of humankind—it was once believed that the earth was flat, the sun revolved around the earth, heavy objects fell more rapidly than light objects, and atoms were indivisible. Modern scientists and social scientists wish to avoid such errors and therefore refuse to make statements of absolute certain "proof."

Consequently, the process of hypothesis-testing involves examining whether the hypothesis can be shown to be false. In a formal sense, although the development of the hypothesis is based on formulating a "testable statement of relationships" between variables, we focus instead on the null hypothesis. As we noted in Chapter 1, the null hypothesis states that no relationship exists between two variables. A null hypothesis might state that "there is no relationship between age and party identification." Before we can conclude that support exists for our hypotheses (e.g. "as age increases, support for conservative parties increases"), we must first reject the null hypothesis. By doing so, we have established that some sort of relationship exists and we are free to consider questions of direction.[2] For these reasons, when writing our research hypothesis, we first state a null hypothesis (no relationship exists, identified by H_0) and then state an **alternative hypothesis** (the relationship we think exists, identified by H_a).

Hypothesis-testing can be seen as the gradual elimination of alternative explanations. If we are trying to identify determining factors in party identification, we might look at age, income, religion, region, parents' income, parents' party identification, and gender. Testing might find that age and region do not appear to contribute to party identification. We would then drop hypotheses related to these variables and continue testing the remaining factors. Over time, others would probably drop from contention and new hypotheses would emerge; we might, for instance, choose to test the impact of education and marital status. Some hypotheses would continue to hold up after repeated testing, while others would be eliminated. If, after repeated testing, income and parents' party identification remain correlated with party identification, we can say with confidence that the hypotheses are supported. We do not state that the hypotheses have been proven.

Summary: Characteristics of a Hypothesis

1. Relationship: It states a relationship between two variables.
2. Comparison: It states a comparison between values of the independent variable.
3. Direction: It states the direction of the relationship if possible.
4. Testability: It is empirically testable.

APPLY YOUR UNDERSTANDING

Developing Hypotheses

Create null and alternative hypotheses for relationships between

- political conservatism and support for deficit reduction;
- age and political party membership;
- regime type and economic system;
- economic system and distribution of wealth; and
- gender and support for national child care.

Causality

Until now, we have been looking for relationships between variables: Does a relationship exist, and, if so, what is the direction of that relationship? While recognizing correlations is important in the social sciences, we often wish to go further; more specifically, we want to know why two variables, A and B, are related. Does A cause B, or is their covariance accidental? Is there a third variable, C, that causes both A and B? Recall from Chapter 1 that an important assumption of the scientific approach to politics is determinism, the belief that cause-and-effect relationships exist and that social scientists can, through research, discover the form of these relationships. Few would argue that the underlying causes of human actions are either clear or certain, but the goal in social science is to find patterns of behaviour and propose causes to explain them.

The term *cause* has been defined as "a person or thing that gives rise to an action, phenomenon, or condition" (oxforddictionaries.com). The key element in this definition is the notion of agency—it is because of the action of the causal variable that the outcome variable exists in its current state. Thus, causal relationships have both a cause and an effect. Variable X causes variable Y when a "change in *X* (sooner or later) produces change in *Y*" or (because some Xs don't change) "*Y*s tend to line up with fixed values of *X*" (Davis 1985, 9). How do we determine which variable is the cause and which is the effect? When one event precedes another in time, it is clear which is the cause and which is the effect. We give a plant water and light and it grows. We cast our ballots and a legislature is elected. When one event occurs in reaction to another, we have **temporal order**. The reacting variable (the effect) is dependent upon the preceding event (the cause): the life of the plant depends upon the supply of water and light, and the composition of the legislature is dependent upon the votes cast.

As we noted in Chapter 1, the influenced variable is known as the dependent variable. The influencing variable—the cause—is called the independent variable: its values are independent of the dependent variable. The availability of water and light does not depend upon the existence of a single plant; the future composition of the legislature does not determine our individual vote, although our expectations about its composition might do so. Some independent variables are descriptive characteristics of the individual, qualities such as age, sex, race, and religion. These variables are known as **prior conditions** and precede in time such dependent variables as political beliefs and behaviours.

We can graphically represent causal relationships with causal models. Figure 3.2a illustrates a simple causal relationship: age (the independent variable) influences income (the dependent variable). The small "+" above the arrow tells us that the relationship is positive; in other words, the two variables change in the same direction. As age increases, income increases. Relationships between a single independent variable and the dependent variable are **bivariate**; there are only two variables being considered. Some causal relationships involve more than one independent variable; these relationships are **multivariate**. Figure 3.2b illustrates a causal relationship among three variables. Both age and education are independent variables, while income is the dependent variable. Note that both relationships are positive.

When there is a chain of influences, with many variables interacting, our causal models become more complex. Figure 3.2c illustrates a more elaborate causal model: both education and age are positively related to income, while income is negatively related to support for socialism. This model suggests that support for socialism decreases as income increases. Note that, in this example, income is a dependent variable to age and education but an independent variable with respect to support for socialism. Causal models help us visualize the relationships between variables; when a large number of variables are involved in a theory, a causal model can often simplify complex relationships.

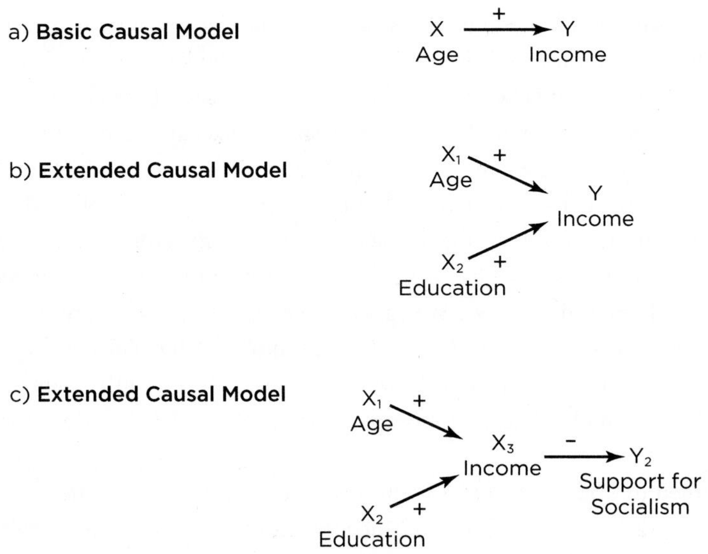

Figure 3.2 Causal Models

Errors in Causal Reasoning

Not all relationships are causal, although many people confuse correlation with causation. If there is a rise in crime at the same time as there is a rise in the number of single mothers, some will argue that single motherhood causes crime. But the world is not that simple. It is entirely possible that a third factor, such as poverty, is related to both crime and single motherhood. When a relationship between two variables can be accounted for by a third variable, it is **spurious**. To test for a spurious relationship, we need to examine whether the relationship between variable A and variable B exists without the influence of variable C. If it does, it may be a causal correlation; if controlling for C causes the relationship between A and B to disappear, the relationship is spurious. We control for the effects of other variables by holding the values of the third variable (the **control variable**) constant.

Returning to our example, we would need to know whether the relationship between single motherhood and crime can be attributed to a third variable: poverty. Consequently, we test if the relationship exists in all socioeconomic groups or if it is isolated to the poor alone. If the relationship between single motherhood and crime disappears when poverty levels are held constant, we have found a spurious relationship; if it exists in all socioeconomic groups, it may be a causal relationship. To be confident that the relationship is causal, we need to be able to eliminate as many alternative explanations of the relationship as possible.

Once we know that a causal relationship is possible, we must consider the order of that relationship. Sometimes social scientists find it difficult to ascertain which variable is the cause and which is the effect. When temporal order is not clear—when events appear to occur simultaneously—causality is difficult to establish. We noted that a correlation between single motherhood and crime might be seen as moving from the former to the latter, that single motherhood causes increased crime rates. It is possible that the relationship could work in the opposite direction: perhaps crime causes single motherhood. For example, violent crime could lead to fathers being killed or imprisoned, leaving the mother alone to raise the children. Many of the relationships we seek to explore in social science can seem like chicken-and-egg dilemmas. When we cannot clearly determine cause and effect, we have less confidence that a causal relationship exists. By modelling carefully, it is possible to be more confident about causal relationships.

One of the most significant errors of analysis occurs when a researcher fails to recognize that a relationship is spurious and not causal. In the example in Figure 3.3, assume that the bivariate analysis showed a relationship between variable A and variable B. Given how the relationship was modelled, the conclusion would be that A causes B. Now, assume that a third variable, C, influences both A and B and causes them to vary. Thus, the initial observed variation between A and B was not causal but was a by-product of C's effect on the other two variables. After taking into account the presence of C, we would conclude that the relationship between A and B is spurious.

Another common error in causal reasoning is that temporal order necessarily implies causality (known as the post-hoc fallacy). This fallacy is similar to assuming that correlation

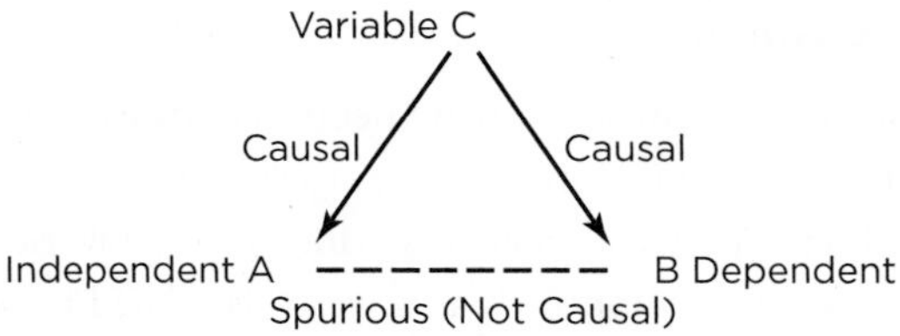

Figure 3.3 A Spurious Relationship

is equated to causation. Just because variable A precedes variable B is not sufficient grounds to argue that A causes B; again, we must ensure that some other variable C does not cause B. Controlling for other possible causes is the only way we can suggest with confidence that A causes B. Unfortunately, we can never rule out all possible alternative explanations for social and political behaviour. In addition, temporal order can be difficult to establish in the social sciences. For these reasons, theory is particularly important to political analysis. Many of the gaps in our knowledge are filled by clear reasoning and logic; good data alone are seldom sufficient.

Finally, we should note the **ecological fallacy**. Imagine a study of electoral support for a local referendum on the amalgamation of municipal governments. In order to test the hypothesis that support for amalgamation will decline as personal income increases, the researchers collect data on average family income and the percentage of "no" votes in each polling district. As the hypothesis predicts, districts with relatively high family incomes were more likely to vote against the amalgamation than were polls with relatively low family incomes. The researchers then conclude that high-income voters are more likely to oppose amalgamation than are low-income voters. In coming to this conclusion, the researchers are committing the ecological fallacy. They are assuming that what is true of the polling district—the ecological unit of analysis—is equally true of individuals within the polling districts. They are assuming that, because high-income districts are more likely to vote "no," so too are high-income individuals.

There need not be any relationship between district characteristics and the determinants of individual voting behaviour. Within wealthy communities, those with lower income may be more supportive of amalgamation than those with higher income, and the same may be true within less wealthy communities. Something other than individual income accounts for the relationship between community prosperity and support for amalgamation. The lesson is that we must be careful in projecting ecological characteristics onto the behaviour of individuals.

Intervening Variables

An **intervening variable** is one that comes between an independent and a dependent variable, but the direction of causality flows from the independent variable to the intervening variable to the dependent variable. The use of intervening variables is one way of providing further elaboration to a theory. Assume that the initial hypothesis is that education leads to participation in politics: the higher one's level of education, the more likely he or she is to have a high level of participation. But why is this the case? What is it about having a higher level of education that leads one to have a higher level of political participation?

A variety of theories could be introduced to explain this relationship, with each specifying an intervening variable. One theory is that people participate in politics when the "cost" of doing so is low. Higher levels of education provide people with a greater understanding of politics, which reduces the cost of becoming informed about the parties during an election campaign. Consequently, the hypothesis follows that people with higher levels of education will participate in politics because the cost to them of doing so is less than for people with lower levels of education. In Figure 3.4, variable C is knowledge about the parties and/or the political process. This model could be extended by including other variables that intervene between levels of education and of political participation, such as having a larger number of social contacts with people actively involved in politics (therefore being more likely to be asked to participate) or having a higher income and therefore taking a greater interest in governmental decisions regarding resource allocation.

Note the difference between an intervening variable and a spurious relationship. In the former, the original independent variable is important because it causes variation in the dependent variable, whereas in a spurious relationship the initial independent variable is not important because its effect on the dependent variable disappears. In each of the examples of intervening variables, higher education levels were hypothesized to affect the intervening variable, that is, to lead to greater political knowledge, more social contacts, or a higher income, which in turn led to higher levels of political participation.

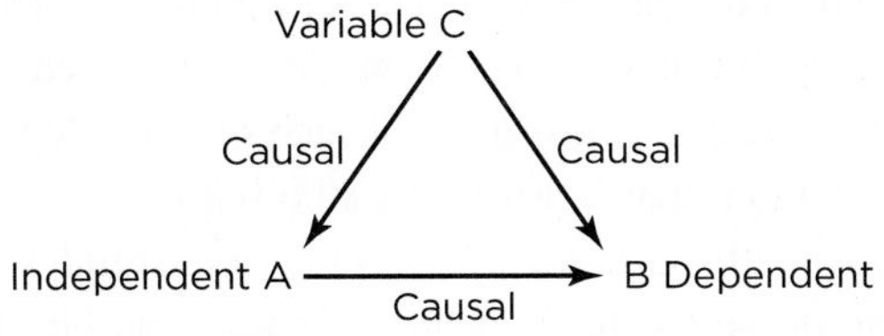

Figure 3.4 An Intervening Variable

Reinforcing Variables

A **reinforcing variable** can strengthen and magnify the relationship between an independent and a dependent variable. Assume that we are examining the effect of gender on attitudes toward abortion. We might find that women are more likely than men to agree that abortion is a matter that should be decided between a pregnant woman and her doctor. A reinforcing variable in this model could be attitudes toward feminism. People who hold views favourable to feminism are more likely to agree that abortion is a personal medical matter. Since women are more likely to be feminists (that is, to hold views favourable to feminism) than are men, attitudes toward feminism reinforce the relationship between gender and attitudes toward abortion. However, attitudes toward feminism do not replace the effect of gender; instead, they complement and reinforce this relationship. This means that the causal connection between gender and attitudes toward abortion persists even after the effect of the reinforcing variable is taken into account.

The causal line from A to C in Figure 3.5 indicates that gender is hypothesized to have an effect on attitudes toward feminism, but in the case of a reinforcing effect, it is expected that a direct effect of gender on attitudes toward abortion will persist even after controlling for feminism. In short, the attitudes toward feminism strengthen rather than replace the direct effect that gender has on attitudes toward abortion. When the two variables are reinforcing, such as in this example, the impact of the independent variable on the dependent variable is larger among women who hold feminist attitudes than among those who do not.

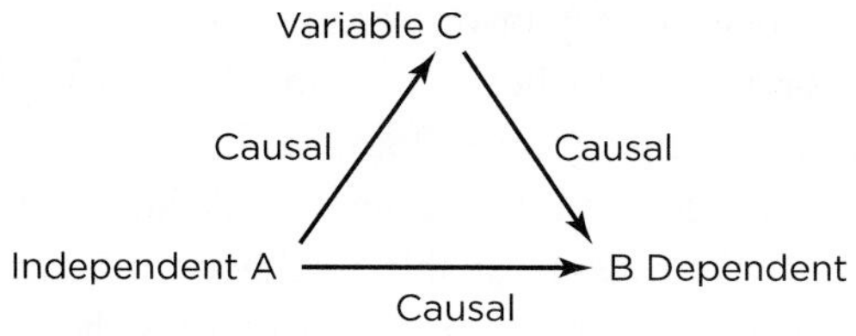

Figure 3.5 A Reinforcing Variable

Multiple Independent Variables

We also could model a set of causal relationships in which a number of independent variables can have an effect on a dependent variable (see Figure 3.6). This type of modelling is quite common when using multiple regression analysis (discussed in Chapter 17) because this technique allows us to examine the effect of each of the independent variables under the *ceteris paribus* assumption, that is, assuming all other things are equal. As a result, we could examine the effect of attitudes toward party leaders, attitudes toward political issues, and party identification on voting to see which of these variables is the most important determinant of voting. Such an analysis would try to answer the question, "Are Canadian elections little more than television-oriented popularity contests among the party leaders or are they the result of policy discussions and debates among the parties and candidates?" To what extent does the government receive a mandate to implement a policy agenda following a Canadian election? Understanding the nature of causality among these competing models provides insight into the character and meaning of Canadian elections and strategic information that can be used by the parties in formulating their election campaigns.

The caution to bear in mind when modelling and empirically testing relationships with multiple independent variables is that the assumption of independence between the causal or independent variables may not reflect the true relationships between these variables in

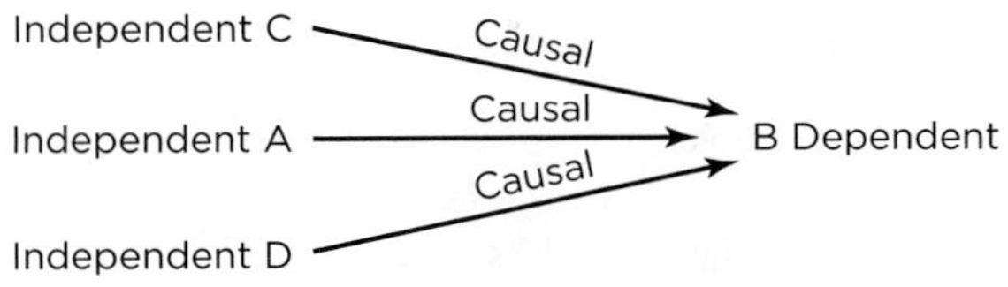

Figure 3.6 Multiple Independent Variables

the real world. In the preceding discussion, is it sensible to assume that attitudes toward party leaders, attitudes toward political issues, and party identification are independent of one another? Is it sensible to think that there is no relationship between attitudes toward Quebec sovereignty, attitudes toward the Parti Québécois (PQ) leader, and support for the PQ? Of course, not all independent variables will be strongly related to one another. But be aware of the assumptions that accompany the modelling of the relationships in your analysis. If there is reason to think that the independent variables are related to one another, you may wish to reconsider how you have accounted for this connection.

Conclusion

This chapter has explored the role of theory in political analysis. Most of the following chapters will explore different ways that we make empirical observations of the social world in our efforts to test our theories and advance our knowledge of the political world. In the next chapter, we turn our attention to defining political concepts.

Working as a Team

1. Discuss what you think is the major causes of the decline in voting among young Canadians. Identify two or more hypotheses that purport to account for the decline.
2. Consider the hypotheses that your discussion group identified. What theory or theories can be said to underlie these hypotheses?

Self-Study

1. Identify a hypothesis that you would be interested in examining. Discuss how, using a deductive versus inductive approach, you would examine this hypothesis.
2. State a hypothesis. Map it by identifying the independent and dependent variables. Identify a possible spurious relationship that can be tested and map the relationship. Then map a relationship with two separate intervening variables.

Notes

1. A notable form of applied research is feminist action research (Reinharz 1992). Indeed, the argument has been made (Lather 1988) that research is feminist only if it is linked to action, to attempts to repudiate the status quo. This does not mean that action research is unable to enrich our conceptual or theoretical understanding of the world; it means only that such enrichment cannot be the sole or perhaps even the primary justification for research projects. Research is seen as an essential part of a larger process of social transformation.
2. As Chapter 15 will discuss, hypotheses sometimes include a specific directionality. Two-tailed tests are used to reject the null hypothesis if no direction is specified, for example, if the hypothesis is simply that some relationship exists between age and conservatism. One-tailed tests are used when the direction of the relationship is specified by the hypothesis.

CHAPTER 4

Defining the Political World
Concepts

Destination

By the end of this chapter, you should be able to

- explain the importance of clear conceptual definitions when conducting empirical research;
- appreciate the difficulties in arriving at clear and consistent conceptual definitions; and
- apply some general rules to the development of conceptual definitions.

The goal of empirical political science is to conduct research in such a way that lawlike generalizations can be made about the political world. Although it is no doubt interesting to know why one voter—say, Cheryl Smith of Saanich, British Columbia—voted for the Green Party in the 2011 federal election, it is of greater interest to know the determinants of voting in Canadian federal elections more generally. The factors that can impinge on voting include many characteristics, such as voters' gender, age, ideology, partisan identifications, attitudes toward party leaders, and so on. But the importance of these factors varies over time and political space. Gender may be more important as a predictor of voting behaviour in the 2010s than it was in the 1960s, as women contest more ridings in which their party stands a chance of winning, political issues are framed in ways that engage women voters, or women become more likely to lead political parties. Likewise, ideology may be a more important determinant of voting in a province such as Ontario, where the parties appear more ideologically distinct, than in Prince Edward Island, where the major parties seem to have a higher level of consensus.

To develop lawlike generalizations about the political world, it is necessary to devise models that enable a comparison of alternative possible causes. We began exploring causal models in Chapter 3; the basic structure of such a model is presented in Figure 4.1. In this simple example, there is one hypothesized causal factor (labelled A) and one outcome (labelled B). Following the discussion from the previous paragraph, B represents the concept that we wish to explain, namely, voting in Canadian federal elections. A represents the hypothesized cause of that outcome, such as attitudes toward the party leaders. These two concepts are joined by a causal arrow, which runs from A to B. The model reads as "attitudes toward party leaders cause Canadians to vote for one party over another in an election."

In the figure, "attitudes toward party leaders" is the independent concept and voting is the dependent concept. Recall that, in empirical research, a dependent concept is the outcome that we are trying to explain. In brief, we hypothesize that variations in this concept are based on, or depend on, variations in other elements inside the model. Put another way, the variance is **endogenous** to the model. In the present example, variation in voting is hypothesized to stem from variation in attitudes toward leaders. The independent concept is the hypothesized cause of the outcome. Variations in the independent concept are hypothesized to depend upon factors outside (that is, **exogenous** to) the model.

Concepts can be independent or dependent, depending on the topic of the research and the way the causal structure is specified. Although the independent concept in our model is attitudes toward party leaders, this concept could be dependent in a different research program. One might hypothesize that women are more likely than men to view Liberal leader Justin Trudeau in positive terms and that men are more likely than women to view another party leader, such as Prime Minister Harper, positively. Attitudes toward party leaders is the dependent concept in this example and the independent concept is respondents' gender.

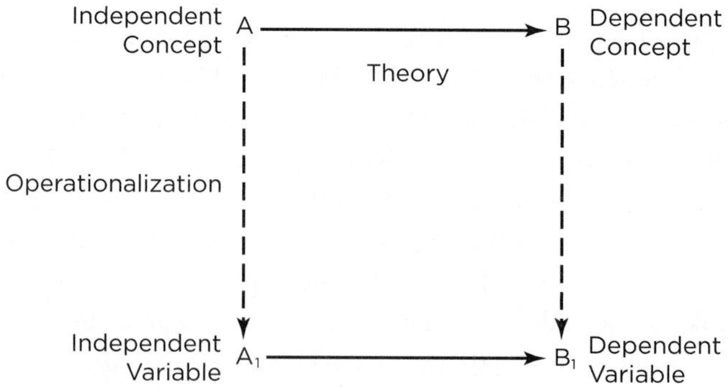

Figure 4.1 Modelling Cause-and-Effect Relationships

Underlying the hypothesized causal connection between attitudes toward party leaders (A) and voting (B) in Figure 4.1 is a theory about the causes of voting. We explored the idea of theory in Chapter 3 and discussed how theories are statements about the relationships between concepts. In the present example, the theory accounting for the relationship between A and B could be that politics in the electronic age is delivered to people in their living rooms via television or social media sites. Since television coverage of politics focuses on party leaders and their images (as opposed to a detailed discussion of political issues and policies), we expect attitudes toward leaders to have an important impact on voting preferences. If the results of the research do not support this hypothesized relationship, our theory is not supported. Particularly in the social sciences, statements about causality arise from theorizing. Hence, our theories, and the concepts embodied in them, are extremely important.

The initial stages in developing an empirical, theory testing research project involve identifying the concepts that will be studied and, drawing on available theory, specifying a hypothesized causal relation between them. At this point, these concepts are defined as relatively abstract entities. To conduct the empirical research, one needs to move from the

APPLY YOUR UNDERSTANDING

The Difference between Concepts and Variables

The preceding discussion suggests that the key difference between a concept and a variable is that a former is abstract, whereas the latter is concrete. Let's see if we can take this distinction a step further.

To say that a concept is abstract does not imply that it is fuzzy or vague. On the contrary, we argue that empirical political researchers try to define concepts as precisely as possible. However, even a precisely defined concept can be measured in many ways. A variable is the way the concept has been measured in the particular study. When we say a variable is concrete and specific, we mean that the researcher can actually assign a value to every "case" in the study. Any clearer?

Consider the concept of attitudes toward party leaders. What does it mean? Can you provide a specific definition of the concept? You might ask, "What kinds of attitudes?" In a study of the 1988 Canadian federal election, Richard Johnston and colleagues (1992) suggested that the relevant attitudes toward party leaders concern their character and competence. Do you agree with their definition? How might assessments of these qualities be measured? Johnston et al. suggest that these dimensions can be changed into variables by asking people four questions concerning competence and another four concerning character. The answers to these questions can be combined into **mean** (average) character and competence ratings for each party leader (Johnston et al. 1992, 174–84; see Chapter 14 for a discussion of the term *mean*). What other ways can attitudes toward party leaders be conceptualized?

level of concepts to the level of variables (designated as A_1 and B_1 in Figure 4.1). Whereas concepts are abstract representations of a phenomenon, variables are the concrete manifestations of that phenomenon in a particular research project. Research on the variables will provide the evidence used to draw conclusions about the hypothesized relationship between concepts. Variables are sufficiently specific that values can be assigned to each person or case in the data set.

In effect, much of the statistical component of empirical research involves comparing the change in one variable with that in another. As we will see in subsequent chapters, there are many statistical methods available to test the strength of the relationship between variables. For the most part, statistical techniques can assess the strength of association, not the direction of causation. The latter is primarily a design matter, in that the researcher hypothesizes a direction of causality and underpins this hypothesis with a more general theory of the causal relationship.

Since empirical analysis is conducted on variables but we wish to make generalizations about the concepts, the variables must be an accurate reflection and precise measurement of the concepts. In other words, the relationship between the variables should mirror the relationship between the concepts. Chapter 5 discusses how operationalization can ensure precision and accuracy in measurement.

Conceptual Definitions

In everyday conversation, we often use terms in a way that presupposes that others understand and agree with our conceptualization. Indeed, effective communication requires that a particular word have the same meaning for each person involved in the dialogue. Yet there is often a degree of ambiguity in our conventional use of words, some of which stems from the different meanings attached to words when they are used in different contexts. For example, after a morning class, you might say to a friend, "Let's go to the Student Union. I'm starving." In this context, the word *starving* might imply that you have not eaten since breakfast. Over lunch, you might read a news story about a famine in East Africa and the rising death toll. Obviously, your comment about your state of hunger was not meant to be equated with the life-threatening condition that starvation presents to many people in the world. In conversation, we are often willing to tolerate a certain measure of ambiguity in conceptual definitions while still being able to communicate effectively.

There are other instances in which such ambiguity in everyday language can lead to ineffective or non-existent communication. A teenager going out at night may tell his or her parents, "I'll be home early." Unless the term *early* is defined more precisely, a misunderstanding will probably arise. In fact, there may be so much difficulty in coming to a shared understanding of the word's meaning that communication might be facilitated by doing away with the terms *early* and *late* and using one that is defined in such a way that both parties agree. It may be preferable to say, "I'll be home at 11" or "I'll be home at midnight." Everyone would then have a common understanding of when the teenager is expected home. Of course, there may be a downside to using this level of precision, if his or her intent is to return at 1:00 a.m. From the teenager's perspective, there may be advantages to arguing over whether 1:00 is early or late compared to explaining why he or she is home one to two hours after the agreed-upon time.

The problem with lack of clarity in conceptual definitions plagues those engaged in empirical political research as well. One of the features that continues to differentiate research in the social sciences from that in the natural sciences is the relative lack of agreement in the former around the meaning of concepts. If the goal of research is to test theories of political phenomena and the expectation is that multiple observers will independently arrive at the same observations and conclusions, it is important to have consistent understandings of the concepts under study. Such consistency is elusive, as the following examples illustrate.

Example: The Impact of Education on Voting

What impact does education have on voting? To begin exploring this question, we can map a causal relationship, as in Figure 4.2. Education is the independent concept (the hypothesized cause) and voting is the dependent concept (the hypothesized effect). Notice that there is a theory underlying this hypothesized relationship. The theory might be that higher educational achievement makes people feel like they are a greater part of the political community and inspires them to higher levels of political activity. Put another way, the higher the level of educational achievement, the higher the level of political activity, such as voting. Since this is a positive relationship (an increase in the value of one concept leads to an increase in the value of the other), we include a + over the causal arrow.

To proceed with this research, we must define the terms *education* and *voting*. The theory being tested concerns the impact of education on level of political activity. In this instance, voting is conceptualized as indicative of a certain amount of political involvement or activity. The research is not concerned with what party a person voted for but simply whether he or she voted. We may wish to refer to this concept as voting turnout rather than simply voting. Furthermore, voting turnout could be conceptualized either as a **categorical** or a **continuous** concept. A categorical concept is one in which the concept's characteristics are separate and distinct. A continuous concept is one in which the categories are joined or connected in a sequential manner. Examining voting turnout in a single election, we see that the characteristics are that one voted or did not vote. This is indicative of separate or distinct activities and therefore is a categorical concept.

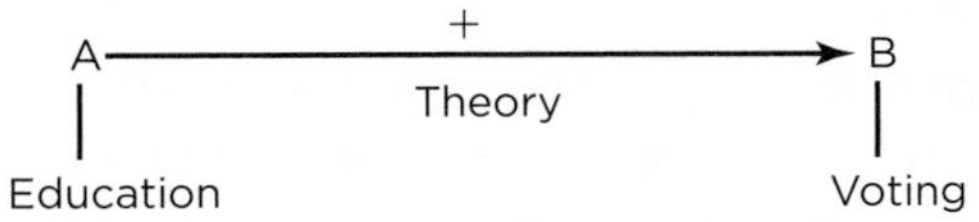

Figure 4.2 The Impact of Education on Voting

Voting turnout could also be conceptualized as a disposition to vote and hence be best measured over time. We could find out the percentage of federal elections the voter actually voted in (when he or she was eligible to vote). This conceptualization would result in a continuous measure of voting, with responses ranging from 0 per cent to 100 per cent. We will see in later chapters that there are important implications regarding the selection of statistics. At this juncture, the key point to remember is that these possible conceptualizations of voting turnout could result in researchers lacking consistent definitions of an important concept in their research.

Once we have settled on a definition of our dependent concept, we must define our independent concept, education. On the surface, this task seems straightforward and uncontroversial: level of education increases with the number of years of formal schooling. Yet a number of questions and concerns challenge this simple conceptual definition. One of the most obvious concerns relates to the change over the past two generations in what constitutes a high or a low level of education. Prior to a major expansion in the Canadian post-secondary education system in the 1960s, a university-level education was relatively uncommon. Indeed, even the successful completion of a high-school diploma was viewed as a mark of significant educational achievement as recently as the period just prior to World War II. Today, a university-level education has become much more widely available and is a much more common achievement.

What are the implications of this change for the way in which education level is conceptualized? On the one hand, we might agree that people today are simply more highly educated than in the past. From this perspective, level of educational achievement is an absolute quality—what is high for one generation is high for others. On the other hand, the conclusion might be that level of education is a relative quality and that those who achieve high levels of education relative to their age cohort should be considered to have high educational achievement. Such a conclusion implies that level of educational achievement must be adjusted for the time the person was enrolled in the educational system.

A second, and possibly more complicated, issue concerns our understanding of how one might achieve a high level of education. We suggested that level of education corresponds with the number of years attending an (accredited?) educational institution. But does education always take place within an educational institution? It would seem self-evident that a considerable amount of learning takes place both inside and outside the classroom. What role does the classroom experience play in the overall educational process? Such questions are raised not to stretch beyond credulity the meaning of the concept of education but to indicate some of the important debates that are currently taking place at universities across the country.

Educators are beginning to ask whether university credits can be given for certain kinds of life experiences, thereby acknowledging that much learning takes place outside the classroom. (This idea can be seen in the emergence of career internship courses and co-operative study programs.) If university credit can be obtained for certain life experiences, such as career experience, are these not part of a person's education, even if one has not applied for and obtained university credit? If university credit is not viewed as the prime indicator of one's level of educational achievement, is it possible to arrive at a uniform agreement on the meaning of *education*? The issue of whether to include life experiences as a component of educational attainment goes to the very heart of the difficulties often faced in the social sciences when trying to agree on the meaning of social concepts.

The third complication that arises in defining the concept of education concerns the connection between years of education and the level of educational achievement. In the secondary education system, there are distinct courses of study: advanced academic streams (the International Baccalaureate program), the regular academic stream, and the lower stream. Does the completion of different academic streams equate to the same level of educational achievement?

Expand Your Knowledge

Changing Definitions of Educational Achievement

In their provocative book, *Transforming Higher Education*, Michael Dolence and Donald Norris (1995, 31–2) contrast post-secondary education by using the model inspired by the Industrial Age with that of the Information Age:

> Under the Industrial Age model, colleges and universities and the training organizations of corporations traditionally created separate, vertically integrated organizations to impart learning. All of the factors of production were included and provided to a largely resident and essentially captive group of learners—geographically isolated learners were served by visiting faculty or remote delivery of instruction. The clustering of the factors of production on the campus was the key competitive advantage. Under this factory/physical campus model of learning, the barriers to entry were huge, and two basic classes of participants existed: providers and learners. During the Industrial Age, higher education has held a virtually exclusive franchise on teaching and certifying mastery in its core areas of interest.
>
> In the Information Age, network scholarship will eliminate much of the advantage of vertical integration and the physical concentration of scholarly resources. Not only can learners be anywhere, they can acquire learning and knowledge from sources in any location or mixture of locations. Owning the physical facility where faculty and other expertise reside will not be a critical differentiator in the eyes of many learners. On the other hand, developing the ability to provide expertise, learning, and knowledge to networked learners will be essential. The capacity to measure demonstrated competence and to certify learning in a way that will be accepted by employers will also be a key differentiator. New learning support roles—facilitators, knowledge navigators, and learner/service intermediaries—will become increasingly important.

APPLY YOUR UNDERSTANDING

Conceptual Clarity

Is there something unusual about the concepts of voting and education that leads to the confusion about their meaning or is conceptual ambiguity common in the social sciences and in political science? To answer that question, think of some examples of concepts that could be used in political science research, and ask yourself whether you could provide one and only one definition of the concept.

Try it with the concept of age. Winston Churchill once said that a person who was a conservative at 20 years old had no heart, whereas a person who was not a conservative at 40 years old had no brain. His statement suggests a connection between aging and political belief systems. To examine this hypothesis, one would have to define *aging*. How would you define this term? Do you foresee any problems with this definition? Do you suppose the process of aging takes place at the same rate, and in the same way, for all people?

How about the other variable in this model—political belief systems? What do you mean by the term *conservative*? Or *liberal*? Do you think all researchers would agree with your definitions? Why or why not?

Of course, in the post-secondary education system, such differences in fields of study are even more pronounced. Students might attend a technical training institute (such as a business college), a technical college, an arts and sciences community college, or a university, including a university with graduate and professional training. Does enrolment at any of these institutions for a similar period of time provide students with a similar level of educational achievement? We might anticipate a negative answer to this question, one that claims that two years at a university provides a higher level of educational achievement than two years at a technical college does. One would need to adjust the definition of the term *educational achievement* accordingly. One might even ask whether students studying in different areas at a university are obtaining the same level of educational achievement. For example, are two years of study toward an engineering degree similar to two years of study toward a Bachelor of Fine Arts, a Bachelor of Arts, a Bachelor of Science, or a Bachelor of Commerce? Furthermore, what impact does different level of performance within the program have on level of educational achievement? Does a student who has completed 15 university courses with an A average have a higher or lower level of educational achievement than a student who has completed 18 courses with a C average?

These issues might seem extremely "technical." You might think that the preceding discussion makes two relatively simple and straightforward concepts overly complex. Everyone knows, you might say, what is meant by the terms *education* and *voting*. We will discover, in fact, that what may appear self-evident to us may not be to others. What is perhaps most important to recognize is the need to be as specific as possible regarding the key concepts in your research. Many of the most interesting debates in political science literature are over the meaning of concepts. Such debates can take place only if researchers provide clear definitions of the concepts included in their analyses.

Example: Party Identification

Party identification was one of the more important concepts to emerge from early studies of voting and elections in the United States. Reporting on some of the first studies on samples of the American electorate during the 1950s, Angus Campbell and his collaborators (1960) at the Center for Political Studies of the University of Michigan developed an attitudinal model of voting. They described the model as consisting of a "funnel of causality." At the wide end of the funnel were the factors that exist in the more distant past or that are further removed (in cognitive space) from the voting decision. As one approaches the narrow end of the funnel, one finds the parts that are most relevant, immediate, and important in the voting decision. These elements are invariably a set of political attitudes and beliefs that impinge directly on the vote. For Campbell et al., the three most relevant factors were party identifications, attitudes toward party leaders, and attitudes toward political issues.

These factors coexist in the sequence outlined in Figure 4.3. This model indicates an important role for party identification in two respects. First, it is one of the three variables that have the most immediate direct effect on voting decisions. Second, it is even more important because of the role it plays in influencing the other two prime determinants of voting. In other words, party identification has an important indirect effect through its impact on attitudes toward political issues and on perceptions of the party leaders.

Before turning to a discussion of party identification, it is noteworthy that the dependent concept in Figure 4.3, vote, differs from the concept of voting in Figure 4.2. Whereas the previous discussion centred on voting turnout, the present example emphasizes vote choice. That is, the concern is not with whether or not a respondent voted but for which party he or she voted. In the United States, the main options are the Democratic or Republican parties, although there is some indication that a broader range of choices may be emerging. In Canada, the options at the federal level include Conservative, Liberal, New Democrat, Bloc Québécois, and Green, together with a host of other parties that do not control parliamentary seats.

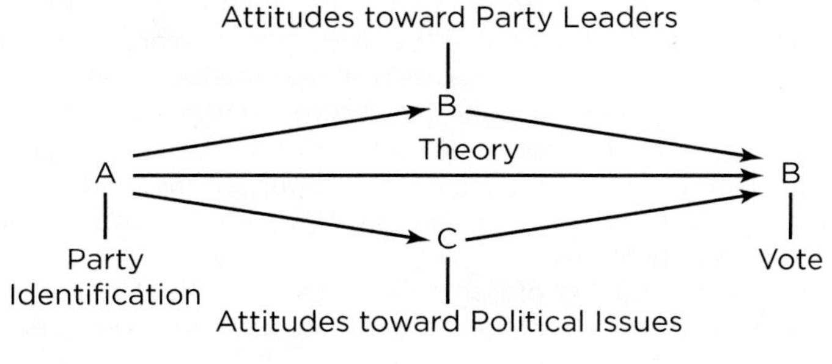

Figure 4.3 The Michigan Model and the Determinants of Voting

The concept of party identification that emerged from the Michigan studies derives directly from the empirical findings of the research. In particular, Campbell et al. (1960) found that only a very small minority of American voters actually join political parties and pay membership fees. Nonetheless, a large majority of Americans think of themselves as being either a Democrat or a Republican. Furthermore, the researchers found that this psychological attachment tended to develop relatively early in life, was often passed from one generation to the next through the socialization process, and was highly stable for most voters unless there was a particularly tumultuous set of political circumstances. Party identification also tended to exert a strong influence on other political attitudes and beliefs, such as feelings toward the candidates or evaluations of political issues (as outlined in Figure 4.3).

Research on the determinants of voting in other advanced industrial democracies borrowed heavily from the pioneering studies in the United States. This is certainly true of Canadian scholarship.[1] The first book-length treatment of Canadian voting behaviour that used Campbell et al.'s principles of social psychology was Harold Clarke, Jane Jenson, Lawrence LeDuc, and Jon Pammett's *Political Choice in Canada*, published in 1979. Similar to the findings of Campbell et al. (1960), Clarke and colleagues found that, in the 1970s, most Canadians had a psychological attachment to a political party. Unlike the American findings, which emphasized the stability of party identification and its long-term impact on other political phenomena, Clarke et al. found that party identification in Canada

Expand Your Knowledge

American Responses to the Michigan Model of Party Identification

Campbell et al.'s (1960) findings regarding the long-term determinants of voting and the stability of party identification generated considerable debate within American political science. Many saw an argument for irrationality in voting, that voters were guided more by the beliefs of their forebears than by an understanding of the issues at stake in elections. In one famous response, V.O. Key (1966) declared, "Voters are not fools!"

Others, such as Norman Nie, Sidney Verba, and John Petrocik (1976) argued that the findings were accurate for the time of the study (the data are mainly from the 1952 and 1956 American National Election Studies) but that the 1950s, under the presidency of former general and war hero Dwight Eisenhower, was a relatively quiet period in American domestic politics. The more turbulent 1960s and 1970s, which saw dramatic increases in the number of protests, demonstrations, sit-ins, and riots in response to the civil rights movement and the Vietnam War, were accompanied by greater instability of party identifications.

The question of the stability of party identification in the United States, and the "rationality" of the electorate, continues to generate interest and research.

tended to be somewhat more complex. Indeed, they argued that party identification in the United States varied along the single dimension of strength of attachment (that is, the range extended from strong Democrat to weak Democrat, independent, weak Republican, and strong Republican), but the psychological attachment to a political party in Canada was **multidimensional**. A multidimensional concept is one in which more than one factor, or dimension, exists within a concept. Clarke et al. suggested that psychological attachments to a political party in Canada consist of three major dimensions: strength, consistency, and stability. Furthermore, they argued that the character of this psychological attachment is sufficiently distinct from the American version to warrant a different name: *partisanship*.

The different conceptualization of partisanship stems from the differences that Clarke et al. (1979) observed in their study of Canadian voters in the 1970s. They found that many Canadians hold different partisan attachments at the federal and provincial levels of government. It was not uncommon for a voter to self-identify as a Liberal when asked about federal politics and as a Conservative at the provincial level. Indeed, in many provinces, different parties compete at the two levels of government. At the time of the study, the main federal/provincial inconsistency was among the provincial Social Credit and federal Liberals and Conservatives in British Columbia, and among the provincial Parti Québécois and federal Liberals in Quebec. More recently, the federal and provincial distinctiveness between political parties has become even more pronounced, with the emergence of federal parties such as the Bloc Québécois and, during the 1990s, the Reform and Canadian Alliance parties. Supporters of these parties are not able to hold "consistent" identifications at the two levels of government. In contrast, cross-level inconsistency of party identification is much less

Expand Your Knowledge

A Comparison of the Conceptualization of Party Identification and Partisanship

Party Identification (United States)		Partisanship (Canada)
Strong Republican	Strength	Strong identifier
Fairly strong Republican		Weak identifier
Weak Republican		Non-identifier
Independent		
Weak Democrat	Consistency	Same federally and provincially
Fairly strong Democrat		Different federally and provincially
Strong Democrat	Stability	Never changed identification
		Changed identification

common in the United States. Since Clarke et al. found that cross-level inconsistency had an important bearing on the character of the psychological attachment to a party, they included this dimension as a component of the conceptualization of partisanship.

The other dimension added to partisanship was stability of party attachment. Once again, this reconceptualization grew out of empirical research on the character of party attachments. Recall that the Michigan formulation of party identification stressed its stability and suggested that it was a long-term attachment to a party passed intergenerationally through the socialization process. In important respects, the transmission of party identification was viewed as similar to the transmission of religious affiliation. Many Americans and Canadians think of themselves as having a religious affiliation, whether or not they formally hold membership in a church congregation. For most, this connection did not result from a period of detailed and systematic study of the major religious

Expand Your Knowledge

Consistency in Party Identifications

A debate between David Elkins and Jane Jenson in 1978 regarding the meaning of party identification illustrates the importance of clarity in conceptual definitions. Elkins (1978, 419–21) states:

> Concepts are like wines; some do not travel well. Thus, a frequent problem concerns whether phenomena with the same label in two societies are really the same. Party identification is a concept which is particularly interesting in this regard. . . . [E]xhibiting different identifications in different party systems should not be considered evidence of inconsistency. . . . Jenson et al. do treat contrary federal and provincial party identifications as a form of inconsistency.

Jenson's view (1978, 437–8) is

> Concepts do not travel; theories do. The distinction is an important one because the concept party identification and its measurement in different contexts provides students of voting with one of a class of problems in comparative analysis. Comparative analysis implies a search for and the development of general laws about human behaviour, laws which are valid across political systems. The way that this search is carried out is through the development, confirmation and modification of theory. . . . The more general and abstract the language, the more comparable phenomena that can be found. The more specific and historical the language, the more different things that will be observed.

texts—the Koran, the Torah, the Bible, and others. Instead, most people learn about religion from their parents and become adherents of a religious faith through the socialization process. Similarly, the Michigan model of party identification suggested that most voters do not become party identifiers as a result of a long period of detailed and systematic study of the major political ideologies and parties.

Empirical research on voting in Canada suggests that this process of intergenerational transmission of party identification is much less pronounced than it was in the United States in the 1950s. Although many voters did receive political "cues" from their parents as they were socialized into the political system, these signals seemed far less powerful in influencing attitudes toward other political phenomena, such as political leaders or issues. Furthermore, for many Canadians, partisan affiliation seemed to change in response to the parties' changing issue agenda or changing leadership. That is, the causal relationship between partisan attachment and attitudes toward issues and leaders appeared to be in the opposite direction: from perceptions of the leaders to partisan attachment as well as vice versa.

This multidimensional conceptualization of partisanship developed in response to empirical applications of the concept of party identification to a study of Canadian voting behaviour. *Partisanship* is therefore defined as a psychological attachment to a political party, which can vary along the dimensions of strength, stability, and consistency of attachment. Those voters with strong, stable, and consistent attachments to a party are referred to by Clarke et al. (1979) as durable partisans, whereas those without one or all of these qualities are called flexible partisans. Durable partisans resemble in many respects the party identifiers discussed by Campbell et al. (1960) in their research; these voters have a long-term, stable tie to a party, which colours their perception of the political world, including their attitudes toward the party leaders and their understanding of political issues and events.

However, in Canada, only about one in three voters is a durable partisan. The rest of the electorate consists of flexible partisans, for whom partisan affiliation is less stable and more likely to change in response to short-term political issues and events. Approximately two in three Canadian voters are flexible partisans, providing Canadian elections with considerable opportunities for change in response to short-term electoral phenomena. The 1993 federal election, which saw the "emerging" success of two parties (Reform and the BQ) and the near obliteration of two "old" parties (PC and NDP), provided a case in point of the dramatic changes that are possible when flexible Canadian partisans go to the polls. So did the 2011 election, in which the NDP seat share in the House of Commons rose from 37 in 2008 to 103 in 2011, and the Liberals dropped from 77 to 34 in the same period. Flexible partisanship can lead to substantial change over a short period of time, and these changes may be magnified by Canada's single member plurality electoral system (which is another matter entirely).

While Clarke and colleagues (1979) argued that party identification in Canada is best understood by the more complex term *partisanship*, analyses by subsequent teams of researchers conducting the **Canadian Election Studies (CES)** adopted a different tack of definition and measurement. In the study *Letting the People Decide*, Richard Johnston and his collaborators (1992) suggested that a key difference between the conceptualization of party identification in the United States and Canada was the way in which respondents could self-identify as being unattached to a party, or as being politically independent. Whereas studies in the United States always provided respondents with the option of identifying as independents, Canadian studies had not included such a choice. The result, according to Johnston et al. (1992, 82), was that "more Canadian than American non-partisans were induced to give what appeared to be a party commitment. This inflated the percentage appearing to identify with some party and made the identifier group appear quite unstable over repeated measurements." The measurement solution to this conceptual problem was to include the option "none of these" in the question probing respondents' party identification. Hence, individuals were asked whether they thought of themselves as Liberals, Conservatives, New Democrats, some other party, or none of these. Not surprisingly, the percentage of respondents indicating that they were not partisans increased from an average of approximately 20 between 1965 and 1984 to 35 in 1988 (Ibid., Table 3-1).

In key areas of research in public opinion and voting, there is an ongoing dialogue between the way concepts are defined and, subsequently, how they are operationalized and measured with questions in our election study data sets. For instance, the reconceptualization of party identification among the Canadian Election Study team continued when André Blais and associates (2001) analyzed the measurement of party identification through a comparison of election study data in Britain, Canada, and the United States. According to the team, party identification has two key components—it is a self-definition among individuals (that is, one does not need to hold a party membership or vote a certain way to identify with a party), and there is a time horizon associated with the identification, in that it consists of an enduring attachment.

Using question-wording experiments in the late 1990s election surveys in the three countries, Blais et al. found that the observed incidence of party identification changed considerably according to the question set used. Specifically, they recommended adopting a set with items that touch on both primary elements. In terms of the self-identification element, they found that using a term such as *normally* when asking about a party self-image helped direct the respondent to an enduring attachment rather than attachment of the moment. They also recommended the use of a cue that enables respondents to indicate that they have no attachment, thereby ensuring that there is no inflated assessment of respondents with a party identification. Both of these recommendations can be seen in the way respondents to the 2008 and 2011 Canadian election studies were asked about their party identification. The question was, "In federal politics, do you *usually* think of yourself as Liberal, Conservative, NDP, Bloc Québécois, Green, or *none of these*?" (emphasis added).

APPLY YOUR UNDERSTANDING

Multidimensional Concepts

One of the prime goals of formulating conceptual definitions is to achieve clarity. This is not to say that the concepts should be simple. As the discussion of party identification and partisanship indicates, concepts in the social sciences may be complex and multidimensional. For each of the following concepts, devise two definitions—one that includes only a single dimension and another that offers a multidimensional explanation

- political participation
- interest in politics
- assessment of party leaders
- neo-conservative ideology
- feminism
- environmentalism

Were you able to develop both unidimensional and multidimensional definitions? You can check how you did by searching for these key terms in an academic journal database. Find a recent article and look for the author's definition of the concept.

Sources of Conceptual Definitions

It is clear that one of the perennial difficulties in the social sciences is defining concepts in such a way that all researchers and observers agree on their meaning. If we wish to conduct research with the goal of formulating lawlike generalizations about the social world, agreement on the meaning of terms would appear to be a basic precondition. Unfortunately, the reality is that such agreement remains elusive. Furthermore, there is no indisputable guide we can turn to for the single, authoritative definition of a concept. We can refer to the political science literature, but, as we have seen, that literature is as likely to document disagreement as it is consensus. This does not mean that concepts either have no meaning at all or that they have any meaning one wishes to ascribe, as suggested by the Mock Turtle in *Alice in Wonderland*:

> "Of course not," said the Mock Turtle. "Why, if a fish came to me, and told me he was going on a journey, I should say 'With what porpoise?'" "Don't you mean 'purpose'?" said Alice. "I mean what I say," the Mock Turtle replied, in an offended tone. (Carroll 1990, 126)

Instead, it is to suggest that debate over the meaning of concepts can be an important topic of scholarly inquiry. Within the debate, inductive reasoning, extrapolation, and intuition all come into play.

Inductive Reasoning

Although most studies begin with a literature review, an account of the conceptual and empirical terrain mapped out to date, this process should not suggest that a researcher can define concepts only in the ways they have been defined in previous research. On the contrary, it is both possible and at times highly desirable to focus a research project on the development of alternative conceptual definitions. Perhaps the most common method of doing so is through **inductive reasoning**, using empirical evidence to help form the definition of a concept. An illustration of this method can be drawn from the afore-mentioned example of party identification. When Clarke and colleagues (1979) examined Canadian voting behaviour in the mid-1970s, they began with the conceptualization of party identification as it was developed in the United States. Their early studies indicated several important differences: they found that many Canadians held different identifications at the federal and provincial levels and that party identifications were not as stable in Canada as they were reported to be in the United States (see Jenson 1975; Jenson 1978; Clarke et al. 1979; LeDuc et al. 1984). In this case, evidence from the application of the concept led to its reconceptualization.

Expand Your Knowledge

Inductive Reasoning and Reconceptualization

A good illustration of evidence from a research project leading to a new and different definition of a concept can be seen in some of the research on political participation. One of the early empirical studies of political participation in the United States was conducted by Lester Milbrath (1965), who argued that there was a hierarchy of participation. The hierarchy, in Milbrath's view, was shaped as a pyramid with many people near the bottom, exhibiting low levels of participation, and with decreasing numbers of people as one moved up the hierarchy. Milbrath labelled those at the high end of the pyramid gladiators, those in the middle participants, and those at the low end spectators.

Sidney Verba and Norman Nie (1972) later found that political participation was not arrayed in such a hierarchical fashion. In particular, they found that many people involved in protest activities such as marches, demonstrations, or sit-ins—including those who were highly involved in such participatory activities—often were not involved in more conventional types of political participation, such as voting, donating money to a political party, or running for elective office. This finding led to the conclusion that there were different types, or "modes," of participation and that these modes may be relatively independent of one another. Furthermore, different factors may account for the level of activity in different modes of participation. Thus, the empirical evidence led to a reconceptualization of political participation.

Extrapolation

An alternative method of changing a conceptual definition is to extrapolate, even borrow, from other fields of study. Political scientists have developed certain conceptual tools for understanding political phenomena, as have economists, sociologists, psychologists, and other social scientists, for their fields of study. At times, the concepts developed for one of the social sciences may have important applicability to others. One well-known example of this type of conceptual borrowing is Anthony Downs's (1957) adoption of a "rational" approach to voting. Downs used **deductive reasoning**, popular in his field of economics, to attempt to explain voters' decision-making and the relative ideological positioning of political parties. The deductive method begins by the identification of one or more postulates, followed by the derivation of expectations and conclusions based on the claims. The postulate often used in economic analysis, and used by Downs in his study, is that voters and the leadership of political parties are rational (that is, self-interested, utility-maximizing) decision-makers. The justification for this extrapolation from economics to politics is that it has a number of insights for economic decisions involving the marketplace and therefore could provide insight into political decisions involving power, influence, and authority. Whether it does so is a matter of ongoing empirical investigation.

Intuition

All the ways of justifying conceptual definitions discussed so far rely to a considerable extent on how other researchers have operationalized a concept. But what about the ideas that are unique and independent to you as a researcher? What if you have thought about a concept in a way that no one else has thought about it before? Is it not possible to bring your own creativity to a research project, to define concepts in new ways that speak more directly to your experience and imagination? The answer to the latter question is a qualified yes. You certainly should not feel restricted to using concepts whose definitions appear less helpful and informative than others that could be imagined. Concepts should be defined to best capture the essence of the quality that is being examined.

Our experience is that students often do not fully appreciate the scope of previous research on a topic. A vast and continually growing amount of research has been conducted and published on topics in political science, and an even vaster amount has been conducted in the social sciences more broadly. The chances are reasonably good that the ideas that occur to you regarding the best definition of a concept, or the best explanation for variation in a dependent concept, have been examined by others in a different context. What may appear new to you as you begin to engage in empirical political science may have occurred to others as well. Two cautionary flags should be raised. First, check the literature thoroughly for examples of other research that has used conceptual definitions similar to those in your study. To acknowledge the work of previous researchers and to connect your findings to those of the wider research community, you must provide citations to the previous research. Second, if you are truly the first researcher ever to define a concept in a particular way, search the literature carefully, highlight the differences between your definition and those in earlier studies, and explain why your conceptual definition is superior to the others.

In summary, defining concepts in clear and concise ways is an important part of using the scientific method. It is useful to begin from the premise that other political scientists may think about this concept differently than you do. To avoid misunderstanding about the research topic, it is helpful to provide precise definitions of the concepts that will be used in your study. It is also important to recognize that your study will be part of "the literature" in an area of study and to provide cross-references to studies that are related to your work and others that depart from it.

Working as a Team

1. One of the central elements of democratic theory, and one of the most common elements of contemporary political debate, is the concept of equality. Discuss various meanings that might be attached to this concept.
2. Did you produce a conceptualization to which everyone in the group can agree? If not, what difficulties did you encounter?

Self-Study

1. Think of a concept that may be of interest in political science research (political ideologies, political belief systems, voting, political stability, democracy, etc.). Identify three journal articles in which this concept is examined. Describe how the authors define the concept in the studies. Provide a critique of the conceptual definitions.
2. Participation in politics is variously called political participation, political involvement, or political activity. It is sometimes defined as a single, simple concept, as a number of (possibly unrelated) simple concepts, or as a complex, multidimensional concept. Find an example of each type of definition in the literature on political participation and discuss the usefulness of each.

Note

1. For a discussion of the more general pattern of American scholarship's influence on research in Canada, see Cairns (1975).

CHAPTER 5

Defining the Political World

Measures

Destination

By the end of this chapter, you should be able to

- explain the process of operationalization and appreciate the research concerns brought to that process;
- state the distinctions among concepts, variables, and indicators;
- distinguish among nominal-, ordinal-, and interval-level variables and discuss issues of accuracy in the measurement of political phenomena; and
- explain the logic behind and creation of scales and indexes.

As political scientists, we often find that the questions we are interested in are stated as abstractions: Which political system is better? Which economic system promotes the greatest social equality? What is the best means to provide health care? When we approach these matters from an empirical rather than a normative position, we seek factual evidence that can be applied to such abstract questions. To obtain such evidence, we need to transform the concepts embedded in our questions into an empirical form. The first step in doing so, as outlined in the previous chapter, is to create a conceptual definition. With that definition in hand, we can then turn to the matter of measurement.

For example, consider the grading of university students. Universities reserve the grade A for those students whose course performance is "excellent." However, academic excellence is an abstract concept. How will a professor know which students have earned an

A and which have not? In the interests of fairness, the professor needs to quantify academic performance so that all students are comparable. He or she may decide that students should be judged on three areas: subject knowledge, research skills, and writing ability. Now the professor needs some method to measure student performance in these three areas. Examinations, homework assignments, and term papers are all methods that might be used. The movement from an abstract concept (academic excellence) to a concrete measure (mid-term examination mark)—is known as operationalization. As we will see, this process is not simple and can be very contentious at times. Think of the potential conflicts and controversies that can swirl around the measurement of academic excellence even in a class such as this one! Seldom can we fall back on widely shared rules to make the decisions required.

This chapter explores the use of conceptual definitions to select variables and the use of indicators to locate individual cases among the variable's different values. In addition, we will discuss how to select and create the best possible variables and indicators for our

APPLY YOUR UNDERSTANDING

Operationalizing University Objectives

The objectives of post-secondary education often come under a good deal of public scrutiny. In their defence, universities often argue that the public and, more particularly, politicians, fail to understand that these objectives entail more than the acquisition of marketable skills.

Suppose that your premier says,

> I will accept your university's definition of its own mission [which might be to produce graduates with a capacity for independent and critical thought and with the research and analytical skills necessary for success in the twenty-first century]. Now, show me the evidence that the university is in fact producing such individuals. Show me proof that universities are not simply taking in bright students, aging them four or five years, and then releasing them back into society with no significant increase in their capacity for independent and critical thought, and without the necessary research and analytical skills. In short, show me that the government and public are getting good value for publicly funded post-secondary education.

Given this challenge, how would you operationalize the university's objectives? How would you measure whether students are becoming better thinkers and whether they are acquiring the appropriate research and analytical skills? What impact has your own education had in these respects, and how would you measure this impact? How might you prove that the government and public are getting good value? Or do we simply ask to be taken on faith? Will such a plea carry much weight in an environment of fiscal constraint? Why or why not?

research questions. It is in this process of operationalization that the conceptual rubber hits the empirical road.

Concepts, Variables, and Indicators

We must be clear about the difference between a concept and a variable from the outset. Recall that a concept is an idea or a term that enables us to classify phenomena; equality, order, social class, political culture, and region are all examples of concepts. Concepts can be relatively abstract (e.g. liberty) or relatively concrete (region)—the more abstract a concept, the more difficult it is to find a definition that is acceptable to one's peers. When we transform our conceptual definition into a quantifiable, observable phenomenon, we have a variable.

The distinction between concepts and variables might best be seen by way of an example. Education is a concept that we might define as "formal training to develop mental abilities and skills." Level of education is a variable that can empirically distinguish between different levels of training. How is this variable different from the concept of education? The variable, unlike the concept, can take on different **values**. We might choose to divide level of education into categories (e.g. low, middle, and high) or we may look at the actual years of education completed by individuals and compare them on a precise basis. The point to stress is that the variable empirically captures the variation within the concept. This is a fine but nonetheless important distinction.

Log on to our website to watch a tutorial on working with variables.

Ultimately, our goal is to acquire knowledge about the concepts. We have already discussed that concepts are the building blocks of theory and that theories use propositions to state the relationships between concepts. Variables are our means of tapping and quantifying these concepts, and hypotheses state the relationships between variables. We test hypotheses in an effort to find support for our propositions and, by extension, for our theory. It

APPLY YOUR UNDERSTANDING

Moving from Concepts to Variables

For the following concepts, provide a precise conceptual definition and select three variables to measure each concept. Do you find it easier to select variables for the more abstract concepts or the concrete concepts? How do your variables differ from the concepts? What is lost by being limited to only three variables? What is lost when you move from concept to variable?

- environmentalism
- political interest
- democracy
- economic growth
- family values

is important to realize that some degree of meaning or understanding is invariably lost as we move from concepts to variables (Manheim and Rich 1981, 45). This loss occurs because we are limited by our variables to those aspects of the concept that can be measured empirically. Often, concepts include intrinsic values or meanings that cannot be captured fully

Expand Your Knowledge

Abuse of Women in Canadian University and College Dating Relationships

A widespread public discussion of the distinction between conceptual and operational definitions in the social sciences occurred in 1993, when DeKeseredy and Kelly released their study examining the abuse of women in Canadian university and college dating relationships. The study's conclusions, widely reported in the media at the time, were shocking: 35 per cent of Canadian students reported having been physically abused, 45.1 per cent had been sexually abused, and 86.2 per cent had been psychologically abused in a dating relationship (DeKeseredy and Kelly 1993, 148–53).

DeKeseredy and Kelly (1993, 146) define *abuse* as "any intentional physical, sexual, or psychological assault on a female by a male dating partner." Using this definition, they identify three types of abuse. The researchers distinguish between the incidence of abuse (a situation that has occurred in the last 12 months) and the prevalence of abuse (has occurred since the students left high school) as well (138). Since the latter covers a longer period of time, the prevalence data invariably are higher than incidence data. The study also compared the responses of male and female respondents, regarding the behaviour of men toward women but not vice versa.

Here is the data on the prevalence rates of psychological abuse:

	Men (*N* = 1,307)		**Women (*N* = 1,835)**	
Type of Abuse	**%**	***N***	**%**	***N***
Insults or swearing	62.4	747	65.1	1,105
Put her (you) down in front of friends or family	25.9	322	44.2	742
Accused her (you) of having affairs or flirting with other men	40.9	495	52.6	901
Did or said something to spite her (you)	65.2	773	72.2	1,216
Threatened to hit or throw something at her (you)	8.0	97	20.6	346
Threw, smashed, or kicked something	30.6	37	37.3	652

Source: DeKeseredy and Kelly (1993, 153)

When the six questions listed in the table were combined, DeKeseredy and Kelly (1993, 153) found that 86.2 per cent of women had experienced at least one of these behaviours since high school. Based on their operational definition of abuse, they by empirical research. For example, many of the benefits that are thought to spring from post-secondary education are not easily captured by empirical measurement. You may be a more thoughtful individual when you finish your degree than you were earlier, but demonstrating this quality to others can be difficult.

concluded that 80.8 per cent of men had been psychologically abusive to a dating partner in the period since high school.

The study's results were so inconsistent with the conventional understanding of the topic that the scholarly community greeted them with widespread disbelief. In the following issue of the *Canadian Journal of Sociology*, commentaries by Gartner (1993) and Fox (1993) appeared. Gartner challenged the validity of the term *abuse* as operationalized by DeKeseredy and Kelly (we discuss measurement validity later in this chapter). She argued that the questions used to measure psychological abuse were derived from a commonly used battery of questions called the Conflict Tactics Scales. These questions are introduced to respondents "by noting both the normality of disagreements and conflicts between partners in a relationship and the range of different ways disagreements are dealt with" (Gartner 1993, 314). The term *abuse* is not used in the questions. Furthermore, as the name of the scale implies, the questions are designed to measure conflict tactics, which may go both ways in a relationship, and not abuse. This latter point is important, Gartner (1993, 316) argues, because previous research shows that "women and men are about equally likely to use verbal aggression." Similarly, Fox (1993, 322) claims that the use of "global" measures of abuse combine the least with the worst offences (e.g. an unwanted kiss with rape). Both scholars argue that conflating the two risks trivializes the more serious offences (Gartner 1993, 318–19; Fox 1993, 322).

In response to their critics, DeKeseredy (1994) and Kelly (1994) justify their operational decisions. Kelly (1994, 83) provides an eye-opening account of her experiences with this study:

> Once the data were collected, there was immediate pressure to release them. From the onset, I was concerned about the release of the psychological abuse items. . . . [W]e agreed to initially release only the marginals for the physical and sexual abuse items and not to release the aggregate of all abuse items and the psychological abuse items until the data had been fully analyzed. Unfortunately, the data were released without my consent, against our express agreement, and in a form that, in my view, distorted the value of the research. . . . [T]he bulk of the media attention was to the combined total abuse figures and the psychological abuse items.

This saga presents a revealing portrait of the challenges facing researchers working in highly sensitive areas within the social sciences. Moreover, it stands as stark testimony to the importance of having consistency between conceptual and operational definitions, illustrating the accuracy of the old adage "The devil is in the details."

When we choose variables, we strive to select those that most accurately capture our concepts and thereby reduce the amount of meaning that is lost. One way to do so is to use multiple variables to tap the same concept. Often, many variables can be seen as legitimate measures of a concept, particularly of more complex ones. Consider the concept of political participation, which we will define here as "acting with the intent of directly influencing the political system." One variable that might tap this concept is voting: Did the individual vote in the last election or not? Voting is empirically measurable and can take on different values (did or did not vote).[1] But other variables provide insight into the concept; party membership, political campaign contributions, lobbying, letter writing, and protest activity are all aspects of political participation.

As Figure 5.1 shows, each of these variables captures a piece—but only a piece—of the concept. Some, such as community participation, may capture part of the concept, even though the bulk of community participation is non-political in character. In the figure, therefore, community participation falls largely outside the conceptual domain of political participation. Even with a number of variables at our disposal, there will still be spaces left, conceptual aspects of participation that remain untapped. (These spaces are represented by the figure's unshaded parts.) Ideally, only small sections of the conceptual domain will be left uncovered by our selected variables.

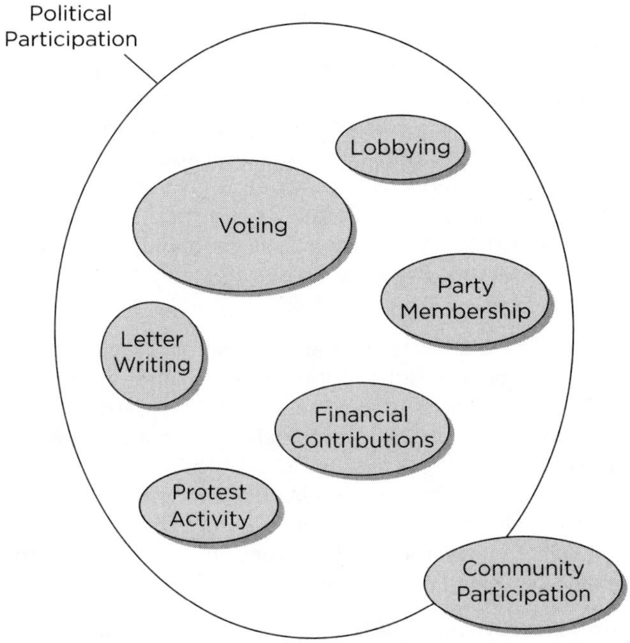

Figure 5.1 Variables Associated with Political Participation

Source: Adapted from Neuman (1994).

This chapter's opening discussion of grading students provides another example of multiple variables: subject knowledge, research skills, and writing ability are all variables that can be used to quantify the concept of academic excellence. When we have multiple variables that appear to measure the same concept, there are likely to be a number of dimensions to the concept. The ability to write is not the same as knowledge of the subject matter, although we hope there is some (positive) relationship between the two.[2] We can sometimes combine variables into an index or a scale, which acts as a **complex multiple indicator**. By using multiple variables to quantify the conceptual definition, we are able to capture more fully the meaning of the concept, as Figure 5.1 suggests. This more complete meaning allows us to be more confident when we use the variables to draw conclusions about the concepts. However, as DeKeseredy and Kelly's (1993) study illustrates, simply choosing more variables to measure a concept is not necessarily a prescription for better measurement if the variables lack validity (see pp. 90–1).

Once we have selected the variables to measure a concept, we still need ways to gather information about them. Such measures are referred to as **indicators**, the means by which we assign each individual case to the different values of the variable.[3] In our university grading example, grades serve as the indictors for the variables: mid-term examination grade is an indicator of the subject area knowledge variable and term paper grade is an indicator of writing ability.

Let's look at another variable, support for feminism. We might understand this variable to alter from high to moderate to low. But what observable facts indicate support for feminism? How do we know whether someone shows high, moderate, or low support? Possible indicators might include stated support in surveys for either feminism or feminist goals, membership in feminist organizations (recorded in membership lists), or financial support for feminist lobby groups (recorded in donation lists). In a study by Keith Archer and Roger Gibbins (1997), support for feminism was measured in part by responses to the following questions:

- Do you agree or disagree that society would be better off if more women stayed home with their children? (Disagreement was interpreted as an indicator of support for feminism.)
- How important is it to guarantee equality between men and women in all aspects of life? (Higher importance was interpreted as an indicator of support for feminism.)

Now think of economic development. Some commonly used indicators of this variable are gross domestic product (GDP), GDP per capita, infant mortality rates, literacy rates, and the proportion of GDP spent on research and development. Information from these indicators can be used to classify countries as developed or developing.

Just as multiple variables may allow us to tap more of a concept, multiple indicators may allow us to reveal more of a variable. Researchers often use multiple indicators of a single variable, even though they will not yield exactly the same results. (If they did, we would need only one.) The United States, for instance, has a poorer record than most Western states with respect to infant mortality, but a better record than most with respect to per capita GDP. Nonetheless, all indicators should point in the same direction; developed countries tend to have higher scores across the board than do developing countries.

To illustrate this point, consider these two fictional examples, one very simple and the other much more complex. The first comes from a questionnaire administered to grade 10 students who had just completed a summer volleyball camp. The students were asked a rudimentary question: Did you enjoy the camp, yes or no? While the camp organizers were pleased that the vast majority of the students said "yes," the questionnaire did little to investigate the various dimensions of enjoyment. Did students enjoy the coaching? The food? The level of competition? The chance to meet new friends? The social atmosphere? Did they like some elements more than others? What did they like least and most? By asking only one question, and an extremely simple one at that, the organizers missed the opportunity to acquire information that might enable them to improve the program. In short, they needed more than a single indicator of the variable "enjoyment."

The second example concerns social class, a concept that has played an extraordinarily important role in the evolution of social science theory. It is one of the truly "big" concepts, particularly in economics, political science, and sociology, and encompasses numerous variables, including income, education, and occupation. Class is more than money, more than education, and more than occupational location, although all three have a significant role to play. Adding to the complexity of measuring social class is the fact that it is difficult to pull together the multiple variables, for they do not always move in sync. Education and income are positively correlated, as are education and occupation and occupation and income, but there are many exceptions to the general rule of positive association. It is the relationship between these variables that affects a person's class position. Because the concept of social class contains theoretical richness and is understood to comprise multiple variables, it should be clear that one indicator is not sufficient; knowing only an individual's annual household income, highest level of education, or current occupation will not suffice. Each of these variables requires one or more indicators.

If social class were measured solely by annual income, two individuals who each earn $150,000 per year would both have a high social class. Suppose that one earned this income as a physician and the other by selling cocaine. Because these two occupations have such a different status in Canadian society, it is no longer apparent that the individuals both have a high social class, even though they have identical incomes. Indeed, the drug dealer has a relatively low social class despite a high income. This type of finding is, of course, not limited to instances in which people are engaged in illegal activities.

Let's look at two respondents who have graduated from law school, which gives them a high score on a variable measuring education. One of them practises corporate law and earns $250,000 annually, while the other works at an inner-city legal aid clinic and earns

$30,000 annually. Which lawyer has the higher social class? In answering this question, be careful to stay within the definition of the concept being measured. Some (idealistic?) students might prefer to work for a legal aid clinic—such a position might be viewed as more socially relevant and, for them, more enjoyable. But the question is about higher social class. If social class is defined as a multidimensional concept comprising levels of education, income, and occupational status, and in which a higher score on each component corresponds with a higher class position, the answer is simple: the corporate lawyer has the higher social class.

In summary, variables are a means of translating concepts into observable and quantifiable phenomena; indicators are the means or operations used to determine the exact values of our variables. As we move from concept to variable to indicator, we move from broad abstraction to narrow precision. Figure 5.2 presents a fairly simple visual representation of how indicators, variables, and concepts fit together. A more complex example using multiple indicators and variables is seen in Figure 5.3.

Given the importance of selecting proper variables and indicators for our concepts, a justification of their selection should be part of any research report. Choices will always be involved, and we need to be able to defend our decisions. By explaining the logic behind our operationalization and demonstrating the links between variables and concepts and then

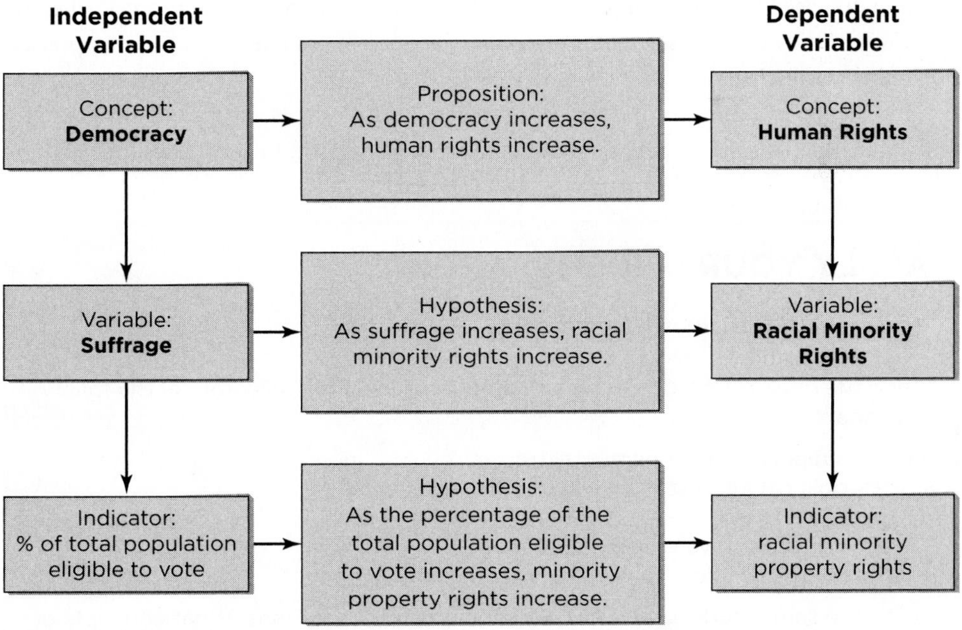

Figure 5.2 A Simple Model of Concepts, Variables, and Indicators

Source: Adapted from Manheim and Rich (1981)

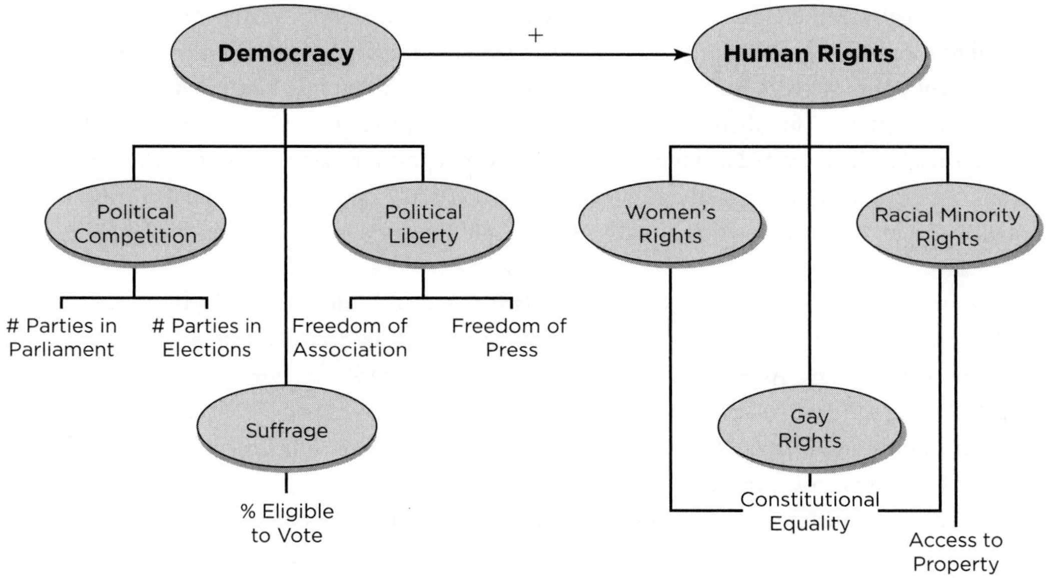

Figure 5.3 An Advanced Model of Concepts, Variables, and Indicators

between indicators and variables, arguments and conclusions are more readily defended. In addition, the need to explain our operationalization choices improves the process: when we know we must defend our selections to our peers, we are more likely to take every precaution to avoid criticism.

In this context, much of the research done by both students and faculty involves secondary analysis of existing data sets (discussed in Chapter 10). In such cases, the primary

APPLY YOUR UNDERSTANDING

Moving from Variables to Indicators

Using the most recent CES or a comparable survey, find indicators of the following variables:

- support for environmentalism
- political interest
- social class
- attitudes toward party leaders
- party affiliation

Using the same study, select five additional survey questions. What concepts or variables do you believe these questions were intended to tap? List all possible uses for each of the five questions.

selection of indicators has already been made by others. If we use data from the Canadian Election Studies (CES), we are locked into the measures selected by the CES research teams. Our choices are therefore limited and we may end up using indicators that are not quite what we would like them to be. The reality is that researchers who rely on secondary analysis must use indicators that may have been designed for other research purposes and agendas.

Precision in Measurement

Our indicators allow us to distinguish between a variable's values. When indicators are designed, the issue emerges as to how precise the distinctions between categories of a variable should be. There are three basic **levels of measurement**: **nominal**, **ordinal**, and **interval**. We will see in later chapters that the level of measurement selected largely determines the type and power of statistical measures available for analysis. The higher the level of measurement, the more powerful the statistics that are available.

What do we mean by *precise*? Think about the difference in precision between describing someone as "young" and as "21 years of age." Both descriptions can be used for the same individual, but the latter is more precise than the former. The designation "young" omits a great deal of information: we do not know the cut-off point between "young" and "not young" or where this person sits within the category. Is he or she at the upper limit of the category (as the case would be if the category "young" ended at age 22) or does he or she still have a few years to enjoy being "young" (as the person would if the category ended at age 30)? If we were to pursue precision to the extreme, we would have an overabundance of information; age could be specified to the year, date, and even time of birth. Fortunately, such detail is neither required nor desirable for most variables or research questions. If we were interested in the impact of age on support for neo-conservatism, we might expect people in their twenties to differ from those in their forties or fifties, but we would not expect to find significant differences between those who are 26 and 27.

Log on to our website to watch a tutorial on levels of measurement.

As we've stated previously, our aim in research is to form generalizations about groups of people, and that goal requires that we categorize individuals on the basis of similar and different characteristics. If we pursue such high levels of precision that we end up with an extremely small number of cases in each category, we will be unable to notice patterns or relationships between variables. Overall, we should strive for the highest level of measurement that is useful for the research question at hand.

Recall that concepts can be conceptualized as either categorical or continuous. Categorical concepts (e.g. religious affiliation) have distinct characteristics, while continuous concepts (e.g. age) have characteristics that are sequentially connected and whose categories can be placed on a continuum. The former result in the selection of nominal-level variables; the latter lend themselves to either ordinal- or interval-level variables. We will outline each level in turn.

Nominal-level variables are those whose categories cannot be ordered or ranked. Religion, region, and gender are examples of nominal variables, as are "yes–no" distinctions. (For instance, "Do you agree in principle with assisted suicide for terminally ill patients?") Differences exist between the categories of the variable—for example, between males and females—and, although numerical values can be assigned to the categories (male = 1; female = 2), there is no mathematical relationship between these values. They are arbitrary and may be assigned arbitrarily (male = 2; female = 1). With a nominal-level variable, the numerical values represent differences in kind (e.g. Liberal = 1, Conservative = 2, NDP = 3, BQ = 4, and Green = 5), not in degree. The categories are distinct, but they cannot logically be ordered. To appreciate how common nominal-level variables and indicators are in political science research, imagine how hamstrung we would be if we could not distinguish survey respondents on the basis of their language, region, sex, religion, or partisan identification.

Ordinal-level variables allow for the ranking of categories. The ranking in an ordinal-level variable is relative to the position of the other categories; we do not know the exact distance between the categories, but we can organize them along a continuum. "Strongly agree–agree–disagree–strongly disagree," "poor–fair–good–excellent," and the "A–B–C–D–F" grading system are all examples of ordinal rankings.

It is common to encounter ranked data in the social sciences, and most people have an intuitive understanding of data presented in this way. However, there are a number of precautions that must be kept in mind when working with ordered data. The first is that we cannot assume that the distance between ranks is the same. If you were asked to rank your first five destinations for a holiday, there may be a much larger perceptual gap between your first and second choices than between your fourth and fifth. You might really want to go to your first choice but be relatively indifferent between choices four and five. Second, and perhaps of greater importance, any order always has a bottom, a lowest, or a worst, but being ranked last does not necessarily indicate the absence of quality. Let's look briefly at two illustrations.

Many universities use student evaluations of faculty to generate decile ratings; some instructors are ranked in the tenth decile, meaning that their student scores are higher than those received by 90 per cent of their peers, while others are ranked in the first decile, meaning that 90 per cent of their peers had better student perceptions. This result does not mean that first-decile teachers are necessarily poor teachers; it means only that 90 per cent of the other instructors are viewed by students as better teachers. It is possible that students in Professor Filibuster's class might describe him as a competent and effective teacher, yet their assessments place him in the first decile in comparison with his peers. When individuals are ranked, someone must finish last regardless of the quality of their performance. Ten per cent of the professors have to be in the first decile. The last-place athlete in an Olympic event is still an excellent athlete.

Our second example comes from a Fraser Institute project—begun in British Columbia in 1998 and subsequently extended to several other provinces, including Alberta and

Ontario—to rank elementary and secondary schools based on student performance measures. The rationale for such a ranking system is that, by combining a number of individual indicators into a global performance score and then publicly releasing the information according to how each school ranks relative to others, "the school report cards allow teachers, parents, school administrators, students, and taxpayers to analyze and compare the academic performance of individual schools" (Fraser Institute, "School Performance").

The problem is that minute differences in the performance measures can have a major impact on rank. Consider data published by the Fraser Institute for Alberta schools in the 2011–12 school year. A school that scored 8.0 on a 10-point scale ranked 26 out of the 279 schools reported on and, according to the rank measure, was in the first decile of "high performing" schools. In contrast, a school with a score of 6.8 (lower, to be sure, but not dramatically lower), ranked ninety-second, placing it in the fourth decile (Fraser Institute, "Alberta"). Thus, relatively minor differences in the measure used to determine rankings can have a substantial impact on the ordering. Students, teachers, and parents associated with the school ranked twentieth in the system could well be depressed by their comparative position, even though the substantive difference between their school and the school ranked first is modest. In a similar fashion, the first-decile teacher may feel depressed and incompetent, even though most of his or her students may feel he or she is doing an effective job.

Interval-level variables can be placed on a continuum as well, but the categories are separated by a standard unit. The distance between 1 and 2 is the same as the distance between 3 and 4. With interval data, then, the value of 4 is twice the size of 2 and 8 is twice the size of 4. Note that this was not the case with ordinal-level data. With ordinal data, 4 is larger than 2, but it is uncertain how much larger it is.

Let's illustrate this difference by comparing an ordinal- and an interval-level measurement of attitudes toward the government's performance. **Agree/disagree questions** are a common way of deriving an ordinal-level attitudinal measure in the social sciences. Respondents could be asked the following:

> On a scale of 1 to 5, where 1 is "strongly disapprove," 2 is "somewhat disapprove," 3 is "neither approve nor disapprove," 4 is "approve," and 5 is "strongly approve," how would you rate the performance of the government?

The higher the respondent's score, the more positively he or she feels about the government. But notice that the size of the units on this variable is not constant. That is, the difference between 1 and 2 (strongly disapprove and somewhat disapprove) is not the same as the difference between 2 and 3 (somewhat disapprove and neither approve nor disapprove). By extension, the value of 4 is not twice the value of 2, in the sense that people scoring 4 are not twice as supportive of the government as those who score 2. Computing an average, or mean, score based on this question would be inappropriate because such a score assumes a constant value between categories (see Chapter 14).

The issue of giving "meaning" or "context" to data, an issue that was at the heart of the dispute over DeKeseredy and Kelly's (1993) study, adds a measure of subjectivity to social sciences data. For example, some would say that money is an interval-level variable or indicator in the social sciences. A dollar is a dollar, and 10 dollars is half of 20 dollars. But it is also true that money has a different meaning for people, depending on the context of their social and economic situation. A government policy designed to increase individual taxes by a flat rate of $1,000 across the board would have a different meaning for people

Expand Your Knowledge

Feeling Thermometers

Researchers sometimes try to impose an interval scale by defining a response set in such a way that it appears to have a standard unit between categories. One frequently encountered illustration of such a pseudo interval-level variable is the "**feeling thermometer**." Canadian Election Studies prior to 1988 (when the studies switched from face-to-face interviews to telephone interviews), introduced the feeling thermometer with the following set of instructions:

> You will see here a drawing of a thermometer. It is called a feeling thermometer because it helps measure people's feelings toward various things. Here is how it works. If you don't have any particular feeling about the things we are asking about, place them at the 50-degree mark. If your feelings are very warm toward a particular thing, you would give a score between 50 and 100—the warmer your feelings, the higher the score. On the other hand, if your feelings are relatively cool toward something, you would place them between 0 and 50. The cooler your feelings, the closer the score will be to zero. (Clarke et al. 1979, 406)

Feeling thermometers are attractive because respondents can use them with respect to a multitude of different topics (politicians, parties, interest groups, countries, or virtually anything). Even so, we cannot assume that the difference between a rating of 20 and 30 is the same as that between 70 and 80; the feeling thermometer is not a true interval-level variable.

An interval-level scale would presuppose that all respondents internalize feelings of like or dislike by using a standard scale, and intuitively this is not to be the case. The trouble is that this differentiation of scales among respondents appears to occur for all attitudinal variables: even if researchers are definitive in the meaning of a response set, it still must be interpreted by the respondents. That process of interpretation, or internalization of the scale, adds a subjective component to its interpretation. In the specific case of the feeling thermometer, most respondents effectively convert the thermometer to a 10-point scale; 40 and 50 are used more frequently than are 43 and 47.

earning $200,000 annually than it would for people earning $25,000 annually. Although the amount is the same, its value varies. Therefore, even "hard" interval-level data in the social sciences can take on ordinal-level characteristics.

Despite these obvious concerns with interval-level data in the social sciences, researchers often assume that their data are at or sufficiently close to this level. The reason, to be discussed in much more detail in subsequent chapters, is that interval-level data are amenable to much higher-level statistical techniques and, in particular, provide opportunities for multivariate statistical techniques that offer more analytical insight than do the bivariate techniques common to nominal- and ordinal-level data analysis. The challenge is to understand the assumptions that underlie the data analysis and to discern to what extent and with what effect the data analytical techniques violate those assumptions. Understanding that process calls for a combination of both the art and science of data analysis.

Notice the precision differences between the levels of measurement. Nominal-level variables have categories, ordinal-level variables have categories that can be ranked, and interval-level variables have categories that can be ranked with a specified distance (or interval) between the categories. As we stated earlier, there are statistical advantages to using the highest level of measurement available. Sometimes, though, it is desirable to move down in precision, such as from interval- to ordinal-level variables. If we do not have enough cases within the categories, we cannot detect patterns, leading us to group interval-level data (e.g. by combining all respondents aged 18–30 into a single category labelled young). Grouped data can be easier to read in a contingency table because of the reduced number of categories. Finally, the calculation of certain measures of strength (addressed in Chapter 16) is easier with grouped data than with interval-level data.

The decision to group data presents yet another decision: On what basis should data be grouped? Consider the variable of age. If we have 100 cases, with ages measured in years, how should we construct groups? Should we have three groups—young, middle, old—or perhaps four—young, young–middle, middle–old, old? What should be the cut-off points between groups? Do we group the data to create equally sized age categories, such as 0–19, 20–39, 40–59, 60–79, and 80–99, or do we categorize age according to our knowledge about life cycle and cohorts, such as under 30, 30–65, over 65? Perhaps we should divide the data so that there are roughly the same number of cases in each category; for example, put the first 33 cases in "young," the next 33 in "middle," and the final 34 cases in "old." However we choose to group the data, we must have some theoretical justification for our choice.

Log on to our website to watch a tutorial on working with IBM SPSS.

One question that should always be asked is, "How have other researchers measured this variable?" Are your indicators consistent with the literature in the area? If so, there usually is no need to provide a detailed justification. But if your indicators differ from the literature, be sure to highlight this fact and discuss its implications with regard to the comparability of the findings. In short, engage in the scholarly dialogue.

APPLY YOUR UNDERSTANDING

Levels of Measurement

What is the most appropriate level of measurement for each of the following variables? Explain why.

- party identification (values = Liberal, Conservative, NDP, BQ, and Green)
- ideological position (values = left, centre, right)
- unemployment rates (values = 0 per cent to 100 per cent)
- development (values = pre-industrial, industrial, post-industrial)
- regime type (values = democratic, fascist, communist, authoritarian)
- population (values = 10,000, 20,000 . . . 10 billion)

APPLY YOUR UNDERSTANDING

Grouping Interval-Level Data

Suppose you are interested in the relationship between age and active involvement in political parties. To pursue this interest, you have accessed the following data set. How might you group respondents into age categories? What categories and what break points might you use, and how would you justify your choices?

Age	Number of Cases	Age	Number of Cases
18	8	31	2
19	16	32	0
20	4	33	2
21	8	34	3
22	12	35	1
23	7	36	0
24	11	37	2
25	7	38	1
26	10	39	3
27	6	40	4
28	4	41	1
29	1	42	0
30	5	43	3

Accuracy in Measurement

We noted earlier that conclusions about a hypothesis are only as good as the variables and the indicators of those variables used. Do the indicators measure the variables? Do the variables represent the concepts? Are the measures stable or are different results obtained with repeated use of the measures? To the degree that we have confidence in the measures, we can have confidence in the conclusions. When we are contemplating the accuracy of indicators and variables, we need to look at two issues: validity and reliability.

Something is valid if it does what it was intended to do. An indicator is valid if it measures the variable, and a variable is valid if it represents the concept. Essentially, measurement validity refers to the "degree of fit" between the indicator and the variable or between the variable and the concept. Take indicators of support for feminism in Canada. One might be the number of members in the National Action Committee on the Status of Women (NAC) as an indicator of support. However, this indicator would be inappropriate because NAC mostly comprises member organizations, such as women's shelters and the YWCA, rather than women who expressly join the NAC. It is possible that many NAC members are not even aware of their membership. Changing the indicator of support for feminism to the number of member organizations in NAC would produce a more suitable measure. But would the measure be complete? How would we deal with groups of different sizes? What about the individual men and women in the population who support feminism and/or feminist principles but who may not belong to organizations falling under NAC's umbrella? And what about all the members of women's groups not affiliated with NAC? A convincing argument could be made that a study of feminism in Canada would need to look further than NAC alone.

To ensure valid measurements, and valid conclusions, we need to select or create measures that are both "appropriate and complete" (Manheim and Rich 1981, 58). The first step in doing so is acquiring knowledge: the more we know about our subject matter, the more certain we can be that our measures are appropriate and complete. Such knowledge keeps us from making avoidable errors. To continue our example, basic knowledge of Canadian feminism would tell us that the anti-feminist lobby REAL (realistic, equal, active, for life) Women of Canada should not be on a list of feminist organizations. The second step to increasing the completeness and appropriateness of our measures is testing and evaluating the measures. There are a number of tests:

- Face validity: On the face of it, is the measure logical? Does it appear to measure the concept? Can you justify your selection of the measure? Would other people see the logic in the selection? For example, few of us would accept pet ownership as a measure of animal rights activism. Face validity tests help address the question of appropriateness.

- Convergent validity: This form of validity compares indicators designed to measure the same variable. Logically, if two indicators are measuring the same variable, they should yield similar results for most cases. Most individuals who score high on one measure of conservatism should score high on a second measure. Since we are using one indicator as a criterion against which the other is measured, it is often preferable that we use a "tried-and-true" measure as the criterion.
- Discriminant (divergent) validity: This test is the opposite of convergent validity. If two indicators predict opposing or extremely dissimilar views, they should yield different results for most cases. Imagine an indicator of feminist views—Do you agree or disagree that "women and men should have equal access to education and employment opportunities"?—and an indicator of anti-feminist views—Do you agree or disagree that "we would all be better off if women stayed home to raise children"? In this case, we would expect a negative correlation between the indicators: most people who agree with one can be expected to disagree with the other. If, on the other hand, we were to find a positive association (those who agree with the former agree with the latter), we would have reason to question the validity of our measure.
- Predictive validity: Does use of the measure help us to predict outcomes? To test predictive ability, we need to pilot test the measure in an appropriate population. If we have a measure designed to tap attitudes about gun control, we could pilot test this measure among self-identified National Rifle Association (NRA; a strong anti-gun-control lobby in the United States) supporters. We would predict that strong opponents of gun control by our measure would be more likely than others to belong to the NRA. If they are not, our measure may be flawed.

Indicators and variables are not themselves valid but are valid (or invalid) with respect to the purpose at hand. Perfect validity is an impossible ideal—we cannot find a variable that perfectly represents its concept or an indicator that perfectly measures its variable. This lack of perfection is inevitable given the losses in meaning that occur during the move from concept to quantification. The very nature of operationalization requires that concepts and variables be simplified and, in the process, made less valid. Hence, when we discuss measurement validity, we are thinking of a continuum between "less valid" and "more valid."

One solution to the perpetual existence of measurement validity problems is to use multiple variables and indicators. The goal here is to have the strengths of one compensate for the weaknesses of the other. The use of multiple variables and indicators ensures that the least amount of conceptual meaning and nuance is lost.

The second factor in assessing the accuracy of our measures is reliability. A measure is reliable if it is consistent regardless of circumstances such as time or subpopulation. If consecutive weighings on a doctor's scale result in identical or near-identical weights, the scale is reliable. If you step on the scale and it registers 70 kilograms on Monday, 95 kilograms on Tuesday, and 45 kilograms on Wednesday, the scale is clearly unreliable. Note that

Expand Your Knowledge

Controversies in Measurement Validity: Seymour Martin Lipset's *Continental Divide*

In *Continental Divide: The Values and Institutions of the United States and Canada*, Seymour Martin Lipset (1990, 1) argued that the differences between Canada and the United States can be attributed to our different histories: "[t]he United States is the country of the revolution, Canada of the counterrevolution." Among other things, the historical background of "counterrevolution" has led Canadians to demonstrate greater deference to authority and elites. Canadians, he argues, are a more lawful and peaceful people. Lipset cites differences in rates of violence, crime, and drug abuse, as well as in attitudes toward both police authority and gun control as indicators of the Canadian "deference to authority."

But do behavioural indicators such as crime rates provide a valid measure of a predisposition such as deference? Lipset's critics argue that his indicators are often inappropriate and that he fails to take into account important national differences in institutional arrangements. What is at issue, then, is whether Canadians behave differently than Americans (e.g. have a lower crime rate) because of their attitudinal predispositions (greater deference to authority) or because of the institutional environment in which they behave. This question boils down to a debate over the validity of different indicators.

reliability does not ensure validity; a scale that is consistently 5 kilograms light is reliable because it provides the same response with repeated measures (that is, 70 kilograms each time). Nonetheless, it is not valid because it fails to measure what it purports to measure (your weight).

Another way of thinking about the difference between validity and reliability in measures is to look at the distribution of errors. **Random errors** exist when a measure is inaccurate but the inaccuracy is not systematic. **Non-random errors** are systematic errors. Consider a 100-point feeling thermometer scale of assessments of the prime minister. If asked to rate the prime minister on this scale, a respondent might place him at 65, which represents a feeling of "warmth" toward the prime minister. But if asked the same question the next day, the same respondent, feeling just as warmly toward the prime minister, might place him at 70. A month later, that same respondent might rate him at 62 and the next month at 65 again. The respondent, with the same feelings toward the same individual, exhibits slight changes in ratings simply through random error: sometimes the score is a little higher, sometimes a little lower.

Now imagine you lived in a country that had an authoritarian regime and you felt that your safety was threatened if you were seen to be critical of the government. If you were surveyed for your feelings toward the political leader, you might choose to inflate your rating (to 100 points on this scale!) for fear that you would be punished if you revealed your true feelings (perhaps you really rate this person at 0). Moreover, each time you were asked this question, you would respond in the same way. This kind of error is non-random, or systematic, error; the error is always in the same direction. A measure is reliable if it is free from random error (that is, there may be non-random error in a reliable measure). A valid measure is free from both random and non-random error.

For an indicator to be reliable across subpopulations, it must receive similar results across all subgroups. If a measure performs differently for men and women, there is a reliability problem. It is possible that men and women are interpreting the question differently or that different social or cultural factors are interfering with the measure. We often hear that women respond to problems by empathizing, whereas men respond to them by suggesting solutions (one indicator of the popularity of this theory is the success of self-help books on this topic). If such generalizations are true, it is possible that men and women would respond differently to a stated problem. With survey questions concerning body weight and height, many young women are socialized to feel that they should understate their weight, whereas many young men feel that they should overstate their height. If such a phenomenon occurred, the measures would suffer from reliability problems.

To increase reliability, researchers often use multiple indicators. Further, it is important that indicators are unidimensional. Take the question, "Are you satisfied with the food and service at this restaurant?" A positive response may mean that the respondent is happy with both service and food or only one of the two. With such "double-barrelled" questions, it is difficult to assess what exactly is being measured. Increasing precision is another way that researchers attempt to increase the reliability of their measures.

Unfortunately, there are occasional trade-offs between validity and reliability: as we decrease abstraction, we increase reliability but decrease validity (White 1994, 158). Of course, our aim is to find measures that maximize both validity and reliability. The balance is a measure that is sufficiently exact to be reliable yet sufficiently abstract that it captures the meaning of the concept and is thereby valid.

Given the importance of measurement accuracy, researchers typically pretest their measures or replicate measures from previous studies. For example, pilot tests can be used to pretest a survey instrument within a convenience sample. (Sampling is discussed in Chapter 8.) The purpose of a pilot test is not to tabulate statistics and draw conclusions about population parameters but to test the validity and reliability of the measures. (Pilot tests can help troubleshoot within the research design as well.) Often, if measures are found to be particularly useful and accurate, they are replicated in future studies by other researchers. The reasons for this practice are threefold: (1) the measures have proven themselves in terms of validity and reliability; (2) replicating measures allows researchers to test the conclusions of others with different samples; and (3) replicating measures allows researchers to detect changes and patterns over time.

APPLY YOUR UNDERSTANDING

Assessing the Accuracy of Our Measures

Suggest three possible survey questions that could act as indicators of the variable environmental activism, indicators that would enable you to distinguish between environmentally active and environmentally inactive respondents. How would you assess the validity of each indicator? What steps would you take, and what conclusions would you make? How would you assess the reliability of the indicators? Would you describe the measures as more valid or more reliable? Formulate three final indicators of environmental activism that you feel are accurate measures.

Thinking through Indicators: Designing Survey Questions

One of the most common research designs in political science is survey research; we use telephone polls, mailed questionnaires, and online or (less frequently) in-person surveys to gather the information necessary to test hypotheses. Survey research methodologies will be discussed at length in Chapter 10 but are useful to discuss here as an example of operationalization. In survey research, indicators are the survey questions themselves. To design accurate indicators, we need to select or design valid and reliable survey questions. Survey research is conducted not only by governments and polling firms but also by private businesses, non-profit organizations, educational and health providers, community associations, and campaign management teams. It is quite likely that many political science students will have the opportunity to participate in the design of a survey at some point in their lives.

When designing a survey, we need to be mindful that all the information necessary for that study must be captured within the survey instrument. We will need questions addressing attitudes, behaviours, and opinions and questions soliciting demographic information such as age, income, and education. All variables of interest—be they dependent, independent, or control variables—must be included in one instrument. Ideally, we will begin by making a list of all the relevant variables that encompass the various concepts to be included in our study and then make a list of all the indicators needed to measure these variables. This process helps us ensure that all information is gathered and prevents us from gathering unnecessary or useless information. We might want to ask questions on every issue from A to Z, but this temptation should be avoided. Time restraints—yours and the participant's—preclude such an approach, as do ethical matters. We want to keep our survey instruments directed at the question at hand; they should not be seen as "fishing expeditions." If we cannot separate the necessary variables and indicators from those that are superfluous, we need to work on our theory.

The researcher needs to choose a question format. **Closed questions** force the respondent to choose among the presented alternatives: Which of the following do you prefer: (1) Coca-Cola; (2) Pepsi Cola; (3) another cola brand; or (4) non-cola beverages? **Open questions** allow the respondent to provide his or her own response, without prompting from categories: Which cola brand do you prefer? There are advantages and disadvantages to each format. Closed questions have a number of design advantages: respondents can answer the questions quickly; it is easy to compare the responses of different individuals; and data entry is less complex. But these questions often ask the respondent to give a simple response to an extremely complex issue and, by providing categories for the respondent, may encourage the statement of opinion or knowledge where none exists.

In contrast, open questions allow a greater range of answers. The respondent is not limited to or biased by preset response categories and may provide answers that lead the researcher into new theoretical waters. However, open questions present a number of data problems: there are many possible answers to any given question, making data entry difficult; respondents will spend more time on open questions, making the questions less efficient; and comparisons between individuals can be complicated.

Selection of question format tends to vary with the type of survey instrument. Telephone surveys typically rely on closed questions, while mail and online questionnaires are more likely to employ a mixture of open and closed questions. Many surveys begin with open-ended questions designed to capture the respondents' "top of the head" impressions before respondents are contaminated by subsequent questions. If the survey is designed to measure public attitudes toward climate change, it would not make sense to ask respondents "What is the most important issue facing Canadians today?" after they had already been exposed to extensive questions about climate change. Front-end, open-ended questions are also used to warm up respondents for the more detailed questions that follow. These questions try, in short, to establish a conversational format.

When designing questions, there are a number of steps that researchers should take to increase indicator accuracy. First, use neutral language. Questions must be designed in a way that does not bias or "lead" respondents. Questions such as "All reasonable people agree that policy A is bad. Do you support policy A?" or "Policy Q will put millions of people out of work. Many children will go hungry as a result of policy Q. Do you support policy Q?" are biased questions. When we use scales, we need to ensure that the response categories are balanced between positive and negative. A scale with categories "excellent–very good–good–satisfactory–poor" is unbalanced; there are three positive categories, one neutral, and one negative.

Second, be clear. To ensure reliable questions, we must first ensure that all respondents interpret the question in the same way. This necessitates that we are specific regarding the exact information sought. Consider the question, "What is your income?" It is not clear if this query means annual income, monthly income, or weekly income. Is the researcher interested in family income, household income, individual income, or net or gross (pre-tax) income? Along with being specific, clarity requires that we keep our questions simple. Avoid double negatives, keep sentences relatively short, and use common language. Do not use jargon or assume detailed knowledge; not everyone knows the definition of GDP or the content of policy Q. Finally, clarity demands that each question be limited to only one topic. So-called double-barrelled questions, such as "How do you feel about the government's policies on military defence and international trade?" will lead to reliability problems.

Third, avoid **response sets**. Some respondents tend to be yea-sayers, agreeing with virtually any statement placed before them, while others tend to be nay-sayers, disagreeing with virtually every statement. It is important in such cases that personality predispositions do not push respondents toward a particular policy position on the questionnaire. If you have five agree–disagree statements designed to test respondents' support for environmentalism, and for each statement "agree" is indicative of a pro-environment position, yea-sayers will tend to show up as environmentalists and nay-sayers as opponents of environmentalism. It is useful, then, to have batteries of questions that require respondents to move back and forth between agreement and disagreement in order to register a consistent position and that place respondents who agree (or disagree) with everything in the middle of the scale.

Fourth, keep response categories **exhaustive**: we need to ensure that all relevant responses (including "no opinion" or "don't know/refuse") are provided for by our response categories. In addition, response categories should be **mutually exclusive**, with no overlap between categories. Think about the problems with the following response categories for the question, "What is your annual personal net (after-tax) income: (1) $10,000–$25,000; (2) $25,000–$40,000; or (3) $40,000–$65,000?" Clearly, not all possible responses are included. There is no room for those whose incomes are below $10,000, for those whose incomes are above $65,000, or for those individuals who refuse to answer the question. Thus, the categories are not exhaustive. A second problem is that there is overlap between the categories. Should an individual whose income is $40,000 be placed in category 2 or category 3? The categories are not mutually exclusive; it is possible for an individual to be placed in two categories. A better set of categories for the same question would be (1) under $10,000; (2) $10,000–$24,999; (3) $25,000–$39,999; (4) $40,000–$65,000; (5) over $65,000; and (6) don't know/refuse.

Fifth, select the highest reliable level of measurement. When possible, we should select interval-level measures above ordinal-level measures. As we have seen, it is possible to move from interval- to ordinal-level data through the grouping of collected data. The reverse is not true: we cannot go from age categories to exact ages. Using higher-level measurements allows us greater flexibility when it comes time to analyze our data. That said, there are some questions, such as income, where we may be inclined to use grouped categories rather than exact numbers. This is because there are some topics that respondents prefer to be more ambiguous about and/or preclude precise answers.

Sixth, pay close attention to **question order**. Remember that respondent reactions to a particular question will be shaped by preceding questions, which provide context. What comes first will contaminate what comes after. Imagine a survey measuring both intended vote in the next provincial election and public reaction to health-care spending cuts. If the health-care questions come first, respondents may be in a different mindset when the voting intention question is asked than they would be if the order was reversed. You should also leave intrusive questions to the end of the questionnaire. Some respondents may become defensive when asked about their income or marital status and may even terminate the interview. If this happens near the end of the interview schedule, most of the information is already in place and the loss is minimized.

Seventh, try to minimize defensive reactions by making the respondent as comfortable as possible. Remember that respondents are under significant social pressure in an interview situation; they want to appear to be knowledgeable and thoughtful. This stress can create a situation in which respondents would rather fabricate a response than not have an opinion or appear not to know the answer. In some cases, therefore, respondents need assurance that a socially incorrect response is all right. For example, questions that ask respondents whether they voted in the last election are sometimes prefaced with a set of acceptable excuses for not voting. It is acknowledged that some people may have been ill, had car or child-care problems, or were called out of town on short notice; the message is that not voting is a perfectly understandable event and that respondents should not be embarrassed by admitting that they did not vote. If these steps are not taken, the result is likely to be an inflated estimate of turnout rates, which would make a comparison of voters and non-voters difficult since some of the latter would be lumped in with the former in the statistical analysis.

Of course, following all of these steps will not guarantee a problem-free research instrument. For one thing, a host of research design and measurement issues will undoubtedly remain. How should missing data be handled? In measuring political and social attitudes, should we use odd-numbered scales that provide a middle response category for respondents or should we use even-numbered scales, which force respondents to lean toward one pole or another? Scales measuring respondents' self-location on the left–right spectrum could provide either six or seven response categories. In the latter case, a response of 4 provides an option for respondents who do not want to identify themselves with either the left or right. If a six-point scale is used, such respondents are forced to choose either 3 (slightly left) or 4 (slightly right).

Finally, we must remember that a fair amount of error is inevitable in survey research. After all, we are dealing with human subjects, who will occasionally fake answers or lie and who will respond to aspects of the interview situation—the sex or age of the interviewer, the artistic quality of the questionnaire, the time of day or night, distractions in the room—as much as they will to the specific questions being posed. The potential sources of error are perhaps best illustrated by questions concerning family income. Some respondents will refuse to disclose their income, while others will inflate it to impress the interviewer. Some people will not know their income; they may know their hourly wage but not their after-tax annual income or the precise income of their spouse. As a consequence, there is a good deal of noise associated with survey measures of income, noise that then may make it difficult to measure income's impact on political attitudes or behaviours.

In any case, researchers should always ensure that their questions are as polite and courteous as possible. Respondents have voluntarily given their time to the research project and should be treated with respect.

Summary: Characteristics of Question Design

1. Use neutral language.
2. Be clear.
3. Avoid response sets.
4. Keep response categories mutually exclusive and exhaustive.
5. Select the highest reliable level of measurement.
6. Pay close attention to question order.
7. Minimize defensive reactions.

Creating Indexes

We have discussed that social scientists will often use a number of variables to capture one concept and a number of indicators to capture one variable. After the data have been collected, indicators can be combined into an **index**, a single measure of the concept or variable in question.

Index construction generally follows a number of conceptual steps. First, we want indicators that are strongly associated or correlated with one another; this is illustrated by the bold line between indicators 1 and 2 in Figure 5.4. (At the same time, we do not want a degree of association so strong that the indicators are obviously measuring exactly the same portion of the variable.) Second, we want to cover as much of the conceptual terrain as possible; hence, the more indicators, the merrier. However, as indexes B and C in Figure 5.4 show, the more indicators we include in the index, the weaker the association is likely to be between those indicators. As our index gets more comprehensive in its conceptual coverage, it becomes less internally coherent. The trick, then, is to balance the competing needs of broad conceptual coverage and internal coherence. Indexes that combine three to six indicators are common in political science research, whereas larger indexes are much less common.

An example of indexes is seen Neil Nevitte and Roger Gibbins's (1990) work. In their analysis of a mailed survey of senior university undergraduates in Australia, Britain, Canada, New Zealand, and the United States, they constructed a number of ideological indexes. One index measured respondent orientations toward feminism and incorporated answers to the following questions:

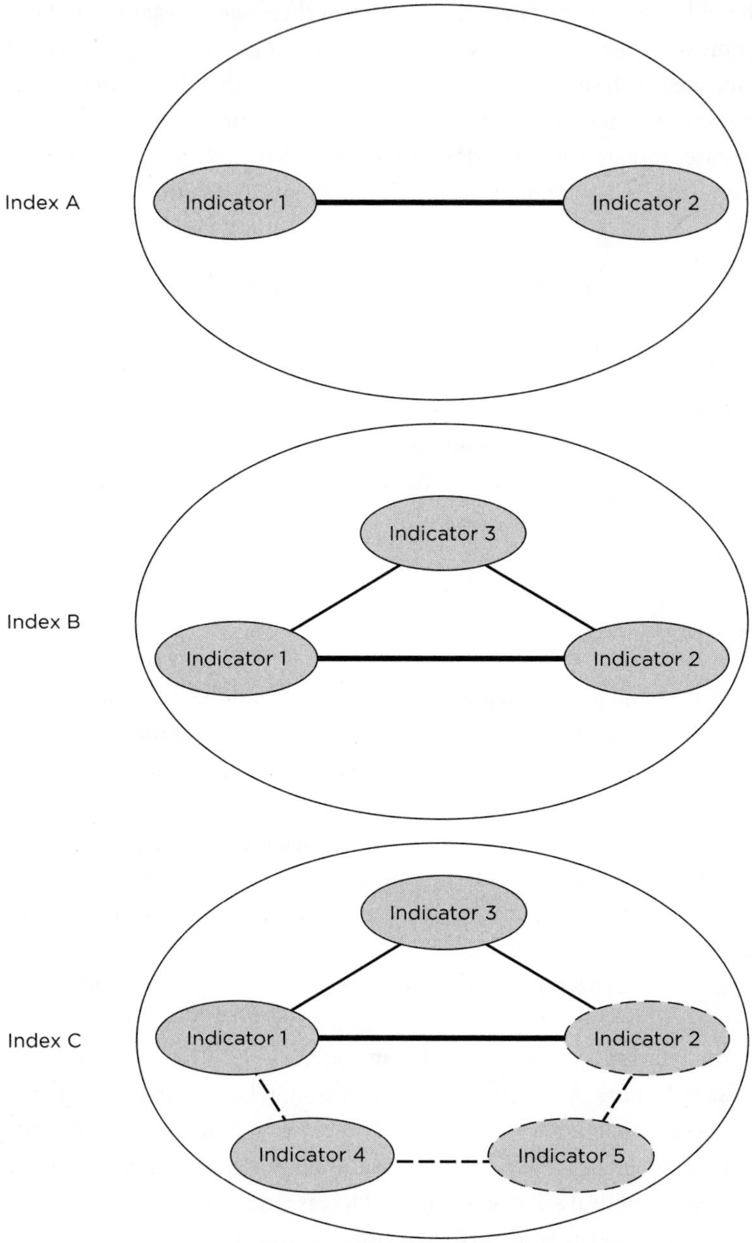

Figure 5.4 A Schematic Illustration of Index Construction

- Respondents were asked to locate themselves on a seven-point scale between two statements: "Women would be better off if they stayed at home and raised families" and "Women would be better off if they had careers and jobs just as men do."

- Respondents were asked to locate themselves on a seven-point scale between another pair of statements: "If women tried harder they could get jobs equal to their ability" and "Discrimination makes it almost impossible for women to get jobs equal to their ability."
- Respondents were asked if they agreed or disagreed with the following four statements:
  - It is the right of a woman to decide whether to have an abortion.
  - If a company has to lay off part of its labour force, the first workers to be laid off should be women whose husbands have jobs.
  - Lesbians and homosexuals should not be allowed to teach in schools.
  - There should be more laws that aim at eliminating differences in the treatment of men and women. (Nevitte and Gibbins 1990, 177, 67)

By combining the responses to these six questions, the researchers were able to create a much more powerful measure of orientations to feminism than would have been provided by any one of the questions alone.

One of the concerns to bear in mind when creating indexes is to do so with questions (or the underlying variables that the questions seek to measure) that are related to one another. A statistical test of reliability designed for this purpose is Cronbach's alpha. This test examines the elements used in the construction of an index (as the example of feminism suggests) and asks whether a person who scores high on one element is likely to score high on the other elements. If so, their score increases. Cronbach's alpha ranges from zero to one[4]; the closer the score is to one, the stronger that element is related to the other elements that comprise the index. Sometimes researchers will remove measures from an index if the Cronbach's alpha score is less than 0.7, although this is not an ironclad rule.

In conceptual terms, the creation of indexes is a reasonably straightforward operation. In practice, it brings into play many of the statistical techniques and measures of association addressed in later chapters.

Working as a Team

1. Examine the code book for a recent CES or a similar survey research instrument. Are there questions that appear to be reasonable candidates for an index of liberalism? Feminism? Conservatism? Environmentalism? What conceptual steps would be involved in the creation of such an index?
2. How would you go about designing a questionnaire to measure teaching effectiveness in a course such as this one? What questions would you ask? Would they be open-ended or closed questions? What would be the advantages and disadvantages of each type? Which strategy would work best: using generic questions that would

enable you to compare this course and its instructor to other courses and instructors or course-specific questions that would enable you to probe the idiosyncratic aspects of this course and its instructor? Give reasons to support your answers.

Self-Study

1. You have been provided with the research opportunity to explore, through survey research, the relationship between environmentalism and the more general ideological predispositions captured by conventional left–right scales. Your theory is that support for environmentalism is correlated with ideological position; more specifically, you suspect that as support for the "left" increases, support for environmentalism increases. In preparation for this research, work through the following steps of operationalization:
   a. State your hypothesis. Provide a conceptual definition for each main concept.
   b. Identify two variables that could be used to quantify each concept. Identify the level of measurement for each variable.
   c. Identify two indicators for each variable. Provide the complete wording for the survey questions, including all response categories.
   d. Select one of the four variables and discuss how you would assess the accuracy of both indicators for that variable.

Notes

1. Surveys that measure voting rates often suffer from "vote inflation," a higher proportion of the sample reports having voted than was the case in the population at large. While the turnout rate in Canadian general elections hovers around 60 per cent, the self-reported turnout rate in CES is often 10 per cent higher. This distortion may be caused by voters being more likely than non-voters to respond to the survey and/or by non-voters in the sample being unwilling to admit that they did not vote.
2. The relationship between independent variables is referred to as multicollinearity. Two independent variables that are related will tend to overlap in their predictive power. For example, we would expect that both knowledge of the subject matter and writing skill will predict academic excellence.
3. The distinction between variables and indicators is often ignored; literature references to variables are often references to what we have termed indicators.
4. Although it is possible for Cronbach's alpha to be less than zero, it is not intuitively meaningful for variables in an index to have less than zero or no relationship to one another.

CHAPTER 6

Research Ethics
People behind the Numbers

Destination

By the end of this chapter, you should be able to

- detail the ethical considerations behind the choice of research topics and methodologies;
- articulate the concerns relating to confidentiality, anonymity, and informed consent; and
- explain how ethical considerations are handled in the social sciences.

As you are drawn into the complexities of statistical and qualitative analysis in the chapters to come, it will be easy to forget that the numbers and quotations encountered in empirical analysis represent real people. For example, in a table showing that 34.1 per cent of 950 respondents in a survey of the Ontario electorate intend to vote for the Progressive Conservative candidate in the next provincial election, we might neglect the fact that this number represents 324 discrete individuals who were disrupted from their everyday routine to answer a survey, who made assumptions about the survey's legitimacy, and who were assured that their anonymity and confidentiality would be respected.

In this chapter, we examine some of the ethical issues and dilemmas that confront political scientists as they collect, analyze, and publish research data. Such ethical considerations emerge from a number of directions. To some degree, they govern the topics we decide to study and, consequently, our choice of research subjects. Ethical considerations may determine the research methodologies we employ. Indeed, the most vigorous ethical standards tend to come into play with respect to data collection: the samples we select, the information provided to subjects or respondents, the precautions taken to ensure confidentiality, and the avoidance of risk. Ethical considerations are also part of our relationships with colleagues, both in specific research projects and within the broader scholarly community. Finally, ethical considerations may determine what we do with research results. Of particular concern is the manner in which research findings can shape the political debate over public policy in democratic states.

The intent of this chapter is to bring the human face of empirical research into sharper focus. As you will see, any assumption that quantitative research is immune from ethical considerations because it deals with numbers rather than people should be quickly discarded.

Risk Assessment and the Medical Model

Many of the ethical guidelines currently employed in the social sciences find their roots in medical research. When research is conducted on the introduction of new medications or on the use of alternative treatments or therapies, there can be a significant potential risk to human subjects. For instance, whether an experimental drug has unwanted side effects is not an "academic question" to the subjects who might experience these effects. If a new treatment is being tested to see if it increases heart surgery survival rates, patients are not indifferent about whether they receive the new or old treatment. In the early days of medical research, though, subjects were often recruited without their consent, much less informed consent. Patients who were institutionalized were particularly at risk. In light of this history, medical researchers have developed elaborate protocols to ensure that research subjects are fully informed about the nature of the research and the potential risks and that their participation is voluntary. These procedures have come to provide the model for similar protocols within the social sciences.

Underlying these protocols is the first principle of medical practice: Do no harm. Social scientists should also adhere to this principle. Any potential research gain with respect to description or theory must be carefully weighed against potential risks to research subjects, to the communities from which they are drawn, and, at times, to the researcher. The *Tri-Council Policy Statement: Ethical Conduct for Research Involving Humans* (hereafter cited as *TCPS 2*) notes that research risks are not limited to participants but may extend to researchers as well, especially when the project engages student researchers. It is suggested that institutional research ethics boards (REBs) may raise such issues, specifically when conducting a research ethics review (CIHR, NSERC, and SSHRC 2010, 25).

But, you might say, surely the potential risks—and thus the ethical considerations—in social science research are much less serious than they are in medical research. It is hard to argue that a respondent to a national Ipsos Reid survey is exposed to the same level of risk as a research subject in a new chemotherapy treatment program. Asking someone his or her opinion on issues of the day seems almost risk-free compared to administering new drugs or food additives. Although most forms of social science research, particularly most forms of survey research, are relatively benign in their potential impact on participants, it would be a mistake to assume that ethical considerations or risk potential are absent. The nature of the risk may be quite different from that of the medical model, but risk is still present. Social science research involves human subjects, and such research cannot escape a concern for the welfare of those subjects. The *TCPS 2* (2010, 8) identifies respect for human dignity as the cornerstone of ethical research involving humans and requires that "research involving humans be conducted in a manner that is sensitive to the inherent worth of all human beings and the respect and consideration that they are due."

Risk is not always obvious. Take the risk associated with self-knowledge. Imagine that you have become an unwitting participant in an experiment designed to see if people will assist strangers in real-life situations and to what extent intervention might be determined by the characteristics of the subject, the "victim," and the event. The researchers have set up a situation in which individuals walking down the street are confronted by strangers apparently experiencing different degrees of distress. The strangers appear to be lost or ill or are being attacked. Let's say that you decide not to intervene and keep walking. At the end of the block, a member of the research team stops you, informs you about the experiment, and, in the debriefing, assures you that no one was actually in trouble. You are relieved to hear that the stranger is unharmed, but you have to confront what might be some disturbing new knowledge: you have been shown to be the kind of person who ignores strangers in distress. This self-knowledge may be enlightening, but it may be the kind that you would just as soon do without. In effect, you have been damaged; you have a diminished sense of your own personal worth, the effects of which may be long-lasting. The question, then, is whether the researchers had the right to inflict this harm. Was the research ethical?

The message here is self-evident but important. Any proposed research must be assessed in terms of both the possible advance of descriptive knowledge and/or theoretical insight and the risk to subjects, communities, and (at times) to the research team. This assessment is first and foremost an ethical exercise.

Selecting the Research Topic

Ethical considerations begin with the selection of the research topic. Our decision about what to investigate always precedes the methodological issues of how the research might best continue. In this context, we must acknowledge the emphasis that universities and colleges place on freedom of intellectual inquiry. If academic freedom means anything, it is surely the licence to pursue research topics that the individual researcher feels are interesting and important. This freedom of inquiry extends beyond academics; it should be a guiding principle for student research. However, it does not exempt researchers from ethical constraints on the conduct of their research or preclude a concern with the research's social relevance. Furthermore, while researchers may be at liberty to pursue any topic that strikes their fancy, funding agencies are under no compulsion to support the research. In fact, funds are most likely to be allocated to projects with some social relevance; research driven solely by intellectual curiosity or theoretical concerns faces an uphill, although by no means impossible, battle for funding.

The definition of what is and is not socially relevant takes us quickly into the ethical domain. There are no empirical criteria by which we can determine social relevance; the issue is a normative one. Admittedly, media coverage and the political agenda may send strong cues regarding the relative importance of various issues, which we might use to identify some research topics as having greater social relevance, and hence funding appeal, than others. That said, social relevancy implies something more than salience: it suggests that certain topics should be pursued and perhaps that others should not.

Much of the discussion in this respect has entailed a variety of problems, both ethical and methodological, that arise when researching sensitive topics. Socially sensitive research includes studies "in which there are potential consequences or implications, either directly for the participants in the research or for the class of individuals represented by the research" (Sieber and Stanley 1988, 49). This general definition could embrace virtually all public policy research. A tighter definition, focused on the presence of risk, is provided by Raymond Lee and Claire Renzetti (1990, 513):

> A sensitive topic is one which potentially poses for those involved a substantial threat, the emergence of which renders problematic for the researcher and/or the researched the collection, holding, and/or dissemination of research data. [Research is more likely to be threatening] (a) where research intrudes into the private sphere or delves into some deeply personal experience; (b) where the study is concerned with deviance and social control; (c) where it impinges on the vested interests of powerful persons or the exercise of coercion or domination; or (d) where it deals with things sacred to those being studied which they do not wish profaned.

There is no suggestion that research should not be conducted in such areas. The point is that ethical considerations are likely to be highlighted when research is conducted in the circumstances identified by Lee and Renzetti.

Lee and Renzetti (1990) acknowledge potential risk to researchers as an ethical consideration. In rare instances, this hazard may involve the physical safety of the research team. In less extreme circumstances, it may entail legal action, including the potential of research material being subpoenaed. (Research material is not protected by the conventions of client confidentiality that apply to medical files and legal counsel.) A more general risk is that of "stigma contagion" for those researching unpopular topics. As Lee and Renzetti (1990, 521) illustrate, "those involved in the study of sexual deviance have frequently remarked on their stigmatization by colleagues, university administrators, and students."

APPLY YOUR UNDERSTANDING

Animal Testing

A great deal of medical research entails testing on animal subjects, generally as a prelude to testing on humans. Not surprisingly, animal testing has been the source of much ethical and political debate centring not only on technicalities—Are the test animals being treated as humanely as possible? Is everything possible being done to minimize their pain and discomfort?—but also on whether such testing should be done at all.

Fortunately, perhaps, very little political science research involves animal testing. Indeed, no cases come to mind. Yet the debate on this subject can be a useful way to "prime the pump" for ethical considerations that are relevant to the field. Consider the following dilemma. A firm has developed a new food additive that may ameliorate lactose intolerance for millions of people around the world. To ensure that the additive is safe for human consumption, the firm intends to feed large amounts of it to lab rats for four weeks and then to dissect the rats to determine if any abnormalities have shown up in larger than expected numbers. The research program, therefore, will necessitate the death and dissection of literally thousands of rats. Does this consequence strike you as a reasonable price to pay, given the potential of the new additive? Would your opinion change if the research animals were cats, beagles, or chimpanzees? Why or why not?

Within political science, such stigmatization could be a concern for researchers studying the extremes of the political left and right, particularly if their research was seen as empathetic rather than critical. It might be a problem for those investigating public policy in areas of high social sensitivity, such as political interrogation, abortion, or child abuse. Consequently, there is a good chance that researchers will avoid topics that carry this risk. Such avoidance means that important topics may be ignored and we may be denied knowledge about them.

It is worth noting that matters of social relevance are of greater importance to some forms of political science research than they are to others. Researchers interested in the complex dynamics of voting behaviour have not been overly preoccupied with the social relevance of their work; the primary concern is to advance theoretical understanding of voting behaviour and electoral choice in democratic societies. Feminist researchers, on the other hand, place a great deal of emphasis on applied or action research. Michele Ollivier and Manon Tremblay (2000) argue that feminist research must be action-oriented, that the research and the feminist thought on which it is based must be directed to social and political change. Feminist researchers also emphasize the importance of involving research subjects in the research enterprise, thereby blurring the distinction between the researcher and the researched. As Shulamit Reinharz (1992, 181) explains: "In feminist participatory research, the distinction between the researcher(s) and those on whom the research is done

APPLY YOUR UNDERSTANDING

Putting Research Subjects at Risk: The Milgram Studies of Obedience

At times, the risk to research subjects can come through increased self-awareness; we may find out that we are not as nice or compassionate as we thought we were. A good example of this risk comes from Stanley Milgram's (1963) famous **experimental research** on obedience.

Milgram recruited male subjects, aged 20 to 50, from the community to participate in what was described as a study of memory and learning at Yale University. Subjects were told that the study's objective was to determine the impact of punishment on learning and were then "randomly assigned" to be either the "teacher" or "learner" in the experiment. In fact, the subjects were always the teacher, and an actor hired for the purpose was always the learner. The learner was strapped into an electric chair apparatus in one room, after which the teacher was led to an adjoining room where there was an electric shock generator with switches ranging from 15 to 450 volts. The switches also had qualitative labels ranging from "slight shock" to "extreme intense shock," "Danger: severe shock," and "XXX." The teacher's task was to administer electric shocks to the learner whenever the latter made a mistake in a word test. Moreover, the teacher was told to increase the voltage each time. The learner, who could be heard but not seen and who was not actually being shocked, began to indicate discomfort at the 75 volt level. At 120 volts, he shouted that the shocks were painful; at 150, he asked to be released; at 180, he screamed that he couldn't stand the pain; at 270, he screamed in agony, and after 330 volts, he made no sound at all.

The experiment was actually designed to determine at what level of shock the teacher would refuse further participation. If the teacher hesitated, he was prodded to continue, with statements delivered in the following sequence:

1. Please continue.
2. The experiment requires that you continue.
3. It is absolutely essential that you continue.
4. You have no other choice, you must go on.

As the study went on, "subjects were observed to sweat, bite their lips, groan, and dig their fingernails into their flesh" (Milgram 1963, 375); some had uncontrollable seizures. If a subject continued to resist, the experiment was stopped.

Milgram's work became famous because many subjects, when prodded, administered extremely high levels of shock. In one of the experiments, 26 of 40 participants administered shocks up to the maximum of 450 volts. The "shock" to readers was that American males were obedient to the point of administering severe and dangerous electrical shocks to compatriots in a university-based research experiment.

What do you think about the ethics of this experiment? Was the knowledge gained sufficient to compensate for the risk to subjects? Were the subjects really at risk? How would you feel if you had been one of the teachers? If a similar piece of research was proposed today, do you think it would receive ethical clearance at your institution? Why or why not? What conditions could be imposed to reduce ethical concerns?

disappears. To achieve an egalitarian relation, the researcher abandons control and adopts an approach of openness, reciprocity, mutual disclosure, and shared risk."

As suggested earlier, part of the hard reality of contemporary social science research is that the availability of research funding may drive the choice of research topics. It is always worth asking whether there is an ethical dimension to the proclivities of funding agencies, whether the unavailability of funding squeezes out research that, on ethical grounds, may have some claim to priority. That said, funding agencies have been instrumental in elevating ethical standards in many cases. The primary funding agency for social science research in Canada, the Social Sciences and Humanities Research Council (SSHRC), has been particularly aggressive in requiring that both universities and individual researchers give careful attention to ethical concerns. The agency also insists that researchers address the social relevance of proposed research and advocates greater attention to **knowledge mobilization** and to the application of social sciences research to social problems. While grant applications are not assessed exclusively on the basis of social relevance, and funding basic research is part of SSHRC's mandate, social relevance remains an important factor in the funding formulas.

Expand Your Knowledge

Tri-Council Policy Statement

In 1998, Canada's three federal granting councils—the Natural Sciences and Engineering Research Council (NSERC), the Social Sciences and Humanities Research Council (SSHRC), and the Canadian Institutes for Health Research (CIHR)—jointly sponsored a statement on the ethical conduct of research, known as the *Tri-Council Policy Statement* (*TCPS*) and overseen by the Interagency Advisory Panel of Research Ethics. The *TCPS* established a framework of ethical guidelines for research on human subjects by researchers in Canada. Beginning in 2008, the policy went through a period of revision and public consultation, the result of which is a substantially revised edition (*TCPS 2*). This document guides REBs established at universities and colleges across the country in their institutional review of research protocols. *TCPS 2* is based on the application of three core principles, as described in the following excerpt:

> Respect for human dignity has been an underlying value of the *Tri-Council Policy Statement: Ethical Conduct for Research Involving Humans* (*TCPS* or the Policy) since its inception. Despite clear recognition of its centrality in research ethics, the term lends itself to a variety of definitions and interpretations that make it challenging to apply.
>
> Respect for human dignity requires that research involving humans be conducted in a manner that is sensitive to the inherent worth of all human beings and the respect and consideration that they are due. In this Policy,

continued

respect for human dignity is expressed through three core principles—Respect for Persons, Concern for Welfare, and Justice. These core principles transcend disciplinary boundaries and, therefore, are relevant to the full range of research covered by this Policy.

Article 1.1 The guidelines in this Policy are based on the following three core principles:

- Respect for Persons
- Concern for Welfare
- Justice

These principles are complementary and interdependent. How they apply and the weight accorded to each will depend on the nature and context of the research being undertaken. . . .

Respect for Persons

. . . An important mechanism for respecting participants' autonomy in research is the requirement to seek their free, informed and ongoing consent. This requirement reflects the commitment that participation in research, including participation through the use of one's data or biological materials, should be a matter of choice and that, to be meaningful, the choice must be informed. An informed choice is one that is based on as complete an understanding as is reasonably possible of the purpose of the research, what it entails, and its foreseeable risks and potential benefits, both to the participant and to others. . . .

Concern for Welfare

. . . Concern for Welfare means that researchers and REBs should aim to protect the welfare of participants, and, in some circumstances, to promote that welfare . . . To do so, researchers and REBs must ensure that participants are not exposed to unnecessary risks.

Researchers and REBs must attempt to minimize the risks associated with answering any given research question. They should attempt to achieve the most favourable balance of risks and potential benefits in a research proposal. Then, in keeping with the principle of Respect for Persons, participants or authorized third parties, make the final judgment about the acceptability of this balance to them.

Justice

Justice refers to the obligation to treat people fairly and equitably. Fairness entails treating all people with equal respect and concern. Equity requires distributing the benefits and burdens of research participation in such a way that no segment of the population is unduly burdened by the harms of research or denied the benefits of the knowledge generated from it. (CIHR et al. 2010, 8–10)

Protecting Research Subjects and Respondents

The ethical guidelines governing social science research raise three interconnected lines of defence around research subjects and respondents: confidentiality, informed consent, and the right to withdraw. We will examine each in turn.

Generally speaking, the assurance of respondent **confidentiality** is a routine aspect of social science research. In survey research, confidentiality is assured primarily through **anonymity**; respondents' names, addresses, and phone numbers are virtually never part of the data record. Although researchers are interested in the characteristics of their respondents—age, sex, regional location, income, etc.—they have no interest in specific identification. It may be very important to know that the research subject is a single white female working at a part-time job and living in Toronto, but it is not important to know her name, phone number, or address. These details would come into play only in the initial selection of the sample or if a survey supervisor wanted to telephone respondents to ensure that the interview had actually been conducted and had not been fabricated by a member of the research staff or employee of the data collection firm. Names are stripped from the survey as soon as authenticity is confirmed. Only in panel studies will names be kept as part of the record, and even here the information is coded so that specific identifiers can be isolated from the primary data set that will eventually enter the public realm. "Juan Gonsalves" becomes "case 1383" before any data are released.

In elite interviewing (see Chapter 9), the identity of respondents is a more contentious issue. An interview with a deputy minister in the federal government takes on additional weight because of the minister's profile. If anonymity is respected, the interview material becomes less useful. The upshot is that protection of anonymity for public officials is not required if the individual agrees to an on-the-record interview and if that agreement is conveyed through signed consent that explicitly waives anonymity. In the event that such consent is not provided, the researcher has little alternative but to fall back on descriptions such as "a senior public servant said" or "an unnamed but senior Liberal Party strategist revealed." Even then, the researcher must be careful that the description provided does not inadvertently reveal the individual's true identity. A published report that describes an interviewee as a "greying deputy minister with a decided limp and sinister goatee" would not protect the person's anonymity.

In many cases, research topics will not place subjects at risk and therefore may not involve questions of anonymity and confidentiality. Picture a conventional public opinion survey in which a thousand randomly selected respondents are asked to identify the most serious issue facing Canada today. If by chance it was revealed that one of the respondents was Ms Irina Buchovski of 115 Bonavista Crescent in Regina and that she had identified unemployment as the most serious problem, the disclosure might embarrass Ms Buchovski but probably would not place her at great risk. Even embarrassment would be unlikely unless the survey addressed some aspects of personal behaviour or opinion on sensitive

Expand Your Knowledge

Privacy and Confidentiality

Research subjects can preserve their anonymity by specifying how their personal information can be used. A key element of anonymity is the right to privacy of personal information. The *TCPS 2* (2010, 55–6) distinguishes between the concepts of privacy and confidentiality in the following way:

> Privacy refers to an individual's right to be free from intrusion or interference by others. It is a fundamental right in a free and democratic society. Individuals have privacy interests in relation to their bodies, personal information, expressed thoughts and opinions, personal communications with others, and spaces they occupy. Research affects these various domains of privacy in different ways, depending on its objectives and methods. An important aspect of privacy is the right to control information about oneself. The concept of consent is related to the right to privacy. Privacy is respected if an individual has an opportunity to exercise control over personal information by consenting to, or withholding consent for, the collection, use and/or disclosure of information. . . .
>
> The ethical duty of confidentiality refers to the obligation of an individual or organization to safeguard entrusted information. The ethical duty of confidentiality includes obligations to protect information from unauthorized access, use, disclosure, modification, loss or theft. Fulfilling the ethical duty of confidentiality is essential to the trust relationship between researcher and participant, and to the integrity of the research project.

topics. Indeed, it is difficult to imagine to whom such information might be disclosed; there is no ready media or commercial market for the identity of respondents to national surveys. If the survey focus was more localized and there was a chance that the researchers know the respondents, breaches of anonymity and confidentiality become more serious, particularly if the research concerns sensitive topics. In research in which participants in an AIDS treatment program or a program designed to eliminate spousal abuse were being questioned about their satisfaction with the program, the inadvertent release of a participant's name could have a serious impact on that individual's employment, community status, and personal relations.

The protection of confidentiality is often woven into broader procedures designed to ensure **informed consent**. Simply put, this means that potential participants (or, in the case of minors, their legal representatives) should be fully informed in writing of the nature of the research project, the identity of the researchers, the potential use of the research findings, and any risks to which participants might be exposed. Potential respondents or subjects should also be advised that they are under no obligation to participate in the research project. According to the *TCPS 2* (2010, 27), "the term 'consent' means 'free, informed and ongoing consent.'" Willingness to participate is conveyed by signing the informed consent form, which signifies that the participant is proceeding with a full understanding of the research project and any risks that might be involved. The signed consent form is kept on record as evidence that the research subjects were, in fact, participating under conditions of informed consent and without coercion.

At times, signed informed consent forms can be problematic. They are impossible to use in telephone interviews, particularly when respondents are being assured that their anonymity is being fully protected. Researchers must fall back on a similar oral statement and upon oral, undocumented consent. It is assumed that the respondent's decision to continue with the interview rather than hanging up is implicit evidence of consent but not necessarily fully informed consent. Many of the same considerations come into play with mailed questionnaires, which are generally returned in a way that does not identify the respondent. Anonymity is thereby protected, but a signed consent form is precluded. Here again, the respondent's willingness to return the completed questionnaire rather than throw it away is taken as evidence of consent. The issue that remains is whether the consent was informed.

Although informed consent means explaining the nature of the research to potential participants, there are limits to that explanation. If participants are informed about the specific research hypotheses, their behaviour may be affected as a consequence. A research

Expand Your Knowledge

Variation from Standard Informed Consent Requirements

The requirement of informed consent is one of the *TCPS 2*'s key provisions. But even this provision is not an ironclad or universal requirement. In the policy's discussion of consent, a section describes "departures from general principles of consent." Article 3.7 provides that REBs may approve research without requiring standard consent procedures if the following conditions prevail:

(a) the research involves no more than minimal risk;
(b) the lack of participants' consent is unlikely to affect the welfare of the participant;
(c) it is impossible or impractical to carry out the research if prior consent is required;
(d) the participant will be debriefed at a later time; and
(e) the research does not involve a therapeutic intervention or other clinical or diagnostic intervention. (*TCPS 2* 2010, 37)

project interested in the relationship between partisanship and support for environmental protection may include questions on both topics in a telephone survey. If respondents know that this relationship is of particular interest to the researcher, they may modify their answers to the environmental questions in order to ensure that their own party is portrayed in the best possible light. The *TCPS 2* (2010, 37–8) states that partial disclosure or deception may sometimes be justified:

> Some types of research can be carried out only if the participants do not know the true purpose of the research in advance. For example, some social science research that critically probes the inner workings of publicly accountable institutions might never be conducted without the limited use of partial disclosure. In some research that uses partial disclosure or deception, participants may not know that they are part of a research project until it is over, or they may be asked to perform a task and told about only one of several elements the researchers are observing. Research employing deception can involve a number of techniques, such as giving participants false information about themselves, events, social conditions and/or the purpose of the research.

The use of deception in research is a particularly sensitive topic, as illustrated with the Milgram experiment previously discussed. The *TCPS 2* provides a framework for assessing the ethical character of research at publicly funded institutions such as universities and colleges. The framework calls for the establishment of REBs, and such boards exist at virtually all public universities and most public colleges in Canada. The *TCPS 2* identifies instances in which research poses minimal risk to participants, which is defined as a level of risk consistent with that experienced in everyday life. Ethics reviews are expedited in instances where the risk is minimal. Furthermore, the *TCPS 2* (2010, 37–9) indicates that, where the project has been identified as minimal risk, an *REB* may approve a project involving deception, as long as the five conditions listed in the previous Expand Your Knowledge box—although applied to deception rather than consent—are met.

Informed consent on surveys is often framed in an extremely bland or abstract fashion: "We are interested in determining public opinion toward a number of current public policy issues, and to that end we would like to ask you a few questions." More specific details about the research hypotheses, information that would distort the data collection exercise, are not included. The use of insipid informed consent statements is partially justified by the rationale that general survey instruments present minimal risk to respondents. Furthermore, it is assumed that identifying the specific research hypotheses would not help potential participants assess the risks of their involvement.

Ethical problems also arise in providing informed consent for participant observation. In this technique, which is discussed in more detail in Chapter 9, the researcher observes members of a group or institution without their knowing his or her role or that their behaviour will be part of published research findings. In some cases, participant observation is the only possible approach for target populations. As Lee (1993, 143) explains, the method avoids problems of reactivity: "Because they do not know they are being studied, research participants are not threatened by the research and do not change their behaviour even though to outside eyes it may be considered deviant."

Still, the ethical problems associated with covert observation are so great that it is seldom used by academic researchers. It is difficult to construct a defensible argument for lying to or misleading people in the interests of social science research. Participant observation negates the principle of informed consent; subjects are not only uninformed about the research, but they also cannot give their consent. At the same time, it should be recognized that, in many cases, participant observation becomes apparent only after the fact. A researcher may work within a political party or community group as a citizen and only later realize that the participation can be blended into subsequent research programs, theoretical explorations, or teaching anecdotes. In such situations, the opportunity for informed consent has passed; the researcher is simply drawing upon life experiences.

The third line of defence for research subjects is the right to withdraw from the research exercise at any time. (This option, of course, cannot be extended to subjects in participant observation, which is just one more ethical problem that the research strategy encounters.) The right to withdraw may not be easy to exercise. Note the following excerpt from a letter sent to The American Sociologist in 1978—the writer is a senior university administrator who had been interviewed by a graduate student:

> In spite of the fact that I was very annoyed at being taped without my permission as well as by the questions and felt increasingly defensive and put down, I did not attempt to terminate the interview. Afterwards I realized how difficult it was to cut off an interview while it is in process. It caused me to reflect on the coerciveness of the interview situation. If as an agency administrator I did not feel free to terminate an interview with a graduate student, it must be almost impossible for the typical subject being interviewed by a "social scientist" to do so when the perceived status differences are reversed. (Cited in Broadhead 1984, 121)

It can be difficult to hang up on someone or to ask an interviewer to leave your house or office. It could be equally difficult for students in a classroom to withdraw from a study being conducted by their instructor. Thus, although informed consent statements should always include the right to withdraw at any time, this right may not be as effective a means of protection as we often assume. When the option is extended, everything must be done to make it possible for participants to exercise it, should they choose to do so.

APPLY YOUR UNDERSTANDING

Discussion of Signed Student Teaching Evaluations

Most universities provide a mechanism for assessing their instructors. If student evaluations are to help improve teaching, it is imperative that they be returned at some point and in some form to faculty members. What is less clear is whether such assessments should be anonymous or signed. They are considered program evaluation or assessment rather than research and hence do not fall under the rubric of the *TCPS* or REBs. However, they do raise important issues of anonymity.

The argument for anonymity hinges on the assumption that students are under some degree of risk, that they might face retaliation by faculty members who were negatively assessed. Such retribution could be manifest through grading in subsequent courses, negative letters of reference, or rumour mongering. To protect themselves, students might inflate their assessments. Anonymity reduces these risks.

The argument can also be made that anonymity strips students of any responsibility for their actions. Students could use the assessments to strike out at instructors with impunity and for reasons unrelated to teaching performance. There would be no check on negative assessments driven by personal malice, sexism, or racism. Consequently, anonymous assessments might be more negative on balance than would be signed assessments.

What do you think? Should the primary concern be to protect the student by using an anonymous instrument? Or should equal concern be placed on protecting instructors by forcing students to take responsibility for their assessments? Is there a middle ground?

Community Consent versus Individual Consent

To this point, our discussion has centred on the researcher obtaining the individual research subject's informed consent. Chapter 9 of the *TCPS 2* discusses the implications of applying the three core principles of research ethics to research on Aboriginal peoples. Upon considering the application of the core principles, the policy concludes that researchers are obligated to "engage" the relevant community regarding the research and to seek the community's consent in conducting it. In a research program involving Aboriginal peoples, *TCPS 2* guidelines indicate that researchers should obtain both the informed consent of each research subject and of the Aboriginal community that is the subject of the study.

Ethical Considerations in Research Design

As we have already discussed, political scientists should pay close attention to matters of confidentiality, anonymity, and informed consent when designing their research projects. The research must be constrained by the requirements of theory or **policy analysis**. Even

Expand Your Knowledge

Forms of Engagement of Aboriginal Communities

The *TCPS 2* (2010, 111–12) recognizes that there are many different contexts in which Aboriginal peoples can participate in a research project:

> The nature and extent of community engagement in a project shall be determined jointly by the researcher and the relevant community and shall be appropriate to community characteristics and the nature of the research.
> . . .
> Community engagement as defined in this Policy can take varied forms. In geographic and organizational communities that have local governments or formal leadership, engagement prior to the recruitment of participants would normally take the form of review and approval of a research proposal by a designated body. In less structured situations (e.g., a community of interest), a key consideration for researchers, prospective participants and REBs is determining the nature and extent of community engagement required. In some situations, if the REB is satisfied that participants are not identified with a community or that the welfare of relevant communities is not affected, the REB may waive the requirement of a community engagement plan (see Article 9.10). In these cases, consent of individuals is sufficient to participate.
> Communities lacking the infrastructure to support pre-research community engagement should not be deprived of opportunities to participate in guiding research affecting their welfare. (See Article 9.14.)

informed consent does not give us a blank slate with respect to the violation of privacy; we should only ask what we need to ask.

In matters of questionnaire design, this practice means restricting oneself to questions that can be justified by the study's theoretical underpinnings. Do not ask respondents a barrage of questions just in the hope that something interesting might later emerge from the data analysis. Such fishing expeditions strain the boundaries of ethical behaviour. If survey respondents are to be asked about their family income or church attendance, there should be a reason for doing so, one that extends beyond "most surveys always ask such questions." In particular, questions that pry into the private lives of respondents or that may embarrass respondents must be asked only if there is a compelling research reason to do so. Even then, every effort should be made to avoid embarrassment and to avoid a situation in which the social pressure of the interview makes respondents reveal information or preferences that they would rather not share. It is not enough to simply assume that respondents are under no compulsion to answer and that, if they do so, no harm has been done. There are very real social pressures at work in interviews. Remember that interviews that intrude on sensitive matters without a valid justification may generate questionable data. The fact that respondents answer does not mean that they answer truthfully. Therefore, close attention to ethical parameters may yield better research instruments.

Research designs should respect participants' privacy and time. As the *TCPS 2* (2010, 12) states, "In designing and conducting research or reviewing the ethics of research, researchers and REBs must be mindful of the perspective of the participant. It may be necessary to consider the various contexts (e.g., social, economic, cultural) that shape the participant's life." Research that is not designed with adequate attention to ethical considerations may yield poor data, particularly if participants are trapped in an uncomfortable situation. Failure to pay due regard to ethical concerns may also "poison the well" for future researchers, which is why sales promotions beginning with the claim that "we are conducting a survey to determine . . ." are so anathema to social scientists. Research participants who are once bitten will be twice shy.

Ethical Considerations in Data Analysis

In most cases, ethical issues arise before the data analysis begins or after the data analysis has been completed and the researcher is considering how best, or even if, to disseminate the research findings. That said, data analysis, be it qualitative or quantitative, is not totally immune from ethical considerations. We will see in Chapter 15 that our tolerance for different kinds of errors is not without ethical implications if the research addresses public policy issues. As the *TCPS 2* argues, the conduct of research involves both freedoms (particularly academic freedom) and responsibilities. Among the latter are "honest and thoughtful inquiry, rigorous analysis, commitment to the dissemination of research results and adherence to the use of professional standards" (*TCPS 2* 2010, 7).

A relatively minor but still interesting issue arises with respect to interview transcripts. When extracts from recorded interviews are used in published research findings (assuming that the respondent has granted written permission for such use), the researcher must decide how faithful he or she will be to the transcript. The problem is that people's spoken language is quite different from written text. In speech, people often use incomplete sentences, strangely constructed sentences, and odd grammatical configurations, all of which may be perfectly understandable within the context of speech, where the listener has access to visual cues, tone, and emphasis. If the spoken words are converted directly to written text, the respondent can appear to be illiterate, bumbling, and incoherent. There is, then, an almost irresistible compulsion to clean up the transcript, to transform the irregularities of the spoken word into more polished written text. But to do so is to alter the data and to change the form and (perhaps) the nuanced meaning of the spoken word.

There is an established convention of asking respondents to review quotations before publication. This practice ensures that the quotation corresponds with the interviewee's meaning. But it also opens up the possibility that the interviewee will change his or her mind and that the quotation eventually used will not correspond with the statement made in the interview.

Janet Finch (1984) draws our attention to another issue: the possibility that the data analysis may be used against the interests of the group from which respondents were drawn. The concern in her case arises initially from interviews with women and with the "exploitative potential in the easily established trust between women, which makes women especially vulnerable as subjects of research" (Finch 1984, 81). She goes on to discuss problems in protecting the collective interests of women, protection that cannot be provided by protecting the anonymity or confidentiality of particular women who might participate in a research project. Indeed, Finch (1984, 85) raises the possibility of betrayal:

> I do not really mean "betrayal" in the individual sense, such as selling the story of someone else's life to a Sunday newspaper. I mean, rather, "betrayal" in an indirect and collective sense, that is, undermining the interests of women in general by my use of the material given to me by my interviewees. It is betrayal none the less, because the basis upon which the information has been given is the trust placed in one woman by another.

Even if the researcher is able to avoid the betrayal that Finch identifies, there is no guarantee that the research material will not be used by others in a way that is contrary to the collective interests of women. The point, then, is that ethical considerations cannot be confined to the mechanics of data collection and analysis and cannot be addressed solely by protecting the interests of research participants.

Ethics and Collegiality

Many of the ethical considerations that are important to the social sciences have less to do with the relationship between researcher and research subject than with relationships within research communities. Ethical considerations extend to how we use the work of others, how we recognize the contributions of others, and how we report research findings.

Students first confront this ethical domain when they learn about the perils of plagiarism. It is unethical to take credit for the work, wording, or ideas of others as if they were your own—we must acknowledge our sources. If we do not, the scientific enterprise is thrown into risk, for there is no way to trace the evolution of ideas and evidence. Plagiarism is a serious offence within universities and within the broader social science community.

Ideas expressed in a research publication, a public presentation, or even a university lecture class are referred to as intellectual property. All universities have policies on intellectual property, and it is useful to review the policy at your institution. A key principle in these guidelines concerns the ownership of ideas. Individual researchers, including students, often retain ownership of the intellectual property that they develop in the course of their research and teaching. Where there is an interest in commercializing the intellectual property, the university's policy may identify that people or institutions other than the creator (such as the university itself) have an interest in the intellectual property.

It is important that intellectual property is recognized in the research community and that its creator is acknowledged. For undergraduate social science students, this recognition generally takes the form of citing the material's source. In this way, one can view research citations both from a legal perspective, by acknowledging the owner of the intellectual property, and as an ethical matter, by not taking personal credit for an idea or finding published by someone else. Citing other's ideas is sound and ethical scholarship.

The avoidance of plagiarism is best seen as a minimal condition of ethical behaviour. The respect shown for one's colleagues should go beyond acknowledging the use of their work and ideas. It should extend to fostering a co-operative research environment where

Expand Your Knowledge

Integrity in Research and Scholarship

The CIHR, NSERC, and SSHRC issued a tri-council policy statement on responsible conduct of research in 2011. The framework document replaced the tri-council policy statement on research integrity. The core of this statement identifies six basic principles:

- Using a high level of rigour in proposing and performing research; in recording, analyzing, and interpreting data; and in reporting and publishing data and findings.
- Keeping complete and accurate records of data, methodologies and findings, including graphs and images, in accordance with the applicable funding agreement, institutional policies and/or laws, regulations, and professional or disciplinary standards in a manner that will allow verification or replication of the work by others.
- Referencing and, where applicable, obtaining permission for the use of all published and unpublished work, including data, source material, methodologies, findings, graphs and images.
- Including as authors, with their consent, all those and only those who have materially or conceptually contributed to, and share responsibility for, the contents of the publication or document, in a manner consistent with their respective contributions, and authorship policies of relevant publications.
- Acknowledging, in addition to authors, all contributors and contributions to research, including writers, funders and sponsors.
- Appropriately managing any real, potential or perceived conflict of interest, in accordance with the institution's policy on conflict of interest in research. (CIHR, NSERC, and SSHRC 2011, 3)

ideas and data are shared openly and quickly, where methodologies are fully transparent, and where current research is effectively connected to the work that has gone before.

Ethical Considerations in the Publication of Research Findings

The publication of social science research and the injection of that research into public policy debate bring us face to face with ethical concerns. The argument that empirical research is normatively neutral provides, at best, a weak defence against ethical considerations, particularly considering that, once the research is in the public domain, it can be used for quite different purposes than originally intended.

The intensity of ethical debate may depend on how the research findings are disseminated. The most common form of dissemination for academic research is through peer-reviewed scholarly publications such as the *Canadian Journal of Political Science* or *Canadian Public Policy*. Dissemination can also take place through the popular press—the argument can be made that social scientists have an obligation to release their findings broadly and publicly. Dissemination through the press often strips away the subtle interpretation that is so important to scholarly inquiry. Complex issues are portrayed as black and white because the academic's fascination with endless shades of grey is not shared by journalists and those who write the headlines. There are, then, unavoidable risks that popular dissemination will distort the research findings and that the findings will be used for political and social ends with which the researcher does not approve. However, lack of dissemination means that the research is not subjected to critical review by other researchers in the field.

One of the more common ethical considerations that arises from the dissemination of survey research findings is their potential impact on social behaviour. Here, the most prominent example comes from pre-election surveys, which might credibly be thought to influence voter behaviour. As a case in point, the 2008 federal election saw considerable variation among polling firms in the predicted vote for the major parties. The result of the election on 14 October was that the Conservative Party received 38 per cent of the vote compared with 26 per cent for the Liberals. An Angus Reid Strategies (2008) poll conducted 9–12 October came very close to the actual result, with the Conservative vote estimated at 37 per cent and the Liberal vote at 27 per cent. But not all polling firms had the same degree of accuracy with their polls. Ipsos pegged Conservative support at 34 per cent and Liberal support at 29 per cent. Similarly, the Strategic Counsel estimated Conservative support at 33 per cent and Liberal support at 28 per cent. Both of these polling firms estimated a difference of 5 percentage points, substantially at odds with the 12-point difference that emerged on election day.

Recent provincial elections suggest that the gap between polling projections and actual election results is growing. During the last week of the 2012 Alberta election campaign, public opinion polls reported that the Wild Rose Party appeared to have an insurmountable lead over the governing Conservatives, leading to widespread predictions of victory for Wild Rose. Yet the Conservatives prevailed in the election, winning a majority government. Similarly, in the 2013 provincial election in British Columbia, the pollsters universally projected an NDP majority government. The party was favoured by up to 20 percentage points over the governing Liberals. As in Alberta, though, the governing party won a majority of seats.

Clearly, something has changed with the validity of public opinion polls. Some of the error may be due to the fact that, during the period between the end of polling and election day, voters might have still been deciding on which party to support, a factor identified by both Ipsos and Strategic Counsel for the 2008 federal election. But there are likely new and significant challenges associated with sampling, particularly with sampling younger electors, who appear to have ever growing residential mobility, often move into and out of the electorate between elections, and often communicate with cellphone and are therefore not included in databases of telephone numbers used by polling firms. All of which means that this degree of inaccuracy in some of the major polls, coupled with the reasonable assumption that poll results can influence the electorate's expectations and behaviour, raises concerns about the widespread use of polls during elections.

Concern over surveys' impact on electoral behaviour has led to some legislative constraints. In Canada, it is illegal to publish survey findings within 48 hours of the onset of a federal election. What remains unclear is the direction of survey effects. Our ethical concerns may depend on whether we believe that surveys lead to a **bandwagon effect**, whereby undecided voters opt to support whatever party is leading in the polls, or an **underdog effect**, whereby voters opt to rally behind the losing side (see Pickup and Johnston 2008). Somewhat ironically, survey research has failed to provide conclusive evidence of either effect, leading to the comforting belief that the effects might cancel each other out.

Surveys and all other types of published research must provide sufficient methodological information about such things as sampling procedures, the nature and size of the sample, the source of funding, and the wording of specific questions. If this information is not provided, being confident about any findings is difficult and replication is impossible. Ideally, the research data—data sets, questionnaires, code books, field notes—will be available to other researchers for secondary analysis. Data that are not released into the public domain within a reasonable period of time can become suspect, even though the failure to release data can often be traced to a variety of factors that have nothing to do with an attempt to conceal information. The researcher may have been slower with his or her analysis than anticipated, may lack the funds to prepare the data for release, or may simply have become overwhelmed by other work.

One of the more difficult problems encountered in the social sciences concerns the publication of negative findings. It is relatively rare to see studies of regionalism in Canada that conclude that the phenomenon has no effect on political values and behaviours or studies of gender politics that show that gender has no impact. Negative findings lack the

APPLY YOUR UNDERSTANDING

Disclosure of Research Findings

Imagine that you are taking an undergraduate course on sociobiology. Everyone in the class has been asked to undertake a specific research topic and to report back through a class presentation. Your project involves looking at instances of rape in the mammalian world. After reviewing a reasonable slice of the published research material, you conclude that rape in mammals is a "natural act." (Whether the research in the field supports such a conclusion is not at issue here.) What, if any, ethical issues should be considered before presenting this finding to the class? Can a case be made that you should not report the findings? Is there any likelihood that the research findings would affect the behaviour of students in the class? That it might heighten perceptions of risk? Give reasons to support your answer.

appeal of positive findings; they are not the stuff of news headlines. Yet, as Matt Shipman (2013) writes,

> you might think that Compound X will prevent Cancer Z from metastasizing. But if your experiments show that Compound X does not prevent Cancer Z from metastasizing you have a negative result . . . If other researchers are also really interested in Compound X they would probably also want to know that your experiments showed Compound X was ineffective . . . But they probably won't find out because most negative results never get published.

At times, the dissemination of research findings may be constrained by prior commitments relating to confidentiality. If access to particular informants has been secured only through the promise that identities and some forms of information not be revealed, the researcher may be unable to publish exciting findings.

Conclusion

Ethical guidelines for social science research are now more than normative, although the normative codes of ethical behaviour that have been adopted by most professional associations are certainly important. Ethical guidelines are generally embodied in specific institutional documents and policed by ethics review committees. It is therefore imperative that researchers of all types, including students building "fieldwork" into term papers and honours theses, know their institution's procedures. Although being ethical is a matter of principled behaviour above all else, it is also a matter of meeting clearly specified institutional requirements that generally entail some form of external review. Given the very serious consequences of failing to observe ethical guidelines and the accompanying procedures, researchers must familiarize themselves with the institutional environment. When in doubt, ask. If still in doubt, ask again.

That said, ethical guidelines are not meant to muzzle the engagement of political scientists in public policy debate. Policy researchers, like other citizens, have every right to express their opinions. At the same time, there is a need to separate the roles of policy advocate and social scientist, to distinguish between empirical research and the normative conclusions that one might draw from that research and wish to inject into the political arena.

Working as a Team

1. Virtually all universities and colleges have formal ethical guidelines in place for social science research. Find copies of the relevant guidelines for your own institution and discuss their coverage.
2. Do your university's guidelines seem relevant to political science research? Why or why not? What concerns, if any, are not addressed or are addressed inappropriately in the context of political science research?

Self-Study

1. Imagine that a political debate has erupted within your community over levels of immigration and immigrants' contributions to Canadian society. A group to which you belong supports increased levels of immigration and is determined to show that opposition is a minority view within the community. You are commissioned to do a survey of community opinion and find, to your surprise and distress, that the majority of respondents oppose increased levels of immigration. Unfortunately, the press has learned that the survey took place and is pressing you for the results. What are the ethical issues involved in releasing or not releasing the findings?
2. Researchers have demonstrated the possibility of cloning a wide array of livestock (sheep, cattle, pigs, etc.). Can such findings be extended to the cloning of human beings? If so, should researchers be allowed to proceed, at least to the point of testing the technology? Who should make this decision: scientists, employers, government, or another group? Give reasons to support your answers.

PART II

Research Design

When conducting research, political scientists must pay explicit attention to research design. Researchers need to be clear about their research questions and hypotheses and about their concepts and measures. They need to specify their population and sample, and they need to make important decisions about data collection and data analysis. Earlier decisions—research questions, concepts, population—influence choices about data collection that, in turn, influence how the data are analyzed. Conscious attention to research design helps researchers ensure that they will obtain the necessary empirical data to answer their research question and/or test their hypothesis.

We begin this section by considering two questions that are pertinent to all research designs, be they quantitative or qualitative: Will the study consider a small number of cases (such as a case study or a "small *n*" comparative research design)? How will the researcher(s) select the cases that will be included in the analysis? After considering these overarching issues, the section turns to a discussion of various data collection techniques. Chapter 9 examines interviews, focus groups, and observation research. Chapter 10 looks at surveys, secondary data, and official statistics. Chapter 11 focuses on experimental research designs. Finally, Chapter 12 explains textual analysis (in the forms of content analysis and discourse analysis). In each chapter, we note the strengths and limitations of the data collection method, as well as the ethical considerations facing the researcher.

CHAPTER 7

Small-*n* Research

Case Study and Comparative Approaches

Martin Gaal, University of Saskatchewan

Destination

By the end of this chapter, you should be able to

- explain the value of the case study's thorough examination of a research topic;
- identify the differences between a descriptive case study and a theory testing/modification case study;
- explain the benefits of the comparative approach; and
- distinguish between most-similar- and most-dissimilar-systems design.

Some research questions require us to consider issues in great depth. For example, political scientists who research Canadian foreign policy decisions are often interested in understanding and explaining why and how events happened, and their research must pay close attention to the specific details. This information might include the geographical context (the Arctic, Haiti, the Middle East), the domestic context (government ideology, public opinion, the economy), the policy stakeholders (the United Nations, powerful actors such as the United States, local individuals/communities), and even the personalities of the decision-makers (the flamboyance of Prime Minister Trudeau, the determinism of Prime Minister Diefenbaker).

To obtain thorough knowledge on a particular topic, researchers often use a case study or comparative approach. Michael Oren (1992) applies the former to expand our understanding of Canadian foreign policy. He scrutinizes in minute detail the context, process, and implications of then secretary of state Lester B. Pearson's diplomacy during the Suez Crisis. Oren's goal is to understand the situation Pearson faced, the subsequent decisions he made, and their consequences. Further, the author seeks to suggest some generalizations regarding both international and Canadian diplomacy.

Another example of using a comprehensive approach to expand our understanding of Canadian foreign policy is Ronald Behringer's (2005) comparison of four human security initiatives supported by middle power states. Each initiative is similar in nature and supported by a like-minded group of states, but the relative success of each varies. The purpose of Behringer's comparative research is to understand how middle power states such as Canada are able to exercise a leadership role in human security. There are significant differences in these two examples: Oren's (1992) work is more historical and nuanced, steeped in greater attention to detail; Behringer's (2005) work is more structured, using a research design that seeks to identify variables that explain the different outcomes. However, they share a commitment to the position that important insight and generalizable findings can be produced by looking at a small number of cases in rich detail.

As mentioned in Chapter 2, this detailed examination and/or comparison of a particular phenomenon is called small-*n* research (where *n* refers to the number of cases being studied, typically ranging from a single case study to a comparative study of a few cases). The particular phenomenon may be a project, policy, decision, process, event, or outcome. Finally, and key to small-*n* research, the process embraces complexity and situates the research in context. It is very difficult, but not impossible, to quantify such research. The multiplicity of variables combined with the inductive nature of most small-*n* research lends itself to qualitative research. This approach stands in contrast to large-*N* research, which employs a large number of cases and, usually, quantitative analysis. In other words, small-*n* research looks at the complex interaction of many variables in a small number of cases, and large-*N* research looks at a few variables in a large number of cases (Ragin 1994; Thomas 2011). Furthermore, small-*n* research allows for greater internal validity than large-*N* research does because the former can have more diverse variables and is therefore open to many potential explanations for the phenomenon (see Chapter 2).

This chapter focuses on small-*n* methods, especially on the case study and comparative research. Besides being important research methods on their own, these two types complement one another. For example, a well-researched case study can contribute to meaningful comparative research by providing the detailed analysis for comparison.

Case Study Research

A **case study** is a detailed analysis of a single discrete phenomenon. All case studies begin from the observation of a **counter-intuitive**, something that does not conform to our expectations. These observations force the researcher to ask questions such as the following: Why did that happen? Why did that happen in that way? How did that come to be? To answer such questions, we need to explore the phenomena without artificial limitations or preconceptions. We need to dive into the phenomena with all its messy complexity.

Oren's (1992) research topic is an instructive example of how a case study begins with a counter-intuitive. The degree to which Canadian diplomats generally, and Pearson more specifically, took a leadership role in the Suez Crisis was not only unprecedented but also posed serious political risks domestically. Prior to World War II, Canadian foreign policy had been dominated by isolationism. Following the war, Canadian diplomats made tentative moves toward internationalism by joining organizations such as the United Nations (UN) and the North Atlantic Treaty Organization (NATO), as well as by participating in the Korean War. However, Canadian diplomacy during the Suez Crisis was qualitatively different. Canadian diplomats were at the forefront of the negotiations, leading rather than following. More surprisingly, they took the two founding nations of Canada—the UK and France—to task. Why did Pearson get involved? Why did he take a leadership position? Why did Canadian Prime Minister St Laurent back Pearson's aggressive diplomacy?

To explain this counter-intuitive behaviour, Oren (1992) followed a qualitative approach, using declassified American, British, Canadian, and Israeli documents to trace Pearson's actions. Through these papers, Oren observed a confluence between two variables: the internalization of an internationalist foreign policy at the institutional level and Pearson's perception that Canada could and should perform a leading role in the crisis. This analysis would be difficult to undertake in a quantitative fashion.

Once the researcher identifies a counter-intuitive, he or she selects the type of case study to use. In political science, there are two broad categories: the descriptive case study and the theory testing case study (Gerring 2004; Levy 2008). The selection of a case study type depends on what information is available and what question is being asked. Sometimes a phenomenon is completely novel or unknown, prompting exploratory questions: What is this? What are the implications of this? These questions lead to descriptive case studies. In other cases, a phenomenon runs counter to theoretical expectations, prompting questions of the theory itself: Why did this case unexpectedly confirm or refute a particular theory? What was it missing? How can the theory better understand or explain social phenomenon? These questions lead to theory testing case studies.

The Descriptive Case Study

The **descriptive case study** is a case study in its purest form. The researcher knows little or nothing about the phenomenon; it is a puzzle, a counter-intuitive. There may be an absence of theorizing or even of any meaningful description. What is left is the case itself. Therefore, the goal of a descriptive case study is to describe the phenomenon as the basis of contributing to an emerging or future research agenda (Stake 1995; Yin 2012).

A descriptive case study sometimes emerges from new information. For example, Herbert Feis (1961) used declassified documents and personal interviews, including one with US President Eisenhower, to explain the decision to use atomic weapons on Japan during World War II and to try to understand the possible consequences of this decision. Other descriptive case studies are based on an emergent phenomenon or the evolution of an existing phenomenon that requires in-depth description. For instance, the end of the Cold War was so unexpected and unprecedented that it dominated debates in the field of international relations for over a decade. A useful case study on this topic is Jeremi Suri's (2002) "Explaining the End of the Cold War: A New Historical Consensus?" In both types of studies, the researcher attempts to get as close to the phenomenon as possible. He or she must have an open mind and follow the story of the phenomenon as it unfolds, looking for variables that could help explain the outcome and, more important, the connections between variables. In writing and presenting the research results, he or she must clearly state the **scope conditions**, the explicit limits to which the research professes to make valid claims.

Because descriptive case studies try to get as close to a phenomenon as possible, it is difficult to make generalized statements from them. In Feis's (1961) work, the scope conditions are limited to understanding the decision to use atomic weapons on Japan and to exploring some possible consequences of that decision. Similarly, the scope conditions of Suri's (2002) article are explaining the end of the Cold War. Thus, the scope conditions of descriptive case study research necessarily restrict insights to the phenomenon being studied, curtailing the ability to generalize to a larger population sample. At most, descriptive case studies can suggest future research or possible implications of the phenomenon under study. Yet the limitations on generalizability do not undermine the importance of such research, as the two examples illustrate. Understanding the decision to use the most powerful weapon in the world or explaining the end of the Cold War is critical, as these subjects are both defining events in international politics.

Heather Cash's (2006) article on Resolution 1593 is another example of a descriptive case study. In 2005, the United Nations Security Council passed the resolution, which referred the ongoing Darfur conflict in Sudan to the International Criminal Court (ICC). This event is a novel situation in that it represents both the first time that the Security Council referred a case to the ICC for investigation and the first referral of a non-signatory to the ICC. (Although Sudan had chosen not to become a state party to the ICC, it was nonetheless being investigated by the court.) In her study of the decision to pass the resolution, Cash traces the legal and political arguments made by key stakeholders leading up to the passing of Resolution 1593 and subsequently assesses the implications of this decision on international legal jurisprudence, the crisis in Sudan, and the ICC. In so doing, she contributes to the research agenda of the ICC and international law. Although her assessment of Resolution 1593 is not generalizable, it suggests implications for future Security Council resolutions vis-à-vis the ICC and provides a rich case for future comparative or quantitative work.

The Theory Testing Case Study

The **theory testing case study** is appropriate if one of two distinct counter-intuitive conditions is met: a phenomenon is expected to confirm a theory but refutes it or is expected to refute a theory but confirms it. The former is a **failed most-likely case** and the latter is a **successful least-likely case** (Eckstein 1975; George and Bennett 2005). Each approach identifies something unexpected and then seeks to discover why it occurs. The ultimate objective is to use the lessons derived from the case study to modify or build theory.

An important distinction between the failed most-likely and successful least-likely approaches is the role of falsification. As discussed in Chapter 1, falsification is an empirical refutation of a theoretical proposition. A failed most-likely case study may falsify a theory if it posits a narrow causality: if a theory argues that A causes B even though our instance of B is caused by something else, the study would falsify the assertion that A is a necessary and sufficient cause of B. This situation is not terribly common in practice, as most theories stipulate complex causal relations. For this reason, a failed most-likely case will usually question the degree of probability or determinism that a theory asserts.

A good example of a failed most-likely case study is Miriam Elman's (1997) examination of the determinism asserted in democratic peace theory (DPT). The strongest example of a general law in international relations, DPT argues that democratic states do not go to war with each other (Bennett and Elman 2007; Elman 1997). It has almost become a rite of passage for international relations scholars to disprove this thesis. Elman (1997) takes two states with solid democratic credentials, Britain and Finland, and notes that Britain declared war on Finland in 1941 after the latter had allied itself with Nazi Germany against the Soviet Union. Further, the countries fought against each other in the Continuation War during World War II. While this case study does not falsify DPT, it questions the degree to which the term *democracy* is a single unified concept. Elman's work suggests that DPT may be on firmer theoretical grounds when the concept of a democracy is disaggregated into a typology of democracies, with each type having its own probability of conflict with other democratic states.

In a successful least-likely case, falsification is rarely the goal because the phenomenon is already expected to fail. This type of study often seeks to relax the scope conditions of the theory, that is, to show that the theory explains more than its proponents claim. As Jack Levy (2008) argues, a successful least-likely case study passes the "Sinatra Inference": if the theory can make it here, it can make it anywhere.

Michael Barnett and Martha Finnemore's (2004) work on the United Nations High Commissioner for Refugees (UNHCR) as a norm entrepreneur is an example of a successful least-likely case study. Norm entrepreneurs are actors who challenge existing ideas, structures, and rules that define appropriate behaviour; examples include abolitionists or suffragettes. Theories of norm entrepreneurship focus on individuals and, to a lesser degree, social movements, which are often represented by non-governmental organizations (NGOs) such as Amnesty International, Oxfam, and Greenpeace. By demonstrating the entrepreneurial role that international organizations have played in international politics, Barnett and Finnemore (2004) argue that restricting the scope conditions to individuals or social movements is too narrow. For example, they show the UNHCR's role in defining the terms *refugee* and *refugee rights*, which included creating and defining new actors with identities and interests in international politics. As a successful least-likely case, the UNHCR example extends theories of norm entrepreneurship to corporate actors.

The ultimate aim of all theory testing case studies is theory modification. A failed most-likely case demonstrates a need to rethink a theory's claims. A successful least-likely case demonstrates the need to rethink a theory's scope conditions. Arguably, the best example of a theory testing case study (in this instance a failed most-likely case) leading to theory modification is Graham T. Allison and Philip Zelikow's (1999) examination of the Cuban Missile Crisis. This crisis was previously understood through the lens of the rational actor model (RAM), a decision-making theory that assumes unitary actors with a set of known and ordered preferences. In this model, the crisis should be explained through the interaction of two unitary actors, the United States and the USSR, who were each attempting to achieve its own instrumental goals and were therefore acting "rationally." Not only was RAM the dominant theory in explaining most foreign policy decision-making, but it was also the basis of much theorizing about nuclear weapons.

However, Allison and Zelikow (1999) discovered serious flaws in explaining the Cuban Missile Crisis through the RAM. Allison also developed two models that are better able to explain some aspects of the crisis, the organizational process model (OPM) and the governmental politics model (GPM). In so doing, the case study undermines the assumptions of the RAM, requiring its advocates to modify their probability claims and to work to incorporate Allison and Zelikow's conclusions. This theory testing case study has therefore led to theory modification in the RAM as well as theory building in the OPM and GPM.

Considerations for Case Study Research

In evaluating a case study, there are four factors to consider. First, are there clear definitions of the subject and object of the case study (Thomas 2011)? This component is an important distinction, as it moves case studies from questions of "what" to questions of "why" and "how." The subject of the case study is the wider phenomenon that contextualizes the study; the object is the "analytical frame" that focuses on what is being analyzed (Ibid., 513). In Allison and Zelikow's (1999) case study, the subject is the respective decision-making by the American and Soviet leaderships, and the object is the Cuban Missile Crisis. If there had been no distinction made between the subject and object, the case study would have only been able to answer the question, "What is the Cuban Missile Crisis?" With the distinction made, the case study answers more analytical questions: Why did the Soviets place missiles in Cuba? Why did the Americans impose a naval blockade? How did the crisis de-escalate? How does this case study question the RAM of decision-making?

Second, does the case study have rigorous and clear conceptualization? Case studies are often highly qualitative and therefore depend on concepts in order to generate meaningful insight (George and Bennett 2005; Gerring 2012). As you will recall from Chapters 4 and 5, concepts are abstract ideas that researchers must define and operationalize to measure indicators of the phenomenon being studied. Concepts are more useful and accurate when they allow greater awareness of the particular phenomenon being studied and when they better situate the phenomenon in the more general context. Case studies are well suited to provide conceptual refinement, whereas statistical research can be at risk of "conceptual stretching," that is, using more general conceptual definitions to increase sample size.

Elman's (1997) work on DPT shows how case studies can result in conceptual refinement. Elman rightly argues that DPT needs conceptual refinement in order to substantiate the claim that democratic states do not wage war on each other. Specifically, she argues that a typology of democracies may provide better analysis by, for example, distinguishing between differing political structures and degrees of executive autonomy. In so doing, DPT would be able to explain more cases and provide better prediction.

Third, does the case study properly employ process tracing? **Process tracing** is the primary means by which case study research generates causal reasoning. It starts with breaking the phenomenon being studied into a series of observations (e.g. decisions, speech acts, events, procedures, and anything else that explains how something came to be). These observations are then used to make an argument that explains the "how" and "why" questions (George and Bennett 2005; King, Keohane, and Verba 1994). Oren's (1992) case study is a helpful example of process tracing. The article disaggregates Pearson's diplomacy during the Suez Crisis into a series of observations: Pearson's early involvement in the Middle East, the historical events of the crisis, and the back and forth of the diplomacy at the UN and between the belligerents. Each of these observations leads the reader through a narrative of evolving Canadian diplomacy, from rhetorical internationalism to bridge-building to Pearson's actions. In so doing, Oren identifies a causal pathway, beginning with Ottawa's changing perceptions of Canada's global role, combining with Pearson's perception of these changes in the context of the Suez Crisis, and leading to the aggressive diplomacy displayed.

Fourth, does the case study make applicable generalizations to a wider population of cases? Essentially, this question asks whether the findings of this case are true in other similar cases. This aspect of case study research is the most difficult. There are two dangers: overgeneralization and undergeneralization. If a case study is overgeneralized, it promises too much and might thus lose credibility. This result can undermine both the generalization and the original argument. If a case study is undergeneralized, it is susceptible to failing the "So what?" test, whereby it examines a phenomenon so narrowly that it is of little interest. The best approach is to qualify the generalization: the case study is certain in its explanation of the phenomenon being studied; it is highly probable to increase understanding on a set of similar cases; and it suggests some interesting questions to ask in the widest population of cases.

Allison and Zelikow's (1999) Cuban Missile Crisis case study illustrates this process. The researchers are confident in their argument that the RAM is unable to satisfactorily explain the crisis and that the OPM and GPM offer important alternatives. They generalize their findings by extending the argument with a high degree of probability to other case studies of American foreign policy. Finally, they claim that their findings could lend important insight into all levels and types of governmental decision-making.

APPLY YOUR UNDERSTANDING

Choosing a Case Study Model

Consider the following research questions. Identify whether each question is best-suited to a descriptive case study, a most-likely theory testing case, or a least-likely theory testing case. How would you structure the studies?

1. To what degree does Canadian foreign policy under Prime Minister Harper fit with the middle power legacy of Prime Minister Pearson?
2. Why is Canada the only state to have withdrawn from the United Nations Convention to Combat Desertification?
3. How can Canada's strong opposition to Russia's intervention in Crimea (2014) be explained in the context of Harper's record of asserting Canada's national interest first and foremost?

Comparative Research

Comparative research is another form of small-*n* research. This type systematically contrasts a number of cases in order to create stronger generalizations and thus broaden our knowledge of the political world. Such generalizations, when supported, allow greater explanatory power and prediction—the ultimate goals of political science.

There are two advantages to choosing comparative research. First, it highlights the degree to which our conclusions about life and politics are filtered through our own preconceptions and are therefore culture-bound. Many of our assumptions about politics and society are context-specific, based on our own experiences and observations. They exist in one person's culture and political system but may not apply to other cultures or political communities. As political scientists, it is critical that we distinguish between the common traits shared among societies and the qualities unique to a particular community. Second, comparative research enables the researcher to examine system-level traits. Examples of such characteristics include federalism, authoritarianism, democracies, revolutionary movements, and developing economies (Bahry 1991). A comparison at the system level drives important political questions. What do particular systems have in common? Do these similarities explain outcomes? Is there variation at the system level? Do these differences explain variance in outcomes? From this type of analysis, it is possible to increase our predictive abilities: if we know that qualities A and B usually lead to condition C, and country Z has both A and B, we have reason to expect C.

Theda Skocpol's (1979) *States and Social Revolutions* is an excellent example of such comparative work. Skocpol is skeptical of theories that explain revolutions in agrarian states through direct action. She builds a structural explanation, identifying two conditions that lead to social revolution in such states. The first condition, a crisis of state, is a challenge that the state cannot overcome due to institutional constraints. The second, a popular uprising, is a bottom-up challenge to the state's authority. In other words, the presence of A (crisis of state) and B (popular uprising) leads to C (social revolution). Skocpol argues that this theory was true in the cases of France, Russia, and China and that the absence of either A or B in the cases of England, Germany, and Japan resulted in top-down reform instead of revolution.

The principal issue when beginning comparative research is the selection of cases. What should be compared to what? Random sampling is ill-suited to comparative research for two reasons. Not all political units are suitable for all research questions (Bahry 1991, 215). In Skocpol's (1979) comparative research, case selection is limited to ambitious agrarian states, which discounts revolutions in, for example, post-colonial states. Of course, this problem could be avoided by creating a sampling frame (a list of all possible cases in the population; in this example, a list of only ambitious agrarian states) and then randomly sampling from that frame. For example, Gary Goertz (2006) has identified a possible population of 12 states, including the original 3 in Skocpol's study. However, the utility of this approach is questionable. As will be discussed in Chapter 8, sampling error increases in random sampling as the sample size decreases. In other words, when sample sizes are small, the benefits of random sampling are lost because it is less certain that the selected cases are truly "representative."

When comparing political units such as states, there is a limited number of potential cases. The population is even smaller when looking at more discrete phenomenon such as Skocpol's (1979) research or some other system-level characteristic. Therefore, the other reason that random sampling is not appropriate for comparative research is that the logic behind random sampling does not hold for such small populations. The alternative is purposive sampling, which best allows the researcher to use specific knowledge of the systems when choosing political units that lead to the most fruitful comparisons. Moreover, there exists an informed knowledge between two principal approaches to comparative research: the most-similar-systems design and the most-different-systems design. These approaches were first identified by John Stuart Mill in 1888 (labelled by him as the method of similarity and the method of difference).

Most-Similar-Systems Design

One approach is to compare very similar systems, seeking to explain differences between them. This **most-similar-systems design** permits researchers to hold constant all shared characteristics between cases in an attempt to explain disparity in the dependent or independent variables (Bahry 1991, 220). Let's look at a concrete example. Political scientists have noted that the United States is unique from Europe in that it lacks a genuine socialist ideological voice. The United States does have "left" and "right" parties (the Democratic and Republican parties, respectively). However, both share a belief in the tenets of liberalism, which includes the principles of individualism, the free market economy, and meritocracy.

There is no viable socialist party that recommends significant levels of state ownership and wealth transfer. Such ideas are in conflict with the "American Dream" and are essentially absent from the national political psyche. But why does the United States lack a true socialist alternative? Louis Hartz (1964) argues that the American settlement was missing a "Tory fragment." The settlers who arrived did not create the strict class system that existed in Europe. Hartz saw this feudal background as a necessary element for the development of socialism. He therefore concluded that the United States' settlement history can explain the failure of socialism on American soil.

However valid this idea may be for the United States, why does it not pertain to Canada? This country has a settlement history and a political culture that is, in many ways, similar to those of the United States. Yet despite the many similarities, successful socialist parties—the Co-operative Commonwealth Federation (CCF) and its successor, the New Democratic Party (NDP)—have emerged in Canada. Moreover, while some may question the socialist credentials of the NDP, its success is not in dispute, as many provinces have had NDP governments and the federal party has been the official opposition since the 2011 election.

In his study of this topic, Gad Horowitz (1966) accepts the thesis that the United States lacked a Tory fragment but argues that the situation in Canada was different. Horowitz identifies a small "feudal fragment" in both the French settlements and, more substantially, in the Loyalists expelled from the United States after the American War of Independence. He asserts that the Loyalists were a second Tory fragment loyal to British traditions and ideas of hierarchy. The Loyalists' influence was felt in Canada because of the country's relatively small population. Horowitz concludes that this Tory fragment allowed Canadian political culture to be more receptive to socialism. By comparing two extremely similar systems, Horowitz was able to focus on a single point of variation. All potential explanatory variables that the two systems held in common were ruled out, reducing the number of factors that he needed to explore.

Most-Different-Systems Design

While most-similar-systems design takes related systems and seeks to explain variation between them, **most-different-systems design** does the opposite: it takes vastly dissimilar systems and attempts to explain commonalities between them (Bahry 1991, 220). In other words, how could such diverse systems produce the same social outcome? As with the previous research approach, the most dissimilar design works by letting the researcher eliminate possible sources of explanation—any variable that does not exist in all systems under study is eliminated. An illustrative example of this design is the work by Ember, Ember, and Russett (1992), which seeks to contribute to the DPT research program by testing its core insight with a set of exceedingly dissimilar cases.

DPT restricts its case selection to a population of modern democratic states, but Ember et al. (1992) apply its logic to traditional societies. The modern state is most generally defined as having a fixed territory, sovereignty, legitimacy, and an established bureaucracy.

It emerged out of Europe through the Treaty of Westphalia, becoming the world's dominant form of political organization. Traditional societies are most often pre-industrial and are much more fluid, defined through family, language, religion, and customary practices. These case sets, then, are greatly dissimilar. The researchers ask whether traditional societies with "wider political participation" are less inclined to engage in warfare with each other than with those with "less participatory political units" (Ember et al. 1992, 579). In other words, their research tests whether DPT can be extended to political units other than the modern state. They conclude that the findings of DPT hold true for traditional societies. Applying the logic of the most-different-systems design, it is possible to eliminate any variable that does not exist in both systems. What is left as an explanatory variable is democratic participation, regardless of the form of political unit.

Selecting an Appropriate Comparative Research Design

Selecting the appropriate comparative research design depends in part on the theory that underlies the study (Bahry 1991, 220–1). If the theory is such that it is possible to predetermine the variables that may be influential, one can choose cases that match these variables, rendering the most-similar-systems design appropriate. Remember the example of a viable socialist party in the United States and Canada. These two systems match significantly on influential variables yet differ on the outcome of such a political party. Therefore, the most-similar-systems design was an appropriate choice for Horowitz (1966). However, if there is less knowledge of influential factors or if it is not possible to match cases properly, the most-different-systems design is appropriate. As our example showed, DPT had been exclusively applied to cases of modern democratic states. These cases varied significantly on important variables from traditional states but demonstrated similar outcomes. Therefore, the most-different-systems design was the better choice for Ember et al. (1992).

Of the two types of comparative research, most-similar-systems-design has more difficulty meeting the necessary requirements (i.e. matching all the variables that may influence the research's outcome). It is often much easier to find cases that differ on influential variables. Further, as Donna Bahry (1991, 221) argues, "a most-different-systems approach offers us somewhat better control over the factors that might influence or bias what we find, and more assurance that our results are valid."

Considerations for Comparative Research

When conducting comparative research, the researcher must be careful about the operationalization of variables. He or she must also be highly cognizant of the social and political context. As we stated earlier, a measure that is appropriate in one culture or society may not be in another. The goal is to have **equivalent measures** and not necessarily identical ones (Bahry 1991, 217–19). Imagine you are conducting a study of women's power in communist and democratic regimes. You decide to compare the number of women holding legislative seats in the national Soviet and American legislatures between 1980 and 1987. You note that the Soviet legislature had a high proportion of female representation, while the American percentage was low. From this observation, you conclude that women have greater political power under communism than under democracy. Would your conclusions be valid? In a word, no. By not recognizing the importance of context, you have inadvertently measured different things in different states. The Soviet legislature had little influence, and its female representatives held very little power, despite their numbers. The assumption that the identical measure of legislative presence has the same meaning in two immensely different cultures is false.

Remember that the aim is to measure a concept. In this example, you are trying to measure women's political power. A particular indicator is merely a means by which to measure such concepts, but researchers must ensure that the indicators they choose actually measure their intended concepts. They may have to use different indicators in different cases or work hard to ensure that the indicators chosen do, in fact, measure the same concept in all the cases under study. Both options require a solid understanding of the cases being considered. Therefore, the importance of context in comparative research cannot be overemphasized. It is worth noting that one source of such context is a well-researched case study. Such sources allow deeper knowledge of causal pathways in context, permitting a comparative researcher to seek equivalency measures.

A second caution for comparative research, known as Galton's problem, is that the researcher must ensure that the units under observation are independent of one another. This requirement can be a problem because societies and cultures do not stay fixed within territorial units. Consider the problem of diffusion with respect to Canada and the United States. Although the countries are technically distinct states and societies, many American influences are felt north of the Canadian–American border. Much of our television programming is American, as are many of our popular bands, magazines, and books. This diffusion

APPLY YOUR UNDERSTANDING

Choosing a Comparative Research Design

Consider the following research questions. Identify whether each question is best-suited to a most-similar-systems design or a most-different-systems design. How would you structure the research in each case?

1. How can we explain the variance between the more ideological Australian foreign policy under the Conservative government of John Howard and the more pragmatic Canadian foreign policy under the Conservative government of Stephen Harper?
2. How can we explain Canada's and Norway's parallel and particularly strong foreign policy regarding opposition to the apartheid regime in South Africa?

of cultural norms and experiences makes cultural comparisons between Canada and the United States incredibly difficult. Such comparisons must also come to grips with the influence of American culture in Canada. As barriers to communication steadily decrease, we can expect diffusion problems to become increasingly problematic for social researchers.

Conclusion

This chapter explored small-*n* research as an in-depth examination and/or comparison of a particular phenomenon. As types of small-*n* research, both the case study and comparative research claim that looking at a small number of cases in minute detail can produce important insights and generalizable findings. Moreover, there is a natural connection between these two methods. A well-researched case study examines phenomenon in context, develops conceptual clarity, and maps causal pathways. Comparative research can utilize such case studies to find equivalent measures to assess the studied concept in multiple cases.

Working as a Team

1. Using Canadian leadership on human security initiatives as an example, think about how you can differentiate between types of small-*n* research. One question on this topic could be why Canada has taken a leading role on such projects as the anti-personnel landmine ban. Other queries might look at a larger sample of like-minded states that have also led to human security initiatives. What other questions can you think of? How many could be answered using a case study method? Should you use a descriptive or theory testing model for these questions? How about questions for a comparative method? Should you use a most-similar-systems design or a most-different-systems design to find answers?

Self-Study

1. In general, what types of questions are better suited to a descriptive case study? A theory testing case? Similarly, what types of questions are better suited to comparative research? When is a most-similar-systems design appropriate? Most-different-systems design? Using the example of DPT, write a specific question for each type of small-*n* research.

CHAPTER 8

Sampling the Political World

Destination

By the end of this chapter, you should be able to

- describe the theory of sampling in the social sciences and explain the logic of drawing representative samples from larger populations;
- summarize and critique several practical techniques for drawing samples; and
- critically assess sampling approaches when reading social science research studies.

In our personal lives, we continually confront situations in which we attempt to generalize from our own experience, or the experience of friends and family, to the larger world. For example, we do better on exams if we cram the night before and wonder if this is true for all students. We feel embarrassed in certain social situations and wonder if everyone feels the same. We react with anger or dismay to an event and wonder if others have the same reaction. To what extent, we ask, are our own experiences, emotions, beliefs, and values typical or idiosyncratic?

This question is fundamental to social science research, where we are always asking whether our knowledge of a particular event, group, or personality sheds useful light on larger phenomena. Thus, if we study a set of elected officials, we seek to advance our knowledge of all elected officials; if we study a set of nation-states, we aim to increase our understanding of all nation-states with roughly similar characteristics. The group that we wish to generalize about is known as a **population** (another commonly used term is ***universe***). Within political science, there are many subjects of interest that involve very large populations. If we wish to discuss the voting behaviour of Canadian females, we are looking at a voting age population of over 12 million individuals. Obviously, we cannot study each member of such a large population, regardless of the research design we select. The solution is to select a sample (or subset) of cases that represents the population of interest and, from the study of this sample, to make generalizations about the whole population. **Sampling**—the process of drawing a sample of cases from a larger population—is an issue of concern for all forms of data collection. Whether conducting a content analysis, survey, interview, or focus group, researchers must think of sampling as part of their research design. This chapter explores the logic of sampling and outlines a number of common sampling techniques.

Populations and Samples

The first step in a research project is to clearly identify the population to be studied. When doing so, three factors must be considered: the unit of analysis (e.g. individuals, political parties, municipal governments), the geographic location, and the reference period (time period under consideration) (Statistics Canada 2013b). Instead of studying members of Parliament, we might study Canadian MPs in the fortieth Parliament (18 November 2008–26 March 2011). If the unit is stated without geographic and temporal qualifications, the population is unclear. Do British MPs count? What about MPs throughout history? Researchers need to be explicit in their thinking about who (or what) their population of study is.

When we study a population, the goal is to uncover its characteristics. How many people vote in municipal elections? What is the preferred taxation policy among Canadian voters? How do feminists feel about neo-conservatism? How do neo-conservatives feel about feminism? For smaller populations, it is possible to obtain information for every unit. If our population is the students registered in a single section of a political science research methods course, we can survey or interview all students with relative ease. With larger populations, such as Canadian citizens in 2015, time and financial constraints and practical considerations (it would be impossible to locate everyone) make it virtually impossible to include all cases in the study. Indeed, even the mandatory short-form census, which attempts to contact every Canadian household, is unable to reach all citizens.

To avoid this dilemma, researchers draw information about a characteristic from a sample of the population. Simply put, sampling is the process of selecting a number of cases from a larger population for further study. The advantages of sampling for large populations are many: using a sample costs less and takes less time, and researchers are better able to monitor the data collection due to the study's smaller scale (Statistics Canada 2013b).

Quantitative research seeks to measure population characteristics in numeric terms. When the responses of each and every member (or case) of the population are measured, the resultant characteristic is known as a **population parameter**. When the responses of a population sample are measured, this information is known as a **statistic**. Researchers use the sample statistics to estimate the population parameters. It is important to remember that we are ultimately interested in the population and its parameters; the sample and the sample statistics are merely a means to these ends.

Qualitative research also strives to use select cases to draw conclusions about a larger population. When designing a research study, the researcher must think through the characteristics of the population that need to be reflected in the sample. As qualitative approaches often have smaller samples, the selection of cases is important.

Expand Your Knowledge

Population Research

Most social science research relies on sample data and therefore entails inferences to population parameters. However, research based on population data is not unknown. Consider the following examples:

- David Lublin and D. Stephen Voss (2002) studied francophone support for Quebec sovereignty in the 1992 and 1995 referenda and the 1993 and 1997 federal elections. Using Quebec's 75 federal electoral districts as their unit of analysis, they considered the relationship between support for sovereignty (drawn from electoral returns data) and a number of demographic factors (drawn from the census), as well as incumbency. Lublin and Voss (2002, 96) found that "francophone support for sovereignty consistently rose with the proportion of francophones" and that support was lower in ridings with high proportions of government workers and agricultural workers.
- Linda M. Gerber (2006) examined how demographic features of federal electoral districts related to party voting in the 2004 Canadian federal election. She combined socioeconomic variables drawn from the census with electoral returns data and concludes that "*riding composition*—in terms of ethnic diversity, affluence and education—and *region* are powerful predictors of voting patterns" (Gerber 2006, 112).
- Matthew E. Wetstein and C.L. Ostberg's (2003) study of the Canadian Supreme Court examined all written judgments published in the *Supreme Court Reports* between 1973 and 2002, considering the records of Justices Dickson, Lamer, and McLachlin. Among other findings, the researchers note differences between the two male chief justices (Dickson and Lamer) and the one female chief justice (McLachlin).
- R. Kenneth Carty and Munroe Eagles (2006) used federal electoral district data to consider the relationship between federal voting and local party factors, such as organization, local party finance, and local candidates. They argue that local campaigns do make a difference to federal voting.

If we are to make generalizations about a population from a sample, we must use a **representative sample**, that is, one that accurately represents the larger population from which it was taken. If the population has approximately 30 per cent Asians, 60 per cent Caucasians, and 10 per cent African Canadians, a representative sample will consist of a similar racial distribution. Keep in mind, though, that we often do not know anything about the population characteristics other than what we can gather from the sample statistics. We would never know, for example, how many Canadians actually support capital punishment or employment equity because the entire population will never be asked. As we will see, population characteristics can be estimated but seldom proved.

Three important factors influence the representativeness of a sample: the accuracy of the sampling frame, the sample selection method, and the sample size. A **sampling frame** is a list of all the units in the target population. If our target population is students at Canadian universities during the 2014–15 academic year, our sampling frame would list all registered students. Ideally, a sampling frame is complete, with no missing cases or inaccurate information. Such a frame is rare, particularly for large populations. Records are often incomplete and are subject to change.

Consider the sampling frame for our population of university students. We would begin by obtaining the 2014–15 student registration lists from all Canadian universities (assuming that the universities were all willing to make such lists available, a highly unlikely assumption), but the lists would not necessarily include students who registered late and would probably include individuals who are no longer members of the target population (e.g. students who had dropped out). Another problem is that, for many populations, no official or even unofficial list that can be used as a sampling frame exists. For example, what is the sampling frame for a target population of Canadians in 2015? Lacking an official list of Canadians, researchers often turn to indirect lists, such as driver's licences and telephone directories. Of course, these lists are also incomplete, failing to capture (in the case of the former) non-drivers and new drivers and (in the latter) those without land lines, new telephone subscribers, and those with unlisted numbers. These incompletions undermine the representativeness of a sample because "the excluded persons usually constitute some distinguishable and homogenous group" (Bailey 1978, 73). Those without telephone service, for instance, are most often poor; the use of a telephone directory as a sampling frame thus leads to the underrepresentation of the group. In addition to exclusion problems, most lists used as sampling frames fail to account for changes to the population caused by birth, death, or migration.

The challenge to researchers is to find a sampling frame that minimizes inaccuracies. One technique popular among telephone survey researchers is the random creation of a list of telephone numbers. The process involves the computer generation of telephone numbers; therefore, the sampling frame is all active numbers. This method is an improvement on the use of telephone directories as a sampling frame because it includes newly listed and unlisted telephone numbers and eliminates cancelled numbers. However, persons without telephone service remain excluded.

Expand Your Knowledge

The Importance of Sampling Frames: The Case of *The Literary Digest*

The most notorious and often-cited example of a poor sampling frame involves a mail survey conducted by *The Literary Digest* in 1936. Attempting to predict the outcome of that year's US presidential election, a contest between Democrat Franklin D. Roosevelt and Republican Alf Landon, the *Digest* staff sent surveys to 10 million Americans. The sampling frame consisted of a number of lists, including automobile registrations, telephone directories, and the magazine's subscribers. From the two million responses gathered, the *Digest* predicted a landslide election for Landon, but Roosevelt was elected.

Although many flaws have been noted with the survey, one of particular interest here is the mismatch between sampling frame and target population.[1] The latter was all eligible American voters, but the former failed to cast such a broad net. Recall that the election occurred at a time when many of the American poor and lower middle class could not afford telephones, automobiles, or subscriptions to magazines such as *The Literary Digest*. Given that support for the Democratic Party in 1936 came largely from these groups, the magazine's failure to include the poor in its sample led to embarrassing results.

What is the moral of the story? Researchers must think carefully when selecting a sampling frame, considering not only who is included but also who is excluded. Efforts must be made to ensure that as much of the target population as possible is included in the sampling frame. If the sampling frame is inappropriate or biased, we cannot make generalizations to the target population with any degree of confidence.

Note

1. Another problem was non-response bias. Mail surveys generate a greater response from the middle class and from those with a greater interest in the study. In this case, both the middle class and Landon supporters (who tended to be more passionate about the election than Roosevelt supporters were) were more likely than other groups to return the surveys, hence biasing the survey results toward Landon.

Not all target populations have a listing (be it direct or indirect) to which we can refer. This absence may be due to an individual's unwillingness to identify publicly with a given population; homeless persons, drug addicts, and sexual assault victims are all examples of such hard-to-identify populations. In such situations, the researcher has difficulty establishing a truly representative sample. We will return to discussing the study of hard-to-access groups later in the chapter.

The second factor is the sample selection method. Sampling techniques can be divided into two categories: probability and non-probability. **Probability sampling** techniques are based on probability theory and allow researchers to use inferential statistics to test the representativeness of their sample. **Non-probability sampling** techniques are not based on probability theory, and researchers are not able to use statistical analysis to make inferences from the sample to the larger population of study. Quantitative research typically uses probability sampling, while non-probability sampling is more commonly used in qualitative research. The discussion of probability and non-probability sampling provides much of the content of this chapter.

The third factor that determines a sample's representativeness is sample size, which we will discuss later in the chapter. At this point, we want to stress only that all three factors are important and that weakness with respect to one cannot be compensated by strength with

Expand Your Knowledge

The Hite Reports

A somewhat less dated example of problematic sampling frames is American sociologist Shere Hite's work on human sexuality. *The Hite Report: A Nationwide Study of Female Sexuality* was first published in 1976, and *The Hite Report on Male Sexuality* was published five years later. Both books, which contain detailed and often vivid accounts of sexual behaviour, were best-sellers, received extensive media coverage, and (along with Hite's subsequent publications) helped establish new empirical norms of sexual behaviour in the United States. But whether the research findings are representative of the American public is unclear when one turns to the sampling frames and methodology.

Hite's report on female sexuality was based on slightly over 3,000 replies to more than 100,000 questionnaires that were distributed through the National Organization for Women, abortion rights groups, women's newsletters, and university women's centres during the early 1970s (Hite 1976, xix). Notices asking readers to write in for copies of the questionnaire were published in *The Village Voice*, *Mademoiselle*, *Brides*, and *Ms.* magazines. Just under 10 per cent of the completed questionnaires came from women readers of the men's magazine *Oui*. The report on male sexuality was based on 7,239 replies to 119,000 questionnaires (Hite 1981, xvii–xix). Here, the sampling frames included men's clubs, church organizations, and male readers of the first Hite report, *Sexology*, *Penthouse*, and *Sexual Honesty: By Women for Women*.

The question is whether this sampling frame, or assortment of sampling frames, could generate a representative sample, particularly given the added problem of low response rates. To be fair, Hite addresses the matter of representativeness with considerable caution and finesse. Indeed, her methodological discussions are well worth reading. However, her publications speak to the broadly defined experiences of men and women. The message, inadvertent though it may be, is that the results denote how American women and men feel, believe, and behave. And yet, unless we have some confidence in the representativeness of the sample, it is difficult to place ourselves against the norms of the Hite reports. Do her respondents in fact reflect the American norm (or at least the norm at the time of the reports)? The norm for men and women in general? Given that we have no independent measure beyond our own limited personal experience, these questions are extremely difficult to answer.

APPLY YOUR UNDERSTANDING

Selecting Sampling Frames

For each of the following target populations, identify a list that could serve as a sampling frame. What limitations (potential inaccuracies and omissions) can you identify for each list?

- Toronto small businesses, 2015
- City hospital admissions, January 2015
- Nova Scotia voters, 2015
- Canadian New Democrats, 2015
- Vancouver heroin addicts, 2015
- Quebec sovereigntists, 2015

respect to another. As we saw in *The Literary Digest* example, a sample drawn from a poor sampling frame does not become better or more accurate by becoming bigger.

Probability Sampling

Sampling based on probability theory allows us to estimate the likelihood that our sample provides a representative picture of the population. Recall that, in quantitative research, our goal is to use the sample to calculate estimates, known as statistics, of the population parameters. For these estimates to be useful, we need to be confident that our sample is an accurate representation of the population. Probability theory gives us this confidence.

Probability sampling can be understood as the **random selection** of a sample. In its truest form, this term means that each case in the population has an equal opportunity to be selected for the sample. To understand how probability sampling works, we first need a basic understanding of probability theory. After this brief introduction, we will discuss the impact of sample size and various techniques of probability sampling.

Introduction to Probability Theory

When we are considering probabilities, we want to estimate the likelihood that a particular outcome will occur. If we roll a die, what is the probability that we will get a six? If we pull a card from a deck, what is the probability that it will be a diamond? In sampling, we are interested in questions such as "What is the probability that we will select person A for the sample?" and "What is the probability that our sample statistic will fall within a given range of values?"

Probabilities can range from zero to one. A probability of zero indicates that there is no chance of an event occurring. A probability of one indicates that there is a 100 per cent chance of the event occurring; that is, it is certain. To calculate the probability of an event occurring, we divide the number of possible favourable outcomes by the total number of possible outcomes. If we have 10 students and 6 are female, our probability of randomly selecting a female student's name from a hat is equal to 6 (number of favourable outcomes) divided by 10 (number of total outcomes), or 0.6. Another way of expressing this likelihood is to state that there is a 60 per cent chance that a female student will be selected. To calculate the probability of a single event, we use the formula $P(A) = r/n$, where $P(A)$ is the probability of event A, r is the number of favourable outcomes, and n is the number of total outcomes.

We are often interested in the probability of two or more events occurring together. The joint occurrence of two events is calculated by the formula $P(AB) = P(A)\,P(B/A)$, where $P(AB)$ signifies the probability of the joint occurrence of events A and B, $P(A)$ is the probability of event A, and $P(B/A)$ is the probability of event B after event A. When events A and B are independent, $P(B/A) = P(B)$. For example, what is the probability of rolling two dice and getting two sixes?

$$P(A) = \frac{1}{6} = 0.17$$

$$P(B/A) = P(B) = \frac{1}{6} = 0.17$$

$$P(AB) = P(A)\,P(B/A) = (0.17)(0.17) = 0.029$$

Each die is independent of the other; therefore, there is a 2.9 per cent chance that rolling two dice will result in two sixes. Incidentally, probability equations use a number of different notations to indicate multiplication: *A times B* may be written as $A \times B$, $(A)(B)$, $A(B)$, or AB.

APPLY YOUR UNDERSTANDING

Calculating Probabilities 1

Calculate the probabilities of the following events:

1. selecting a face card from a deck of cards
2. flipping a coin and getting heads
3. rolling a die and getting a four
4. buying three home lottery tickets and winning the prize, assuming 200,000 tickets were sold and only one prize is given

Events A and B are dependent when the outcome of A influences the outcome of B. If we are selecting cards from a deck, what is the probability that we will select two diamonds in a row?[1] Note that, after we have selected the first diamond, both the number of diamonds (r = favourable outcomes) and the number of cards (n = total outcomes) are reduced:

$$P(A) = \frac{13}{52} = 0.250$$

$$P(B/A) = \frac{12}{51} = 0.235$$

$$P(AB) = P(A)\,P(B/A) = 0.250(0.235) = 0.059$$

There is a 5.9 per cent chance that we will select two consecutive diamonds from a full deck.

APPLY YOUR UNDERSTANDING

Calculating Probabilities 2

Calculate the probabilities of the following events:

1. You have the names of 16 Liberals, 12 Conservatives, and 5 New Democrats in a hat. What is the probability that, upon selecting three names, you will select all Liberals? All Conservatives? All New Democrats?
2. What are the odds of rolling a die and getting six five times in a row?
3. You have bought a ticket in a raffle. The raffle procedure is to return all 10,000 tickets to the draw after each prize is awarded, thus ensuring that everyone is eligible for every prize. If there are three prizes, what is the probability that you will win one of them? What is the probability that you will win all three?

Probability Theory and Sampling

This basic knowledge of probability theory is necessary to understand the principles of random sampling, both how it is conducted and why samples based on probability theory produce accurate estimates of population parameters. The principle of random sampling is rather straightforward in that each case has an equal probability of being selected: $1/n$. **Simple random sampling** is the process by which every case in the population is listed and the sample is selected randomly from this list. (Computers simplify this process.) There are practical limitations to the application of simple random sampling, but the principle underlies all forms of probability sampling.[2]

As previously stated, probability theory allows us to determine the likelihood that our calculated sample statistic is a good estimation of the population parameter because statisticians have found that sample statistics (used to estimate the population parameter) distribute themselves around the population parameter in a normal (bell-shaped) distribution. An example will help clarify this point.[3] Consider the following data set:

Name	Number of Pets
Arnie (A)	3
Beth (B)	1
Carlotta (C)	2
Dimitri (D)	0
Elke (E)	2
Frank (F)	4

The population size in this example is six; our universe is restricted to the six individuals. The population parameter we are interested in is the mean (or arithmetic average; discussed in Chapter 14), which is equal to the sum of the individual scores (3 + 1 + 2 + 0 + 2 + 4 = 12) divided by the total number of cases (6); hence, the mean number of pets owned is 2 (12/6). However, if we take samples from this population, we will find sample means that differ from the population parameter. If our sample size is 2, there are 15 possible samples, each with its own sample mean, as Table 8.1 illustrates.

Taken together, all the possible sample means for a given sample size create a **sampling distribution**. The sampling distribution of means for this two-case sample illustration is presented in Table 8.2 and graphically presented in Figure 8.1. The sampling distribution is created by totalling the number of combinations that present the specified sample mean. For example, in the two-case samples there are two combinations (CD and DE) that have a mean of 1.

Table 8.1 All Possible Samples of Size 2, with Sample Means

Combination[1]	Mean	Combination	Mean
AB	2.0	CD	1.0
AC	2.5	CE	2.0
AD	1.5	CF	3.0
AE	2.5	DE	1.0
AF	3.5	DF	2.0
BC	1.5	EF	3.0
BD	0.5		
BE	1.5		
BF	2.5		

1. AB = the sample composed of Arnie (A) and Beth (B); AC = the sample composed of Arnie (A) and Carlotta (C); etc.

Table 8.2 Sampling Distributions from the Pet Illustration

Sample Mean	Number of Samples	Probability
0.5	1	0.07
1.0	2	0.13
1.5	3	0.20
2.0	3	0.20
2.5	3	0.20
3.0	2	0.13
3.5	1	0.07

We can apply probability theory to determine the odds of selecting any particular mean. In our two-case samples, the probability of obtaining a sample mean of 2.5 is equal to 0.2 (3/15 = 0.2); there is a 20 per cent chance that we will select a sample mean of 2.5. As Table 8.2 suggests, our probabilities of obtaining a sample mean close to the population parameter (which, as you will recall, is 2) are higher than our probabilities of obtaining sample means that diverge greatly from the parameter. That is to say, you are more likely to get a sample mean that is close to the parameter than one that is not. In our example, the probability of getting a sample mean that is within 0.5 units of the parameter (i.e. between 1.5 and 2.5) is 0.6 (9/15 = 0.6). The range of values within which the population parameter is likely to fall is known as a **confidence interval**, a concept we will return to in Chapter 15.

The difference between the sample statistic (the estimated value) and the population parameter (the actual value) is referred to as **sampling error**. In this example, a sample mean of 1.5 has a sampling error of 0.5, since it is 0.5 units off the population mean of 2.0. A large sampling error indicates that the sample statistic deviates greatly from the population parameter, whereas a small sampling error indicates that the sample statistic is close to the population parameter.

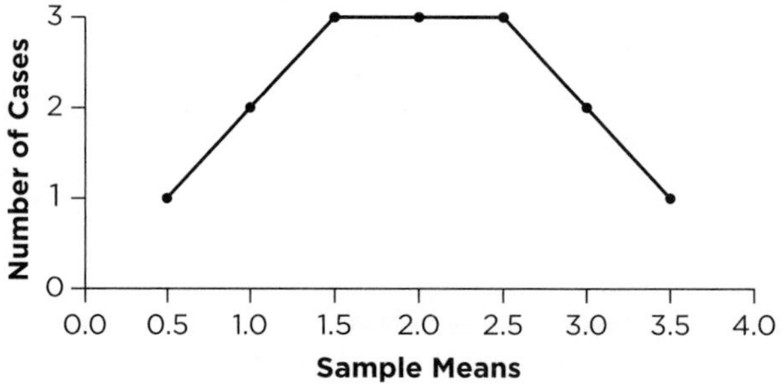

Figure 8.1 Sampling Distribution (sample means for n = 2)

Sample Size

When probability sampling techniques are used, sampling error is reduced as the sample size increases. Given that our goal is to reduce error, it is not surprising that we prefer large samples over small ones; we desire sample statistics that are as close to the population parameter as possible. Yet larger and larger samples are also more and more expensive samples. Since resources are always limited, how large should our sample be? To determine the appropriate sample size, we need to consider a number of factors: the homogeneity of the sample, the number of variables under study, and the desired degree of accuracy.

APPLY YOUR UNDERSTANDING

Calculating Sampling Distributions

Using the number of pets data set from the previous example, calculate a sampling distribution for sample means from samples containing three cases. (There should be a total of 20 combinations.) What is the probability of selecting each of the sample means? What is the probability that a selected sample mean will fall between 1.5 and 2.5? What is the sampling error for the sample ABC? For ABD?

Homogeneity refers to how similar a population is with respect to salient variables, while **heterogeneity** refers to how dissimilar a population is. The goal of our studies is to explain variation. What we as researchers need to estimate is how homogeneous or heterogeneous our population is: a highly homogeneous population allows us to use a smaller sample, but a highly heterogeneous population requires a larger sample. The appropriate sample size increases as we move along the continuum from homogeneity to heterogeneity (see Figure 8.2).

The number of variables we wish to explore also influences sample size. More complex studies require larger sample sizes. The need for a larger sample stems from the desire to look at subgroups within the sample and to impose statistical controls. A sample of 500 voters might have only 10 individuals with a post-graduate education. If the education variable is necessary to your study, you will need to greatly increase your sample size to randomly generate a large enough subgroup for analysis. (Alternative techniques are discussed later in this chapter.)

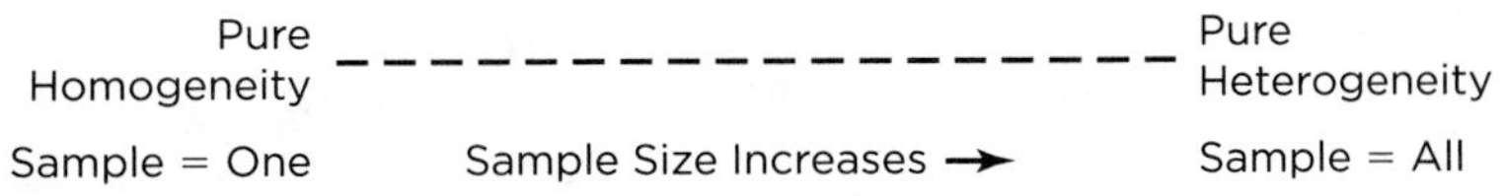

Figure 8.2 Continuum of Homogeneity

A third factor that influences sample size is the desired degree of accuracy. Recall that, for probability samples, sampling error decreases as sample size increases. Before conducting an analysis, researchers can state the **margin of error** they are willing to accept, or tolerate (expressed as a percentage). Knowing the margin of error allows researchers to state their sample statistics as a confidence interval. For instance, a research team may conduct a survey to determine the level of public support for same-sex marriage. If the survey finds that 57 per cent of the respondents support same-sex marriage and if the sampling error is ±5 per cent, the survey's sponsors can conclude that between 52 per cent and 62 per cent of Canadians support same-sex marriage. Researchers can preset the margin of error they want and then, using the information illustrated in Table 8.3, determine the minimum sample size required to yield such a **confidence level**.

It should be clear from the table that the law of diminishing returns applies to sample size: at a certain point, dramatically increasing sample size results in only modest improvements in accuracy. With a population of 500,000, moving from a sample of 384 to one of 784 takes us from 5 per cent error down to 3.5 per cent; roughly doubling the sample size results in a substantial reduction in error. However, to increase accuracy to the 1 per cent margin of error, one would have to increase the sample size to 9,423. Given the significant financial costs in increasing sample size, researchers are willing to tolerate some error. Note that, as population size increases, the minimum sample size needed to obtain a particular margin of error narrows—the minimum sample size for a 5 per cent margin of error for a population of 500,000 is only three cases greater than the minimum sample size for a population of 50,000. This explains why national public opinion polls in the United States are generally of the same size as those in Canada, even though the American population is 10 times as large.

In summary, we need to consider the homogeneity of our population, the complexity of our study, and the degree of accuracy desired when selecting sample sizes. In general, a larger sample is always preferred to a smaller one, but obtaining large samples is a costly process in terms of both time and money. Bernard Lazerwitz (1968, 278–9) argues that the ideal sample is representative, obtained by probability sampling, "as small as precision

Table 8.3 Minimum Sample Sizes at a 95 Per Cent Confidence Level

Population Size	5.0%	3.5%	2.5%	1.0%
100	80	89	94	99
500	217	306	377	475
1,000	278	440	606	906
10,000	370	727	1,332	4,899
50,000	381	772	1,491	8,056
100,000	383	778	1,513	8,762
500,000	384	783	1,532	9,423

Source: Adapted from Boyd (2006).

Expand Your Knowledge

Sampling Error in Pre-Election Polls

Pre-election polls are now commonly reported in the media with a specified margin of error. A Forum Research Inc. (2013, 2) telephone survey conducted shortly before the 2013 Nova Scotia provincial election was based on 961 interviews, and the margin of error for the total sample was estimated to be 3 per cent with a 95 per cent confidence level. Put somewhat differently, if the survey found that 40 per cent of the sample intended to vote for party X, we could assume that, within the population of all voters, there was a 95 per cent chance that between 37 per cent (40 per cent – 3 per cent) and 43 per cent (40 per cent + 3 per cent) would vote for party X. There is also a 5 per cent chance (100 per cent – 95 per cent) that party X would get either less than 37 per cent of the vote or more than 43 per cent. The odds would be small but not negligible.

Let's apply this logic to the actual results of the survey, which were that 48 per cent of the respondents intended to vote for the Liberals, 26 per cent for the NDP, 23 per cent for the Conservatives, and 3 per cent for the Greens. Thus there was a 95 per cent chance that the level of support for the Liberals within the electorate at large was between 45 per cent and 51 per cent (48 per cent ± 3 per cent), and that the level of support for the NDP was between 23 per cent and 29 per cent (26 per cent ± 3 per cent). At one extreme, the Liberals could end up with 51 per cent of the vote and the NDP with only 23 per cent. At the other extreme, the Liberals could end up with only 45 per cent and the NDP with 29 per cent.

In the election, the Liberals received 46 per cent of the vote, compared with 27 per cent for the NDP—outcomes very close to those predicted by the survey.

considerations permit, as economical as possible, and gathered as swiftly as its various measurement techniques permit." We seek samples that are just large enough to ensure the precision necessary; any larger is a waste of resources.

Conducting Probability Samples

In simple random sampling, all the cases are listed and assigned numbers 1 to *N*. Through computer selection or use of a table of random numbers, cases are selected until the desired sample size is met. If we had a population of 10,000 and a desired sample size of 2,000, we would number the cases individually from 1 to 10,000 and then randomly select 2,000 cases to serve as our sample.

Occasionally, researchers will use **systematic selection**. In this method, a selection interval ($1/k$) is calculated based on the sample size needed. If we want 5 per cent of the population to be included in the sample, we need to select one out of every 20 cases ($1/20 = 5$

per cent), and our selection interval is therefore 20. If we want 1 per cent of the population included in the sample, we need to select one out of every 100 cases (1/100 = 1 per cent), and our selection interval is 100. Once our selection interval is determined, a random number is selected to serve as a starting point; this number is known as a random start.

If our selection interval is 20, we begin by selecting a random number between 1 and 20—let's use 6. We then add the selection interval until the sample size is reached: cases numbered 6, 26, 46, 66, 86, 106, and so on are selected. Recall that numbers correspond to individual cases and that the numbers selected represent the cases that will be included in the sample. Systematic sampling can be more practical and efficient than simple random sampling, but it is less random and thus less accurate. In addition, it necessitates a random sampling frame; a list of the population that is ordered (e.g. alphabetically) may lead to biased results.

Stratified sampling involves breaking the population into mutually exclusive subgroups, or strata, and then randomly sampling each group. If we are interested in differences between undergraduate and graduate students, we could break the population into two groups—undergraduates and graduates—each with its own sampling frame. We would then randomly sample from each list and combine the subsamples to construct our larger sample.

Stratified sampling allows us to focus on small subgroups within the population. If a particular group of interest is small, we may choose to sample a larger proportion of that subgroup to ensure numbers large enough to produce significant statistics. For instance, if the population of subgroup A is 100 and the population of subgroup B is 1,000, we may choose to include 50 per cent of A in the sample (for a total of 50 cases) but only 10 per cent of B (for a total of 100 cases). This procedure, known as disproportionate stratified sampling, is routinely used in Canada to deal with variance in provincial populations. Imagine that you have the money to do a national survey of 1,500 respondents on a matter of public policy interest. It is important that you report not only on Canadians at large but also on provincial differences. Because Ontario and Saskatchewan have, respectively, 39 per cent and 3 per cent of the Canadian population (based on the 2013 post-censal population estimate), in a purely random sample, 585 respondents could be expected from Ontario (1,500 × 0.39 = 585) and 45 from Saskatchewan (1,500 × 0.03 = 45). You would have more than enough respondents to provide a reasonable read on Ontario opinion—you would have "oversampled"—but you would not have enough for Saskatchewan.

Therefore, disproportionate stratified sampling could be used to increase the number of Saskatchewan respondents and to decrease the number from Ontario. The catch is that your final sample would no longer be representative of the Canadian population, for you would have too few Ontario respondents and too many Saskatchewan respondents. To reconstruct a representative national sample, it is necessary to assign weights to respondents. If we had sampled 200 individuals from each of the two provinces, we would assign a weight of 2.925 to each Ontario respondent (585/200 = 2.925) and a weight of 0.225 (45/200 = 0.225) to each Saskatchewan respondent. Although this procedure makes mathematical sense, it can be difficult to explain in public forums.

Cluster sampling is the process of dividing the population into a number of subgroups, known as clusters, and then randomly selecting clusters within which to randomly sample. This method is best understood by considering geographic units. Let's say our population is Canada as a whole and we are conducting individual door-to-door interviews. If we were to

Expand Your Knowledge

The Census Debate

Sampling theory became a national news story in the summer of 2010, when changes to the Canadian census were announced. The Canadian census includes both a short and long form. Sent to all households in the country, the short form includes questions about the number of household residents and their ages and sexes. The long form includes questions about language, ethnicity, income, and employment and was sent to only 20 per cent of Canadian households, selected based on probability sampling techniques. Completion of the census was mandatory for Canadians; individuals failing to return the form(s) faced possible fines or jail time. (In practice, jail time was not used.)

On 29 June 2010, the Harper government announced that it would be replacing the mandatory long-form census with a voluntary long form. (Completion of the short-form census would remain mandatory.) Industry Minister Tony Clement stated that the government was making the long form voluntary because of privacy concerns. He announced that the 20 per cent mandatory sample would be replaced by a 33 per cent voluntary sample and claimed that this increase would compensate for the anticipated drop in response rate. This claim drew harsh criticism from Canadian statisticians, who stated that the voluntary long-form census would greatly undermine data quality because some social groups would be more likely to respond than others.

The National Statistics Council urged the government to reverse its decision; more than 200 groups (including universities, industry and medical associations, non-profit organizations, and think-tanks) voiced opposition and more than 15,000 Canadians signed a petition opposing the move to the voluntary long form. Most dramatically, Statistic Canada's chief statistician, Munir Sheikh, resigned when Clement claimed that the organization had advised that a voluntary census would result in reliable data. (Documents revealed in August 2010 demonstrated that Statistics Canada had in fact expressed concerns about the voluntary census [CBC News 2010c].) When asked by the House of Commons Industry Committee if the voluntary census could adequately replace the mandatory survey, Sheikh replied clearly, "It cannot" (CBC News 2010b).

Sheikh's prediction proved accurate. The voluntary National Household Survey (NHS), which replaced the mandatory long-form census, had a response rate of 68.6 per cent, considerably lower than the 2006 long-form census response rate of 93.5 per cent. In October 2013, researchers reported strong concerns about data quality, particularly with respect to income measures (Grant 2013). Sheikh stated, "The irony is, we've spent more money compared to a census to get data which is largely useless. Why anyone would want to do this is beyond me. Why would you spend $600-million for this?" (Ibid.)

randomly sample all Canadians, we could end up with cases all over the country, resulting in considerable travel costs. Instead, we could use cluster sampling. We would need to first divide the country into clusters such as federal electoral constituencies. There were 308 constituencies in the 2011 federal election; let's say we randomly select 2 of them. These constituencies are then further broken down into clusters of similar population size, for example, city blocks, and again a number of them are randomly selected, say 10. We now have 10 city blocks within 2 federal constituencies. The randomly selected but geographically concentrated housing units located in those 10 city blocks serve as the sample.

Cluster sampling allows the researcher to greatly reduce costs and increase efficiency while using probability sampling for a large population. However, this approach can appear to or actually produce samples that, on face value, are not representative. In the preceding example, the sample's representative nature could become suspect in the public's eyes if you had poor luck at the first stage of the sampling procedure. If you drew two constituencies in northern Ontario, would you have a sample that was representative of the Canadian population? As Statistics Canada (2013b) notes, "It is usually better to survey a large number of small clusters instead of a small number of large clusters. This is because neighbouring units tend to be more alike, resulting in a sample that does not represent the whole spectrum of opinions or situations present in the overall population."

Researchers can employ a number of approaches to obtain probability samples. The odds of any individual case in the population being selected into the sample depend on the random sampling method used. The general advantage of probability sampling is that it allows us to use sample statistics to estimate population parameters. But not all research problems allow the use of probability sampling, which requires complete sampling frames.

Non-Probability Sampling

Non-probability sampling methods do not employ random selection of cases. The non-random selection means that we cannot identify margins of error or confidence intervals; thus, it is more difficult to make generalizations and draw conclusions about the general population. Qualitative research designs often use non-probability sampling. Non-probability samples also usually have smaller sample sizes; for example, researchers using an interview research design would typically conduct fewer than 50 interviews (Ritchie, Lewis, and Elam 2003, 84).

Non-probability sampling is appropriate when researchers are not seeking to make generalizations about a larger population but are pursuing more in-depth descriptive information. This sampling is also valuable when probability sampling is not feasible, such as when sampling frames are inadequate, members of the population are likely to refuse to participate, or the population of study is extremely small. In such instances, the researcher often must make use of the cases available or abandon the study.

Non-probability sampling can be accidental or purposive. In an **accidental sample**, also known as a convenience sample or haphazard sample, the researcher gathers data from individuals whom he or she "accidentally" encounters or are convenient. An example is "person on the street" opinion polling, often done by news programs. Designed to tap the "pulse of the city," such samples are actually quite biased. A poll taken on a downtown corner at noon on a weekday is limited to those individuals who tend to be downtown during the week for lunch, typically office workers. Many other people in the city, such as students, union workers, homemakers, and the retired, have a much lower probability of being included in the sample; consequently, what is stated to be the common opinion is actually the opinion of only a small group.

A related, similarly biased form of sampling is any sample that involves **self-selection**, such as call-in programs on the radio or television or mail-in surveys for magazines and newspapers. In such samples, the participants are limited to those who opt in to the study, and it is possible that they are unrepresentative of the larger population. As Bethlehem (2009, 2) explains, "Researchers have no control over the selection mechanism. Selection probabilities are unknown. Therefore, no unbiased estimates can be computed, nor can the accuracy of estimated be established."

Purposive sampling (also known as judgmental sampling) involves researcher selection of specific cases; the researcher uses his or her judgment to select cases that will provide

Expand Your Knowledge

University Classes as Samples of Convenience

It is not surprising that many professors turn to their classes as samples of convenience. After all, students are close at hand, inexpensive to survey, and generally predisposed or at least resigned to playing the respondent role. In some psychology departments, there is a formal expectation that students will act as subjects for faculty, graduate, and undergraduate research as long as that research is conducted according to approved ethical guidelines.

Of course, there are also disadvantages to using student respondents or subjects. The primary drawback is that students are not typical or representative of the general population. Seldom are we interested in making generalizations from student samples to the student population; the population that is of interest is broader, but generalizations in this respect are suspect. At times, however, research with student populations can reveal dynamics and relationships that are at least suggestive of wider population dynamics and relationships. A 1994 study of 2,114 students at l'Université de Montréal (Blais, Martin, and Nadeau 1995) explored the relationship among concerns about the language situation in Quebec, expectations about the short- and long-term economic costs of separatism, and support for sovereigntist and federalist options. The findings that economic expectations had greater weight than linguistic expectations in explaining support for sovereignty and that long-term economic considerations outweighed short-term economic expectations provide useful insights into the broader dynamics of referendum voting in Quebec.

the greatest amount of information. Cases are selected both "to ensure that all the key constituencies of relevance to the subject matter are covered" and "to ensure that, within each of the key criteria, some diversity is included so that the impact of the characteristic concerned can be explored" (Ritchie et al. 2003, 79). Researchers will often use purposive sampling for interview or focus group research. For example, they may interview experts on a particular topic or stakeholders with respect to a specific policy area. As Ted Palys (2008, 698) explains, "Research participants are not always created equal—one well-placed articulate informant will often advance the research far better than any randomly chosen sample of 50—and researchers need to take this into account in choosing a sample."

Snowball (or **network**) **sampling** is often employed to study social networks. The researcher begins by identifying a few cases, from which he or she gets referrals to others and continues to branch out. He or she might interview three self-identified environmentalists and, at the conclusion of the interview, ask each respondent to suggest three others who could be interviewed. The researcher would then interview the suggested nine environmentalists and again ask for further referrals. This process would continue until sampling is completed. Just as a snowball rolled down a hill picks up snow and grows in size, the sample picks up more cases over time and becomes larger until logistical and financial considerations force the researcher to stop.

When accidental or purposive sampling is combined with stratification, the result is known as **quota sampling**. The researcher identifies a number of target groups (strata), such as men and women, and then sets a quota number that must be met for each group. For instance, the researcher may decide that he or she needs to sample at least 15 men and 15 women. How the researcher meets the quota can vary; he or she may use accidental sampling or use his or her knowledge to create a purposive sample.

This chapter has explored the need for a representative sample in our research. It was noted that representativeness is determined by three factors: sampling frame, sample size, and sampling method. Sampling is an important consideration in data collection. The following chapters will consider a number of different data collection techniques, each with unique sampling considerations.

APPLY YOUR UNDERSTANDING

Choosing a Sampling Approach

For each of the following, select a sampling technique and explain your choice.

1. An Internet survey of Canadian public servants to discuss career satisfaction.
2. A telephone survey of Canadians to assess voting intentions.
3. A mail survey of elected officials in your province to assess the impact of gender on policy preferences.
4. Interviews with members of the gay and lesbian community to discuss experiences with discrimination.

Working as a Team

1. Imagine that your group has been commissioned to conduct a study of drug use among teenagers aged 14 to 18. The agency that commissioned the study is particularly interested in drug users; issues of concern include frequency and type of use, peer pressure, religious beliefs, and degree of social integration. Up to 200 interviews will be funded, and the results of the study will be used to provide policy recommendations to the provincial government. Define the population for your study. Is there a sampling frame? What sampling method would you use? What ethical issues might you encounter?

Self-Study

1. You wish to conduct a study of youth participation in Canadian political parties. Answer the following questions, providing reasons for your answers.
    a. What are your target population and sampling frames? What possible problems can you identify with the latter?
    b. How would you conduct a simple random sample for this study?
    c. How would you conduct a systematic sample for this study?
    d. Which sampling procedure is best for your research question?
2. You are conducting a study of the career paths of provincial public servants, specifically individuals currently working as policy analysts in your provincial government. How could you create a sampling frame? How could you conduct a probability sample and a non-probability sample? Which sampling procedure would you use and why?

Notes

1. This example is adapted from Hayslett (1968, 38–9).
2. Lazerwitz (1968, 279) notes that the limitations are the need for a complete listing and the assumption that cases are statistically independent of one another.
3. The example is modelled on one presented in Singleton et al. (1988, 140–4).

CHAPTER 9

Interview, Focus Group, and Observation Research

Destination

By the end of this chapter, you should be able to

- explain interview, focus group, and observation data collection strategies and their basic steps;
- identify the types of research questions suited to interview, focus group, and observation research and explain how these approaches can inform political analysis; and
- appreciate the ethical issues that must be considered when conducting qualitative research.

Many political science research questions require specialized or "inside" information. We may wish to understand the dynamics of a party caucus, the leadership style of a certain political leader, or the decision-making process of a specific public policy. We may wish to understand why individuals act the way that they do or feel the way that they say they feel about a particular political issue. We might also want to observe exactly how political events occur rather than rely on second-hand information.

This chapter examines three qualitative research techniques: interviews, focus groups, and observation. Such approaches are particularly valuable for inductive research. Recall from Chapter 3 that, unlike deductive hypothesis-testing, inductive research seeks broad information to aid in the formulation of new theories and hypotheses. When little knowledge exists about a subject or when researchers wish to go beyond existing theories and approaches, qualitative research can help to establish a rich understanding of the topic. Additionally, qualitative approaches allow us to make important new discoveries. With more structured forms of research (such as surveys), the relevance of particular issues has been predetermined and only issues that are addressed in the questionnaire are included in the study, whereas in a less structured approach (such as interview research), respondents are able to indicate what they feel is important. By indicating their own priorities and concerns, respondents may suggest to the researcher a new way of approaching the research question or new avenues to be explored.

Interviews

Interviews take on the tone of a conversation, but some important differences exist. In interviews, one person asks questions and the other answers. In a "normal" conversation, each individual contributes equally and there is an exchange of ideas. (Of course, we have all had conversations in which the level of contribution is unbalanced; when it is the other person who is dominating the discussion, we often consider him or her to be a bit of a bore!) In ordinary conversation, if we do not wish to answer a question, we have the option of changing the subject or making a joke. Usually, the other person picks up on such cues and lets the issue pass. In an interview, however, the interviewer is likely to return to these questions in an effort to obtain the necessary data.

Interviews are an important tool for political science research. Through interview research, political scientists are able to expand our understanding of political and governance practices. Many political and policy research questions require an understanding of context or political processes. Research on political or policy-making processes often requires interviewing. As Putt and Springer (1989, 144) explain, "Organizations rarely run completely by stated procedures. Program processes and procedures are shaped and reshaped as the program evolves. Intensive interviewing of program managers and staff is an important means of documenting current procedures used in organizational processes. Interviews also provide insight into the conditions that affect these procedures and the ways in which they have evolved."

Explanatory research is also well served by interviews. Why was a particular decision made? Who were the key actors? What were the organizational procedures? What were the circumstances surrounding a particular event? Answers to such questions often cannot be found in written documents, and the questions may not be well suited to a survey or other data collection technique.

Political scientists often turn to interview research when dealing with **small** or **hard-to-reach populations**. Certain individuals, including politicians, deputy ministers, and business leaders, are less likely to respond to a survey than to an interview. Individuals or groups with access to the specialized information we need are referred to as elites; in this context, the term is not used in the conventional sense, which suggests privileged political or economic elites (although they may be the group you are studying). Elite interviewing can be a critical source of research information. For some elites, being selected for an interview presents a welcome opportunity to talk at length, to explain personal and political choices. Such interviews can give the researcher a rich understanding of historical background.

Further, elites can provide invaluable assistance in directing and informing research. As Patton and Sawicki (1993, 98) explain, "Often the analyst must quickly obtain data that have never been organized or tabulated. Experts in the area may be the best source of such information; they will often know where to locate unpublished material or who else to contact." In many cases, the interview respondent wishes to be of maximum assistance to the researcher and makes valuable suggestions for the study. For example, a respondent may direct the researcher to contacts for additional interviews or to particular documents, records, or sources that will advance the research.

Overall, a key advantage of interviewing is that researchers can obtain very detailed, directed, and often private, otherwise inaccessible information. Information and opinions that a respondent would feel uncomfortable describing in an e-mail or that would be too complex for a telephone survey can often be addressed in an intensive interview. The personal contact that occurs during an interview allows for rapport to develop between the interviewer and the respondent; over the course of the interview, trust grows and the interviewee is more likely to discuss the issues of interest. Moreover, the respondent sets aside a greater amount of time for a personal interview than for telephone or mail surveys or for e-mail communications. More time allows for more detailed data than can be accessed by other means.

Interviews are not appropriate for all research questions. Obviously, the process is extremely time-consuming. Along with the time spent on the interview itself, the researcher needs to factor in the possibility that respondents will have difficulties fitting the interview into their busy schedules. This issue can lead to delays in data-gathering. Given the demands placed on both the researcher's and the respondents' time, interviews should not be used when the necessary information can be more efficiently obtained through other means.

It is important to always keep in mind that interviewing is reactive: the respondents are aware that their answers will be used in a research study, and this awareness may lead them to alter the information given. People do not wish to look unknowledgeable and prefer to be seen in the best possible light. The desires for self-promotion and self-protection can lead people to embellish or downplay certain issues; the temptation to act as one's own spin doctor is great. In addition, interviewees may mislead, lie, or present information that they believe to be true but is in fact erroneous. Thus, a researcher might collect data that are either partially or completely false. If a respondent reports that the majority of Canadians support a carbon tax, the onus is on the researcher to verify the fact, in this case, by exploring opinion poll data.

The first step in interview research is to figure out who you want to interview. Which individuals have the information to answer your research questions? You may generate this list based on job descriptions (e.g. public managers, members of Parliament, leaders of non-profit organizations), memberships (members of political parties or interest groups), social groups, or other criteria suited to your research question. Interview research is almost always based on non-probability sampling, with a relatively small number of cases selected. Because of the limited number of cases, researchers typically use purposive sampling, carefully selecting individuals to interview.

Your next task is to contact potential respondents and request an interview. One strategy that can be effective is to first contact the individual in writing and then follow up by telephone. It may be easier to get a response from potential respondents if you are able to mention an individual whom they know, mention an organizational affiliation, and/or write the letter on organizational letterhead. (You must be certain that you have clear permission from the noted individual and organization before you do so.) In your written communication, be certain to clarify the purpose of the discussion and the anticipated length of the interview. It may require a number of attempts before you are able to schedule an interview with a respondent. If, after you follow up by telephone, a potential respondent fails to respond to your request, Pierce (2008, 121) suggests that you "write again. Attach a copy of your earlier letter. Be gently persistent." In following up in such cases, it is important to be cautious not to badger or annoy the individual or his or her staff. Similarly, if a potential respondent declines your request, accept the refusal gracefully and do not attempt to convince him or her.

Bardach (2009, 92–3) suggests that researchers be strategic when they schedule interviews over the research process. Individuals who are likely to be helpful or particularly knowledgeable should be interviewed in the early stages of your research because they can direct you to additional sources and may provide access to both information and people. Individuals who are likely to be very busy or potentially hostile should be interviewed at a later stage, allowing you to go into the interview as informed as possible.

Before conducting the interview, it is important to be clear on the data you are seeking. Interview time can pass quickly, and many respondents are fascinating people; the interview time might expire before you have obtained all the necessary information. As we stated earlier, time is scarce for many people, researcher and respondent alike. For these reasons, it is advisable to have an **interview framework** before entering an interview. The framework is merely a set of questions to ask the respondent. Using a framework keeps you on track during the interview and ensures that you ask the core questions in each interview. This practice allows you to compare answers provided by different respondents. That said, you will still be flexible during the interview, inserting questions as they fit naturally into the discussion (rather than necessarily sticking to a preset ordering) and inserting additional questions when necessary. The framework is only a guide to aid the interview rather than a strict outline that must be followed absolutely. It also provides a useful cue to interviewees that their time is not being wasted by inadequate preparation and that you are not making it up as you go along.

How do you create a framework? Start by asking yourself the following questions: What do I want to know? What topics need to be addressed? What issues are of less importance? In essence, you must distinguish between what knowledge is wanted and what knowledge is needed, ensuring that the questions tapping needs are given higher priority than the questions addressing wants.

To ask productive questions, you need to have a basic familiarity with the subject matter and context. You should learn as much as possible on your own prior to the interview and incorporate this learning into your interview framework. Doing so creates personal credibility and demonstrates respect for your respondent's time. It may make you aware of major controversies or sensitivities and thus allow you to avoid missteps or gaffes during the interview. An additional advantage of doing background research is that it allows you to learn the language relevant to your research question. Understanding and using the appropriate terminology establishes rapport and reduces the "interviewer as outsider" tone (Putt and Springer 1989, 148).

Question ordering is important. The initial questions should lead into the subject area without threatening the respondent in any way; you may opt to start with simple, factual questions that the respondent can answer with relative ease. Difficult, controversial, or sensitive questions should be left for later in the interview, after a sense of rapport and comfort has had a chance to build. Always aim to end the interview on a positive, or at least neutral, note by asking more neutral questions (Patton and Sawicki 1993, 102). Woliver (2002, 677) recommends ending interviews with broad questions, such as "Is there anything you would like to tell me about which I haven't thought to ask you?" This approach allows the respondent to bring unexpected information to your attention.

Ensure that the questions are clear and not phrased in ways that lead the respondent. As the goal is to promote discussion, questions that can be answered in a yes–no or other abrupt manner should be avoided. You should also plan segues between discussion topics and probes (follow-up questions) to provide direction and encourage more comments.

Besides drawing up an interview framework, you should prepare by investigating the background of the interviewee. The purpose of this step is twofold. First, it gives insights into the personality and style of the interviewee. Rapport is formed most easily when we confront people who are similar to us in dress and energy; if you are aware that your interviewee is extremely formal in speech and dress, matching him or her on these details can help build the initial comfort level of the interview. Second, background research helps prevent wasting interview time on information that can be found elsewhere; for example, the interviewee's position in the government and the duties associated with that position might be found in public records. The interviewee has every reason to assume that you have done your homework before conducting the interview; a researcher who devotes considerable interview time to information that can be easily found elsewhere may annoy individuals who see their time as scarce.

Interviews should be prescheduled to ensure that the interviewee has sufficient time to spend with you. At the beginning of the interview, briefly explain the purpose of the meeting and take care that the information provided does not reveal your specific hypotheses, should you have any. Recall that one problem with interviewing is that the process is subject to reaction: respondents consciously or unconsciously alter their behaviour and responses to fit the researcher's expectations, resulting in biased data. During the interview, avoid leading interviewees with your body language or facial expressions. If you show disapproval at certain types of statements, interviewees may begin to guard their statements.

Meticulous notes should be taken throughout the interview, regardless of whether you make an electronic recording. Recordings may have technical or sound problems (e.g. inaudible statements) and cannot capture non-verbal communication such as body language. The interviewee's body language and voice intonation can prove as interesting as his or her statements; it is useful to note if the respondent became nervous when a particular topic was broached or scowled when a certain name was mentioned. If you use a recording device, you must first secure the interviewee's consent. When taking notes, be as clear and thorough as possible—if a statement is particularly important, record it word by word so you can quote verbatim. Write up your notes and transcribe the recording as soon as possible after the interview. It takes very little time for the memory of the interview to fade, particularly if you are interviewing more than one person.

Expand Your Knowledge

Interviews and Sample Size

A perennial question in qualitative research and particularly interview research is, "How many cases are enough?" With quantitative research based on probability sampling, answering such a question is relatively simple: we consider the population size, determine our desired margin of error and confidence level, and use existing statistical tables or online sample size calculators to determine a precise number. This approach clearly does not apply with non-probability sampling and qualitative research.

To examine the issue of sample sizes with qualitative interviewing, Sarah Elsie Baker and Rosalind Edwards (2012) consulted 19 social scientists for their opinions and advice. Not surprisingly, the study's respondents argue that researchers should focus on the quality of information being obtained rather than on the number of interviews completed. One common suggestion is that researchers stop interviewing once they have reached **data saturation**, the point at which the interviews no longer provide the researcher with new relevant information. In the words of one respondent, Harry Wolcott, "In general the old rule seems to hold that you keep asking as long as you are getting different answers, and that is a reminder that with our little samples we can't establish frequencies but we should be able to find the RANGE of responses" (as quoted in Baker and Edwards 2012, 3–4; capitals in original). Overall, the scholars consulted feel that the appropriate number of interviews depends upon factors such as research objectives and resources.

Interviewing skills take time and practice to develop. Although it may appear simple in theory, interview research can be challenging. That being said, interview research skills are a valuable skill set for political scientists, and it is worth taking the time to learn how to conduct interviews effectively.

APPLY YOUR UNDERSTANDING

Constructing an Interview Framework

Suppose that you are investigating if male and female candidates enter politics for similar reasons. As part of your research design, you have decided that interviews are essential. But whom would you interview and why? Outline the topics you would wish to explore in the interview. What questions could be used to get the information you need? Draft an interview framework.

Focus Groups

When hearing the term *focus group*, many people immediately think of market research, in which a small group sits in a room and discusses the pros and cons of a product. Is it too harsh? Too bright? Too expensive? Focus groups are also important research tools for policy research, political parties, and campaign organizers. They enable researchers to probe beneath the surface of public opinion, to explore what people really like or dislike about political parties, leaders, policies, or advertisements.

While a questionnaire in a survey research project may get hundreds and perhaps thousands of individuals to address a topic for a few minutes, a focus group will pull a small handful of people together to discuss the same topic in a structured conversation for an extended period (usually one to two hours). Focus groups are not designed to be representative but to bring together a group of individuals to discuss a specific product or issue at length and in depth. For instance, in her study of rural women's political participation, Louise Carbert (2006) conducted 14 focus groups with a total of 126 women in Atlantic Canada. The focus group approach allowed for a more fulsome understanding of women's political engagement.

There are numerous advantages to focus group research: "focus groups are an economical, fast, and efficient method for obtaining data from multiple participants," and the social aspect of focus groups can promote discussion and information sharing (Onwuegbuzie et al. 2009, 2). Focus groups can provide a useful complement to conventional survey research. They allow the researcher to dig beneath the surface opinion captured by the larger survey, to probe for details and nuance. Gupta (2001, 164) writes, "Focus groups can shed light on complex areas of public policies and other important issues that might be missed by a survey, which can be too structured." Luntz (1994) presents a similar argument: "Unlike traditional quantitative research, focus groups are centrally concerned with *understanding* attitudes rather than *measuring* them" (emphasis in original).

Although focus groups present a number of research advantages, they are more appropriate to some research questions (and some types of research subjects) than to others. Carey and Asbury (2012, 16, 18) argue that focus groups are a suitable technique when "members are knowledgeable, willing, and capable of communicating; the topic and group setting are compatible to group interaction; and the group facilitator has adequate skills. . . . However, when group rapport and trust cannot be established, the data collection will be too compromised to be of value." Without trust within the group, individuals may either censor their statements or start to conform to the dominant group opinions, limiting the value of the focus group data (Ibid., 30). Trust can be a particular issue if individuals within the group know each other outside the focus group setting. For example, if participants work together, they may have reasonable concern that comments made within the focus group may be repeated within their work environment.

Focus groups typically have 6 to 12 participants; "[t]he rationale for this range of focus group size stems from the goal that focus groups should include enough participants to yield diversity in information provided, yet they should not include too many participants because large groups can create an environment where participants do not feel comfortable sharing their thoughts, opinions, beliefs and experiences" (Onwuegbuzie et al. 2009, 3). The composition of the focus group can be key to its success. Homogenous groups often work best. Luntz (1994) writes,

> Human behavioral studies have consistently proven that people will reveal their innermost thoughts only to those they believe share a common bond. For example, if your goal is to study the real, in-depth *feelings* of whites and blacks toward affirmative action, welfare, or crime, you cannot have an integrated focus group. Similarly, women will not talk freely and emotionally about abortion if men (including a male moderator) are present. This is just a fact of life. (Emphasis in original.)

Likewise, Smithson (2000, 116) argues,

> A particular strength of the [focus group] methodology is the possibility for research participants to develop ideas collectively, bringing forward their own priorities and perspectives . . . Participants themselves use the groups in ways not always anticipated by the researcher. This can be especially useful for highlighting issues for disadvantaged or minority groups by validating and publicizing their views, although this only works when these 'minorities' form the majority within a focus group.

Typically, a focus group will have both a moderator (also known as a facilitator) and a note-taker, to allow the moderator to focus his or her attention on the ongoing discussion.

Focus groups are often videotaped (to allow for study of group dynamics and non-verbal communication, such as body language) or audio recorded and then transcribed for the purposes of qualitative data analysis. As ensuring trust is key to a successful focus group, logistical details such as the physical space (including room size and furniture layout) are important considerations. Participants are typically offered some type of food and beverage: "Food is a surprisingly important aspect. . . . Food facilitates presession conversation and provides group members with something to do. The presession chatting, often around the food table, helps break the ice socially, but more important, it allows the facilitator to observe the members' characteristics and to arrange optimal seating" (Carey and Asbury 2012, 47). With regards to seating, Carey and Asbury note that facilitators may wish to sit next to more dominant personalities (to better control their participation) and across from more quiet personalities (to allow for better eye contact).

Running a focus group effectively is a challenging task. Managing the interpersonal dynamics and drawing out opinions without imposing the researcher's own biases are art forms in themselves. The moderator begins the session by providing a short introduction that establishes the purpose of the session, sets group rules that will guide the discussion (such as speaking order), and outlines ethics considerations (such as how data will be protected). Once the discussion begins, questions are open-ended and the moderator must guide the group discussion to remain focused on the topic. To do so, he or she must be clear about the goals of the focus group; he or she will have a number of scripted questions and prompts but will be flexible in moving between them as the conversation naturally unfolds.

Moreover, the moderator must be flexible in allowing the discussion to veer off course on occasion, as such tangents may allow for unanticipated but valuable information. The moderator must manage the group to ensure that one or two participants do not dominate the discussion and must be aware of "the tendency for certain types of socially acceptable opinion to emerge" over the course of discussion (Smithson 2000, 116). Focus groups typically conclude with an overarching question that allows participants to raise any final issues: "It can be very useful for facilitators to ask a last question that often elicits the most important data, because members are engaged in the topic and rapport has been established. A common phrasing is, 'If you could tell the people in charge just one thing, what would it be?'" (Carey and Asbury 2012, 54).

Focus groups are often combined (or triangulated) with other methodologies, such as surveys. Focus group research is also used to provide context and community perspective around a broader issue. For instance, in their assessment of the Vancouver food system, Barbolet et al. (2005) conducted focus groups with "workers in and clients of the City's charitable food resources," analyzed municipal and provincial food security documents, and developed and mapped a database of food resources.

The non-random selection of focus group participants makes generalizations to larger populations hazardous at best. Chapter 2 noted that qualitative approaches such as focus groups seek results that are transferable and in some way applicable to other environments rather than results that are necessarily representative of the larger population. As Copsey (2008, 9) argues, "those who dismiss focus groups as too 'soft' and unrepresentative to be of use misunderstand their purpose. Focus groups . . . complement quantitative data."

Observation Research

One problem with research instruments such as interviews and surveys is that they leave the researcher dependent upon reported behaviours. At times, there can be significant disjunctures between reported and actual behaviour, in part because many things have normative social value. Because voting is seen as a social responsibility, many people claim to have voted when in fact they did not. Often the respondent truly believes he or she engaged in a particular action—for example, voting for the popular winning party rather than the "losers"—when he or she actually did not. The possibility of faulty recall is particularly high for past events; as the months and years go by, we can forget whom we voted for, how many news programs we watched, and even what organizations we supported financially. This situation is an example of the background noise that is common to empirical research in political science and that can lessen the power of statistical analyses.

In addition to problems of reporting false behaviour, there is a tendency to over- and underestimate certain behaviours. Let's say you ask Nathan how many hours he studies every day. He reports four hours of concentrated study per day, yet his grades are much lower than classmates who study for the same amount of time. You wonder what is going on, so you decide to watch Nathan study. Something interesting emerges: although he does indeed spend four hours in the library, much of that time is spent doing activities other than studying. Nathan spends 10 minutes arranging his papers, goes on three 20-minute coffee breaks, checks social media regularly, stops studying to check all incoming e-mail and text messages, and devotes almost a full hour to rewriting his class notes (a highly inefficient study technique). When all these factors are considered, he has actually devoted less than two hours to effective studying and has exaggerated his study time by 100 per cent. When we observe actual behaviour rather than rely solely on reported behaviour, we are conducting **observation research**.

Observation research (also known as field research and ethnography) has the advantage that the events of interest occur in natural circumstances, which means that the external validity of our study can be quite high. We engage in observation research on a casual basis in our everyday lives; people-watching can be an enjoyable pastime. Observation allows us to explore interpersonal dynamics, and it is therefore useful for studying group dynamics and political processes. In such research, we pay particular attention to context; cultural settings and power relations figure prominently.

Observation research can be obtrusive or unobtrusive (Manheim et al. 2002, 332). **Obtrusive observation** occurs when the subjects are aware that they are being observed. In private forums or small group settings where the researcher's presence is sure to be noticed, research must be overt—the researcher informs the subjects that they are being observed as part of a research project. For instance, a researcher may receive permission to sit in on a committee session and watch the dynamics: who speaks and for how long, what are the responses, what is the mood, and so on. Of course, reaction problems are a possibility because, if the subjects know that they are being watched, they may begin to alter their behaviour. This phenomenon is known as the **Hawthorne effect**. To minimize this effect, the researcher must take care not to reveal the study's hypotheses or to take extensive notes. The goal is for the group or individual to proceed with their activities as if the researcher were not there, which requires the researcher to be as inconspicuous as possible. If the researcher is taking detailed notes, his or her presence is felt more readily. For this reason, the researcher should develop extensive notes immediately after the observations have been completed for the day.

Unobtrusive observation occurs when the subjects are unaware of the researcher; they do not know about the research study and proceed with their activities in a normal manner. For example, a researcher might sit in Parliament and observe MPs' behaviour without informing the members. When the forum is public, this method can be the best way to conduct observation research.

Expand Your Knowledge

The Hawthorne Effect

The Hawthorne effect is named after a famous set of experiments that took place in Hawthorne, Illinois (near Chicago) in the 1920s and 1930s at a factory owned by Western Electric. The experiments' original purpose was to determine whether changes to the physical conditions of workers—including improved lighting, more rest breaks, and altered working hours—affected their productivity. Each time one of the work conditions improved, productivity increased.

The researchers then began to change the working conditions so that they were worse (the lights were dimmed, breaks reduced, etc.). They found that, even when working conditions deteriorated, productivity gains were not lost. The conclusion from the research was that it was not necessarily the type of change in conditions that led to increased productivity as much as the fact that the workers were aware that they were being studied.

As a result of the Hawthorne effect, it is common for researchers to introduce controls, such as the use of a control group that receives either no treatment or treatment with a placebo (no treatment disguised as a treatment), to ensure that the results are not confounded by participants' expectations (for more on control groups and placebos, see Chapter 11).

One particular type of unobtrusive observation research is **participant observation**. In this strategy, the researcher becomes part of the community being observed. To study the dynamics among political campaign staff, he or she may volunteer for a campaign. One advantage of participant observation is that it allows for greater understanding of context: by becoming a member of the group, one has maximum access to that group's beliefs and world paradigm. An action may have significantly different meaning in a particular group context than in the world at large, and in some cases being a member of the group is the only way that a researcher can access this information. Finally, there are some subgroups that can be accessed only through covert participant observation. Consider a sociologist exploring a particular religious cult or a police officer investigating drug smuggling. Neither group could be penetrated unless the researcher assumed the identity of a group member.

Participant observation is very context-driven and less structured than other forms of observation research. As with other forms of observation research, note-taking should be kept to a minimum in the presence of the research subjects. In the case of covert observation, note-taking might be restricted to times when the researcher is completely removed from the subjects.

For participant observation to work effectively, the researcher must be accepted into the group. The process of building trust and rapport can be time-consuming, but it is necessary for valid data. To access extremely sensitive information, the researcher must obtain high levels of trust and respect in the group, which can involve adopting the dress, speech patterns, social interests, and personal style of group members. The researcher needs to not only "talk the talk" but also "walk the walk" if he or she is to be trusted with group secrets and viewpoints. In some cases, assuming the status as a group member can be a difficult task. In the late 1950s, John Griffin sought to study the black community of New Orleans. A white man, he used drugs prescribed by a dermatologist to darken his skin and shaved his head to conceal his straight hair. He then experienced life as a black man and recounted his experiences in the classic *Black Like Me* (1977).

Participant observation carries a number of risks. First, certain forms may put the researcher at physical risk should his or her purposes be discovered. After the publication of his study, Griffin was hanged in effigy and his family harassed. A second risk comes from the association with the group. Let's imagine that a researcher studying neo-Nazism in Canada joins a neo-Nazi group. After completing the study, he or she will always be plagued by that association; if the situation is taken out of context, he or she may be seen as a true supporter of the group. Some affiliations can be difficult to shake and may be used to damage the researcher's credibility. In 1963, Gloria Steinem took a job as a Playboy Bunny (a waitress position, not a Playmate, which is a nude model) to investigate how women were treated in the Playboy clubs. Later, Steinem became a leader in the mainstream feminist movement, and the former Bunny association, taken out of context, proved at times a liability. She reports "[c]ontinuing publishing by *Playboy* magazine of my employee photograph as a Bunny amid ever more pornographic photos of other Bunnies.

The 1983 version [of the Steinem photo] insists in a caption that my article 'boosted Bunny recruiting'" (1983, 69).

A third potential problem with participant observation involves exiting the group. It is possible that one can do such a good job convincing others of group status that disengagement is problematic. The researcher may have developed friendships that are difficult to leave. Finally, the researcher faces the risk of becoming so entrenched in a group and so identified with its positions that objectivity is lost (Chadwick, Bahr, and Albrecht 1984, 214). Sympathy for the group and its causes may lead researchers to forget why they are

Expand Your Knowledge

Participant Observation with the Reform, Canadian Alliance, and Conservative Parties

It should come as no surprise that many political scientists move back and forth between the study and practice of politics. Indeed, much of the richness and excitement of the social sciences in general comes from this interplay. Political scientists have a wide array of applied skills and knowledge: they have substantive expertise, an ability to write and to think analytically, often a detailed understanding of the public policy process, and, in many cases, a comprehensive grasp of empirical research methodologies. In this last case, they know how to collect data, orchestrate surveys, design questionnaires, and make complex data stand up and sing for diverse sets of clients.

However, participant observation means more than applying or marketing one's analytical skills. It entails working for governments, parties, interest groups, social movements, or community associations with the objective of improving one's understanding of the political process. Participant observation, therefore, goes well beyond providing a source of anecdotes and illustrations to use in class.

Tom Flanagan, a (now retired) professor from the Department of Political Science at the University of Calgary, has considerable experience working with political parties. From 1991 to 1992, he was the director of policy, strategy, and communications for the Reform Party of Canada. Flanagan's experiences were woven into his 1995 book *Waiting for the Wave: The Reform Party and Preston Manning.* (A second edition was released in 2009.) The book draws on Flanagan's participant observation and goes well beyond his direct experience in providing a detailed historical account of the party and a theoretical treatment of the Reform party's place in the Canadian political landscape.

Flanagan also worked with Stephen Harper for a number of years, first with the Canadian Alliance and then with the Conservative Party. He retired from the latter after the 2006 election, when Harper became prime minister. He has written about his experiences with these parties in *Harper's Team: Behind the Scenes in the Conservative Rise to Power* (2007; updated in 2009).

there and, rather than provide a balanced analysis of the group, turn them into apologists. This bias may lead to dubious conclusions.

Observation research, be it obtrusive or unobtrusive, can vary in the degree to which it is structured. When observation is unstructured, the researcher typically is not looking for any particular patterns; the research is mostly inductive and exploratory. However, even with unstructured research, the observer should develop a number of areas that he or she wishes to explore and that will help direct the study by leading him or her to pay greater attention to particular issues and dynamics. In unstructured observations, data are collected as **field notes**, detailed descriptions of events and their subjective meanings.

More structured (and thus more quantitative) research is necessary for hypothesis-testing. In this research, the observer considers only the actions that occur. Prior to the observations, he or she draws up an **observation schedule**, which is essentially a checklist for recording behaviour. In our study of parliamentary behaviour, we might create a checklist for who spoke and for how long. Our prior research has suggested ways to classify behaviours; all we do during the observation research is note frequencies of behaviour. After the session, we examine the data to see if the results fit our hypotheses.

When creating the observation schedule, we must ensure that our indicators are clear; if we leave categories broadly defined, we may have trouble deciding if a given behaviour fits into a particular category. For example, imagine that you are observing a city council session to see if female politicians are more consensual than their male colleagues. How are you going to determine what counts as "consensual" behaviour? Will voice tone be included? Efforts to compromise? An explicit desire to avoid arguments? Clearly, observing consensual behaviour can be quite subjective if specific indicators of such behaviour are not included. In addition, if we do not have clearly defined ideas of what a given behaviour is, we may be inconsistent between observations. At one council meeting, we may be in a good mood and see everything as efforts to compromise. At a meeting later in the week, after a long day that included a minor car accident and getting yelled at by a co-worker, the world may not seem so rosy and very little actions might be seen as consensual. Using specific indicators of behaviour can help overcome such problems; researchers should first operationalize their key concepts to develop valid measures and should ensure that the categories available are mutually exclusive and exhaustive (that all possible categories are included in the schedule).

Overall, **observational designs** are an important means by which researchers can explore what really happens in groups. They give the role of context its due and provide a richer understanding of social dynamics. However, the method requires a great deal of the researcher's time: it is not a method for the uncommitted! In the realm of politics, there are a number of areas that are not open to observation, such as cabinet dynamics. In such cases, researchers must rely on first-hand accounts through elite interviewing or written documentation.

APPLY YOUR UNDERSTANDING

Constructing an Observation Schedule

Your task is to explore the interpersonal dynamics of political science professors at the annual faculty retreat. You suspect that, as seniority increases, faculty members are more likely to raise "thorny" issues and vigorously defend their positions. In other words, you suspect that a sessional instructor will not raise such issues but that an associate professor will and that the assistant professor is more likely to back down than is the full professor. Develop your schedule and identify your key concepts. How will you define *thorny issues*? How will you categorize the faculty? What will constitute raising and/or supporting an issue?

Ethics and Qualitative Research

As noted in Chapter 6, it is important to ensure that research participants are not harmed as a result of your research. Doing so may include protecting the participant's identity, which can be a particular concern with qualitative approaches. With interviewing and focus groups, the researcher must clarify prior to the data collection if data will be attributed to the individual or if identities will be concealed in the reporting. Protection of identities for individuals holding public office is not required if the individual agrees to an on-the-record interview and if that agreement is conveyed through signed consent that explicitly waives anonymity. Although the researcher should do his or her best to ensure confidentiality in focus groups, he or she is unable to promise the same degree that one would expect with an interview, given that focus groups involve multiple people. For this reason, focus groups are often not appropriate for the discussion of sensitive information.

Regardless of your approach, it is important to be clear and honest about the purpose of your research. This practice not only ensures more ethical research but also facilitates your current and future research. Bardach (2009, 77) writes,

> Your informants will often be acquainted with one another and will occasionally talk among themselves about you and your work. Since you want such discussions to serve your interests rather than to work against them, you should try to develop a reputation as a competent, knowledgeable, and energetic researcher who is likely to produce something of intellectual or political significance. The best way to develop such a reputation is to actually be such a person.

Working as a Team

1. With a partner, conduct a mock 10-minute interview. (Yes, you will feel ridiculous doing so, but push through it!) One partner will assume the role of a provincial deputy minister of health and the other the role of the researcher who is interested in why the government has not committed to building a new children's hospital in your city, despite public pressure to do so.
2. After the interview, share your thoughts on the following:
   a. Interviewer: How difficult was it to take notes and conduct the interview at the same time? What note-taking strategies would you adopt in the future?
   b. Interviewee: Where there any questions that you felt unable or unwilling to answer as a senior public servant? If so, why? How might the interviewer have reworded the question to get the information he or she needed?
3. With your group, brainstorm five political science research questions that could be examined by using observation research. Select one question and discuss how you would design your observational study. What type of observation research (obtrusive or unobtrusive) would you use? Discuss the extent to which your study would be limited by political, practical, or ethical considerations.

Self-Study

1. Your research project is to explore the leadership style of a prominent young politician with a reputation for his or her confrontational approach to politics. How could you use interviewing to gain insights into this style? Whom would you interview? What questions would you ask?
2. Imagine that you are considering how environmental and business interests in your province perceive current water protection policies. You are planning to use focus groups to inform your research. How many focus groups would you hold? Would you distinguish among types of business interests (e.g. agricultural, energy, manufacturing)? What types of questions would you ask? Would the questions differ across the focus groups? Why or why not?

CHAPTER 10

Survey Research and Official Statistics

Destination

By the end of this chapter, you should be able to

- describe how researchers use survey data to assess social trends and measure public opinion;
- outline the advantages and disadvantages of using various means of gathering survey research data;
- explain the attention that should be focused on issues such as question type and question wording;
- outline the advantages and limitations of using secondary data and official statistics; and
- explain the distinction between aggregate and individual data.

Survey research, including telephone, Internet (or web-based) mail, and (less frequently) face-to-face surveys, is a major component of quantitative social research. In addition to providing a great deal of the empirical database for the social sciences, surveys inform political and social commentary in the media. Survey research is a ubiquitous feature of modern life, from massive pre-election polls to the notice that "four out of five dentists surveyed recommend sugarless gum for their patients who chew gum." It is difficult to read an issue of a major newspaper without running across one or more stories that draw on survey "evidence" of some sort or another.

Public opinion polls are used for insight into everything from voting and consumer behaviour to public policy preferences and sexual behaviour. They offer important glimpses into how the average Canadian, the mythical "person in the street," sees the world. In so doing, they enable us to compare our own beliefs, values, and preferences to societal norms. Are we typical, different, or even deviant compared with our neighbours, colleagues, and fellow citizens? Polls provide us with a point of comparison, a standard against which we can place our own worldviews. We can judge whether we sleep more, drink less, exercise more frequently, watch more television, or have fewer pets than others around us do. We can compare the values and beliefs of Canadians to those of other nationalities. We assume, not always correctly, that polls offer a broader, less biased insight into the world than we can get by talking to friends, neighbours, and colleagues.

But surveys do more than enable us to compare our beliefs and behaviour to others. They are used by a diverse set of individuals and organizations to gain insight into the attitudes and behaviour of citizens. Governments are active consumers of survey research, particularly with respect to identifying the public's policy preferences, and assessments of program initiatives. Generally, the expectation is that there is a distinction between government's polling of attitudes toward policy issues and the more partisan polling in which political parties may be engaged with assessments of attitudes toward political leaders and the parties. Public attitudes toward policy preferences are also of interest to non-governmental organizations, interest groups, think-tanks, and industry, as each is involved at various points in the public policy process. News organizations are another significant consumer of survey research, particularly on matters relating to the "horse race" character of politics, knowing which party is ahead in public preferences at any given time, which leader is most popular, and the like. Similarly, political parties and individual candidates (either for leadership or in a constituency election) often rely on public opinion polls to measure their relative standing with the electorate. Indeed, contemporary Canadian politics is positively infused with survey research data and analysis.

Ideally, and if ethical guidelines were to permit, the researcher would like to peer inside people's heads without disturbing their thoughts. In practice, however, doing so is impossible. No matter how skillfully designed questions might be, they do disrupt pre-existing patterns of thought, and clumsy questions cause even more disruption. Respondents can be highly sensitive to the research environment and, in the case of in-person or telephone surveys, may react to the physical (including voice) characteristics and mannerisms of the interviewer, particularly if the interview touches on sensitive topics. In such a context, respondents may watch or listen to the interviewer to try to gauge how their answers are received and then tailor later responses to produce a more favourable social response from the interviewer. This general phenomenon is known as the **interviewer effect** and is more problematic than one might expect.

There is also a concern that, in some cases, survey research may create opinion as much as measure it. In an interview, as in other social situations, there is an innate desire to please.

As we stated in previous chapters, respondents may make up answers to questions they have never thought about because they are unwilling to display a lack of knowledge or are simply trying to be helpful.

Even if we are measuring rather than creating, we are often measuring the potential profile of opinion should an issue emerge for public debate. Thus, when you read about a survey that concludes that 48 per cent of Canadians believe X or would prefer Y, do not assume that some 16 million individuals are carrying those beliefs or preferences in a conscious, active way. A more appropriate interpretation of the poll would be to conclude that, if all Canadians were in fact confronted with the question posed to the survey respondents, close to 16 million would likely believe X or opt for Y.

In this context, we should never assume that public opinion is or should be translated in some immediate or automatic fashion into public policy. Public opinion is only one element in an extremely complicated political process; it is sifted and weighed by political actors who must take into account the general distribution of opinion and the intensity with which particular views are held and by whom they are held. Governments, moreover, not only are influenced by public opinion but also seek to shape it as it relates to matters of public policy.

Furthermore, when we encounter polls on voting intentions, we must keep in mind that the popular vote is filtered through an electoral system that does not faithfully translate votes into legislative seats. To know, for example, that the Liberal and Conservative parties each have 30 per cent of the national vote (in terms of individuals' stated vote intentions) in a recent poll tells us little about how well they might do in terms of seats; it all depends on where the respective party support is concentrated, on the extent to which Canadians turn out to vote, and on whether they vote the way that they said they would. Surveys, therefore, provide a valuable window on the political process, but they provide far less than the complete picture.

Conducting survey research can be a very complex undertaking. In essence, however, virtually all survey research follows a similar template. We begin with a population in which we have some research interest, such as Canadian voters, supporters of a particular party, members of an interest group or religious faith, female MPs, or holders of a specific ideological orientation. We then devise means to draw a sample from this larger population; Chapter 8 discussed a variety of ways to sample, some good and some bad. The next step, examined in Chapters 4 and 5, is to come up with a set of questions to measure the underlying concepts, values, or beliefs in which we are interested. We may want to supplement the empirical information with more qualitative data as well; selected means of doing so were covered in Chapter 9. Once the survey data are in hand, they must be tabulated and described. Then we find a way of working back from the sample data to the population in which we are interested. Here, the tools of descriptive and inferential statistics, discussed in Chapters 14 through 17, are indispensable.

Survey Data Collection Options

Survey data collection can take many forms: face-to-face, telephone, mail, and Internet. Most people are most familiar with telephone and Internet surveys, but the face-to-face and mail types continue to be used for survey data collection. Each approach has its strengths and limitations.

Face-to-face surveys provide the most versatile methodology because respondents can be presented with a mix of question formats and visual aids. These surveys are known as paper and pencil interviewing (PAPI) when responses are recorded by hand and as computer-assisted personal interviewing (CAPI) when responses are recorded onto a computer. The direct human contact can result in higher response rates and permit longer surveys, as respondents may be more inclined to complete a survey when the interviewer is directly in front of them. At the same time, face-to-face interviews may be most prone to the interviewer effect.

Expand Your Knowledge

Surveys on Aboriginal Populations

Although political scientists are often interested in studying the behaviour and attitudes of subpopulations, doing so can be challenging with survey research because of issues of sample size. The study of Aboriginal political participation presents a good example of these challenges. Aboriginal Canadians are a growing population; the 2011 National Household Survey found that over 1.4 million Canadians reported Aboriginal identity (Statistics Canada 2014b, 6). However, Aboriginal people remain a relatively small percentage (4.3 per cent) of the overall Canadian population and, in a survey based on random sampling, the number of Aboriginal respondents is typically too low to allow for meaningful analysis. This is particularly true if researchers wish to control for geography (province of residence; urban, rural, and on-reserve populations) and/or population (First Nation, Métis, and Inuit). An additional challenge for research is that Aboriginal Canadians, especially urban Aboriginal populations, can be harder to access with telephone surveys.

Because of these data restrictions, empirical studies of Aboriginal political participation in Canada are limited. Yet researchers are increasingly using Aboriginal oversamples and Aboriginal-specific surveys to fill the knowledge gaps. In 2009, the Environics Institute conducted the Urban Aboriginal Peoples Study, in which Aboriginal interviewers conducted face-to-face interviews with 2,614 urban Aboriginal peoples living in large Canadian cities (Environics Institute 2010). The face-to-face approach, combined with snowball sampling, allowed the researcher to include hard-to-reach populations such as the homeless and those with temporary housing.

These surveys are less frequently used than other forms because they are expensive and can be difficult to conduct in a security-conscious environment where people are uneasy about admitting strangers into their homes. Examples of face-to-face surveys include Statistics Canada's Canadian Community Health Survey, which combines CAPI with telephone data collection approaches, and the standard Eurobarometer, a face-to-face survey of approximately 1,000 individuals in each of 34 European countries.

Telephone surveys are the most common format for contemporary survey research. They are less expensive than face-to-face surveys and, when coupled with computer-assisted telephone interviewing (CATI) technologies, provide for question versatility, quick data summaries, and speedy analysis. Telephone surveys avoid some of the security problems confronted by the face-to-face format, although voice mail and call-screening are causing new and potentially serious problems for locating respondents. There are numerous examples of telephone surveys, including Statistics Canada's General Social Survey (GSS) and the Canadian Elections Studies (CES)' campaign period and post-election surveys.

Mail surveys provide an even less expensive way of conducting survey research. Mail questionnaires can be longer and more complex than telephone surveys and can include visual presentations, such as images or symbols. One advantage of mail surveys is that the respondent may be more willing to address controversial questions honestly, since there is no interviewer present (in person or in voice) to make judgments. Interviewer effects are therefore eliminated. An important disadvantage is that researchers cannot be certain that the individual completing the survey is the individual for whom the survey was intended. Another disadvantage is that, in cases where the survey question may be unclear, the respondent is unable to pose clarification questions to the interviewer. The CES often combine detailed telephone interviews with follow-up mail surveys.

Internet surveys (also known as web or online surveys) have increased in popularity tremendously in the past decade, particularly because survey companies have developed groups of people (known as panels) to serve as members of an ongoing pool of respondents who can be contacted relatively easily and inexpensively. Early trials of Internet surveys in the 1990s tended to produce disappointing results because the portion of the population that had ready access to the Internet was both limited and highly skewed in favour of young people. As online access has spread and the user group has become much more diverse, survey firms increasingly look to it for survey respondents. The advantages of this survey method are that it is relatively inexpensive to administer and that it potentially offers a rapid turnaround between the time that the survey is released and the time that the responses are gathered. In addition, the survey instrument can be designed with fairly complex questions. The most significant disadvantage is the challenge associated with securing a representative sample. Not only is there self-selection bias among online survey responders, but the sampling frame may also be sufficiently distorted so that the resulting sample is unrepresentative. With appropriate weighting of the sample, at least some of the distortion can be mitigated. The 2011 CES included a web survey, and the

Comparative Provincial Election Project conducted online surveys after each provincial election in the 2011–14 period.

These four survey techniques have been adapted to incorporate commercial research opportunities and limited research budgets through the use of **omnibus surveys**, which allow researchers to add a few questions to a larger survey. Many commercial firms conduct regular national surveys with standard demographic questions and some questions of particular interest to the firm. The rest of the questionnaire space is then sold to clients, including private firms, government departments, interest groups, political parties, think-tanks, and academics. A single omnibus survey may have questions on a wide range of disjointed topics: voting intentions, consumer preferences, reactions to government policy initiatives, and lifestyle issues. The disadvantage to academic researchers is that they do not know the context in which their questions are being asked; the advantage is a tremendous cost-saving, since the expense of the national survey is spread over a number of clients.

Across all survey forms, a key concern is the representativeness of the resulting data, as researchers need to be aware that the results may be biased in some way. One issue is **coverage bias**, in which the survey data collection mode or some other factor excludes particular groups from the sampling frame. Early telephone survey research suffered from coverage bias because telephones were not present in many homes, and Internet surveys are limited in their ability to contact individuals without home Internet access.

Another concern is **non-response bias**, a sampling error that occurs if the individuals who opt to participate in a survey are in some important way dissimilar to those who choose not to participate. Survey non-response rates are increasing over time, largely due to increasing refusal rates. This change raises concerns about the representativeness of survey results, as "[t]he assumptions underlying probability sampling are violated when increasing numbers of sample members cannot be contacted, cannot participate or are unwilling to participate. This is why non-response is one of the major threats to survey quality" (Stoop 2012, 122). A number of reasons have been identified to explain increasing refusal rates, including time pressures and the growing number of survey requests that individuals receive (Stoop 2012).

The data collection mode is relevant to response rates. According to Hibberts, Johnson, and Hudson (2012, 73), "[t]he sample response rate depends greatly on the type of survey method used. Though response rates vary from survey to survey, there is some agreement that face-to-face surveys have the highest rate of response, followed by telephone surveys, with mail or self-administered surveys having the lowest response rates." Specific to telephone surveys, response rates from cell phones and land line phones are similar—and similarly low: "Today, only rare official surveys can achieve response rates above 50%. . . . [G]eneral telephone surveys (e.g., opinion polling) are typically below 20% or, more realistically, below 10" (Vehovar, Slavec, and Berzelak 2012, 280).

Most surveys are **cross-sectional** in that the respondents are interviewed only once and all approximately at the same time. Thus, a detailed snapshot of opinion at that particular point in time is produced, but change over time is difficult to assess. Although one can compare snapshots taken at two different points in time, it is difficult to decide if the difference between them is caused by change in the composition of the respondent groups or by a real change in social and political attitudes.

By contrast, **longitudinal studies** (also known as **panel studies**—not to be confused with online survey panels) interview the same respondents at different points in time, thereby facilitating the study of change. Longitudinal research provides a valuable means by which to study change over time, but such studies can be expensive to conduct because contact with respondents must be maintained or renewed; the longer the time interval between survey waves, the more complicated the task of tracking respondents becomes. As a consequence of attrition, it is sometimes necessary to replace panel members as the study progresses and early respondents move, die, or lose interest in the project. The 2004, 2006, and 2008 Canadian Election Studies included a panel component.

In all forms of survey research, there are tradeoffs among complexity, cost, and response rates. As a consequence, there is no best way to do a survey; it all depends on the resources you have and the research questions that need to be addressed. The external validity of survey research depends heavily on the sample chosen—if the sample is large and randomly selected, and if response rates are good, external validity can be high. The internal validity of survey research depends on the questions chosen for the study, which is our next topic.

Expand Your Knowledge

The Bibby Reports

One of the most high-profile mail surveys of Canadian public opinion is *The Bibby Report*, published by sociologist Reginald W. Bibby from the University of Lethbridge. Bibby's first study was conducted in 1975 and was based on a mail survey of 1,917 respondents. The sample size, the study's focus on prominent social issues of the day, and Bibby's energy in publicizing the study's findings quickly established the report as a benchmark for Canadian social trends. Bibby repeated the survey every five years until 2005, and each survey included a substantial number of respondents from past surveys, thus providing an important panel component. The surveys were all mail surveys and averaged 1,500 respondents, with very respectable response rates (over 60 per cent). The questionnaires were long, detailed, and covered a wide swath of Canadian social and political life. The accumulated Bibby reports provide a useful series of snapshots of Canadian society and demonstrate how much can be done with relatively modest resources.

Measures: Survey Questions

The goal of survey research is to obtain an accurate (valid) and reliable assessment of the attitudes or behaviour of the sample population (for discussion of measurement validity and reliability, see Chapter 5). The responses to the survey questionnaire serve as the data for subsequent analysis; hence, the quality of the data analysis ultimately depends on good-quality measures drawn from survey responses. When we consider measures, we must think about question type, question wording, and question ordering.

Question Type

It is important to distinguish between open-ended questions, which allow respondents to provide whatever response they deem appropriate to the question, and close-ended questions, which allow respondents to choose from a response set that identifies all the answers. Neither question type is inherently better, and the choice depends on whether the researcher has confidence that he or she knows all the response categories to include in the close-ended question or whether there is an interest in obtaining an uncued or unfiltered response from the participants.

An open-ended question is often used when the question may have a wide variety of responses and the researcher is interested in having the least amount of influence on the answers provided. For example, he or she may be interested in obtaining respondents' assessment of why they voted the way they did in a recent election. The researcher might feel that there are a large number of potentially significant factors that explain the voting decision and may probe this issue with an open-ended question such as the following: What factors were most important to you in voting for the __________ Party in the last election? He or she could use this question to see what kinds of factors were essential to voters (the impact of party leaders, long-standing party attachments, the issue stances of the parties, media coverage, the role of a local candidate, etc.) and could make this assessment by examining what factors were mentioned by respondents and in what order they were mentioned. Therefore, a strength of open-ended questions is that they provide a "raw" form of response, unconditioned by perceptual or analytical frameworks that may be introduced by the researcher.

Open-ended questions have a number of analytical challenges. For one thing, they often produce an extremely long list of response categories when used in survey research. As you can imagine, asking people to tell you why they voted as they did in the election may produce a wide variety of responses, some of which may be subtly different from one another. One respondent may say he voted for the Conservative Party in 2011 because he liked the party leader, Stephen Harper; another might have liked the leadership displayed by Harper on specific policy issues; and others might have viewed Harper as a better leader than his opponents. While all of these respondents mentioned *leader*, there were subtle differences in the meaning attached to this term. The analytical challenge is to capture the nuance in these multiple meanings when analyzing the data. As noted in Chapter 3, our goal in empirical political science research is to develop models that simplify the political world, yet the detailed data available through open-ended questions invites analysis in a more complex manner.

To conduct statistical analysis on the data from open-ended questions, it is often necessary, or at least desirable, to reduce the amount of diversity in responses and to regroup the data into a smaller number of somewhat more generic categories. To continue with our example regarding the reason for vote choice, other respondents likely would mention factors such as a specific policy put forward by one of the parties, the general economic circumstances in the country, or perceptions of the government's performance. Some respondents might state that they continued the family tradition of voting for a particular party. Others might mention things that were seemingly trivial—they might not like a certain leader's moustache, might think that one of the leaders looks untrustworthy, or might be punishing a party for perceived transgressions of a year, a decade, or a generation ago. In short, there are so many categories of responses with open-ended questions that it may be necessary to collapse all of the respondents who mentioned leadership into a single category, thereby losing the diversity of response that the open-ended question was designed to provide.

Although it may seem a relatively minor point, the use of open-ended questions has the added drawback of generally requiring an additional step in recoding the data before they can be used in quantitative analysis. When the timeliness of data release is important, it is less likely that open-ended questions will be used. Commercial public opinion surveys, particularly those that are conducted and published during election campaigns, are less likely to rely extensively on open-ended questions. One of the goals of such surveys is to release the data as quickly and with as much fanfare as possible so that the polling company can benefit from the subsequent publicity. Since open-ended questions generally take longer to code, and hence to analyze, they tend not to be featured in such surveys.

Close-ended responses are by far the more popular question type in survey research, both the commercial and academic variety. In many instances, the question pertains to a situation in which there are a limited number of responses; therefore, presenting these responses in the question is sensible. Questions such as a person's age, party identification, religion, or education are all generally close-ended questions. In addition, a number of standardized response sets have been developed that enable a number of questions to be asked and the results analyzed from a comparative perspective. One common approach is agree/disagree questions, which present a statement and ask respondents to rate their agreement on a continuum of agree/disagree responses (see Chapter 5). Here is an example:

Free trade with the United States has been good for the Canadian economy.

1. Strongly agree
2. Agree

3. Neither agree nor disagree
4. Disagree
5. Strongly disagree
6. No opinion/Don't know

A variation of the agree/disagree question is to ask respondents to rate their support or opposition to a statement on a continuum of support/opposition responses. Another common question is the feeling thermometer, in which respondents indicate their warmth toward a subject using a standard response scale, such as (0) very cold, (25) cool, (50) neutral, (75) warm, and (100) hot. An example is, "On a scale of 0 to 100, where 0 indicates 'greatly dislike' and 100 indicates 'greatly like,' how do you rate your feelings about labour unions?"

A third type of close-ended question is the **forced choice question**, which asks respondents which of a limited number of statements best reflects their personal views; these statement are often viewed as opposites on an opinion scale, such as "Which of the following statement comes closest to your view: The government's primary job in the economy is to keep inflation under control OR Government policy should put employment ahead of inflation in its economic policies?" In each kind of close-ended question, the result is a limited set of common responses that can be used for analysis.

Close-ended questions can influence the percentage of respondents who answer a question and are perceived as having an opinion, an effect based on whether respondents have the option to say that they don't know or have no opinion on a matter. This issue arose, among other places, in analyses on Canadians' partisan attachments. As discussed in Chapter 5, prior to the 1988 Canadian Election Study, the question about respondents' partisan identification was asked without including a "don't know/no opinion" option. From 1988 onward, the question has contained this option. The matter has also surfaced when Canadians in the CES have been asked to indicate their family income in the previous year. Responses to this question often indicate that upward of 20 per cent of respondents do not know what their income is. In this instance, the "don't know" response is likely a euphemism for respondents who actually know their income but want to convey to the interviewer that it is none of his or her business.

Close-ended questions are not without limitations. Perhaps the most significant challenge is that the researcher forces respondents who may not have had an opinion on the topic to make a choice. Rather than measuring a pre-existing attitude among respondents, the researcher may be creating the attitude that he or she is measuring. The research finding may be presented as an analysis of the electorate's attitudes toward some policy or another, when in reality it consists of an analysis of non-attitudes. Moreover, the use of close-ended questions presupposes that the researcher is aware of and has included all the possible and appropriate responses in the response set. When the list is incomplete or incorrect, the findings necessarily will be similarly mistaken.

Question Wording

The way questions are worded has a significant impact on the quality of survey data. Poorly worded questions can be worse than having no information at all, since they can lead to the assumption that the data provide a meaningful insight into the values, beliefs, and behaviour of the sample when, in fact, they may do nothing but provide a misleading understanding.

A goal in designing survey research questions is to have each question measure only one quality, whether that is one attitude, one belief, or one specific behaviour. When questions have multiple stimuli—for example, in which individuals are asked to respond to more than one attitude—the interpretation of the answer is **non-singular**, or is open to different interpretations. An agree/disagree question in which the statement is phrased as, "The Northern Gateway pipeline will create jobs and provide access to Asian markets" has two separate stimuli. A respondent might believe that the pipeline will provide market access but not that the pipeline will create jobs. Therefore, it is not evident how he or she should answer the question or how one would interpret an answer of either agree or disagree. A question that includes only one stimulus can resolve this dilemma.

A second issue that arises in question wording is the use of **ambiguous questions**. The objective is to use questions that are clear and commonly understood by all respondents (and subsequently by all users of the data); failing this, questions are likely to be unreliable. A question can be ambiguous for a number of reasons. For instance, it may use a concept that is not defined in the question and for which respondents may hold different interpretations of its meaning. A question may also be ambiguous if timelines or other parameters

Expand Your Knowledge

Push Polling and Political Advocacy

As consumers of survey research, we must distinguish between true survey research and advocacy efforts that use survey technology for other purposes. The latter is commonly known as push polling because the communications within the "survey" are intended to "push" voters and the public toward certain positions. As Rothenberg (2007) explains, "Push polls are really advocacy calls aimed at thousands of recipients. They are like television or radio ads, except they are delivered over the telephone. . . . Advocacy calls are not, in any shape or form, public opinion surveys." Push polls are typically extremely short (less than five minutes) and often do not include basic sociodemographic questions, as their purpose is persuasion rather than analysis. Professional market research associations argue that push polls are both unethical and damaging to the reputation of their industry.

are not specified. For this reason, questions are often very specific, such as "What was your total before-tax household income in 2013?"

Questions should be worded so as not to lead respondents to answer one way or another. This can be done by ensuring that value statements are not included, either implicitly or explicitly, in the wording of a question. One might be interested in people's evaluations regarding the media's objectivity in covering the proposed Northern Gateway pipeline. A leading, and hence inappropriate, question would contain a value statement about the media's purported ideological bias, such as "Do you think that Canada's liberal-dominated press provides fair and unbiased reporting of debate regarding the much-needed Northern Gateway pipeline?" In this instance, the respondent is cued to think that there may be a generally liberal orientation among the media and that the pipeline is needed. Leading questions are likely to **skew the opinion** expressed among survey respondents.

Question Order

If you have ever participated in a survey, you might have answered all the questions without being aware that there was a definite order in which the questions, or question types, were asked. Question order is obvious in those instances in which the question design is one of root and branch—that is, when one set of questions logically follows from an answer to an initial question. When asking about a person's party identification, the root question often begins, "Do you usually think of yourself as Conservative, Liberal, NDP, Green, some other party, or none of the above?" This question is followed by branch questions. Respondents who indicate that they identify with one of the parties are then asked which party that is. Those who don't identify with a party are asked, "Do you usually think of yourself as being closer to one of the parties?" In this case, the logic of responses to the initial question determines the order of the subsequent question.

More generally, there is an order in the presentation of survey questions. It is common to include a few innocuous and non-threatening questions at the outset of a survey, such as "Have you noticed that a provincial election campaign is underway?" or "Do you usually pay much attention to political ads on TV?" Next, it is common to see the key "horse race" questions. These questions, the responses to which often lead newscasts, include, "If an election were held today, which party would you vote for?" "On a scale of 1 to 10, how would you rate the leader of the X Party?" The reason these questions occur early in the order is that they are often the basis for the survey company's overall assessment of voting intentions. It is generally desirable to obtain information on such questions before asking respondents to assess factors that might influence their voting decision or opinion of the leaders. If there were a series of questions about the parties' stands on issues and a respondent indicated a preference for the position of party Y, it could create mental stress for the person to indicate an intention to support party X.

Once the vote-intention questions have been asked, questions about issue influences and perceptions, the party leaders or their personal characteristics, and general deep-rooted values and beliefs follow. If the survey is administered during an election campaign, questions about the campaign are asked. These questions can be either open- or close-ended, depending on the needs of the researcher and the timeliness of their use. Once the full set of attitudinal and behavioural questions are asked, the final section of a survey asks about respondents' personal characteristics—their age, marital status, gender, income, education, and the like. These questions generally are placed at the end of a questionnaire because some respondents do not like to answer them and because asking them too soon could lead people to wonder whether they will really retain their anonymity. Further, such questions are considerably less interesting, and leading with these questions could result in greater termination (and thus non-response) rates.

Pretesting Survey Questionnaires

Researchers take great care in designing clear questions that have only one stimulus per question and in ordering questions to conform with standards used by other researchers. However, prior to conducting the survey, it is a good practice to administer it to a small number of respondents who are similar to the people in the survey's sample frame. A pretest will assist with a number of administrative matters: How long does it take to administer the questionnaire? How does the survey flow? Do respondents lose interest? It will also help ensure that seemingly straightforward questions are clear when people hear them for the first time. Are there any technical terms that confuse, for example, the difference between a government debt and a deficit? Are any questions offensive or off-putting to respondents? Do questions that use a close-ended response set include all the responses needed to assist people to convey their sentiments? Considering the time and expense involved in conducting a survey of 1,000 to 4,000 respondents, including the valuable time of the respondents themselves, a pretest of 5 to 10 people is a small price to pay for confirming that the survey will produce high-quality information.

Using Secondary Data Sets

Although much political science research involves the creation of new research materials through primary data collection, it contains the secondary analysis of data collected by others as well. There are a number of key sources of **secondary data**, that is, data that is not directly collected by the researcher. An important source of survey data for students of Canadian politics is the CES. This comprehensive set of **cross-sectional studies** began with the 1965 federal election and now encompasses the federal elections between 1968 and 2011 (excluding 1972), along with the 1992 constitutional referendum. The series tracks many variables over time, although its focus and format have changed in terms of the research teams, our understanding of electoral dynamics, and the nature of the political landscape. The CES concentrate on their respective elections and on explaining the vote, but they also pick up a good deal of attitudinal and sociodemographic information that can be used to address a wide range of other research topics. The data sets are generally available to the political science community at large—including students—within a year of an election. Much of the empirical work on Canadian public opinion and political behaviour published in the *Canadian Journal of Political Science* is rooted in CES data sets.

Another main source of secondary data in Canada is the GSS, which covers a wide range of topics. The 2014 GSS (Cycle 28) examines criminal victimization and public perceptions of crime and the justice system, while the 2008 GSS (Cycle 22) examines social engagement, including voting and civic participation.

Secondary survey data at the international level enable comparative analyses. The World Values Survey includes over 50 countries and examines individuals' beliefs and values, using questions about democracy, religion, gender roles, and the environment, among other topics. The Comparative Study of Electoral Systems (CSES), a cross-national election study that includes over 50 countries, features post-election survey data exploring vote choice and related questions. The International Social Survey Programme (ISSP) is an annual, cross-national survey research collaboration involving over 50 countries; the topic of study, which varies by year, has included the role of government (1985, 1990, 1996, 2006), national identity (1995, 2003), and family and gender roles (1988, 1994, 2002, 2012).

Secondary data present both advantages and challenges. A key advantage is efficiency and cost-savings. By using secondary data, the researcher saves data collection time: rather than spending months designing and implementing a study, he or she can access data almost immediately. Using secondary data sets also saves the researcher the (often considerable) costs associated with data collection. Many data sources are freely available from public websites; the CES make full data sets available online, with no costs charged for download, and the Elections Canada website includes both web-based summary tables and raw electoral returns data files for download. Other data sets (or select portions) can be accessed through university research data libraries.

Another advantage can lie with research design. Some secondary data sources are longitudinal. Longitudinal data allow researchers to consider change over time and to clarify if certain events preceded others, thereby enabling researchers to better assess causality. Examples of this data type include the Survey of Labour and Income Dynamics and the National Longitudinal Survey of Children and Youth, both conducted by Statistics Canada. Moreover, some secondary sources have sample sizes well beyond those possible in individual research studies. Though survey research is often limited in its ability to draw conclusions about subgroups in the population because of a small number of cases in a particular subgroup, some secondary data sources, such as electoral returns data, are based on the full (or nearly full) population. Others are based on very large samples; for example, the GSS has had a sample size of 25,000 respondents since 1999.

Using secondary data sets presents numerous advantages, but there are some limitations. One chief drawback is that secondary data sets often include some measures of interest to the researcher but not all of what he or she would have included in an original design. Similarly, the questions included in the survey may be worded differently than the researcher would have preferred. As discussed in Chapter 5, to achieve measurement validity we want to have measures that fit and that capture all aspects of the concept of study; our ability to achieve these goals is sometimes hampered when we use secondary data.

Beyond Survey Research: Official Statistics

In some cases, **official statistics**—that is, statistics that are made available by governments and international organizations—are the only possible source of the indicators of interest. Researchers are often interested in comparing jurisdictions across key indicators, such as GDP, health outcomes, or infant mortality. Obviously, an original survey about GDP or infant mortality makes no sense, and official statistics must be used. To conduct such analyses, we must look to the data presented by agencies such as Statistics Canada and Elections Canada (for national data) and the World Bank (for comparative international data). These agencies offer a breadth of information. The World Bank data sets provide comparative information on education, environment, agriculture, rural development, economic policy, health, social development, infrastructure, and poverty, among other topics; additional comparative data are available from numerous other data sets. Similarly, Statistics Canada, Canada's leading statistical agency, has created data sets on topics related to the population, society, economy, environment, and government. More information can be obtained from other government agencies, including Elections Canada and its provincial counterparts and provincial statistical agencies.

Where do the government's official statistics come from? In many cases, such as statistics about crime, the environment, and government revenues and expenditures, official government data are derived from government administrative sources. In other cases, official government data are derived from census data. A census is a record of the full population, as opposed to a sample (or subset) of the population. The census has a long history in Canada; indeed, the Constitution Act, 1867, requires that census population figures be used to determine the allocation of MPs to provinces and to adjust district boundaries, and the first post-Confederation census was taken in 1871 (Statistics Canada 2009b). Since 1956, the Canadian census has been taken every five years, a practice that was put into law with the Statistics Act of 1971. As discussed in Chapter 8, statisticians and social scientists have expressed concerns about the sampling methodologies used in the 2011 long-form census.

A vast number of comparative data sets are available online through the International Monetary Fund (IMF), the World Bank, the United Nations, and other entities. Organizations and research institutes create these data sets by compiling and standardizing country-specific data. Some examples of comparative data sets used in political science research include the following:

- The World Bank's *World Development Indicators* data set includes measures for 214 countries and economies, including all World Bank member countries and all other economies with populations above 30,000.

- The *Correlates of War* project compiles and disseminates available data sets relevant to international relations. Topics covered in these data sets include wars, militarized disputes, military expenditures, territory change, world religions, and intergovernmental organizations.
- The Quality of Government Institute's *Quality of Government* (QoG) data sets present comparative information on corruption, democracy, bureaucratic quality, election rules, social fractionalization, economic and human development, environmental sustainability, gender equality, and other topics.
- The *Polity IV* data set includes measures for 167 countries (specifically, major independent states with populations of 500,000 or more) over the 1800–2012 time period. The data set considers political competition, constraints on executive authority, and executive recruitment, among other measures of regime authority.
- The Union of International Organization's *Yearbook of International Organizations Online* presents a database of over 66,000 international organizations, with information on such areas as types of organizations, geographic locations of secretariats, geographic distribution of meetings, and meeting size.

An important shortcoming in using official statistics is that researchers are typically limited to **aggregate data**—that is, grouped data for a specified geographic area. Access to non-aggregated **microdata** files from Statistics Canada surveys is highly restricted because of strict confidentiality rules.[1] Aggregate data present challenges for analysis. First, they are not always available in the manner that a particular researcher prefers. As Statistics Canada (2009a) writes:

> Not all aggregate data contain the combination of variables from the microdata that a user may desire. For example, a patron may be looking at whether alcohol use and gambling are correlated and wishes to know if these variables differ between men and women, by age group, and whether the results vary across Canada. Although data in the Canadian Community Health Survey (CCHS) 3.1 are collected about the respondent's geography, gender, age, Canadian Problem Gambling Index, and alcohol use, this combination of variables may not have been used in creating an aggregate data product.

Second, because aggregate data provide group-level (as opposed to individual-level) information, researchers must be careful to ensure that their conclusions do not imply individual-level behaviours. An analysis of aggregate electoral returns data may find that districts with greater proportions of high-income households tend to have greater support for the Conservative Party than other districts do. From this result, it is tempting to assume that high-income individuals are more likely to vote Conservative. Although this assumption might be true, the aggregate data do not support it; lower- and/or middle-income individuals living in higher-income ridings might also be more likely to vote Conservative or the relationship between income and vote choice may be spurious. When we assume that group-level patterns imply individual-level patterns, we fall victim to the ecological fallacy, as discussed in Chapter 3. To avoid this problem, researchers must be cautious in their language when describing their results. In their analysis of Alberta electoral returns data, Edward Bell, Harold Jansen, and Lisa Young make clear reference to districts as the unit of analysis. They write that "[h]aving a higher proportion of immigrants was associated with higher levels of Liberal voting," but they do not imply that immigrant voters were more likely to vote Liberal (Bell et al. 2007, 41).[2]

Expand Your Knowledge

Electoral Returns Data

Many political scientists are interested in questions of voting, including voter turnout and vote choice. Electoral returns data, available from Elections Canada for federal elections and from provincial elections organizations (e.g. Elections Manitoba, Elections Ontario) for provincial elections, provide population-level data on voting. These data can be used to describe voting in specific geographic units, such as ridings or polling stations.

Canadian researchers have used electoral returns data to analyze on-reserve First Nations voting. Because electoral returns data are available at the polling station level, it is possible for researchers to isolate on-reserve polling stations to draw conclusions about on-reserve First Nations voting. Such research has considered on-reserve voter turnout (Bedford 2003; Bedford and Pobihushchy 1995; Guérin 2003) and vote choice (Berdahl, Adams, and Poelzer 2009; Kinnear 2003; Pitsula 2001); the data suggest that voter turnout is lower at on-reserve polls than at non-reserve polls and that the provincial New Democratic parties typically receive a higher percentage of votes at the former. These data tell us something about on-reserve First Nations voting but cannot be used to describe Aboriginal voting more broadly because the data do not include off-reserve First Nations, Métis, Inuit, or Non-Status Indian persons.

Political scientists have combined Statistics Canada data with electoral returns data to consider the relationship between constituency-level socioeconomic variables and voting. Statistics Canada provides census population data according to federal electoral districts (FEDs). The FED profiles include variables such as age, marital status, median income, immigrant status, and other key sociodemographic variables. Researchers can use FED-level Elections Canada and census data to look for constituency-level sociodemographic variations in voting. In such analyses, the variables are often univariate descriptive statistics (discussed more in Chapter 14), such as percentages (e.g., "percentage of the district population who report being retired") and medians (median age, median income in district), and not raw count data. For example, Linda Gerber (2006, 108) describes her variables as follows: "census variables were compiled for each riding, converted to percentages and rates, and merged with the results of the federal election of 2004—as the percentage voting for each party—to provide the database for the following analyses."

Ethical Considerations When Using Secondary Data and Official Statistics

Given that secondary data and official statistics are already collected, ethical considerations are focused on the use of the data. When using this information, it is critical that researchers carefully review the technical documentation—referred to as **metadata**—associated with the data file. It is extremely easy to unintentionally misuse or misrepresent secondary data and official statistics. Here are some areas to watch for:

- *Conceptual definitions and associated measures:* Data sets may contain multiple measures of similar concepts, and the researcher must be clear in reporting the measure used. The 2011 census included a number of questions on the following topics to identify the Aboriginal population: Aboriginal ancestry, Aboriginal identity, Registered Indian status, and Band or First Nation membership. The different measures provide considerably different counts for the Aboriginal population: over 1.8 million Canadians reported Aboriginal ancestry; 1.4 million reported Aboriginal identity; 697,505 reported Registered Indian status; and 75,485 reported Band or First Nation membership (Statistics Canada 2014a). It is incumbent on the researcher to select the measure that best fits the research question and to clearly specify the measure in the analysis.
- *Question wording:* When researchers compare data sets (such as data sets across countries), they should watch for differences in question wording and response categories. Such differences may influence the results, and researchers should acknowledge this effect in their analyses.
- *Geographic boundaries:* Researchers should also watch for variations in geographic boundaries across different data sets. For example, electoral district boundaries change over time, and additional districts are occasionally added. (The 2013 Representation Order includes 338 seats, compared to 308 federal districts in the 2003 edition.)
- *Population of study:* Data sets differ in who is included in the population of study. Some data sets consider individuals and may vary in terms of a certain parameter. Statistic Canada's Canadian Community Health Surveys include individuals aged 12 and over, while its General Social Surveys include individuals aged 15 and over. The agency's Longitudinal Survey of Immigrants to Canada was limited to immigrants who met particular criteria. Some surveys, such as Statistics Canada's Survey of Household Spending, are based on households rather than individuals. Researchers should clearly report the population of study in their analysis.
- *Data cautions:* Organizations and research teams often provide caveats or cautions about the use of their data in the technical documentation. Researchers must respect this advice. For instance, Statistics Canada (2009c) provides the following note with respect to Aboriginal identity data:

> Caution should be exercised in analyzing trends for Aboriginal peoples based on previous census data. Over time, patterns in Aboriginal self-identification have changed. In recent years, a growing number of people who had not previously identified with an Aboriginal group are now doing so. Changes in the participation of First Nations people living on reserve in the census over time also affect historical comparison.

Given this warning, researchers should either not report trends in Aboriginal identity data or report the concerns about the data in their discussion.

Working as a Team

1. Select a topic or theme you and your group would like to know about (e.g. people's attitudes toward left/right distinctions; assessments of the prime minister's performance; their vote decision, etc.). Develop close-ended and open-ended questions (at least three of each) that help measure people's attitudes toward this topic. Make sure that your response set is comprehensive and complete.
2. Select a small group (such as 10 classmates) and administer the questionnaires created in the previous exercise. Compare the results by using the different question formats and discuss the advantages and disadvantages of each.
3. Identify 15 electoral districts. For each district, use the census FED data to identify the constituency's characteristics based on average family income, age, educational attainment, and ethnic composition. Discuss any trends that you see in terms of the regional or urban/rural character of the constituencies.
4. Using Elections Canada data, insert a new variable in the data set—percentage vote for the Conservative, Liberal, NDP, Bloc, and other parties in the most recent federal election. Discuss any trends that you see. (Depending on the technical expertise of the group, you may wish to import the data for all federal constituencies into a statistical package, such as IBM SPSS, and run similar analyses for the country as a whole.) Discuss the findings among the group.

Self-Study

1. A number of reputable commercial polling companies use web surveys quite extensively. You have quite likely received and possibly completed an Internet survey. List some of the strengths of and limitations to the use of web public opinion surveys.
2. What techniques could be used to ensure that the information obtained from Internet surveys is as free as possible from random and non-random errors?

3. One of the challenges associated with using aggregate data is the risk of committing the ecological fallacy. Provide an example in which such a problem may occur.
4. Discuss the strategies that could be used to decrease the likelihood of committing the ecological fallacy.

Notes

1. Statistics Canada (2009a) defines microdata as "the data directly observed or collected from a specific unit of observation," such as "an individual, a household or a family." Researchers can access Statistics Canada microdata through Research Data Centres after completing a rigorous application process, but doing so can be time-consuming.
2. Researchers who wish to make individual-level inferences from aggregate data can use specific ecological regression analyses. For an example, see Lublin and Voss's (2002) analysis of francophone support for sovereignty.

CHAPTER 11

Experimental Research

Alexandre Morin-Chassé, Université de Montréal
Erick Lachapelle, Université de Montréal

Destination

By the end of this chapter, you should be able to

- understand how randomized controlled experiments make it possible to isolate causal effects;
- differentiate between internal and external validity;
- describe the different types of experiments and identify strengths and weaknesses associated with each type;
- read, understand, and evaluate published research that uses experimental designs;
- explain how to design an experiment to test your own hypotheses; and
- recognize practical and ethical limits of experimentation.

Experimentation in political science is a relatively recent phenomenon. In the past, many political scientists questioned the **feasibility** of applying experimental methods to their preferred objects of study. Was it possible for researchers to intervene in the social and political world in such a way as to isolate a variable's effect on an outcome of interest? Substantive preoccupations with systemic and institutionalist theories of politics in the 1970s and 1980s largely precluded this type of analysis. In addition, the application of experimental methods in the political realm raised important ethical issues. For example, even if one really could randomly assign segments of the population to a new poverty reduction program, on what grounds was it ethical to deny others in need? While recognizing these practical and ethical constraints, the experimental method has long served as a benchmark for evaluating the quality of causal inferences made in political science. Indeed, the controlled experiment is often referred to as the gold standard for making causal inferences providing a clear logic and degree of control that other methods strive to replicate (Blalock 1964).

Today, experimentation is much more common in political science, and studies drawing on experimental methods are increasingly finding their way into the discipline's leading journals (Dunning and Nilekani 2013; Druckman et al. 2006). In fact, the recently created *Journal of Experimental Political Science* restricts submissions to ones that either employ experimental methods or apply experimental reasoning to naturally occurring phenomena. Many reasons contribute to this increased use of experimental methods, including a growing desire among researchers to uncover the micro-foundations of political phenomena, the development of guidelines to assuage ethical concerns for research involving humans, and innovations in the way researchers apply experimental logic through seizing opportunities presented by naturally occurring randomized assignment in the political and social world. Technology has also clearly played an important role in making experiments more feasible. Most important, however, experimental methods offer important advantages in terms of making stronger causal inferences, which has become a central goal of political science (King et al. 1994).

This chapter explores experimental data-gathering techniques as they relate to political science research. We begin with a discussion of causal inferences and an explanation of how experiments manage to isolate **causal effects**. We then outline in greater detail how experiments work and describe key issues that researchers should consider when designing an experiment. Several types of experiments are discussed with reference to concrete examples drawn from a wide range of subfields in the political science literature. Finally, we examine important limitations related to this method.

Experiments and the Search for Causality

Causal thinking is an important part of human existence. In fact, people make causal inferences all the time. In some cases, the simple co-occurrence of two events might suggest that a causal relationship exists. If your coffee cup is hot, it's probably because there is coffee (or another hot substance) in it. If you see a group of people wearing scarves and toques on the first of September, the weather is likely unseasonably cold. In both instances, the association between cause and effect has been observed so many times before that you may automatically infer a causal relationship based on the simple concurrence of two events. However, the cup may have recently contained coffee, but your roommate may have just gulped it before leaving for class. The people wearing warm clothes may be a group of tourists from

Central America for whom 16 degrees Celsius indicates that winter has arrived. If constant conjunction of events is relatively unproblematic for making causal inferences in day-to-day life, the same cannot be said of making them in political science, where the standards of evidence are much higher.

As noted in Chapter 3, correlation does not necessarily imply causation. Suppose that Canada adopted a system of proportional representation to elect members of Parliament and that voter turnout in the subsequent election increased by 10 per cent. This increase may be the result of changes to the electoral system, but the reform is probably not the only thing that changed between elections. There might have been new party leaders (and certainly some new candidates); new issues may have motivated more people to vote; there may have been bad weather in parts of the country on the day of the previous election; and the composition of the Canadian population may have changed between elections. Given all the factors that could have potentially influenced turnout in both elections, it is impossible to say with absolute certainty that this 10 per cent increase was caused by the change in the electoral system. This is because we do not actually observe causal effects but must infer them from our observations. And since our observations are necessarily limited, we have no way of knowing whether we have considered all relevant factors or whether the outcome of interest would have still occurred in the absence of a presumed cause.

To illustrate this problem further, we can formally represent the causal effect as

$$E_X = Y_t(u) - Y_c(u)$$

where E is the causal effect of the independent variable X (changing the electoral system), u is the unit of observation (an election in Canada), Y is the measurable outcome of interest (the per cent of eligible voters who vote), and t and c refer to the unit in its treated (proportional representation) and untreated (first-past-the-post) states, respectively. The causal effect, then, is the difference in turnout between an election held using a system of proportional representation (the treatment) and the same election using the existing first-past-the-post system (the control). The problem, often referred to as the **fundamental problem of causal inference** (Holland 1986), is that we cannot observe given subjects—in this case elections—in both their treated and untreated states. To actually observe the causal effect of changing the electoral system, we would have to observe the outcome of an election with the existing system and then replay history after changing nothing but the electoral process. Short of having a time machine or access to a parallel universe, it is impossible to actually observe causal effects in the real world.

In response to these inferential problems, the social sciences have imported experimental methods from the natural sciences. Experimental methods are best suited to making causal inferences because an experimental design mimics causal thinking. If we believe that X causes Y, it follows that, if X changes, Y will subsequently change as well. This process is exactly what an experimental researcher sets out to do. We manipulate X and observe if changes in Y follow. Most biomedical sciences use randomized controlled experiments to test the causal effects of new medications in randomized control trials. In so doing, researchers exploit two key characteristics of the experimental method: **planned intervention** by the researcher and **random assignment** (Green 2004).

In contrast to observational studies, in which the researcher plays a passive role in collecting naturally occurring observations and looks for patterns after the fact, experiments involve an intervention by the researcher, who then tracks the consequences for the outcome of interest (Green 2004). This planned intervention is precisely what distinguishes the two types of data: whereas observational data are generated by forces beyond the researchers' control, experimental data are generated from the researcher's deliberate involvement. For example, a researcher may be interested in studying the effects of electoral reform on strategic voting. An observational study might gather data from multiple electoral surveys and compare instances of strategic voting in several regions to see whether turnout varies across different electoral systems. An experimental approach might involve randomly assigning subjects in a lab to identical elections, save for the way of counting votes, in order to assess whether electoral rules affect the likelihood of strategic voting.

A second main component of the classic experimental method is random assignment (Green 2004). This element enables the researcher to create at least two groups: the **experimental group** that receives the treatment and the **control group** that does not. Assuming that the sample size is sufficiently large and that treatment assignment is entirely determined by chance, we can be sure that the treatment and control groups are, on the aggregate, identical in terms of all attributes, both measured and unmeasured. Given that the groups are similar in all respects, we say that they are the same in expectation. That is

Expand Your Knowledge

The Power of Randomization

Consider a village of 7,000 inhabitants who have a mean age of 45 years old. This population is randomly divided into two groups (for each individual, we flip a coin to decide which group he or she belongs in). To the extent that each individual has the same probability of being assigned to one or the other group, there is a very strong likelihood that the mean age in both groups of 3,500 people will be close to or equal to 45 years old. Yet the strength of the randomization process is that the groups will be equivalent for all other characteristics, both observable (e.g. sex, eye colour, educational attainment, and church attendance) and unobservable (e.g. self-confidence). Moreover, randomization implies that groups will be identical, even for variables that we have not thought about. Randomization is thus the procedure that makes the treatment and control groups equal in expectation, and thus, amenable to an experimental design.

to say, absent an exposure to the treatment, we would expect no real difference between the experimental groups in terms of all possible attributes, including the outcome of interest. Through the power of randomization, therefore, any observed differences in the two groups post-treatment may confidently be attributed to the experimental intervention.

Internal and External Validity

Despite the ability of experiments to make strong causal inferences, experimental methods have their limits. As is true for all methods, one's ability to infer causality after experimentation largely depends on a study's internal and external validity (introduced in Chapter 2). Internal validity here means the extent to which the measured change in X really causes a change in Y inside the experimental setting. In other words, does the experiment provide an unbiased environment that enables the researcher to unequivocally attribute a measured change in the dependent variable to the experimental treatment? Threats to internal validity include any uncontrolled aspect of the experimental environment that may interfere with the design or distract subjects from a given task. A study's internal validity may also be compromised by biased measurement tools (e.g. a sensitive question that will lead some subjects to abandon the experiment) and violations to the randomization procedure (subject self-selection and other forms of selection bias).[1]

External validity refers to the extent that results obtained from an experiment may be generalized to other subjects, experimental settings, and/or populations. In other words, how robust are the results outside of this one experimental setting? External validity may suffer from three main types of threats. The first occurs when the experiment is conducted with a sample whose characteristics greatly differ from the population to which inferences are made. For instance, testing the efficacy of campaign messages about pension plans on undergraduates may tell us little about their impact on people nearing retirement. The second happens when the experimental design differs too much from the investigated phenomenon's usual function in non-experimental contexts, as in the shopping mall experiment discussed in the next section. Third, experiments may also suffer from the Hawthorne effect (discussed in Chapter 9), in which subjects behave differently because they know they are being observed. As illustrated throughout the rest of this chapter, different types of experiments raise different types of validity concerns.

Designing an Experimental Study

As is the case in any research project, researchers interested in applying experimental methods must consider a number of key issues in their design. A central item in this process is the selection of what to study. Unlike observational researchers, who may rely on information collected for other purposes, experimental researchers must be clear about the hypotheses they want to test and collect exactly the type of data they need to test their ideas. This step implies that, before conducting the experiment, researchers must be clear about what treatment they want to test for. Such clarity is essential to the experimental method and must receive serious attention.

Once the researcher has a clear idea of the causal effect to test, he or she can proceed to defining the sample and experimental context. Both definitions should be informed by attention to practical constraints and theoretical expectations. For instance, determining the target sample involves important trade-offs. On one hand, a larger sample yields greater **statistical power**, that is, the ability of a study to discern medium or small effects. On the other hand, generating a larger sample size will require more resources, time, and money. Practical and theoretical considerations also impose a number of limitations over the type of sample and the experimental context that can test the hypothesis.

For instance, it might be unwise to test whether subjects are responsive to the subtleties of a TV political advertisement if they are recruited in a mall while doing last-minute Christmas shopping. The absence of an effect in this convenience sample will inform us more about the subjects' level of attention at the time the experiment was conducted than about whether political advertising may have an impact. Contemplation of the experimental context is also crucial. In one study about the effect of political advertisement, Iyengar (2002, 9) reports: "It is possible, of course, for the experimental setting to be too realistic. During the early days of our campaign experiments, we provided subjects with access to a remote control device, only to discover that a subject used it to fast forward the tape during the commercial breaks." This famous example reminds us that experimental realism must not compromise the researcher's ability to administer the treatment.

Regarding the type of subjects, it is extremely common for psychologists to conduct a pilot study with their students, since these subjects are easily accessible and very cheap to recruit. American researchers can now recruit and compensate subjects from a more heterogeneous pool on the web, using crowdsourcing websites. It is also essential that, during recruitment, researchers inform participants that they are subjects of an academic research project and obtain their consent to participate (see the discussion of ethics in Chapter 6). Each university has its own ethical regulations and standards; therefore, you should gather information about these rules and follow them when planning and conducting your experiments.

As discussed earlier, an experiment's ability to isolate causal effects depends crucially on the integrity of its random assignment. For randomization to be completely successful, every subject must have an equal chance of being assigned to each experimental condition included in the design. In practice, this situation can be achieved by simply flipping a coin or rolling a dice. Nowadays, most experiments use computer-assisted randomization algorithms. This technology has greatly facilitated the implementation of more complex research designs, in which subjects are randomly assigned to more than just two (treatment and control) groups. Computer-assisted randomization has also made it easier to implement randomized controlled experiments in much larger samples. It is often a good idea to perform randomization checks after the procedure to ensure that the groups are equivalent. In some cases, however, such tests may not be appropriate, especially if sample sizes are relatively small (Mutz and Pemantle n.d.).

In some experimental designs, it is important that subjects remain unaware of the randomization process and of the existence of other groups exposed to different treatments. Knowledge of the design may induce some subjects to guess the study's hypothesis or to share information with people assigned to other conditions, potentially biasing results. To guard against such contamination effects, researchers may decide to design their study as single- or double-blind. An experiment that blinds the subjects to the randomization process is a **single-blind design**. For experiments with an individual administering the treatment, the gold standard is a **double-blind design**, in which both subjects and treatment administrators are unaware of the effect being tested. This second condition ensures that the administrator will not undeservedly induce subjects to react in a certain way or notice some aspects of the subject's reactions.

With the hypotheses, sample size, recruitment procedure, and experimental setting defined, researchers must next decide on the details of their experimental protocol, including the precise stimuli that the experimental group(s) will be exposed to and the experimental design itself. In developing the **stimulus** (the treatment intervention), researchers have to be creative and strike a balance between the desire to test for an effect and the need, in most cases, to be as realistic as possible. For instance, when investigating the impact of different issue frames in political advertising, a researcher could record the advertisements in a studio, using professional actors and presenting them in the same way as subjects likely encounter them in everyday life. Though subjects know that neither the political party nor the candidate is real, the fact that the video looks authentic may compensate for this drawback and prevent subjects from perceiving the stimulus as having little credibility.

Furthermore, the researcher must give careful attention to the overall experimental design, that is, to the number and size of groups to which the stimulus is presented. If the sample's size permits, the researcher may create a **placebo group**, in which subjects are exposed to a fake treatment (e.g. a sugar pill) in order to better isolate treatment effects.[2] In some cases, researchers benefiting from large samples may also assign different versions of a stimulus to different groups in order to verify if slightly altered experimental conditions generate stronger or weaker effects.

Regardless of the number and types of groups, researchers typically compare different experimental conditions to a **control condition**, which acts as a baseline for comparison (McDermott 2002a). In a **between-subjects design**, subjects are randomly assigned to various treatment and control groups and examined post-treatment (and sometimes pre-treatment as well). In a **within-subjects design**, researchers evaluate subjects before and after they receive the treatment relative to the before and after scores of subjects who did not receive the treatment and infer causality based on any differences observed (Mutz 2011). Whether analyzing different scores measured before and after treatment or comparing

Expand Your Knowledge

Framing Political Issues

Entman (1993, 52) defines issue framing as the act of selecting "*some aspects of a perceived reality and mak[ing] them more salient in a communicating text, in such a way as to promote a particular problem definition, causal interpretation, moral evaluation, and/or treatment recommendation* for the item described" (emphasis in original). In a classic experiment, Nelson, Clawson, and Oxley (1997) exposed students to different media coverage of a Ku Klux Klan (KKK) demonstration and found evidence of how such framing can affect public perceptions of a political event. In this study, research subjects were randomly assigned to one of two very similar versions of a recorded video stimulus. The only difference was that, in the first news report, protesters were framed as demonstrating in favour of free speech, while the second video framed the same demonstration as an instance of public disorder that erupted during the rally. The study revealed that subjects exposed to the "free speech" frame expressed more tolerance toward the KKK than did the group exposed to a video of "social disorder."

This simple experiment suggests that the public may be influenced by subtle differences in the way the media insist on some aspects of an issue and ignore others, that is, in the way that the media frames political events. A prolific subfield of research that involves both political communication and political psychology has subsequently begun to unpack the psychology and complexities of framing effects (Scheufele 1999; Chong and Druckman 2007, 2013).

treatment and control groups, researchers may test for post-treatment differences using a variety of statistical techniques (such as those discussed in Chapters 14–17).

While the steps we have outlined apply more or less to all situations in which researchers design their experimental protocol, experimentation can take different forms. The next sections explore four types of experiments that are increasingly being used in political science.

Laboratory Experiments

Laboratory experiments are likely what most people have in mind when they hear the word *experiment*. As their name suggests, laboratory experiments are defined primarily by the location in which they occur; subjects are recruited to a common place where the researcher exerts a relatively large degree of control over the experimental setting. Such in vitro environments limit the risk of unknown influences and thus increase confidence that any *ex post* differences (i.e. differences after the experiment takes place) observed between treatment and control groups are due to the experimental manipulation. The laboratory experiment resembles experiments carried out in a biology, chemistry, or physics lab, except for the fact that, in the social sciences, it typically takes place among students, in a room on campus. As previously mentioned, the student body provides researchers with a relatively large and accessible pool of cheap and willing subjects, and many university professors, particularly in psychology, political psychology, and political communication, regularly publish their work based on experiments with student samples in such settings (e.g. Druckman 2001).

Today, social science experiments have benefited from the construction of actual labs in which researchers administer sophisticated experiments in a controlled setting, expanding the realm of possibilities for political science research along the way. For instance, computer labs with on-screen survey administration software have come to replace paper questionnaires. Unlike traditional surveys, these lab-based versions tend to be relatively cheap to administer, allow for some possibility of deliberation in a controlled setting, and give the researcher a greater degree of control over the environment in which subjects answer questions. In the lab, networked desktop systems can also be programmed to simulate interactions among actors operating in a particular environment created by the researcher. Though still in their relative infancy, laboratories can now be equipped to measure biomarkers and physiological responses to stimuli, including measurement of galvanic skin response, heart rate, blood pressure, skin temperature, respiration, and even ECG. This context offers researchers an opportunity to verify if manipulating aspects of the virtual environment influences these physiological outcomes, as well as associated variables related to emotion, cognition, and individual decision-making processes.

Initially more common in political economy (Palfrey 1991), political psychology (Lupia 1994), and political communication (Iyengar and Kinder 1989), laboratory experiments are increasingly making their way into other areas of political science. For instance, they have been used to examine the prevalence of strategic voting under different electoral rules (Blais et al. 2011) and to demonstrate the impact of electoral systems on the decision of whether or not to vote (St-Vincent 2013). Other political scientists have employed experiments in the lab to test theories of particular relevance for international relations. In one such study, Tingley and Walter (2011) explored decision-making dynamics in a series of iterated games. They found that, under certain conditions, individuals will invest in reputation-building and that reputations for being "tough" can deter other players from engaging in aggressive behaviour.

These in vitro experiments give researchers an unprecedented degree of control over the lab environment. By manipulating a very small number of variables while controlling for virtually all others, laboratory experiments enable researchers to isolate causal effects in ways that are not possible by any other means. However, this strong internal validity is counterbalanced by doubts about the representativeness of subjects (for instance, student populations drawn from mostly Western, educated, industrialized, rich, and democratic (WEIRD) societies), and by scepticism around the artificial nature of the setting in which the experiment takes place (Henrich, Heine, and Norenzayan 2010).[3]

Survey Experiments

In contrast to experiments in the lab, **survey experiments** have a relatively longer history in political science. This is because survey researchers have embedded experiments in the instruments used to measure public opinion. Survey experiments are administered in the context of survey research[4]; that is, respondents are randomly assigned to one or another version of the survey questionnaire. In light of variation in the survey instrument (the treatment), researchers look to identify differences in the responses given. The classic example of a survey experiment is the split-ballot used to examine question order and question wording-effects (Schuman and Presser 1981; Morin-Chassé 2010). For instance, using a split-ballot design, one study found that the proportion of Americans open to allowing reporters from communist countries into the United States during the Cold War was significantly greater when such a question was preceded by one asking whether Americans should be allowed to report from such communist countries as Russia (Schuman and Presser 1981). In addition to these methodological concerns, experiments are commonly used to address substantive questions and can be administered through various types of surveys, including mail-back, telephone, and, increasingly, Internet.

Whether researchers deploy survey experiments by mail, telephone, or the web ultimately depends on their research objectives and the financial resources available. In the past, when mail-back surveys were more common, researchers were often limited to split-ballot designs that compared responses to only two versions of a single survey. Over time, the development of computer-assisted telephone interviewing (CATI) greatly facilitated the administration of complex experimental designs involving multiple interventions in a single survey. Though more expensive, telephone surveys using random-digit dialling also have the benefit of administering surveys to random probability samples, assisting with the external validity of results (Mutz 2011). Web surveys tend to be cheaper, since most rely on non-representative opt-in panels to recruit eligible subjects. This survey type helps recruit younger people, who are notoriously difficult to reach by phone, and allows researchers to integrate images, sounds, and video in order to examine how subjects respond to different sensory stimuli.

Combining the best of both worlds, some firms and research teams have assembled probability-based web panels, which can be used to draw random samples of the population for Internet-based survey experiments. While this is generally more expensive, collaborative efforts, like the Time-sharing Experiments for the Social Sciences (TESS), allow researchers to share time on web surveys administered to random probability samples. Time on the TESS is competitive and based on intellectual merit, so researchers in the early phase of their research may decide to first try out their survey experiments on student samples in a lab or on relatively cheaper opt-in panels using such crowdsourcing software as Amazon Mechanical Turk.

Expand Your Knowledge

Time-sharing Experiments for the Social Sciences (TESS)

Originally led by Diana Mutz (University of Pennsylvania) and Arthur Lupia (University of Michigan), TESS provides a platform for researchers interested in conducting web-based survey experiments. Academics and students from around the world (including you) are invited to submit experimental protocols that can be implemented in an online questionnaire. Projects must involve an experiment and the topic must be within a field of the social sciences. After a formal review process, some projects receive approval for inclusion on TESS. All winning experiments are implemented by the American research firm GfK (formerly Knowledge Networks) on a representative sample of residents in the United States, at no cost to the researcher. After the survey is conducted, TESS makes the data available to the entire academic community. Because they are better able to achieve higher levels of both internal and external validity, TESS experiments provide the researchers with valuable data that have the potential to make important contributions to the social sciences.

Today, survey experiments are commonly used to address substantive questions in addition to methodological preoccupations. For instance, Lachapelle, Montpetit, and Gauvin (forthcoming) replicated a web-based survey experiment to examine the role of risk frames in shaping public perceptions of policy expertise. From this experimental design, the researchers found that perceptions of expert credibility depend on the fit between a policy expert's framing of risk and a subject's underlying values and worldviews. In a different study using a similar Internet poll, Press, Sagan, and Valentino (2013) examined the taboo against nuclear weapons and found that, under certain conditions, the American public is more likely to support the use of nuclear weapons over that of conventional warfare to destroy critical targets. Both of these studies exploit the advantages of administrating a complex survey design over the web, and their larger and more heterogeneous sample sizes also help with the generalizability of results. However, answering questions on the phone or in front of the computer is not necessarily like being in the real world, where people are exposed to a variety of information opportunities and not just the treatment a researcher wants to test. Moreover, treatment effects found in a one-shot survey setting may not endure (Gaines, Kuklinski, and Quirk 2007). From this perspective, a recurrent critique of laboratory and survey experiments is that their context is not realistic (Barabas and Jerit 2010). Would subjects react the same way if they had been in a real-life setting?

Field Experiments

One way to guard against the potential shortcomings of laboratory or survey experiments is to implement a **field experiment**. Here again, treatment assignment is randomized, but this time "a researcher's intervention takes place in a subjects' natural environment" (Morton and Williams 2010, 46). Compared to the other types, a field experiment often necessitates that the researcher invest more resources and find original opportunities to reach or recruit subjects. Indeed, catching the attention of potential subjects is likely more difficult in a real-life setting than it is in a lab, where subjects may receive precise directions. However, from a scientific perspective, such investment may be worthwhile because conducting an experiment in this more authentic environment has a great advantage: it gives the researcher a more realistic assessment of treatment effects.

Consider Bertrand et al.'s (2007) field experiment investigating corruption in India. This study followed 822 men in Delhi as they tried to obtain their driver's licences. Subjects were randomly assigned to a control group or one of two treatment groups. The first treatment (bonus group) was promised a monetary reward if they obtained their licences quickly. Subjects in the second treatment (the lesson group) were offered free driving lessons. Results showed that subjects in both treatment groups were more likely to obtain their licences than those in the control group. The process was also faster in the bonus group. As it turns out, many in the bonus group managed to use some of the money to pay for the illegal services of middlemen who had connections within the public administration and could accelerate the licensing process. Finally, the experiment revealed that this corruption has concrete consequences: among those who had received their licences, subjects from the bonus group had a higher probability of failing a surprise driving test than either the lesson group or the control group subjects did.

Other field experiments have investigated such topics as the efficacy of "getting-out-the-vote messages" (Green, Gerber, and Nickerson 2003) and the influence of cultural conventions on ethnic voting (Dunning and Harrison 2010). One of the most interesting features of field experiments is that their real-life setting often provides the researcher with an opportunity to measure treatment effects on more substantive behaviours than the typical attitudes or behavioural intentions that are usually measured by other data collection methods, such as traditional surveys. In contrast, field experiments can produce results associated with a high degree of both internal and external validity, if done well. Thus, in principle, field experiments are particularly well placed to make a significant contribution to our understanding of politics.

However, this type of experiment also comes at a potential cost. Unlike laboratory experiments, any increase in realism associated with experiments conducted in the field may result in a certain loss of control for the researcher (McDermott 2002b). For instance, in the classic example of Green et al.'s (2003) randomized voter mobilization experiments, it is possible that subjects exposed to different messages about voting exchanged information about the different treatments. This cross-contamination also likely shrinks the difference in outcomes between the different groups, thus biasing results and leading the researcher to underestimate causal effects.

Naturally Occurring Experiments and Quasi-Experiments

In some cases, researchers do not actually design experiments in the field; they find them (Remler and Van Ryzin 2011). Because the researcher does not interfere in the underlying data-generating process, these studies are technically observational. However, the term ***natural***, or ***naturally occurring, experiment*** is sometimes used to describe a situation in which an exogenous change alters the natural course of events in the same way that a researcher would if he or she could (Dunning 2012). Recall that pure randomization to treatment and control conditions is a key characteristic that makes experiments the best method to establish the existence of a causal relationship. However, under some real-life circumstances, it is possible that a change in an independent phenomenon (X) is so outside anything related to another phenomenon under study (Y) that the researcher may credibly claim that any association between the two must therefore indicate that X causes Y. In other words, when treatment assignment occurs naturally, as if by random chance, it may be possible for a researcher to exploit the strength of experimentation without actually having to design the experiment or intervene.

One example is a recent study of private members' legislation put forth by Canadian MPs. As of 2004, the order in which backbench MPs are given the opportunity to submit a piece of legislation (or motion) for study (or vote) in the House of Commons is determined by a lottery. Loewen and colleagues (2014) exploited this law as an opportunity to examine the Canadian electorate's responsiveness to more active backbenchers and, as a corollary, whether this new method of proposing legislation may lead to some sort of electoral gain in subsequent elections. In this example, the law ensures that allocation to treatment (i.e. having the opportunity to propose something in the House) occurs as a matter of chance, completely satisfying the "as if" random assumption. Indeed, winning this type of lottery is by definition exogenous in the sense that it is completely unrelated to any other factor that may be related to the outcome of interest (i.e. performance in subsequent elections). Loewen and colleagues may thus confidently compare the electoral performance of MPs who won the draw to those who did not, in order to see whether more legislative activity improves chances of re-election.

More often than not, however, it is difficult for researchers to make a credible claim that assignment to some treatment occurs as if by random chance in a natural setting. Moreover, researchers may want to exploit situations in which the assignment of a treatment is in fact planned and intentional, such as studies that treat instances of electoral reform as "interventions" in the experimental sense of the term. Such studies are perhaps better labelled as **quasi-experiments**, given the inherent difficulty in making "as if" random assumptions and the inability to control for the fact that some interventions (e.g. electoral reform) are consciously implemented to influence precisely the desired outcomes (electoral turnout). An example of a quasi-experiment is Gomez, Hansford, and Krause's (2007), which is one of the most extensive studies of precipitation's impact on voter turnout in the United States. In another interesting study, Healy, Malhotra, and Hyunjung Mo (2010) suggest that factors unrelated to politics—such as a home-team college football win—may affect voters' mood and thus influence electoral outcomes. Although precipitation and college football wins may indeed be unplanned and affect observed patterns of political behaviour, such events may be correlated with some other geographically distributed demographic characteristics. If not completely exogenous, these characteristics may thus bias results.

Because practical and ethical constraints prohibit using randomized controlled experiments to study certain types of research questions, naturally occurring and quasi-experimental designs broaden the range of phenomena to which experimentation can be applied and thus play an important role in accumulating knowledge. For instance, quasi-experiments are sometimes necessary when researchers want to evaluate the consequences of particular policies and, for this reason, are commonly used by academics (Campbell and Ross 1968) and multilateral institutions (e.g. the World Bank) in policy evaluation. Given that they take place under real-life conditions, naturally occurring and quasi-experiments may succeed in achieving higher levels of external validity (as is also true of field experiments). To the extent that the assignment of conditions is beyond the researcher's control, however, pure randomization is rarely achieved in the strict sense. Thus, in contrast to the types of randomized controlled experiments described earlier, researchers exploiting naturally occurring experiments cannot claim to control for all possible observed, unobserved, or unobservable confounders. This inability may weaken the internal validity of studies relying on natural events (see Sekhon and Titiunik 2012).

Ethical Issues and Other Limits of Experimentation in Political Science

Though unrivalled as the gold standard for making valid causal inferences, experimentation in political science, like all methods, has its limits. Some have already been mentioned with reference to internal and external validity. Others are more fundamental and relate to the desirability of the experimental techniques used. These types may be referred to as the ethical and practical limits of experimentation in political science.

As we have alluded to, it is sometimes impossible for researchers to manipulate variables of interest to political science. Given the practical constraints of what researchers may feasibly control, experiments (at least of the classic type) tend to be more fruitfully applied when individuals (as opposed to larger political communities) are the units of observation.

As a result, some of the "big" questions in political science—the causes of war and peace or the effects of institutions on politics—may be addressed only by naturally occurring or unplanned events that have some resemblance to a randomization procedure in the real world but lack more targeted intervention and control. This being the case, some of the most influential theories in politics carry assumptions about human nature (e.g. rationality), which may be tested by various types of experiments (Tversky and Kahneman 1974). Thus, while not all questions are as amenable to an experimental study, there are very likely some corollaries that are tractable using experimental data-gathering techniques.

Another important practical constraint relates to what McDermott (2002a) would call the illusion of total control. Although experiments are much better at controlling for confounding variables, there is always the possibility that some extraneous factors may unduly influence the way that some subjects interpret a stimulus and thereby bias results. Though experiments are extremely good at discerning whether a variable has (even an extremely small) effect on an outcome of interest, such designs may have more difficulty tracing detailed interactions and estimating relative effect sizes across a range of potentially interrelated variables in more complex models of political processes (Imai et al. 2011; Bullock, Green, and Ha 2010).

Of potentially greater concern, experiments may raise important ethical issues when they are implemented in practice. This is because, as opposed to playing a more passive role in observational studies, experimental researchers often manipulate aspects of an environment to see how human subjects react. In some studies, randomly withholding a program from part of the population for the purpose of making valid comparisons may be morally reprehensible on the grounds of equity and fairness. More often than not, political science experiments do not deal with the random assignment of government programs but on the randomized administration of some stimuli—for example, different rules in a game, question wording in a questionnaire, or political advertisements during a campaign.

At times, this intervention implies some form of deception, which is necessary in order to get subjects to buy into the artificial environment created by the researcher and to limit interactions with other subjects, who may have received different conditions under the same experimental setting. Deception in experimental designs can range from the relatively benign withholding of information (as in a single- or double-blind study) to the somewhat more intrusive practice of deliberately misleading someone to believe that something fake is actually real (for a striking example, see Milgram 1974). Under such conditions, a subject might feel threatened, offended, or uncomfortable. But in no cases should an experiment compromise a subject's health.

The *Tri-Council Policy Statement* (CIHR 2010) gives an official position on deception and other ethical issues in experimental research. Though the document offers general guidelines, it is ultimately up to the institutional review boards that govern the research ethics across North America's largest research institutions to determine whether a proposed study's risk to human participants is outweighed by its scientific contribution. To satisfy this requirement, researchers must develop a convincing case that such risks have been minimized by a detailed protocol outlining how eligible subjects are to be recruited, how researchers are to receive informed consent, how researchers will deal with the confidentiality of the data, and, crucially, how a debriefing will inform participants about the nature and purpose of the deception (if involved). When followed, this procedure helps ensure that the rights of subjects—including the right of refusal—are completely respected while also providing the researcher with an opportunity to make substantive strides in the accumulation of knowledge.

Conclusion

This chapter discussed the challenges related to making valid causal inferences, the advantages of using random assignment, and the different issues to consider when preparing an experiment. It also highlighted many of the benefits and drawbacks associated with experimental data-gathering techniques, as well as practical and ethical limitations.

To be sure, an artificial environment, combined with samples often drawn from WEIRD and student populations, certainly raises important questions about the external validity of experimentation in political science. However, such a critique is not always appropriate, particularly in the context of experiments conducted on representative samples (as in the case of population survey-based experiments) or experiments conducted in the field. Moreover, as McDermott (2002b, 334) concisely points out: "Without internal validity, there can be no external validity." In other words, because there is no significant contribution made by generalizing flawed results, external validity should become a concern only as a research agenda progresses and as internal validity is strengthened. The experiment's unique strength in improving the quality of causal inferences thus plays a key role in the accumulation of knowledge and can be expanded through the replication of existing studies using different experimental designs and in different experimental settings.

A more fundamental limit concerns the applicability of experimental designs to particular questions of interest to political scientists. Indeed, many interesting hypotheses in political science cannot be tested by randomly assigning an independent variable. For instance, if survey data suggest that women preferred Hillary Clinton to Barack Obama during the 2008 US Democratic primary, it will always remain impossible to randomly assign someone's gender to improve the validity of this causal inference.

Though experimental methods have their limits, they also present researchers with enormous opportunity. Much like clinical trials test a new drug before putting it on the market, the fact that experimental researchers generate their data makes it possible to test for the effects of novel political features that are not yet available in the real world. For instance, in Bond et al.'s (2012) "61-million-person experiment," researchers designed a

Facebook application allowing users to inform their friends that they had voted. The study found that, compared to a control group of Facebook users who did not use the app, users receiving cues from friends fulfilling their civic duty actually voted in a higher proportion. Like the St-Vincent (2013) study mentioned earlier, Bond et al.'s work provides an example of how experiments allow researchers to test the causal effects of novel political features—such as electoral systems and Facebook apps—that may one day become more prominent in the real world.

Experimental designs also make it possible to break causal processes into more tractable pieces and dig deeper into causality in order to investigate more complex causal effects. For example, Gerber and Green (2000) test the efficacy of different get-out-the-vote messages, including some that emphasize the civic duty of voters to participate in democracy and others offering a gentler nudge simply reminding people to vote. The delivery of these different messages was also randomly assigned, so that messages were communicated via face-to-face canvassing, postcard, or pre-recorded phone calls. Since the experimental design randomized both the message content and the communication media, researchers could arrive at more sophisticated conclusions about which combinations succeeded best at increasing turnout. These types of field experiments hold the promise of making valid causal inferences while achieving high levels of external validity as well. Maximizing the inferential leverage of naturally occurring, "as if" randomized treatment assignment also provides another promising avenue for future research.

Experimental designs are increasingly becoming an important part in the political scientist's methodological tool kit. We invite students interested in conducting experiments to begin with more modest designs, such as lab experiments with student samples or survey experiments using crowdsourcing, to replicate past studies in new contexts. Ultimately, experimental methods hold much promise for young scholars interested in testing their ideas and making valid causal inferences. The increased use of experimentation in political science is a welcome development contributing to knowledge accumulation in various fields, and the trend toward more common use of these methods is therefore likely to continue.

Working as a Team

1. Brainstorm several causal research questions of interest to political science. Once you have a list of four or five, select two or three and work your way through the steps of designing an experimental study. What is your hypothesis? What type of treatment might you test for? What type of experimental design might you use? Where might you recruit subjects? Once you have settled on a design, go back and evaluate your proposed research project in terms of its limits (e.g. any concerns you may have with internal and external validity). What ethical issues might your design raise? Are some

of your research questions more amenable to an experimental design than others? Why or why not?

2. Do experiments allow researchers in political science to finally solve the fundamental problem of causal inference? Why or why not?

Self-Study

1. On the chart below, locate how lab experiments (L), survey experiments (S), field experiments (F), naturally occurring experiments (N), and quasi-experiments (Q) stand with regard to internal validity and external validity. Use an uppercase letter when randomization is initiated by the researcher and a lowercase when it is not.

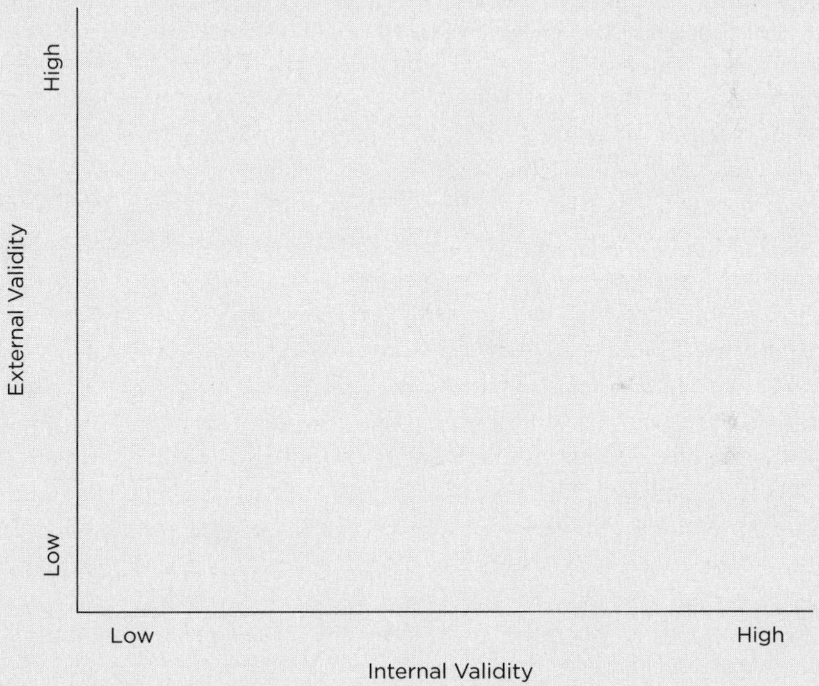

Notes

1. For more information about potential threats to internal validity, see McDermott (2002a).
2. Suppose an experiment measures the impact of watching a three-hour political debate on people's level of cynicism about politics. Although the experiment is interested in testing the causal effect of the actual debate, forcing people to stay immobile for that long may tire or bore them, potentially inducing them to provide cynical responses independent of what they actually think about the debate. Hence, the measured effect in this example does not actually reflect the real impact of watching a political debate per se but is instead a by-product of watching a three-hour debate,

be it political or not. To better control for such confounding effects related to treatment assignment when the number of research subjects is sufficiently large, researchers might consider implementing two control groups: one with no treatment and one with a placebo treatment. The demonstration of a placebo effect is in itself a scientific contribution as it may lead to questioning the validity of previous experiments. When the number of subjects is not sufficient, researchers should ponder the pros and the cons of each option in order to justify their choice afterward.

3. Experiments conducted in a lab inherently face greater threats to their external validity, but studies have found that student subjects behave in ways that are not that different from the broader population in certain types of experiments (Kühberger 1998, cited in Druckman 2001). Moreover, despite the artificial environment in which they occur, laboratory experiments can help shed light on micro-level cognitive factors that shape strategic behaviour and calculation that are also likely to operate in real-world settings.
4. Although some define survey experiments narrowly to include only those administered to random probability samples (Mutz 2011), survey experiments can also be administered in a relatively small sample that is not probability based (Nock and Guterbock 2010).

CHAPTER 12

Textual Analysis

Linda Trimble, University of Alberta
Natasja Treiberg, Athabasca University

Destination

By the end of this chapter, you should be able to

- define textual analysis and understand why it is used in political science research;
- apply quantitative and qualitative textual analysis methods when conducting original research;
- explain the strengths and weaknesses of quantitative and qualitative textual analysis research methods; and
- describe the ethical considerations related to textual analysis.

Textual analysis is the systematic examination of the messages and meanings conveyed by texts. A **text** is any form of communication, be it written, visual, spoken, or even sung (Neuman and Robson 2009, 221). The conversations you have with your friends constitute texts because they feature **content**, defined as any message—words, meanings, symbols, or themes—that can be communicated (Neuendorf 2002, 227). Political actors use texts to "promise, threaten, insult, plead and demand" (Halperin and Heath 2012, 311). Political scientists analyze texts because of what they reveal about the ideas, goals, motivations, and activities of politicians, political organizations, and institutions. Additionally, textual analysis can shed light on political issues and events. For example, Kern and Nam (2013) explored how value commitments were activated and used to mobilize a large-scale anti-globalization movement by examining the tactical briefings providing detailed information and instructions to participants in the Occupy campaign.

Researchers interested in political messages scrutinize political party manifestos, government and party websites, records of legislative debates, court decisions, and, of course, actual legislation. The speeches of American presidents are among the most widely studied political texts. Because "presidents exist in the public imagination largely through their words" (Coe and Neumann 2011, 728), their speeches are a gold mine for researchers, who sift through them to identify beliefs, agendas, and persuasion techniques. But plenty of overtly and subtly political content is embedded in texts produced by non-government actors. Everything from political graffiti to talk radio debates, protest signs and slogans, and country music lyrics can be analyzed systematically for the political meanings they convey and for what they say about the societies producing these meanings. Mass media texts are also ripe for political analysis, as there is a great deal to be learned from investigating mainstream news coverage of politics on television, on radio, and in newspapers and from looking at web-based texts such as blogs, websites, and social networking sites. A wealth of messages is readily available for textual analysis.

This chapter presents both quantitative and qualitative approaches to analyzing texts. **Content analysis** is a quantitative research technique used to explore the message characteristics in any form of communication (Neuendorf 2002, 1; Neuman and Robson 2009, 221). By employing this method of gathering and analyzing information, researchers can methodically and rigorously account for the content in texts. **Discourse analysis**, in contrast, is a qualitative approach that focuses on the meanings reflected in, and created by, discourses. **Discourses** are sets of "meanings, metaphors, representations, images, stories, statements and so on that in some way together produce a particular version of events" (Burr 1995, 48). Discourses expose everyday understandings about social and political life; therefore, discourse analysis seeks to "uncover how discursive practices construct meanings through the production, dissemination, and consumption of various forms of texts" (Halpernin and Heath 2012, 311). In short, content analysis reveals overt patterns in texts, while discourse analysis reveals what discourses signify in the context in which they are communicated and understood (Sampert and Trimble 2010, 326).

Why Use Textual Analysis?

Very few people join political parties or interest groups, participate in direct political action, or support political causes. Most of us are spectators to political life, and the information we gather and impressions we form are based on texts. We learn about political events and issues second-hand, by watching political news on television, following politicians on Twitter, accessing government or political party information online, or engaging in debates with friends on Facebook. Systematic analysis of these texts can tell us what is being said about politics and what is assumed or understood to be "true." Political communications are actions designed to achieve particular goals or outcomes. As a result, the texts created by political actors, be they elected politicians or "ordinary" citizens, reflect the norms, assumptions, and values resonant in the society within which these texts are created and consumed. Moreover, texts reveal how different actors construct different versions of the political world or different understandings of social reality.

Political scientists use content and discourse analysis to determine how political issues, events, and actors are represented in a text's structural features and to identify what its substantive features communicate. Analysis of **structural features** focuses on the communication's format and the content's presentation. For example, *The Globe and Mail*'s increasing use of photographs in its coverage of Canadian federal party leadership contests shows that the newspaper is embracing television's visual storytelling techniques (Sampert et al. 2014).

The question of how political messages are presented is an increasingly important topic because a revolution in web-based technology allows politicians and citizens alike to communicate via social media platforms such as Facebook, Twitter, and YouTube. Barak Obama's 2008 presidential campaign is considered an exemplar of this trend, with its more than two million Facebook "friends," a popular Twitter page, and, perhaps most important, an online fundraising campaign that raked in over half a billion dollars (Small 2012, 169). On a much smaller but no less successful scale, Calgary mayoral candidate Naheed Nenshi's sophisticated social media campaign propelled him from a distant third place to an electoral victory in 2010 (CBC News, 2010a). Why does the medium matter? According to communications scholar David Taras (2012, 4), Internet technologies fuel the permanent campaign, perpetuating the never-ending election cycle. As illustrated by the Occupy and Idle No More movements, social media allow activists to quickly and effectively mobilize support, organize protests, and communicate the movement's goals. But does the medium change the message? Is the content any different, any more (or less) informative or engaging? Textual analysis can also address these sorts of questions by exploring the substantive meanings communicated by texts.

The **substantive features** of a communication are measured by focusing on what is said and what it means; that is, how words, themes, ideas, symbols, frames, metaphors, and rhetorical devices convey particular meanings, norms, and assumptions. With substantive measures, it is important to note the distinction between manifest and latent content in communications. **Manifest content** is the literal, or surface, meaning of the message (Neuman and Robson 2009, 223). **Latent content** is the underlying or implied meaning (Sumser 2001, 200). Of the two types, manifest content is much easier to account for and measure objectively with a quantitative approach such as content analysis.

Researchers often use qualitative discourse analysis to identify latent content because its meanings are frequently a matter of interpretation. For example, determining whether a politician's looks are discussed in newspaper stories is a fairly straightforward task. A researcher can count the number of references to a politician's body, clothes, styling, and grooming. Many studies have found that reporters are significantly more likely to comment on the physical appearance of female politicians than on the looks of male politicians (see, for instance, Campus 2013, 82–3). But quantitative analysis leaves important questions unanswered. What does it mean when the media highlight women's hairstyles and wardrobes yet ignore the sartorial elements of men's political identities? Qualitative analysis allows researchers to explore what these representations reveal about gender and political leadership norms (e.g. Falk 2010).

How to Conduct Textual Analysis

Both content and discourse analysis engage with theory, but they are guided by a different logic and have different approaches to theory construction. The former is usually descriptive and objective and the latter interpretive and subjective. To put the distinction very simply, content analysis takes a scientific approach to measuring manifest content, answering "how many" and "how often" questions about the messages communicated by texts. Because discourse analysts see texts as embedded within socially constructed meaning structures, researchers begin with theory and adopt a deductive approach, observing how discourses reflect, reinforce, and perhaps even challenge relationships of power, historical social structures, and institutional norms.

Content Analysis

The first stage in content analysis is to craft a research question for the study to answer. A clear, concise research question is essential because a vague or imprecise query cannot be operationalized. As discussed in Chapter 5, operationalization is the "process of moving from the conceptual definition of a construct to a set of specific activities or measures that allow a researcher to observe it empirically" (Neuman and Robson 2009, 395).

The second step is to pose at least one hypothesis for the study to test (see Chapter 3 for a discussion of hypotheses). However, content analysts do not invariably test hypotheses, especially if the research is exploratory and there is insufficient evidence to hypothesize. For instance, Roberts (2013) wondered if web-only campaign advertisements disseminated by American presidential candidates during the 2004 and 2008 elections differed in content and tone from traditional televised advertisements, or "spots." Because there has been little investigation of the use and content of online-only ads, Roberts could not draw on the literature for hypotheses and his research question reflected the preliminary nature of the project. He asked: "How are web-only spots different from traditional broadcast spots in efforts to acclaim, attack or defend policies and/or character?" (Roberts 2013, 29). The findings of his study—that traditional TV ads were significantly more likely than web-only spots to acclaim candidates via positive statements about their credentials and that web-only spots were more often deployed to attack opponent's credentials—will guide the hypotheses of future research in this area.

Expand Your Knowledge

A Step-by-Step Guide to Content Analysis

1. Develop a clear, precise, and answerable research question.
2. Based on the relevant literature, draw at least one hypothesis for testing.
3. Identify the texts to be analyzed (the population).
4. Determine how many texts will be analyzed (a census or sample).
5. Choose the portion of the text that will be analyzed (the unit of analysis).
6. Specify what you are looking for in the text and how you will measure it.
7. Gather the data via rigorous, systematic, and replicable coding procedures.
8. Quantitatively analyze the data to determine whether the findings support the hypothesis, or hypotheses, for the study.

In the third step, the researcher decides which texts will be analyzed. It is crucial to identify the population of texts most appropriate to answering the research question and testing the hypothesis (Manheim et al. 2008, 181–2). Some texts may be readily available but inappropriate for answering the research question. Researchers need to be particularly careful to take the validity of the data source and the context of the communication into account when designing their research projects. Who produces the text, and under what circumstances and conditions? What is the intended purpose of, and audience for, the communication? What are the biases of the data source? Texts are produced with particular audiences in mind, under particular rules and conditions, and through particular routines. An analysis of the prime minister's Facebook page may indicate what he wants Canadians to know about his private persona, but these texts cannot provide an authoritative account of his policy agenda. Choosing the population is often very difficult. For instance, analyzing media coverage of a political issue or event requires making hard choices, as there are many media organizations and outlets to choose from.

Even if the field is narrowed to newspapers, the researcher needs to decide which ones should be included in the study. Then another decision awaits: Should the study contain a sample of articles from the selected newspapers or all the coverage of the event (a **census**)? These choices represent the fourth step. The census approach worked for Abu-Laban and Trimble's (2010) content and discourse analysis of Canadian newspaper coverage of Muslim Canadians during the 2000, 2004, and 2006 Canadian federal elections because, even though they searched 8 newspapers, only 67 news stories met their search criteria. But if the universe (the entire population of texts available) is large, it must be confined to a manageable number.

Determining the number of texts to be analyzed depends on available resources, including time. One option is to carry out a purposive sample based on certain criteria that are logical and clearly related to the research problem. For instance, a researcher could choose to reduce the number of sources or restrict the time frame under examination. Had Abu-Laban and Trimble's search produced a large number of news articles, they could have opted to narrow the time frame to one or two elections. Another option is to carry out a random sample of the texts, thus eliminating sampling bias. (Sampling was discussed in Chapter 8.) The choices made with respect to selecting the population need to be justified as appropriate to answering the research question.

Fifth, the researcher must choose the **unit of analysis**, the smallest portion of the text that will be coded. It can be the entire text, though content analysis often breaks the text into smaller segments so that they are more easily analyzed. The segment of the text to be analyzed can be a single word, image, or symbol; a sentence or paragraph; a theme; a character; a narrative; or a metaphor. It depends what the researcher is looking for. Trimble and Sampert (2004) focused on headlines in their study of national newspaper coverage of the 2000 Canadian election because they wanted to find out if the *National Post*, whose editorial stance favoured the Canadian Alliance Party, was more likely than *The Globe and Mail* to name the Alliance and its leader and to express a positive opinion of the party. They chose headlines because these prominent features are written by news editors and are thus more likely than articles to display the news organization's partisan preferences.

With the sixth step, the researcher decides what to look for in the text and how to precisely account for it. Because content analysis uses objective and systematic counting and classification procedures to "produce a quantitative description of the symbolic content in the text" (Neuman and Robson 2009, 221), it looks for categories that can be quantified. This process is called **coding**. The researcher develops a **codebook** that lists the items to be coded (variables) and specifies how they will be coded (values). For instance, one of Trimble and Sampert's (2004) variables was the newspaper that produced the headline. *The Globe and Mail* was assigned a code of 1 and the *National Post* a code of 2. Coding can identify several characteristics of a text, including idea, frequency, direction, intensity, prominence, and size. The following list defines and gives an example of each type.

- **Idea** refers to the issue or message being communicated: Do speeches by the minister of the environment refer to the concept of climate change?
- **Frequency** means whether or not something occurs in a text, and if it does, how often: How often does the minister of the environment mention climate change in her speeches?
- **Direction** means identifying the type of message by situating it along some sort of continuum or classification scheme: When the minister mentions climate change, is she accepting the phenomenon as a fact, expressing skepticism about its very existence, or denying the phenomenon outright?
- **Intensity** is another measure that can be used in content analysis: Is climate change emphasized with strong, emotive images or metaphors?

- **Prominence**, which can be gauged by the message's location in the text, indicates the importance of the topic or event to the text's creators: Is climate change the first issue mentioned in the minister's speeches?
- The **size** of a message measures how much space or time it takes within the text: What proportion of each speech is devoted to the topic of climate change?

Creating a codebook that establishes clear coding categories and protocols is time-consuming but very important. Values must be mutually exclusive (not overlap) and collectively exclusive (include all the possible answers to the question). In the sample codebook provided in Table 12.1, taken from a study by Trimble, Way, and Sampert (2010), one of the variables is designed to measure whether voters are depicted in editorial cartoons published during election campaigns. The values, "yes" or "no," are mutually exclusive and exhaust the possible answers to the question: are voters represented in the text?

But assigning values, or coding, is not always this straightforward. If the researcher wanted to conduct exploratory research to determine who (or what) is represented in political cartoons about elections, it would be difficult to list all the possible answers to this question in advance of data collection. Because it is important to include all relevant answers, the researcher might want to employ **open coding** before settling on a concrete list of values. Open coding requires listing, for each case, all the possible answers that appear in the texts. These answers can later be categorized for **closed coding**, coding each case based on a specific list of values. For instance, you might observe that editorial cartoonists depict a wide range of actors and organizations, including political parties, citizens, media, interest groups, and political institutions.

Regardless of the coding approach used, a codebook should outline consistent rules so that all coders are provided clear criteria for judgment. These coding notes may include observations about items the researcher decided to include or exclude as he or she went along, or detailed instructions for coding latent content. For example, Trimble, Way, and Sampert's (2010) codebook explains that voters can be depicted by being drawn into the cartoon as figures, mentioned in the editorial cartoon's caption or speech bubble, or represented with signs or symbols. It is important to test and retest the coding frame on a sample of the cases to resolve any coding issues. If results are inconsistent on a particular variable, the problem must be resolved before coding begins.

Once the researcher has confirmed that the coding process is reliable by checking to see that different coders arrive at the same answers, he or she can proceed to the seventh stage of the content analysis process: coding the texts. To facilitate systematic and reliable data collection, a **coding sheet**, on which coders can record the values for each case in the sample, is created (see Table 12.2). Guided by the codebook, the coder records the codes for each case and each individual variable on the coding sheet. As well, each case is assigned a **case identification** number as a way of locating it in the database.

Table 12.1 Codebook for Cartoons during the 2004, 2006, and 2008 Federal Elections[1]

General Coding Note: For editorial cartoons to be selected for coding, their focus must be the federal election.

Variable #	Variable Name	Values and Value Labels
Structural Variables		
1	Case ID	Coding Note: Case identification number begins with a C (for Cartoon), then the initials of the paper being coded (NP for *National Post*, GM for *The Globe and Mail*), followed by the sequential number: CNP1, CNP2; CGM1, CGM2, etc.
2	Election	2004 2006 2008
3	Newspaper	1. *National Post* 2. *The Globe and Mail*
Substantive Variables		
4	Frame	What is the main frame of the cartoon? Game frame Issue frame Other (specify in variable 34) Coding Notes: Determine which is the dominant frame of the cartoon. **Game Frame:** This frame reflects a preoccupation with winners and losers, conflict, strategy, and personalities. References to polls and to game images or metaphors (e.g. the horse race or boxing match) will be prominent in the cartoon. **Issue Frame:** This frame reflects a focus on campaign issues, party platforms, party ideologies, or the government record on particular issues. References to particular campaign issues, or party policy pronouncements, will be prominent in the cartoon.
5	Liberal	Is the Liberal Party depicted in the cartoon? Yes No Coding Note: Code as "yes" *only* if the party is named (there is a separate measure for the party leader, below) *If the party's symbol is included, code as "yes."*
6	Conserv	Is the Conservative Party depicted in the cartoon? Yes No
7	NDP	Is the NDP depicted in the cartoon? Yes No
8	BQ	Is the Bloc Québécois depicted in the cartoon? Yes No
9	Voters	Are voters depicted in the cartoon? Yes No Coding Note: Code as "yes" if voters are drawn into the cartoon as figures, mentioned in the editorial cartoon's caption or speech bubble, or represented with a sign or symbol.

1. This example does not replicate all the variables included in the study.
Source: Trimble et al. (2010).

Table 12.2 Sample Coding Sheet

Case ID	Election	Paper	Frame	Liberal	Conserv	NDP	BQ	Voters
CNP1	1	1	1	2	1	2	2	2
CGM1	1	2	2	2	2	2	2	1
CGM2								
CNP2								

Source: Adapted from Trimble et al. (2010)

Analyzing or making sense of the data is the crucial eighth and final step in the textual analysis process. The data recorded on the coding sheet are entered into a database for analysis. Typically, researchers create SPSS or Excel files featuring an identification number for each variable and its corresponding values. It is advisable to run frequencies on each variable to find and correct any data entry errors. From this point, the quantitative data analysis can be conducted, including means (see Chapter 14), crosstabulations (see Chapter 16), and regression analyses (see Chapter 17). The researcher analyzes the findings, determining whether or not the hypothesis was supported. He or she must also reflect on how well the research question was answered by the findings and decide whether or not to test alternative hypotheses.

Discourse Analysis

Before we begin itemizing the how-tos of the qualitative approach to textual analysis, it is important to note that we use the term *discourse analysis* very loosely to refer to a wide range of research techniques and strategies. It is, in fact, impossible to identify a generic format for discourse analysis research. While we offer these steps as a guide, we encourage you to examine the works of various discourse analysts in order to understand the different approaches. You will notice that one recurring aspect is a desire to understand the "ways in which discourses give legitimacy and meaning to social practices and institutions" (Halperin and Heath 2012, 311).

Researchers who use qualitative forms of textual analysis want to go beyond exploring what is manifestly expressed by the text: they want to understand its meanings and their implications for political life. As such, their first step is to identify the problem to be investigated. In this process, discourse analysts are guided by theory and a concern for the role of discourses in reflecting and reinforcing existing power relations. For instance, because **critical discourse analysis** (CDA) investigates the ways in which discourses reflect, reproduce, and reinforce relationships of dominance, the analysis is structured around a theory about power, oppression, or inequality (see Fairclough 2001 and van Dijk 2008). Thomas W. Hairston (2013, 230) was concerned with race-based power relations, so his study of President Obama's speeches on education analyzed "how Americans hear perpetuations of racism through the call for neoliberal educational policies."

Expand Your Knowledge

A Step-by-Step Guide to Discourse Analysis

1. Guided by a theoretical or conceptual framework, identify the problem to be investigated.
2. Identify the discourse strand and sector of the discourse plane that are appropriate to investigating the problem and situate them within their discursive context.
3. Determine which discourse fragments (texts or portions of texts) need to be studied.
4. Gather the data (e.g. through a three-stage qualitative coding process).
5. Analyze the data based on the theoretical or conceptual framework guiding the study.

In the second stage of the discourse analysis process, the researcher identifies the **discourse strand** (the theme or issue to be investigated) and **plane** (or sector of a plane) in which the theme is expressed (Jäger 2001, 52). Discourses operate on various planes, defined as "the societal locations from which 'speaking' happens," including politics, media, science, business, and "everyday life" (Jäger 2001, 49). Researchers decide which particular discourses to analyze by focusing on those most likely to illuminate the problem or issue being investigated. Say you are interested in the articulation of anti-gay sentiments (the discourse strand) in everyday media discourses (the discourse plane). You could focus on a particular sector of a discourse plane, for instance, by examining homophobic discourses articulated by callers to a popular talk radio program (a sector of the media plane). This plane can be narrowed further by investigating a specific discursive event, such as an incident that sparked discussion on a particular program (e.g. the January 2014 decision by the Obama administration to recognize the marriages of 1300 same sex couples in Utah who were left in limbo by the Supreme Court). It is important to then identify how the ideology of homophobia is expressed. In other words, the researcher needs to determine which discourses help formulate and express this ideology. How is homophobia expressed in characterizations of prominent LGBT figures, reactions to political decisions such as the repeal of the "Don't Ask, Don't Tell" policy, or in conservative arguments about the alleged decline of the American family and degeneration of American values due to the legalization of same sex marriage?

Considering the character of the discourses being analyzed is a crucial part of this selection process. How are the discourses disseminated? What is their intended audience? Who is creating the discourses and for what purposes? Examining Americans' reactions to Obama's decision, for instance, will reveal social assumptions about the appropriate role of the state in fostering social change, but will not illuminate the government's ideological positions. This is because discourses are produced by particular actors operating within specific circumstances and reflect "antecedent choices, conditions or processes" (Riffe, Lacy, and Fico 2005, 10). As Jäger (2001, 48) puts it, they are entangled within a particular discursive context.

Let's look at an example that illustrates the complicated process of choosing discourses for analysis. Berger and Naaman (2011) were interested in the visual representation of women combat soldiers, particularly the extent to which they are sexualized and trivialized in widely disseminated photographs. As a result, the researchers identified the mass media as the appropriate discourse plane. Since it would be enormously time-consuming to analyze the meanings embedded in all such photos, they had to choose the discourse strand carefully. They identified photographs of Israeli women soldiers as a fruitful site of analysis because these images would communicate understandings about women engaged in active combat roles. A key discursive event guiding their selection was the participation of women in the 2006 Lebanon war, and they analyzed photos of women soldiers at major points in the conflict. The character and context of the discourses was an important consideration as well. Because they wanted to determine whether female Israeli soldiers were represented differently by photographs produced by different actors and for different audiences, Berger and Naaman also looked at photos published by the Israeli army's official magazine (which is circulated within the army), newspaper photographs published during the 2006 Lebanon war, and images of women combat soldiers in mass circulation men's and women's magazines.

The third step involves determining which **discourse fragments** to explore and how they will be interpreted. Discourse fragments are the texts, or the portions of texts, chosen for analysis because of the themes or meanings they are likely to convey. Jäger (2001, 54) refers to this stage as "processing the material." To continue with the example of Berger and Naaman's (2011) study, the researchers selected particular fragments (photographs) for analysis and scrutinized each image and its accompanying caption, examining poses, gestures, facial expressions, clothing and equipment, props and backdrops, and setting and context.

Depending on the research problem, the discourse analyst may want to examine some or all of the text's surface features, syntactical structures, thematic structures, narrative structures, frames, rhetorical devices, ideological assertions, or silences. Each of these elements is summarized below, with an example to illustrate how it can be identified and analyzed. However, this is by no means a complete list of the features that can be observed through discourse analysis.

- **Surface structures** include the form, format, structure, and layout of the text. For example, a newspaper article can take one of several forms: a news brief, a regular news story, a feature, an editorial, an editorial cartoon, a letter to the editor, a captioned stand-alone photograph, or an opinion column. Each format has a different purpose and goal (see Franklin 2008). For instance, editorials assert the opinion of the newspaper, but letters to the editor reflect the (carefully selected) reactions of news audiences.

- **Syntactical structures** are the arrangements of words, symbols, or images in the text. A news story includes a headline, a lead paragraph, and a concluding paragraph and may also feature quotations, photos or illustrations, captions, and text boxes. These structural elements both reflect and create meanings. For example, quoting a source directly confers legitimacy by signalling that his or her words are important to understanding the issue or event. Using scare quotes around a word or phrase allows the newspaper to distance itself from the sentiment being expressed. (See van Dijk [1991] for a discussion of the semantic roles of different newspaper story features).
- **Narrative structures** are standard storylines, or narrative devices, used to create tension and keep an audience's attention. Narratives reveal how societies apply moral reasoning, "establish commonalities, promote goodness, and discourage wickedness" (Johnson-Cartee 2005, 149). For instance, Anker (2005, 22) argues that the television news' melodramatic renderings of the September 11 terrorist attacks signified the United States as a "morally powerful victim," thus justifying its desire to seek heroic retribution.
- Gitlin (1980, 7) defines **frames** as "persistent patterns of cognition, interpretation, and presentation, of selection, emphasis and exclusion, by which symbol-handlers routinely organize discourse." For example, elections are routinely framed by the news media as horse races. This frame emphasizes who is winning and why, focusing on the strategies used by parties to "get ahead." Excluded, or elided, is discussion of the ideational elements of campaigns, such as ideological differences between parties or the distinct policy choices they offer (Trimble and Sampert 2004). Frames resonate with audiences because they draw on familiar myths, themes, or cultural values. As a result, frames are particularly valuable to discourse analysis because they illustrate the norms and values circulating in a given society.
- **Rhetorical devices**, or semantic techniques of persuasion, include irony, hyperbole, and metaphor. Metaphors are particularly powerful rhetorical devices and are widely used in political speech and media accounts of political life. Falk (2013) observed that the US media used a playing-the-gender card metaphor in its accounts of Hillary Clinton's campaign for the 2008 Democratic presidential nomination to subtly communicate negative assumptions about the role of women in politics and to hide relations of power and dominance.
- **Ideological assertions**, such as those about human nature, power, or political values, are often implicitly or explicitly articulated in politically relevant discourses, as they are concerned with "establishing one version of the world in the fact of competing versions" (Gill 2000, 186). For example, Hairston (2013) specifically

examines how Obama's speeches situate education within the neo-liberal ideology, thus perpetuating racism and inequality.

- Noting **silences and omissions** can be very important in analyzing discourses, as certain "ways of thinking and seeing become invisible because they are assumed to be truthful and right" (Halpernin and Heath 2012, 312). Abu-Laban and Trimble's (2010) assessment of Canadian newspaper coverage of federal elections focused as much on what was not said about Muslims as it did on what was said about this heterogeneous group of Canadians.

After establishing what will be observed in the texts, the researcher proceeds to the fourth stage of the discourse analysis process: gathering the data. The three-stage qualitative coding process used by some qualitative researchers is detailed in Chapter 13. Others refer to this step as akin to taking a "long preliminary soak" in the material before looking for patterns and identifying latent meanings (Falk 2013, 194).

The fifth step is to interpret the data. This process is conceptual rather than numerical. As illustrated by the example provided in the next section, the researcher makes sense of the qualitative information, linking it to the conceptual framework for analysis. Rather than offering numerical data, the analyst provides a detailed description, explanation, and evaluation of the discourse, relying on themes, narratives, images, words, or quotations to illustrate generalizations and arguments.

Discourse Analysis: Sample Discourse Framework

Trimble et al.'s (2010) qualitative analysis of editorial cartoons was directed by the following research question: Did "the cartoonists represent voters as being pulled, or attracted, to the polls—compelled to participate, out of engagement with the issues, a sense of citizen duty, or a feeling that the outcomes really mattered?" (Trimble et al., 2010, 71). While content analysis of the cartoons found that voters featured quite prominently, discourse analysis revealed that they were not represented as active agents in the democratic process.

The researchers arrived at this finding by applying a detailed framework for data-gathering and analysis. They took detailed notes on each cartoon, based on a series of questions about how the symbols, messages, and meanings in the cartoons represented voters or non-voters. The first two questions were designed to gauge how cartoonists represented voter roles and motivations (Trimble et al 2010, 71):

1. How do the cartoons represent the roles and functions of voters in the campaign? What are voters (or members of the voting-age public) depicted as doing? Are they shown as actively engaged in the electoral process, or as mere observers, or as fully disengaged?
2. How are the attitudes and motivations of voters (and non-voters) represented? Are voters portrayed as interested or apathetic? Are they represented as hopeful and efficacious or as cynical and disillusioned?

This analysis produced four categories, or clusters: non-voters and disengaged citizens, innocent bystanders, critical spectators, and active citizens. Since several of the cartoons could be read in more than one way, and thus fit into multiple categories, the researchers assigned them to the cluster that most strongly reflected the cartoon's core message.

To determine how the cartoonists allocated responsibility for the efficacy of the electoral process, the researchers added the following question to their discourse framework (Trimble et al. 2010, 76):

> How did the cartoonists evaluate the roles and motivations of voters (and non-voters)? Are voters assessed as important and integral to the electoral process? If problems with the electoral process are identified, are they portrayed as the fault of voters, or of other political actors, or the electoral system more generally?

Their analysis found that cartoonists tended to blame political organizations and institutions rather than voters for declining electoral participation.

Strengths and Weaknesses of Textual Analysis

A primary strength of textual analysis is its use as a methodological tool for many approaches to political science research, including cross-sectional, comparative, case study, longitudinal and experimental research designs. Textual analysis is often used as part of a mixed methods design. For instance, Iyengar (1996) coupled content analysis with an experiment to investigate how particular approaches to telling news stories shape the viewing public's understanding of, and attribution of political responsibility for, political issues. As Iyengar's study shows, mixed-method designs can address a major drawback of textual analysis. Neither content nor discourse analysis can get at media effects—the impact of texts on their intended audiences. Other research methods, such as interviews, surveys, and experiments, must be used to answer questions about how the meanings produced by texts are interpreted by audiences (Neuendorf 2002, 69).

The availability of texts is both a strength and weakness of textual analysis. There is an abundance of politically relevant texts available online, but some are more readily accessed than others. For example, newspaper databases such as Factiva and LexisNexis do not include news photographs. Television news programs are rarely available in video or digital form. Social media texts pose particular challenges for researchers because they are so transitory. It is often necessary for the researcher to gather these sorts of texts himself or herself or to analyze them when they are available.

Both quantitative and qualitative approaches to textual analysis have virtues and drawbacks. As previously noted, content analysis is effective in quantifying the nature, quantity, and placement of messages in a text and discourse analysis is often required to assess what these messages mean and what they communicate about the society, person, or organization producing them. We argue that content and discourse analysis can be used in concert because the strengths of one approach can compensate for the weaknesses of the other. This combination is not always an easy marriage, as theorists on either side often critique each other's methods. For example, many discourse analysts would dispute the claim that content analysis is objective.

Let's look at content analysis specifically. One of the key assets of this method is the reliability and validity of its findings. Categories of measurement are precisely defined and consistently applied, so it should produce the same or very similar results if conducted by someone else. For example, from reading the newspaper and watching TV news, you might believe that media coverage of electoral politics is quite critical of parties and their leaders, but, without evidence to back up your observation, it is merely an unsubstantiated impression. Quantitative analysis provides reliable evidence, as illustrated by Stuart Soroka and Blake Andrew's (2010, 114) content analysis of 6,694 articles about the 2004 and 2006 national election campaigns published in seven major daily newspapers across Canada. They found that most coverage was neutral. However, reporting was much more likely to be negative than positive when evaluations of political parties and their leaders were offered.

Because Soroka and Andrew examined all the coverage and tested for **intercoder reliability** (checking to see that different coders came up with the same interpretation), their findings are dependable. In other words, these researchers can say with confidence that newspaper evaluations of parties and their leaders in recent Canadian elections were predominantly negative in tone. But these data do not tell us whether the negative assessments are more critical for certain parties than for others. Nor can they answer the question of whether the assessments reflect ideological presumptions about particular parties. These sorts of questions are better answered through qualitative analysis.

When carefully designed and carried out, content analysis can examine large volumes of texts, make comparisons within and between texts, and measure changes in content over time. But content analysis is much better at accounting for manifest content than at analyzing latent content. Linda Trimble (1997) wanted to know if electing more women to the Alberta legislature generated more legislative debate about women's experiences, issues, and policy demands. This project meant looking at a large time frame—1972 to 1994—to include periods when there were few women in the legislature to periods when the percentage of female MLAs met or exceeded 15 per cent of the total number of elected legislators. Trimble compared the amount of attention to women's issues by different legislative actors (cabinet ministers, backbenchers, government members, or opposition members) and by discrete time periods based on the number of women in the legislature. She demonstrated that electing more women did generate more attention to women's concerns, though typically female opposition MLAs were at the forefront of this discussion. But while the study measured the topics addressed by legislators, it did not reveal whether the speakers or the speeches were sympathetic or hostile to women's policy needs and claims. So Trimble used discourse analysis was used to identify the tone and direction of the comments, with feminist theory as a conceptual framework for analyzing the meanings conveyed by the Alberta MLAs in their discussion of women and women's issues.

Other drawbacks of content analysis can similarly be mitigated with discourse analysis. The emphasis on **rigour** in quantitative measurement may mean that important messages are not captured by content analysis because of its reductionist tendencies. Discourse analysts see a discourse as a unified whole whose meanings cannot be disaggregated, or reduced to specific words, phrases, or symbols. The contextual meaning is often lost as a result. While it is easy to code the overt references within a text, it takes some ingenuity to identify the messages that are excluded or marginalized. Discourse analysis, on the other hand, is ideally suited to teasing out latent messages and meanings and situating them within their particular ideological or historical context. However, there is considerable potential for bias when accounting for underlying messages in texts or identifying patterns in discourses. The validity, or trustworthiness, of this methodology cannot be assumed, and it is important to carefully examine the assumptions underlying the research design as well as the rigour with which the research was carried out (Hackett, Gilsdorf, and Savage 1992). Discourse analysis should be clear and transparent about the theoretical presumptions guiding the study and the textual material under review. Furthermore, it should provide an interpretation of the material that is plausibly related to, and demonstrated by, the textual evidence (Halpernin and Heath 2012, 317).

Ethical Considerations

One of the most important strengths of textual analysis is that it is unobtrusive and non-reactive (Krippendorff 2004, 40; Riffe et. al. 2005, 38). Analyzing texts does not impact the time or convenience of others. If they have already been produced and published, there is no danger of texts being affected or influenced by the research process. On the other hand, if the texts being analyzed are part of an ongoing conversation (e.g. a Twitter exchange), the researcher's interventions could influence their content.

Most texts analyzed by political scientists are in the public domain. Consequently, studying them does not involve ethical issues such as the need to obtain the participant's informed consent or to guarantee his or her confidentiality. However, if the researcher wishes to analyze communications that are considered personal or private, ethical concerns are raised and issues of consent and confidentiality must be considered in the research design.

Working as a Team

1. Your team plans to conduct a textual analysis of provincial Throne Speeches to identify the evolving issue priorities of your provincial government. (For an example of how researchers analyze Speeches from the Throne, see Stuart Soroka, *Agenda-Setting Dynamics in Canada*, Vancouver: UBC Press, 2002, 64–6.) Each team member should analyze one Throne Speech. Decide how the team will choose which speeches to analyze and whether it will take a quantitative or qualitative approach to data-gathering and analysis. Then determine what, precisely, the team will look for and how to measure it.
2. Develop a codebook or discourse framework for your Throne Speech study and collect and analyze the data from each speech.

Self-Study

1. You want to find out if the authoritative voices of television news about politics are more likely to be male than female, thus reflecting dominant power relationships in Canadian political life. Because the CBC has a legislative mandate to be inclusive in its representations, you could hypothesize that the public broadcaster will have more women in these roles than its privately funded competitors do. Your project will compare the presence of women as news anchors, reporters, and experts on the CBC's *The National* with the equivalent national news show produced by a private broadcaster (e.g. CTV or Global). Choose one weekday for your study and watch the three broadcasts, which are available online. Using the coding sheets provided, record the number of men and women in each category for the top five politically relevant stories in each broadcast. Tabulate and analyze your results. Do the data support the hypothesis?

CBC	Topic	Anchor(s)		Reporter(s)		Expert(s)	
		Male	Female	Male	Female	Male	Female
Story #1							
Story #2							
Story #3							
Story #4							
Story #5							

CTV or Global	Topic	Anchor(s)		Reporter(s)		Expert(s)	
		Male	Female	Male	Female	Male	Female
Story #1							
Story #2							
Story #3							
Story #4							
Story #5							

2. As you code the news stories, you may notice that men are more likely to appear as reporters or experts for certain kinds of stories, such as those about the economy, elections, or political conflict, while women reporters and experts are more prevalent when the stories are about consumer issues, policies affecting the family, or matters of human interest. In the "Topic" column of the coding sheets, use open coding to identify the broad topic of each story. Is there a relationship between the gendered division of labour amongst those telling the stories and the types of stories being told?

PART III

Data Analysis

Once researchers have collected and cleaned their data, they turn to data analysis. Chapter 13 focuses on qualitative data analysis and introduces qualitative data-coding techniques. Chapters 14 through 17 concentrate on quantitative data analysis and introductory level statistics. Chapter 14 examines univariate statistics, or statistics used to describe a single variable. Such descriptive statistics are of interest not only in their own right but also as a foundation for statistics used in later chapters. Chapter 15 introduces inferential statistics, which assess whether the sample statistics are reasonable estimates of the population parameters. (Recall that we are interested in the population itself, not just the sample!) Chapter 16 considers relationships between two (bivariate) or more (multivariate) nominal- and ordinal-level variables, and Chapter 17 introduces the more advanced statistical technique of regression analysis. Finally, Chapter 18 looks at the next step, writing the research report.

The quantitative analysis chapters provide an overview to the step-by-step hand calculation of key statistics used in political science research. Understanding the mechanics of the statistics better equips political scientists to use the data appropriately. In real life, one rarely calculates such statistics by hand; instead, computer software programs such as SPSS, Stata, SAS, and R are used to quickly conduct the sometimes cumbersome calculations. However, it is the researcher who decides which statistics to run in the computer program, who ensures that the statistical assumptions are met, and who interprets the statistical results. For this reason, we suggest that you familiarize yourself with the individual statistics.

By introducing the basics of qualitative and quantitative data analysis, this section offers a general level of research literacy. On completing the chapters, you should be able to read and understand political science research that presents data analyses. You should also be able to conduct your own basic analyses and have a general foundation for pursuing more advanced study of data analysis techniques.

Log on to our website to watch a tutorial on IBM SPSS.

CHAPTER 13

Analyzing Qualitative Data

Jared Wesley, University of Alberta and University of Manitoba

Destination

By the end of this chapter, you should be able to

- explain the three-step process of qualitative data-coding;
- identify the coding techniques that can increase trustworthiness; and
- describe how to present qualitative data in written analyses.

Quantitative analysis cannot respond to every research question. Many things in politics may be measured according to their frequency, salience, or intensity, but some phenomena are more difficult to "count." Imagine quantifying a concept like national identity or reducing the entire meaning of the Geneva Convention to a series of numbers. Even if such numbers were attainable—through opinion polling or content analysis—the authenticity of the findings would remain in question. In short, as Albert Einstein famously suggested, "not everything that counts can be counted, and not everything that can be counted counts."

This maxim challenges students to learn non-quantitative ways of studying political life. Whether applied to interviews, textual analysis, or any other methodology discussed in this textbook, these qualitative approaches involve unique strategies and techniques for dealing with data. To be sure, they involve distinct styles and standards of measurement compared to those applied in quantitative political science. Yet there are obvious bridges between the two traditions. As discussed in Chapter 2, quantitative and qualitative approaches share common allegiance to certain norms about data collection, analysis, and reporting. To advance beyond casual, "armchair" interpretations, disciplinary standards require all political scientists to adhere to certain rules. The "raw materials" of politics only become scientific "evidence" when treated systematically, and certain standards apply to scholars employing quantitative and qualitative methods alike.

Coding Qualitative Data

Empirical qualitative research may be conducted on a variety of raw materials, ranging from documentary sources and oral histories to field notes and interview transcripts to television commercials and comic books. In order to treat qualitative evidence empirically, researchers must systematically code and then analyze their data. Some analysts refer to qualitative data analysis as a process of "soaking and poking"—a choice of words that implies less rigour than is actually involved (Putnam 1993, 12; King et al. 1993, 36–43). Although it is true that qualitative analysts must immerse themselves in their data for an extended period of time, the picture of a researcher casually bathing in a sea of texts, images, or sounds understates the amount of systematic analysis required. Indeed, over time, the social science community has developed a widely accepted, three-step procedure for coding qualitative data (see Neuman and Robson 2007, 336–40; Creswell 1998, 139–46; Hesse-Biber and Leavy 2006, 279–91; Boyatzis 1998; Marshall and Rossman 2006, 151–76; Richards 2005, 85–103).

As displayed in Figure 13.1, the first stage of the process involves open coding. In the initial review of the raw material, the researcher obtains a general sense of its major themes. Whether reviewing field notes, reading party platforms, listening to speeches, viewing debate footage, or analyzing interview transcripts, he or she records any noticeable

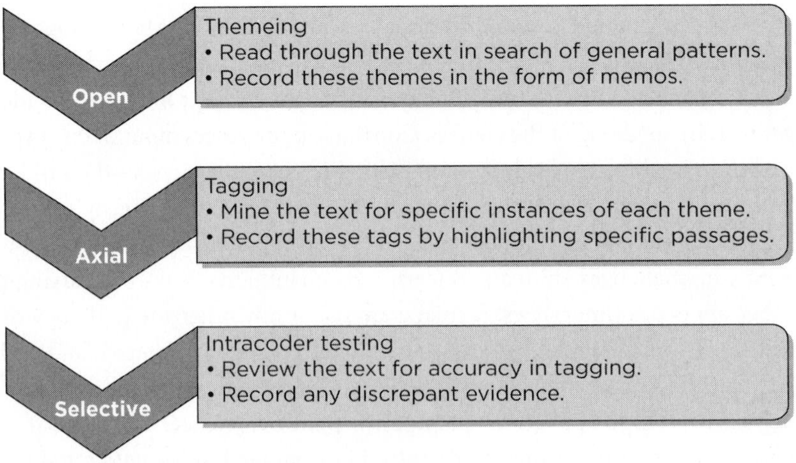

Open
Themeing
• Read through the text in search of general patterns.
• Record these themes in the form of memos.
Axial
Tagging
• Mine the text for specific instances of each theme.
• Record these tags by highlighting specific passages.
Selective
Intracoder testing
• Review the text for accuracy in tagging.
• Record any discrepant evidence.

Figure 13.1 The Qualitative Coding Process

patterns. Do certain parties emphasize comparable policies? Do certain politicians speak with the same sort of rhetoric? Do certain leaders employ similar hand gestures? Do certain respondents fit into identifiable schools of thought? Are there trends over time or patterns across different communities or cases? Depending on his or her preferences, the researcher stores these conceptual categories in a series of index cards, a notebook, or an electronic journal or uses **computer-assisted qualitative data analysis software** (CAQDAS). Because it involves writing a series of memos about these emergent themes, open coding is also referred to as **memoing** or themeing.

Depending on their familiarity with the subject matter and research topic, analysts may bring a range of prior knowledge to the open coding stage. Sometimes, there is little existing research upon which to rely. Under these circumstances, the researcher's approach is primarily inductive, as he or she searches for meaning in the interview scripts, documentary sources, or other bodies of data. Other times, a researcher may enter the coding process with a higher level of knowledge about the subject area, whether rooted in personal experience or grounded in the existing literature. Here, the researcher may approach the data with a pre-conceived set of codes or categories, which he or she then seeks to test and fill.

Once this first stage is complete, many qualitative analysts pause for reflection. What do these themes mean, and how do they relate to each other? Why do right-of-centre parties emphasize policies on crime and punishment in their manifestos, whereas left-of-centre parties are virtually silent on the issue? Why do conservative politicians speak with a greater

Expand Your Knowledge

Blending Quantitative and Qualitative Techniques

In Chapter 2, you learned how researchers often "quantize" their qualitative research (just as many "qualitize" their quantitative research). When it comes to the open coding stage, quantitative tools such as word clouds can be quite useful in helping to uncover themes and patterns by identifying commonly used words and phrases, particularly when massive amounts of data are involved.

Imagine that you are comparing the content and tone of American presidents' speeches to the United Nations to their State of the Union addresses, a project that requires you to analyze a large body of text. The open coding process can be daunting, confusing, and time-consuming without some frame of reference with which to access the texts. Some researchers may rely on secondary research for models, theories, or others' observations about the differences between the speeches. Another approach would be to feed the full-text versions of these texts through a word cloud generator (e.g. Wordle.net). This method is by no means a shortcut or replacement for the full reading of the texts required in the open coding process, but the resulting images would give you a general idea of what themes may appear during that analysis.

sense of urgency and gesture with more aggressive motions than do liberals, who project certainty and a calmer demeanour? Why do rural interviewees of various backgrounds tend to agree on most issues of public policy? In search of answers, the analyst will typically turn to existing research, conducting a thorough literature review to provide theoretical support for any hypotheses that may have arisen during the open coding stage.

With this backing, the researcher re-engages the data in the second step, this time with a more refined sense of purpose and a set of coding categories. During this stage of **axial coding**, the analyst takes more detailed notes about the content found in the raw materials, categorizing specific phrases, events, or **passages** as belonging under the broad themes identified in stage one. This part of the process is referred to as **tagging**, with the analyst highlighting important sections of a party platform, transcribing important portions of a speech, splicing together pivotal moments in a televised debate, or copying-and-pasting key responses offered during an interview. These elements (also known as bits or **chunks**) are then labelled according to one or several of the emergent themes. Once again, depending on the original materials' format and the researcher's preferences, this process may be conducted by hand or electronically. Some researchers use more sophisticated CAQDAS programs to record their notes during the axial coding stage. Others use more rudimentary techniques, ranging from the "Comments" or "Sticky Note" function in programs such as Microsoft Word or Adobe Acrobat to physical marginalia, coloured flags, or Post-it Notes on the printed page.

For researchers new to the qualitative tradition, this second stage of the coding process can be the most daunting. Many struggle to identify relevant chunks and worry whether their choice of categories is appropriate. Given the idiosyncratic, relatively subjective nature of qualitative inquiry (discussed in Chapter 2), there are no pre-defined answers to these questions. Researchers are best advised to treat the qualitative coding process as a creative, interpretive one. They should scour the source material for evidence supporting, and disconfirming, the themes identified in the open coding stage. Tags should be treated more as (re)movable labels based on the researcher's own interpretation at this stage in the process rather than as permanent markers of some fixed characteristic of the source material. The objective of this second stage is to identify specific evidence of a more general theme—to identify specific elements of more general sets of patterns.

During the third stage of qualitative analysis, the researcher mines the raw materials a final time, examining the data for additional and discrepant evidence. Jones and McEwen (2002, 167) describe this **selective coding** process as one in which the researcher seeks "saturation of categories . . . which means that further analysis produces no new information or need for additional categories. In short, all the data are captured and described by key categories, and a core category emerges that tells the central story." In other words, the researcher must ask if all the excerpts drawn from the platforms, speeches, debates, or interview transcripts really fit under the themes identified. Do more passages need to be added to substantiate the argument? Are there any passages that appear to contradict the general theme? If so, how can they be explained? In this sense, selective coding is a form

Expand Your Knowledge

When Raw Materials Become Data

Just as quantitative analysis involves transforming raw material into a series of numbers, typically through counting, qualitative analysis converts raw materials into useable data of a different kind. Revisit Table 2.2, on page 33. You will notice how qualitative research involves producing non-numerical data (words or images) by identifying emergent themes in the source materials. The data recording instrument is much more fluid than in quantitative research, in that the themes and patterns identified in the open coding process often shift and become more refined as you proceed through the axial and selective stages. Unlike the mathematical processes involved in quantitative research, qualitative data processing is far more conceptual, resulting in the verbal reporting of findings (rather than a series of summary statistics, tables, or graphs). The entire empirical qualitative approach is premised on the researcher's ability to produce plausible results, such that other researchers may be reasonably expected to follow the same processes and reach similar conclusions.

of intra-coder reliability testing and data cleaning, ensuring that all of the data fit into the assigned categories and adding, modifying, or deleting tags as necessary.

Throughout this three-stage process, the researcher remains open to revising or refining any of these categories, collapsing some under broader headings, or adding or deleting any as necessary. Any additional notes may be recorded in the margins of the documents or added to any existing index cards, notebooks, or electronic journals.

A pair of examples may be helpful in understanding this three-stage coding process, one hypothetical and one drawn from a recent research project.

Hypothetical Example of Qualitative Coding: Political Culture and Identity

A researcher is analyzing transcripts derived from a series of focus group sessions aimed at understanding political culture and identity in Canada. The moderator has asked each group a series of questions such as, "What does it mean to be 'Canadian'?" and "Are there any particular values that appear to unite us as Canadians?" Not surprisingly, participants have offered a wide variety of responses. One focus group member stated that Canada is a "mosaic" of different cultures, while another felt it was more of a "melting pot." In another group, one participant suggested that Canada is defined by "not being American"; another added that the country has strong ties to its British heritage. Still others highlighted unique political cultures in Quebec, the West, and Atlantic Canada, as opposed to a single pan-Canadian identity. How is the researcher to analyze these raw materials (transcripts) and transform them into data?

During the open coding stage, she reviews all the transcripts, making notes about how different statements (or respondents) appear to fit together under different categories. For instance, the "mosaic" and "melting pot" comments may be grouped under the heading of multiculturalism, whereas those concerning the role of geography in defining separate subcultures may be considered evidence of regionalism. Other comments may not fit easily into categories at this point in the analysis, forcing the researcher to leave their coding for later stages.

In stage two, any identified themes are used to tag specific statements during the second read-through of the transcripts. This axial coding process consists of labelling various passages as belonging to one of the various categories identified during the previous stage. This tagging may be done by hand (underlining or highlighting segments of text on paper) or electronically (using the "Comments" or "Captioning" functions found in many word processing or CAQDAS software packages). This could include tagging passages like "Canadians appreciate ethnic diversity more than Americans do" or "If you move to the States, you'd better be prepared to be American." Once this stage is complete, the researcher proceeds with selective coding, reviewing the transcripts once more in search of improperly tagged segments, discrepant evidence, or any excerpts that may have been missed. A coder may have categorized a phrase that, upon further reflection, was taken out of context or misinterpreted. This can occur, for example, when authors or focus group members employ sarcasm or irony, neither of which is immediately evident in the written word.

Real-World Example of Qualitative Coding: Provincial Political Party Platforms

As a second example, consider the coding process employed during a recent qualitative analysis of provincial party campaign literature (Wesley 2011).[1] Here, the researcher was guided by the question, "Have dominant political parties in Alberta, Saskatchewan, and Manitoba helped to cultivate the three distinct political cultures found on the Canadian Prairies?" In other words, can we find evidence of Alberta's conservative ethos in the campaign rhetoric of its most successful parties and premiers? By the same token, have Saskatchewan's social democratic traditions resonated in the rhetoric of its dominant leaders, and have Manitoba's political parties promoted the province's image of modesty?

An initial review of several hundred pamphlets, speeches, brochures, party platforms, and other election documents revealed stark differences between the campaign discourses in each province. During this open coding stage, the analyst identified a series of distinct rhetorical themes. In Alberta, parties tended to campaign on, for example, notions of liberty and anti-conformity, whereas parties in Saskatchewan tended to emphasize the importance of community and solidarity. Note that these observations were not grounded in a quantitative analysis of the number of times various parties used these terms explicitly. Rather, they emerged from a qualitative "reading" of the texts.

The researcher recorded these observations as memos to himself, using a combination of traditional notebooks and an electronic journal created using a standard word processor. These notes proved useful when operationalizing the codes employed in subsequent stages of analysis and for creating an "audit trail" for the final report.

A round of axial coding helped to refine these themes, as the analyst highlighted and tagged key passages as belonging to the unique code of that particular province. As the documents had been scanned and stored in Portable Document Format (PDF), this tagging could be done electronically, using Adobe Acrobat's "Comments" and "Sticky Note" functions. By highlighting a passage of text and attaching a comment box, the researcher was able to take and store notes about various segments of text.

Drawing on the rhetoric of prominent Social Credit leaders such as William Aberhart and Ernest Manning and successful Conservatives such as Peter Lougheed and Ralph Klein, campaign literature in Alberta was littered with tags relating to freedom and liberty, including references to individualism, populism, and provincial autonomy. By contrast, axial coding of Saskatchewan platforms involved tagging passages relating to security, with prominent leaders such as Tommy Douglas, Allan Blakeney, and Roy Romanow emphasizing the importance of collectivism, strong government, and polarization. A similar, systematic review of campaign literature in Manitoba revealed a provincial code grounded in moderation—a discourse combining more progressivism and pragmatism and a looser conception of partisanship than those found elsewhere on the Prairies.

The names of these various themes were derived in two ways. Given that the terms were used repeatedly in the source documents, some themes (such as freedom, security, and progress) were drawn directly from the raw materials. This is referred to as in vivo coding, with patterns named after manifest content in the texts. In other instances, the researcher imposed his own conceptual codes, in effect paraphrasing the nature of the discourse in his own words.

To complete the process, selective coding was conducted to verify these findings. In some instances, certain passages were reclassified as belonging under a different coding category. For instance, a promise to "preserve the power of the Saskatchewan state against the ill-wishes of the business elite" could be tagged as being evidence of a party's strong government rhetoric. Alternatively, it could be interpreted as an attempt to polarize the discourse between the forces of left and right. In such cases, a third and closer reading is necessary to uncover the deeper context, and ultimate meaning, of each coded statement.

At the same time, the researcher was on constant alert for discrepant evidence. The active search for data to disconfirm one's hypothesis is a crucial component of the positivist approach to political inquiry (see Chapter 1). In this vein, the researcher reported several competing interpretations of the data. Though Alberta party platforms were dominated by references to freedom, Saskatchewan by the notion of security, and Manitoba by progress, he noted that all three terms were found in campaign discourse throughout the region. All Alberta premiers acknowledged the importance of a strong provincial government,

APPLY YOUR UNDERSTANDING

Analyzing Campaign Advertisements

Not all qualitative analysis involves examining texts. Many researchers use visual images, videos, and recordings as their raw materials. For example, the political science community has conducted a considerable amount of quantitative research on campaign advertisements, systematically counting the proportion of negative ads over time and counting the number of positive versus negative mentions in each individual advertisement. Conventional wisdom suggests that American political campaigns have become increasingly negative over the past half-century, with so-called attack ads emerging as a primary means of reaching the public. The trend can also be analyzed qualitatively, however, to determine not just whether campaigns have become increasingly negative (and with what speed and to what degree) but how.

The Living Room Candidate initiative (livingroomcandidate.org) has compiled United States presidential election advertisements produced from the 1950s to today. Using the raw materials on this website, devise a qualitative research design to answer the following question: How have American presidential campaign ads evolved over time in terms of their negativity? Randomly select a sample of six advertisements and test your research design using the three-stage qualitative coding techniques described in this chapter. What are the results of your preliminary inquiry? Do you suspect your results are trustworthy (see Chapter 2)? How might you improve the trustworthiness of your analysis? How would your analysis have been different if, instead of using videos as your raw materials, you used written transcripts of those ads?

just as all Saskatchewan leaders recognized the importance of preserving individual rights. The difference, he argued, lay in the differing levels of emphasis granted by each group. Whereas Alberta politicians contended that "there could be no security without freedom," Saskatchewan leaders maintained that "there could be no freedom without security." Caveats and nuances such as these are critical elements of any trustworthy qualitative analysis, as they place reasonable boundaries on the researcher's interpretations (see Chapter 2).

In summary, the three-part coding process involves a combination of inductive inquiry (stage 1), data mining (stage 2), and data cleaning and intra-coder reliability testing (stage 3). Each stage of the procedure may be conducted manually or electronically, depending on the nature of the raw materials and the proclivities, skills, and resources of the researcher.

Computer-Assisted Qualitative Data Analysis

The relationship between the technological advancements of the late-twentieth century and the growth of quantitative analysis is obvious. Regression analyses that once took days by hand or hours by punch-card readers now take fractions of a second thanks to the advent of the personal computer and statistical software packages. Large-*N* survey analysts, in particular, have benefited most from these advances. By the same token, the quest for precision and impartiality has led many researchers in the qualitative tradition to develop automated means of coding their data. Today, many documents can be fed into **optical character recognition (OCR)** scanners designed to convert the text into digital/electronic format. With advances in voice-recognition software, it is now also possible to convert orally delivered speeches to text. This process makes the materials conveniently searchable by using keyword or Boolean techniques. Once in electronic format, this data can then be analyzed using any number of programs, which help researchers record, file, organize, store, and retrieve their notes.

For the electronically inclined, developments in CAQDAS have rendered index cards, notebooks, and Post-it Notes obsolete. Rather than filing their documents in hard-copy form, recording their notes in handwritten memos, repeatedly transcribing text segments, or tagging passages in the margins of a written page, CAQDAS enables researchers to store, code, search, retrieve, manipulate, report, and build theories directly from their data. Most programs feature a combination of quantitative and qualitative tools, with many offering the researcher the option of automatically coding data using a series of pre-defined and user-defined dictionaries and thesauruses. In addition, memoing, tagging, and themeing can be conducted on-screen, with codes and information stored in a convenient, linkable, and fully searchable collection of databases.

This text is not the place to compare qualitative software programs like ATLAS.ti or NVivo. Each has its own tools, drawbacks, and benefits; choices between them depend on the skills of the researcher and the nature of the inquiry. Suffice it to say that, just as automated quantitative analysis offers certain advantages over manual analysis, so too does computer-assisted analysis offer a more reliable and systematic approach to qualitative inquiry. At the same time, researchers must be wary of sacrificing validity, especially when turning to purely automated forms of coding.

Reporting Qualitative Data

It takes talent to summarize quantitative findings effectively in the form of tables, charts, graphs, or other figures. Similarly, qualitative scholars must hone their skills to provide convincing yet concise reports of their research findings. The latter face unique challenges in presenting their data, however. On one hand, they are expected to provide sufficient support for their arguments. In most cases, this task means including lengthy excerpts from interview transcripts or direct quotations from source documents, both of which require a great deal of space. On the other hand, qualitative scholarship is expected to conform to the same tight word limits imposed by publishers, editors, and instructors.

These expectations force analysts in the qualitative tradition to strike a delicate balance between presenting data and providing analysis. If researchers present too much direct evidence, they are criticized for simply transcribing the raw materials. The result is a collection of quotations rather than an academic analysis (Morse and Richards 2002, 188). On the other hand, if researchers focus too heavily on their own interpretation of the data, they are criticized for failing to provide enough evidence. As Platt (2006, 111–12) puts it, "the problem is how to show that the data do indeed support the interpretations made without presenting the reader with all of it."

But how much evidence is enough, and how much is too much? How many quotations do researchers need to provide to substantiate their arguments? The answers to these questions will differ from instructor to instructor, researcher to researcher, and reviewer to reviewer. In general, a safe rule of thumb is to include a broad cross-section of at least three pieces of evidence to support each interpretation (Berg 2004, 270). For instance, to establish that multiculturalism is a key component of Canadian political culture, the researcher should provide at least three chunks of data, drawn from disparate sources, to substantiate this interpretation. Quotations could be taken from younger and older members of the focus group, and paraphrases could be provided to offer a general overview of the data.

Conclusion

The political world may be counted or rendered, with each approach requiring its own set of tools and skills. Qualitative research may be less structured than quantitative analysis, but—to be considered empirical—it must be equally rigorous. The qualitative coding process may be more interpretive and the reporting of qualitative findings more impressionistic. Yet, as with quantitative research, all stages of qualitative analysis must be conducted systematically in order to be considered a legitimate element of empirical political science.

As a series of guidelines, this chapter has outlined a proven three-step coding process designed to ensure the soundness of any interpretations drawn from qualitative data. Conducted as part of the initial read-through of the raw materials (be they interview transcripts, political documents, or any other form), stage one of the process involves open coding the data to identify general themes. A second step, one of axial coding, is then conducted to tag specific elements of the data as evidence of these various themes. A third stage (selective coding) involves a combination of intra-coder testing and data cleaning to verify the accuracy of the interpretations. This three-step process imparts the same level of precision involved in quantitative coding while maintaining the flexibility necessary to make sense of qualitative data. Einstein was correct that "not all that counts can be counted." But make no mistake: methods count, whether counting or not.

Working as a Team

To complete the following exercises, use the documents available from the Poltext Project (poltext.org).

1. Divide your group into three subgroups: one in charge of researching Liberal parties, a second responsible for New Democratic parties, and a third for Progressive Conservative parties. Using the coding process outlined in this chapter, have each subgroup analyze its respective party's most recent platforms from the following three provinces: Nova Scotia, Prince Edward Island, and New Brunswick. Then, as a group, answer these questions:
   a. Which themes emerged from each group's open coding analysis?
   b. Did these themes change during the process of axial coding?
   c. What types of discrepant evidence emerged during the selective coding stage?
   d. How did these themes differ from party to party? Was there any overlap?
2. Create three new subgroups. This time, one will analyze all three parties' platforms in Nova Scotia, while the other two subgroups will study platforms in PEI and New Brunswick, respectively. After the analysis, answer these questions as a group:
   a. Which themes were identified during this coding analysis?
   b. What type of evidence was marshalled to support these interpretations?
   c. Did this second qualitative analysis affect your perception of the trustworthiness of your findings in question 1? Why or why not?

Self-Study

1. The Financial Crisis (or "Great Recession") of 2007–10 had a large but uneven impact on political systems across the globe. Using the Poltext Project website, locate 2009 Budget Speeches for any four Canadian jurisdictions. Conduct a systematic qualitative analysis of these speeches and then answer the following questions:
   a. How did the style of rhetoric differ in these four jurisdictions? How was it similar?
   b. How did each government's response to the recession differ? Were there any common solutions? If so, what were they?
   c. How would you explain these differences and similarities?

Note

1. All excerpts in this section are taken from Wesley (2011).

CHAPTER 14

Describing the Political World

Univariate Statistics

Destination

By the end of this chapter, you should be able to

- construct and interpret frequency distributions;
- compute and interpret the descriptive statistics used to measure the central tendency of and variance within data sets;
- explain the properties and characteristics of the normal curve;
- calculate standardized scores from datasets; and
- compare distributions between subgroups.

We are all used to describing the world in terms loosely based on statistical concepts. Think of how often you use such words and phrases as *typical*, *representative*, or *on average*. The goal of this chapter is to sharpen your conceptual language by introducing a number of specific terms used to measure both the average, or **central tendency**, of data sets and the manner in which individual cases are dispersed around the average. When we calculate measures of central tendency or dispersion, we look at just one variable at a time, hence the term *univariate analysis*. As we will see, **univariate** analysis provides the foundation for more complex forms of statistical analysis.

Many of the distinctions between the various measures of central tendency will refer to the measurement levels discussed in Chapter 5. Therefore, you should refresh your memory with respect to nominal, ordinal, and interval levels of measurement before reading the following pages. You should also keep in mind that this chapter is initially concerned with the statistics used to describe sample data. However, as we move through the chapter to discuss the normal curve, the focus will shift toward inferential statistics and the estimation of population parameters.

Measure of Central Tendency

The description of virtually any data set in the social sciences, particularly those drawn from survey research, begins with the identification of central tendencies, or (in more common usage) averages. Survey findings in the press frequently start with phrases such as "a majority of Canadians believe that" or even "Canadians believe that." There is no assumption that all Canadians believe the finding, and the article will likely go on to point out specific levels of agreement and disagreement. Still, we begin with the average, or typical, response and then fine-tune the analysis. Determining this **central value** (referred to as the central tendency of the data) is not as straightforward as you might expect, for we have three different measures of central tendency at our disposal. There is no correct measure for all situations, although there are more or less useful measures. Our choice often depends on the level of measurement used; interval-level variables provide more options than do nominal-level variables.

Log on to our website to watch a tutorial on working with variables.

Our assessment of the central tendency of variables in a data set usually begins with the visual inspection of **frequency distributions**, which record the possible values of the variable under discussion along with the number of cases associated with each value. Table 14.1 provides a hypothetical frequency distribution of the number of political science courses taken by graduating majors in political science and the number of graduating students associated with each value. For example, 14 graduating majors had completed 16 courses, and 7 had completed 22 courses. No students completed 26 courses, although it would be possible to do so. Most frequency distributions report not only the number of cases but also the percentage of cases associated with each variable value. In Table 14.1, then, we find that 11.3 per cent of the students (13 out of 115) had completed 19 courses. Finally, frequency distributions sometimes report cumulative percentages. In our example, 68.7 per cent of the students (79 out of 115) had completed 20 courses or fewer. Cumulative percentages build from lower variable values to higher values; the cumulative percentage for a given score is the proportion of cases with that score or lower.

A close visual inspection of a frequency distribution can tell us a good deal. We can see, for example, where the majority of scores fall and whether scores tend to cluster toward high or low variable values. However, it is very difficult to articulate visual impressions for others, or at least to do so with any numerical precision. It is even more difficult to compare such impressions. Hence the need for simple summary measures of central tendency, and here we have three options: the mode, the median, and the mean.

Table 14.1 Number of Political Science Courses Taken by Graduating Political Science Majors

Number of Courses Taken	Number of Students	Percentage of Students	Cumulative Percentage
15	10	8.7	8.7
16	14	12.2	20.9
17	15	13.0	33.9
18	16	13.9	47.8
19	13	11.3	59.1
20	11	9.6	68.7
21	9	7.8	76.5
22	7	6.1	82.6
23	9	7.8	90.4
24	5	4.3	94.8
25	3	2.6	97.4
26	0	0.0	97.4
27	0	0.0	97.4
28	2	1.7	99.1
29	0	0.0	99.1
30	1	0.9	100.0
Total	115	100.0	100.0

The **mode** refers to the most frequently occurring value in a distribution of scores. In a 2013 online Angus Reid survey (*N* = 2,028, +/- 2.2 per cent, 19 times out of 20), 35 per cent of the respondents said they would vote Conservative in the next election, 22 per cent Liberal, 29 per cent NDP, 6 per cent BQ, and 6 per cent intended to vote for the Green Party (Angus Reid 2013). The modal value is Conservative or, more precisely, the intention to vote Conservative. In Table 14.1, the mode would be 18 courses; more graduating students have taken 18 courses than any other number.

Log on to our website to watch a video tutorial on measures of central tendency.

The mode is the least useful of the three available measures of central tendency, in large part because it incorporates only one value—the most frequently occurring—in a range of values. It therefore fails to make use of much of the data. The mode is not a particularly stable measure, since it can change if only a few cases change. In Table 14.1, the mode would change from 18 to 17 if just one student taking 18 political science courses had dropped a course. Finally, the mode is highly sensitive to how measurement categories are constructed. If we grouped respondents in the Angus Reid survey into just two categories, those who intended to vote Conservative and those who intended to vote for a different party, the mode would no longer be a Conservative voting intention because 63 per cent of the respondents indicated that they would not vote Conservative.

Nevertheless, the mode is not without some utility. First, it is the only measure of central tendency available for nominal data (such as sex, party identification, and religious affiliation), although it can also be used for ordinal and interval data. Second, it is an appropriate measure of central tendency for J-shaped distributions, illustrated in Figure 14.1a. In such cases, the frequency distribution would be highly skewed (discussed later in this chapter) toward one side of the measure, and the mode would aptly describe where the bulk of cases fell. Third, the mode can be of considerable descriptive utility if we expand the definition from the most frequently occurring *value* to the most frequently occurring *values*. If we describe a distribution as unimodal, bimodal, or polymodal, as illustrated by Figures 14.1b to d, the description immediately conveys useful images. Finally, finding the mode does not require any calculation; visual inspection of frequency distributions will suffice.

The **median**, a measure of central tendency that can be used with both ordinal and interval data, refers to the value above which and below which 50 per cent of the cases fall. It is the midpoint in the distribution of cases, not the midpoint of the scale upon which those cases are distributed. To find the median, we order the cases from low to high—hence the need for ordinal or interval data—and then find the middle observation if the number of

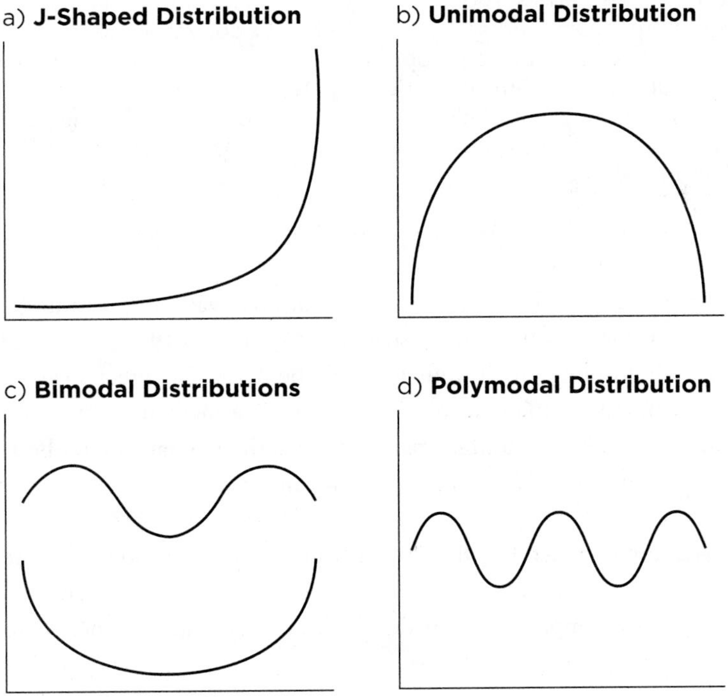

Figure 14.1 Modal Distributions

Expand Your Knowledge

Practical Usage of the Mode: Anthony Downs and Party Competition

In his *An Economic Theory of Democracy* (1957), Anthony Downs used unimodal, bimodal, and polymodal images of the electorate to develop some remarkably useful representations of party competition. As noted in Chapter 3, Downs's models assumed that all voters could be placed along a single left-right continuum and that their placement would determine the nature of party competition and the number of parties likely to enter the competition.

If the electorate is distributed in a unimodal fashion, as in Figure 14.1b, party platforms are likely to converge on the mode as parties compete for the greatest concentration of voters. In this situation, party platforms will be similar and only two primary competitors will survive, one placed slightly to the left of the mode and one slightly to the right, with the parties competing for the same modal voters. Minor parties may exist at the tails of the distribution, but there will not be enough voters at the extremes to propel such parties into office.

If the distribution of the electorate is bimodal, as in Figure 14.1c, the major parties will locate themselves at the two modes. There will be no convergence in party platforms; parties will appeal to their own constituencies and will not attempt to encroach upon the turf of other parties. A polymodal environment (Figure 14.1d) will promote a multi-party system, again marked by the absence of convergence among party platforms. Parties will concentrate on mobilizing voters at their own modes and will not venture off in pursuit of the small number of voters in the troughs between modes.

Downs's work shows both the power of economic models and the utility of simple distributional diagrams in illustrating some of the important dynamics of party formation and electoral competition.

cases is odd or the midpoint between the two middle observations if the number of cases is even. In Table 14.1, the median for the distribution of scores is 19. (Note that the midpoint of the scale running from 15 to 30 courses would be 22.5.) The precise calculation of the median can be difficult if it falls within an interval. The median of 19 courses is not an interval because a student cannot take partial credits; the median cannot be 19.1 courses. Formulas do exist for calculating medians for such interval data, but you probably will not have to do such a task.

The most common, useful, and stable measure of central tendency is the arithmetic mean ($\overline{X}$), which is calculated by adding all scores in a distribution and dividing by the total number of cases (sample means are designated by $\overline{X}$; population means are designated by σ):

$$\text{Mean} = \overline{\text{X}} = \frac{\Sigma X}{N}$$

The mean for Table 14.1 is found by multiplying each value by the number of cases, summing the scores,[1] and dividing by the total number of cases; the result is 19.3. Unlike the mode but like the median, each and every value is included in the calculation of the mean. However, this equation uses precise scores, whereas the calculation of the median uses only the order in which scores fall. When most people talk about averages, they are talking about means.

Mean scores should be calculated only if we have interval data. We can compute your grade point average (GPA), which is a mean score, because the precise distance between the various grades is known. An A grade is not somewhat better than an A–; it is exactly 0.3 better on a four-point scale ranging from 0.0 (F) to 4.0 (A). Yet means are often calculated

Expand Your Knowledge

The Use of Mean Scores with Ordinal Data

Given that the mean score provides a concise summary of central tendency and that the mean corresponds more closely to common understandings of the word *average* than does the median, it is not surprising that means are often calculated in circumstances where a different measure of central tendency might be technically correct. In a 2007 report, André Turcotte looks at young adults' attitudes regarding different citizen-oriented behaviours. He uses 2005 International Social Survey Programme data, in which respondents were asked to "Rate the importance of each of the following on a scale of 1 to 7 where 1 is 'not at all important' and 7 is 'very important'" (Turcotte 2007, 13). For such data, we cannot be sure that, in respondents' minds, the distance between 2 and 3 on this scale was the same as that between, say, 3 and 4 or 6 and 7. Although the mean scores reported by the author in this case do make intuitive sense and provide useful insight into the thinking of young Canadians, the mean is often not the most appropriate measure of central tendency.

Examples of the data are provided in the following table. How do these perceptions of relative importance of civic behaviours square with your own views?

Behaviour	Mean Score for 18–30-Year-Olds
Serve in the military	3.55
Always vote in elections	5.62
Keep watch on government	5.73
Never try to evade taxes	5.88
Always obey laws	6.07

Source: Adapted from International Social Survey Programme 2005, as presented in Turcotte (2007, 13).

for ordinal data. This practice commonly occurs with scales measuring public opinion or political attitudes, scales that may range from strongly agree to agree, disagree, and strongly disagree. It is not unusual to see numbers attached to these values (strongly disagree = 1; disagree = 2; agree = 3; strongly agree = 4) and then to have mean scores computed. The problem is that we cannot assume that the gap, for instance, between agree and strongly agree is the same as the gap between agree and disagree. Regardless, means are frequently used with ordinal measures.

The values of central tendency measures for a certain distribution of scores are seldom identical. Suppose that a political science department requires students to take 15 courses for a degree with a major in political science and that most students take the minimal number of political science courses needed for their major and degree. The mode could be 15, while the mean would be higher, inflated by the smaller number of students who take more than 15 courses en route to their degree. The general rule is that, as an arithmetic average, the mean is affected by or is sensitive to extreme scores. Therefore, it is less useful as a measure of central tendency than is the median when distributions are skewed or asymmetrical, with extreme values falling to only one side of the distribution. Measures of average income can be significantly affected by relatively few individuals with extremely high incomes; thus, the mean can give a distorted impression of central tendency. The advantage of the median in such cases is that it is insensitive to extreme scores.

Let's look at another example. A professional sports team has 10 players with salaries ranging from $1 million to $4 million. The mean and median salaries are both $2 million, and the distribution of salaries among the players is symmetrical about the mean. If the team releases a $3-million player and hires a superstar with an annual salary of $10 million, the median salary for the team will be unchanged. But the salary distribution is now skewed toward the high end of the scale, and the mean salary will increase from $2 million to $2.7 million. If the superstar demanded and received a salary increase to $20 million, the mean salary for the team would increase but the median salary would not. In summary, "when the score distribution is symmetrical, the median has a value equal to the mean. If the distribution is skewed, the median usually lies closer to the bulk of the scores than the mean does" (Wright 1976, 93). In this case, "skewed" refers to the mean being pulled in the direction of extreme scores. The mean, then, would be greater than the median. The difference between the mean and the median provides a rough measure of how skewed a distribution of scores might be; the greater the difference, the greater the skew.

Measures of central tendency are used to compare individuals or groups all the time. We talk, for example, about how the average doctor makes more than the average welder or how the average professional hockey player makes many times the income of the average political science graduate (assuming that the two are mutually exclusive categories!). We compare GPAs, batting averages, average heights, average weights, average election turnouts, and average votes received by different political parties. However, comparing groups by looking at differences in central tendencies alone can be a risky endeavour. Figure 14.2 displays a number of possible distributions that all have the same mean score but that

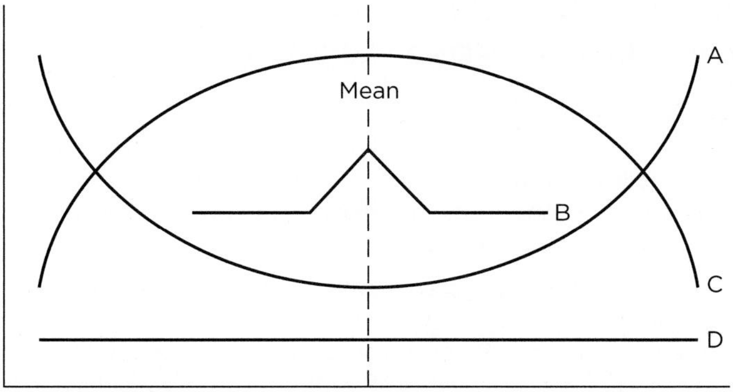

Figure 14.2 Differing Distributions with Identical Means

differ dramatically in other respects. For a more useful and meaningful group comparison, we also need to know something about the distribution of scores around the measure of central tendency.

Expand Your Knowledge

Median Measures of Average Income

Because the median is unaffected by extreme scores, it is the preferred measure of central tendency for income distributions. For example, Statistics Canada (2013a) reported that the median after-tax income for families of two persons or more was $65,500 in 2010. Median after-tax incomes varied by place of residence:

Alberta	78,100
Saskatchewan	70,100
Ontario	69,300
British Columbia	67,000
Canada	**65,500**
Manitoba	64,500
New Brunswick	58,900
Quebec	58,100
Nova Scotia	56,800
Prince Edward Island	56,400
Newfoundland and Labrador	56,300

Source: Statistics Canada (2013a)

APPLY YOUR UNDERSTANDING

Selecting a Measure of Central Tendency

For each of the following, which measure of central tendency would be best for expressing the average: the mode, median, or mean? See Table 14.2 for a summary of the three types. Explain your decisions.

- the average salary paid to all actors in a blockbuster movie
- the average salary of public servants
- the average (or typical) supporter of the Liberal Party of Canada
- the average age of undergraduate students in political science
- the average age of first-time voters in federal elections
- your GPA at college or university

Table 14.2 Summary of the Three Measures of Central Tendency

Measure	Level of Data	"How to"	Pros	Cons
Mode	Nominal Ordinal Interval	Use the frequency distribution to find the most frequent value.	Only measure for nominal data; appropriate for J-shaped distributions	Fails to use all information; varies with category construction; unstable
Median	Ordinal Interval	Place all cases in order and find the middle value.	Stable; not affected by extreme scores; uses all cases	Does not use precise values
Mean	Interval	Sum all scores and divide by the total number of scores.	Most reliable; uses all information, including precise values	Affected by extreme scores

Measures of Variation

Statistical measures for the dispersion of scores around the central tendency are termed **measures of variation**. Just as there are a number of ways to measure central tendency, there are a number of descriptive statistics to measure the dispersion, or variation, within a set of scores. As with measures of central tendency, our choice is determined in large part by the level of measurement.

For nominal data, the only available measure of variation is the **variation ratio**, the number of cases that are not in the modal category. A high variation ratio indicates that the data are more dispersed, while a low variation ratio indicates that the data are more concentrated. To calculate the variation ratio, we use the following formula:

variation ratio = 1 – (number of cases in modal category/number of total cases)

If there are 25 cases in the modal category and 100 cases in the full sample, the variation ratio equals 0.75: 1 – (25/100). This ratio suggests that the data are more dispersed. Given that there is a high variation ratio, it is possible that the mode is not very representative of the data taken as a whole.

For ordinal- and interval-level data, researchers have additional measures of variation to contemplate. The simplest but least useful is the **range**, which is the difference between the lowest and highest values in a distribution of scores. If we found that the highest annual income among the 75,000+ medical doctors in Canada was $1.2 million and the lowest was $30,000, the income range would be $1.17 million (the highest value minus the lowest value). However, the range would tell us something about only the highest paid and lowest paid of the 75,000+ physicians, and we would have no idea if most doctors were near the bottom, top, or middle of the range. The measure ignores all information but the two most extreme scores.

Sometimes the range is calculated by taking the difference between the highest and lowest scores and then adding 1. To illustrate why this is the case, imagine a set of scores ranging from 1 to 5. If we subtract the lowest score from the highest score (5 – 1), the range is 4. In fact, five scores are possible: 1, 2, 3, 4, and 5. Therefore, adding 1 gives us a more precise estimate of the range:

$$\text{range} = \text{highest score} - \text{smallest score} + 1$$

While we can easily calculate how much any particular score deviates from the mean, it is not as easy to put that deviation into perspective. Is it relatively small or relatively large? To answer this question, we need to measure the average deviation from the mean and, at the same time, locate individual scores relative to both the mean and the other scores in the data set. The catch is that deviations about the mean will always sum to zero. If we have 10 scores and we subtract the mean from each score and sum the deviations, the total will always be 0. Because mean deviation does not provide a useful measure of variation about the mean, we need to turn to more complex measures.

The variance measures the degree of dispersion in a dataset and is defined as the sum of the squared deviations from the mean, divided by the number of cases. Although the variance may be initially difficult to grasp conceptually, its properties become more readily apparent if we work through the calculations. The variance for a set of scores is calculated by the following steps:

1. calculate the mean for the set of scores;
2. subtract the mean ($\bar{X}$) from each individual score (X);
3. square each difference, that is, each $X - \bar{X}$;
4. sum these squared differences (this figure is known as the **sum of squares**); and
5. divide that sum by the number of cases.

The variance is symbolized by S^2 and the five steps are summarized in the following formula:

$$S^2 = \frac{\Sigma(X - \bar{X})^2}{N}$$

The problem with the variance is that it is difficult to interpret; because it involves squaring the deviations, the units of measurement for the variance are the squared units of measurement of the original cases. In other words, if the data were measured in dollars, the variance would represent dollars squared.

The solution to this issue is rather straightforward: we simply take the square root of the variance to return to the original unit of measurement. The resulting measure is known as the **standard deviation** and is the most common measure of average deviation from the mean. It is represented by the following formula:

$$S = \sqrt{S^2} = \sqrt{\frac{\Sigma(X - \bar{X})^2}{N}}$$

Note that the values for the variance and standard deviation are always positive; it is impossible to have a negative standard deviation. When you think of it, how could there be less than zero variance? If all scores are identical, each score would equal the mean, there would be no deviation from the mean, and both the variance and the standard deviation would equal zero.

To illustrate the calculation of both the standard deviation and the variance—if you can calculate one, you can do the other—imagine a set of five scores: 4, 4, 4, 4, and 9. The steps are as follows:

1. Find the mean:

$$\text{mean} = \bar{X} = \frac{\Sigma X}{N} = \frac{25}{5} = 5$$

2. Subtract the mean ($\bar{X}$) from each score (X):

Score (X)	**$X - \bar{X}$**
4	−1
4	−1
4	−1
4	−1
9	4

3. Square the difference between the mean and each score $(X - \bar{X})^2$:

Score (X)	**$X - \bar{X}$**	**$(X - \bar{X})^2$**
4	−1	1
4	−1	1
4	−1	1
4	−1	1
9	4	16

4. Total the sum of the squared differences (sum of squares):

$$\Sigma(X - \bar{X})^2 = 1+1+1+1+16 = 20$$

5. Divide the sum of the squares by the number of cases:

$$S^2 = \frac{\Sigma(X - \bar{X})^2}{N} = \frac{20}{N} = \frac{20}{5} = 4$$

6. Take the square root of the variance:

$$S = \sqrt{S^2} = \sqrt{4} = 2$$

Fortunately, this calculation is routinely done by computer-based statistical packages; therefore, you will not need to do it by hand for large data sets.

APPLY YOUR UNDERSTANDING

Calculating the Variance and Standard Deviation

You have been asked to calculate the average age of a group of NDP voters and to find out how typical this average is. To this end, calculate the mean age, variance, and standard deviation for the following set of respondents. Round all calculations to the nearest decimal point (e.g. 34.567 = 34.6 years).

Respondent	Age (in years)	Respondent	Age (in years)
A	21	L	56
B	27	M	62
C	46	N	19
D	65	O	47
E	23	P	58
F	37	Q	51
G	83	R	45
H	22	S	72
I	29	T	18
J	47	U	40
K	41		

The standard deviation is a useful measure for discussing the spread of cases around the mean. The larger the standard deviation, the greater the variability in scores. When variability is low, the mean is more representative of the bulk of the scores than it is when variability is high. Put somewhat differently, the mean is a better predictor of individual scores when the standard deviation is low than when it is high. Consider two sample datasets: sample A has a mean of 50 and a standard deviation of 10; sample B has a mean of 50 and a standard deviation of 4. In this case, the data are more dispersed in sample A than in sample B, and the mean is more representative of the data in sample B than in sample A. Overall, the size of the standard deviation depends on how tightly the scores are clustered around the mean; more tightly clustered data will have a smaller standard deviation and more dispersed data will have a larger standard deviation.

Like the mean, the standard deviation incorporates each and every case in the distribution of scores and is sensitive to extreme scores (as is the variance on which it is based).

Expand Your Knowledge

Means and Standard Deviations

The utility of having measures of both central tendency and variation is demonstrated in an analysis by Michael A. Goldberg and Maurice D. Levi (1994), which examined annual growth rates in provincial and territorial economies from 1962 to 1991. As the mean scores in the following table show, the provinces and territories have differed significantly in their annual growth rates. This disparity, however, is only half the picture. They differ in variability as well; Alberta and Saskatchewan, for example, have had much more volatile economies—reflected in the larger standard deviations—than has Ontario or Quebec. Clearly, if we want to make sense out of the relative economic performance of provincial economies, we need to take both average growth and volatility into account. The variability of the resource-based Alberta economy was also seen in the province's economic downturn in 2008–09.

	Mean Growth Rate	Standard Deviation of Growth
Yukon and Northwest Territories	6.84	8.14
British Columbia	4.87	3.52
Alberta	5.25	6.39
Saskatchewan	3.37	8.24
Manitoba	3.15	3.16
Ontario	4.09	3.30
Quebec	3.67	2.65
New Brunswick	4.29	4.76
Nova Scotia	4.09	3.41
Prince Edward Island	4.46	4.95
Newfoundland	4.39	3.45
Canada	**4.06**	**2.55**

Source: Goldberg and Levi (1994)

Table 14.3 Summary of the Measures of Variation

Measures of Variation	Levels of Measurement		
	Nominal	Ordinal	Interval
Variation ratio	✓	✓	✓
Range	×	✓	✓
Variance	×	×	✓
Standard deviation	×	×	✓

If outliers exist, the standard deviation will not accurately reflect variability among the bulk of the scores. Look back at our example on pages 268–9. Most of the variance in that case came from a single score (9). As the calculations show, it is because the deviations from the mean are squared that extreme scores have such a disproportionate effect on the calculation of the variance. That effect is moderated in the calculation of the standard deviation in that, by taking the square root, the impact of squaring deviations from the mean is reduced.

Overall, by combining measures of central tendency with measures of dispersion we get a more complete understanding of our data. We can combine knowledge of the centre of the data with a sense of how data spread around that centre. Table 14.3 provides a summary of the types of measures we have discussed and their use with the three measurement levels.

Normal Curve

The **normal curve**, or what is often known as the bell-shaped curve, is a particularly useful statistical concept. Normal curves need not have identical shapes; the example in Figure 14.4 (see p. 274) is perhaps the most typical, but other normal curves could be more or less peaked than our illustration. However, all normal curves and the **normal distributions** that they contain share a number of characteristics:

- The normal curve is bilaterally symmetrical; its shape is identical to the left and right of the mean.
- As a consequence, the mode = the mean = the median of the normal curve.
- The tails of the normal curve are asymptotic; they approach but never quite meet the horizontal axis. As a consequence, any value can be placed under a normal curve—the tails stretch to infinity.
- The total area under the normal curve = 1.
- Almost all cases fall within three standard deviations of the mean: 68.3 per cent fall within ±1 standard deviation of the mean: 95.4 per cent fall within ±2 standard deviations of the mean; and 99.7 per cent fall within ±3 standard deviations of the mean. (This is referred to as the 68–95–99.7 rule, the empirical rule, or the three-sigma rule; the last title reflects the fact that the sigma is the symbol used to denote

standard deviation.) If the mean of a normal distribution is 50 and the standard deviation is 5, 68.3 per cent of the cases will fall between 45 and 55, 95.4 per cent will fall between 40 and 60, and 99.7 per cent will fall between 35 and 65.

The importance of the normal curve does not arise because real data are distributed in a normal fashion; "the normal distribution is a mathematical distribution that is not found in the real world" (Elifson, Runyon, and Haber 1990, 149). Real-world distributions, which we often think of as normally distributed, do not actually fit the conditions in the list. We may think of IQ, weight, or height as being normally distributed. Yet, if they were, any score would be possible, no matter how unlikely. We could have, for instance, adults who were 20 metres or 20 centimetres tall. The real world, then, is not normal, but large parts of the statistical and mathematical worlds are. This fact is of considerable importance in the chapters to come.

One way to think about how the normal curve is derived, and in particular the importance of the central-limit theorem in research that uses probability sampling, is to ponder what happens when we toss coins. Assume that we have an unbiased coin, that is, one that is equally likely to land on heads or tails. If we tossed the coin 10 times, we would expect to produce 5 heads and 5 tails. In practice, though, we find that sometimes we get 4 heads and 6 tails, 6 heads and 4 tails, 3 heads and 7 tails, or 7 heads and 3 tails. There might even be rare occasions when we get 10 heads and no tails. If we flipped a coin 100 times, we would find that the distribution of samples would approximate a normal curve as shown in Figure 14.3a.

If the "true" result of tossing coins is an equal number of heads and tails, the samples will be normally distributed around this value. The distribution in Figure 14.3a indicates

Expand Your Knowledge

The Central-Limit Theorem

Although real-world data are not normally distributed, many statistics are. If we take repeated samples of the same population, a given statistic (for example, the mean) will follow a normal distribution. Indeed, this is the case even though the data on which those statistics are based are not normally distributed. As Allen Edwards (1969, 123) points out, "The fact is, that regardless of the shape or form of a population distribution, the distributions of both the sum and the mean of random samples [taken from that population] approach that of a normal distribution as the sample size is increased. This statement is based on an important theorem known as the central-limit theorem." Note the role that sample size plays in this theorem; statistics generated by large samples are more normally distributed than are statistics generated by small samples.

that, although not all samples will exactly produce the true value, they are likely to approximate it. Furthermore, as is discussed later in this chapter, we know what proportion of the cases falls within given standard deviations of the mean under the normal curve, a fact that proves very useful when testing hypotheses about the statistical significance of findings.

The other significant implication of the central-limit theorem is that, as sample size increases, the distribution of cases more closely approximates a normal curve. With large populations, the likelihood of producing results that deviate substantially from the true value is small. Let's say that, instead of tossing a coin 10 times over 100 samples, you tossed a coin 100 times over 1,000 samples. (This presumes, of course, that you have a lot of time on your hands!) The larger sample size will ensure that more of the samples will approximate 50 heads and produce the distribution shown in Figure 14.3b.

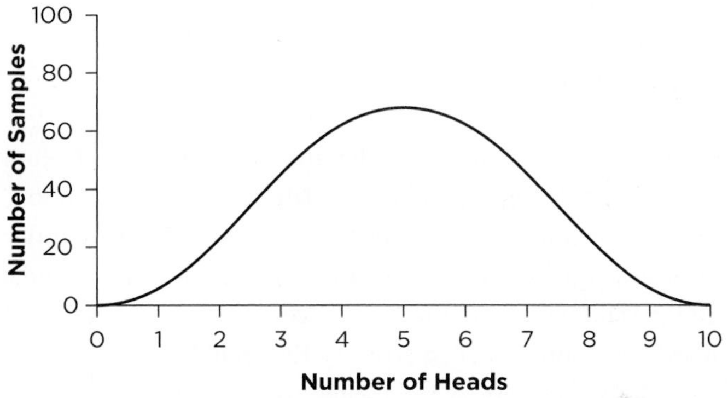

Figure 14.3a Distribution of Samples in which 10 Coins Were Tossed 100 Times

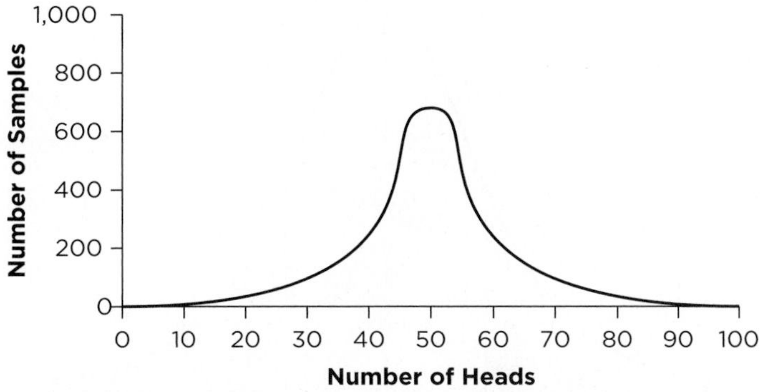

Figure 14.3b Distribution of Samples in which 100 Coins Were Tossed 1,000 Times

We can use the idea embodied in the central-limit theorem when we are testing hypotheses. In probability sampling-based research we draw samples to test hypotheses about the causal relationship between variables. Of course, we are never sure if our particular sample measures the true value of a variable and of the relationship between variables. We do know that samples are normally distributed around the true value and, the larger the sample size, the more closely the samples approximate this value.

Take a look at Figure 14.4. Notice that 95.4 per cent of the normal curve's total area falls within ±2 standard deviations of the mean, and 99.7 per cent falls within ±3 standard deviations. The area of the normal curve encompassed within ±1.96 standard deviations from the mean includes 95 per cent of the cases, and the area encompassed within ±2.57 standard deviations from the mean includes 99 per cent of the cases. These latter percentage distributions come into play with statistical significance and confidence intervals, which we will explore in the next chapter.

Standardized Scores

We are sometimes interested in knowing how far an individual case is from the mean. We often hear references to cases being "2 standard deviations from the mean" or "0.5 standard deviation from the mean." Another way to express such findings is with **standardized scores** (also known as ***z*-scores**), which are scores expressed as the number of standard deviations they fall from the mean of the total distribution of scores. If the mean of a distribution was 150 and the standard deviation was 20, a score of 120 would be −1.5 standard deviations from the mean. Therefore, the score of 120 expressed as a standardized score, or *z*-score, would be −1.5. Unlike the standard deviation, standardized scores can be positive or negative. Scores greater than the mean yield positive standardized scores, and scores falling below the mean yield negative standardized scores. In either case, they allow us to compare scores in terms of their relative distance from the mean.

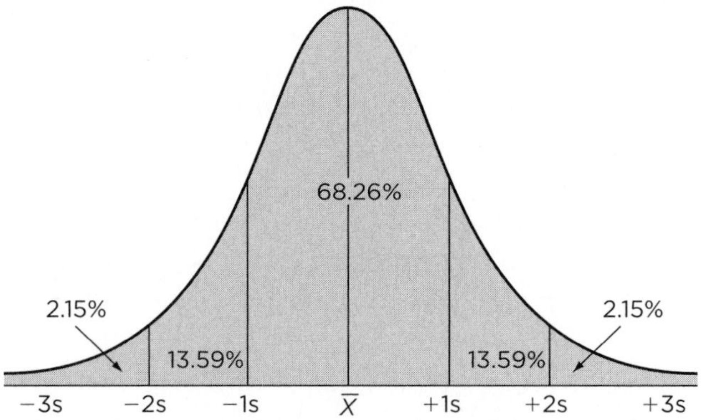

Figure 14.4 The Normal Curve

Standardized scores enable a comparison of scores across different populations. In surveys, respondents are often asked to indicate their feelings toward the party leaders by using a 100-point feeling thermometer. Let's focus for a moment on hypothetical assessments of Liberal leader Justin Trudeau and Prime Minister Stephen Harper. The average rating of Trudeau in this "study" was 55 on the scale, with a standard deviation of 15, and the mean for Harper was 48, with a standard deviation of 18 units. We could draw two conclusions from these data: Canadians felt more positively toward Trudeau than toward Harper ($\bar{X} = 55$ versus 48), and there is greater consensus regarding attitudes toward Trudeau than toward Harper ($S = 15$ versus 18).

We can extend the analysis from the aggregate data (mean and standard deviation) to the individual level of analysis by comparing raw scores and standardized scores. Assume that one respondent (Jane Porter from Halifax) rated both Harper and Trudeau 60 on the 100-point thermometer. By examining the raw score, we might conclude that the party leaders had no effect on her voting intentions, since both were assigned the same score. However, by using standardized scores, a different portrait—and possibly a different conclusion—emerges. We can compute the standardized scores with the following formula:

$$Z = \frac{X - \bar{X}}{S}$$

Jane's rating of 60 for Trudeau is slightly above the average ($\bar{X} = 55$) and well within the standard deviation ($S = 15$). Her *z*-score for Trudeau is $(60 - 55)/15 = 0.33$. The conclusion would be that Jane's feelings toward Trudeau were 0.33 standard units above the mean. For Harper, the calculation is as follows: $(60 - 48)/18 = 0.67$. In this instance, Jane's evaluation of Harper was 0.67 standard units above the mean. Compared with other voters, Jane rated Harper more positively than Trudeau. We could hypothesize that this more positive evaluation may be relevant to her voting intentions.

Let's examine another illustration of the use of *z*-scores, one that is closer to home for many university students, particularly those wishing to be admitted to graduate or professional schools. Let's say that your major is political science and that your GPA is 3.2, that the average GPA of political science majors as a whole is 2.4, and the standard deviation is 0.6. Your friend, and potential competitor for a valued place in law school, is a psychology major. Her GPA is 3.4, and the average GPA for psychology majors is 2.8 with a standard deviation of 0.6.

Which of you should be admitted to law school? Your friend's higher GPA (3.4 versus your 3.2) suggests that she might be more likely to win the place. But let's compare performance by using *z*-scores. Your score, which would be called your standardized GPA, is $(3.2 - 2.4)/0.6 = 1.33$. Your friend's standardized GPA is $(3.4 - 2.8)/0.6 = 1.0$. Thus, your standardized score in relation to all political science majors is higher than hers in relation to all psychology majors. Leaving aside arguments about the potential superiority of psychology students in relation to political science students overall (they did attain higher GPAs),

APPLY YOUR UNDERSTANDING

Calculating *Z*-Scores

You have been told that the average GPA for political science majors is 2.7 and the standard deviation is 0.8. Using this information, convert the following GPAs to *z*-scores. How would you verbally express such *z*-scores to someone without a statistics background?

Schulmit:	3.41
Andrew:	2.76
Christine:	3.01
Malinda:	3.17
Scott:	3.56

the *z*-scores might lead one to conclude that you should be offered admission to law school ahead of your friend. The purpose of *z*-scores is to try to standardize the base of comparison between groups.

Comparing Univariate Statistics between Two Subgroups

The discussion to this point has stressed that measures of central tendency and dispersion are closely connected, not only in their calculation (as in the case of the mean and standard deviation) but also in the role they play in interpreting empirical data. To illustrate the interplay between measures of central tendency and of dispersion, consider Figures 14.5a and b, which present two quite different comparisons of the relative physical strengths of men and women. The figures show hypothetical distributions of two subgroups, men and women, across a scale measuring physical strength; the higher the score on the horizontal axis, the stronger the individual. The means for women are identical in both figures, as are the means for men. In both figures, the mean score for men is higher than the mean score for women; hence, men, on average, are stronger than women. The difference between the two figures comes from the dispersion of scores around the means; in Figure 14.5a, the scores are tightly bunched around the mean, whereas in Figure 14.5b the dispersion is much looser.

Now suppose a fire department is hiring new staff and decides that a minimum strength of 150 is needed to perform satisfactorily as a firefighter. As was often done in the past, sex is used as a proxy for strength. Instead of actually measuring the physical strength of individual applicants, the fire department decides that any man who applies is strong enough and that any woman who applies is not. What errors would be made? In Figure 14.5a, the lighter shaded section shows the women who might be strong enough to do the job yet who would not be hired, and the darker shaded section shows the men who might be hired even though they would not have sufficient strength to do the job. In both cases, the errors that would be made by using sex as a proxy measure of strength would be quite small.

But if we turn to Figure 14.5b, the potential for error increases dramatically. There are now many more men who might be hired even though they lack sufficient strength and many more women who would be denied employment even though they have the necessary strength. Sex, therefore, serves as a poor proxy of strength in this case, and a fire department that relied upon it rather than on individual measures of strength would end up with suboptimal firefighters. (And, in a modern context, a host of legal challenges!) Figure 14.5b, we would suggest, illustrates the job discrimination women faced in the past when sex was used indiscriminately as a proxy of strength.[2]

Figures 14.5a and b can show some of the complexities in the long-standing debate about sex differences in mathematical ability. Let's presume that, on average, men do have a greater aptitude for math than do women, that men have a higher mean score on some measure of mathematical ability. As we have seen from the firefighter example, the relevance of this difference depends on the dispersion of male and female scores around their

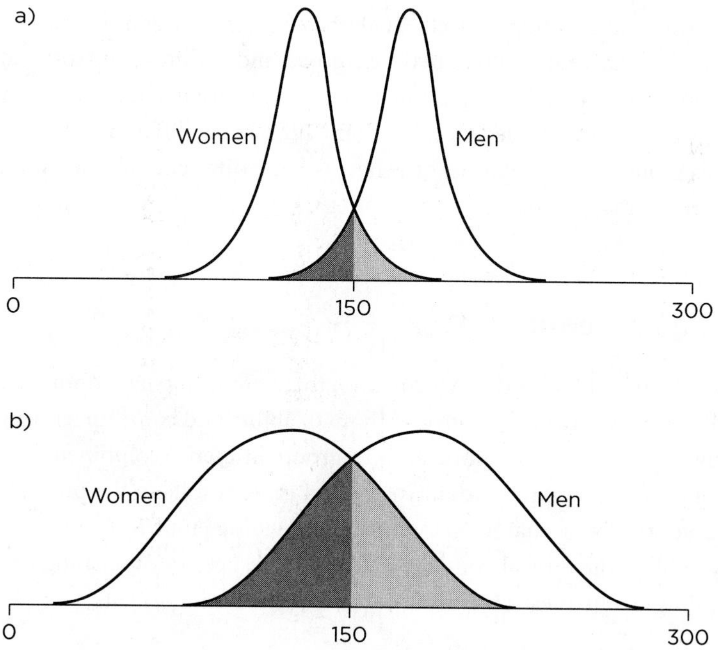

Figure 14.5 Sex Differences in Strength

respective means. If the distribution resembles Figure 14.5a, we could use sex as a proxy of mathematical ability and assume that, as a rule, men are better at math than women. But if the distribution resembles Figure 14.5b, sex cannot be used as a proxy for mathematical ability. In this latter case, there is no rule; knowing an individual's sex provides little assistance in predicting his or her ability in math. The sex difference in mean scores is irrelevant.

The point to emphasize is that the contrast between the figures stems not from differences in mean scores but from differences in the dispersion of scores around the means. Thus, to make sensible intergroup comparisons and provide a complete descriptive profile of data sets, we need information on both central tendency and the manner in which scores are distributed about those measures of central tendency. We also need a statistical measure of differences in mean scores to which we can attach levels of confidence. Is the difference in mean scores significant or did it occur by chance? We will look at how to assess this question in the next chapter.

The hypothetical sex differences in strength and mathematical ability illustrate the conceptual underpinnings for the **analysis of variance (ANOVA)**, one of the most useful statistical techniques in the social sciences. In one form or another, social scientists are often interested in subgroup differences—between men and women, Liberals and Conservatives, Canadians and Americans, Quebecers and western Canadians—that are conceptually analogous to the differences in group means just discussed. As we have seen, however, the difference between groups is only half the story; we need to know about the dispersion, or variance, of scores within groups as well. Analysis of variance provides a systematic method for comparing the relative strength of between-group and within-group differences. Simply put, and as illustrated by the examples, between-group variance takes on greater importance as within-group variance declines. In other words, small differences between relatively homogeneous groups can be significant, whereas large differences between relatively heterogeneous groups may not be.

Working as a Team

1. Return to Figures 14.5a and b. Assume first that your group has conducted a survey of racial differences between two groups in math ability and come up with a pattern similar to the second figure: a significant intergroup difference combined with substantial intragroup variability. How would you report these results to the public? How would you counter the likely charge that you were providing empirical support for racism?
2. What would be the ethical considerations with respect to publishing or suppressing your findings from question 1?

Self-Study

1. As a class project, you have asked 22 of your fellow students to place themselves on a 7-point left–right scale with values ranging from 1 (far left) to 7 (far right). To protect the respondents' anonymity, a letter of the alphabet has been assigned to each respondent. The left–right scale locations were as follows:

A = 6	B = 1	C = 3	D = 7	E = 6	F = 4
G = 4	H = 2	I = 7	J = 5	K = 3	L = 1
M = 6	N = 6	O = 2	P = 1	Q = 3	R = 4
S = 5	T = 2	U = 6	V = 1		

   a. Construct a frequency distribution for the set of scores.
   b. Calculate the cumulative percentages for the frequency distribution.
   c. Find the mode, median, and mean for the distribution of scores.
   d. Calculate the standard deviation and variance for the distribution of scores.

Notes

1. The symbol for "sum of" is Σ.
2. There were, of course, other reasons for discriminating against women, and strength criteria were often used to mask sex discrimination.

CHAPTER 15

Assessing the Political World: Inferential Statistics

Destination

By the end of this chapter, you should be able to

- summarize the conceptual nature of significance tests and the roles that inferential statistics play in hypothesis-testing;
- describe various types of data distributions;
- distinguish between Type I and Type II errors and appreciate the factors to consider in choosing between the two types;
- explain the difference between parametric and non-parametric statistics; and
- select and calculate appropriate significance tests.

We have stated throughout this text that we conduct research on samples in an effort to gain knowledge about populations. The descriptive statistics that we calculate—be they the univariate statistics of Chapter 14, the bivariate statistics of Chapter 16, or the multivariate statistics of Chapter 17—provide us with concrete information about the sample. We can calculate sample means or uncover relationships between two or more variables within the sample, but these are of theoretical interest only to the degree that we can use them to make inferences about the population from which the sample was drawn. This chapter will explore **inferential statistics**, which test the probability that sample statistics are reasonable estimates of population parameters. Inferential statistics provide the bridge between what we know about samples and what we would like to know about populations.

Recall that the principles of random sampling are based on probability theory. Inferential statistics address the questions, "What is the probability that the relationship we found occurred by chance in the sample?" "Was the sample finding a fluke or was it reflective of a relationship in the population?" If the sample statistic is found to be representative of the population, we say that it is statistically significant.

Inferential statistics are a crucial step in hypothesis-testing. Hypotheses, which have been discussed in a number of previous chapters, assert the existence of a relationship between two or more variables. When we gain support for our hypothesis, we gain support for the underlying theory. In order to support our hypothesis, we must first reject the null hypothesis, or the supposition that no relationship exists between the variables in the general population. We ask whether there is sufficient evidence to reject the null hypothesis, to conclude that the relationship observed in the data reflects a similar relationship in the larger population. In other words, is the observed relationship significant or insignificant? Do we conclude that the sample relationship is not sufficiently robust to provide compelling evidence for a similar relationship in the population from which the sample was drawn? It is only once we have rejected the null hypothesis that we can begin to argue in favour of our alternative hypothesis and the theory from which it is drawn. Therefore, a lot is at stake with tests of significance.

The five basic steps of hypothesis-testing are as follows:[1]

1. Formulate the null and alternative hypotheses.
2. Select a confidence level.
3. Calculate the appropriate inferential statistic.
4. Using the table for the test statistic, find the critical value (expected value) at the selected confidence level.
5. If the calculated statistic equals or exceeds the critical value, reject the null hypothesis.[2]

The first of these steps was addressed in Chapter 3; this chapter will explore the remaining stages. Before we begin, however, two key points must be addressed.

First, when we discuss significance in this chapter, we are focusing on *statistical* significance, on tests that allow us to assess whether sample statistics are acceptable estimates of population parameters. Yet there are some instances where rather weak relationships are found to be statistically significant. Significance tests are affected by sample size; the larger the sample, the more likely it is that a relationship of a given strength will achieve the statistical standard necessary to be considered significant. As a result, some trivial relationships from large samples will be statistically significant and other potentially interesting relationships from very small samples will be statistically insignificant. The point to stress is that statistical significance does not always entail substantive significance. A relationship or a statistic is substantively significant if it is theoretically important, if it plays a role in elaborating, modifying, or rejecting the theory. The need for substantive significance as well as statistical significance requires that the researcher rely not only on inferential statistics but also on an assessment of the supporting descriptive statistics and contingency tables. In other words, we need to look at all parts of the data analysis rather than rely on summary statistics alone.

Log on to our website to watch a tutorial on statistical inference.

Second, inferential statistics are either statistically significant or not. Some relationships are not "more significant" than others. The desire to make such a claim arises from confusion between substantive and statistical significance. If we wish to argue that one relationship is stronger than another and not more significant, we need measures of association (discussed in Chapter 16) rather than inferential statistics. Statistical

Expand Your Knowledge

Pre-Election Surveys and Predicting Election Outcomes

In most forms of survey research and virtually all forms of attitudinal research, we never know what the population parameters are. Surveys provide the best estimate we have of those parameters, but there is nothing that we can compare the results with to see if they are accurate or correct. We do not know, for example, what proportion of Canadians might support a more liberalized immigration policy; we know only the survey proportions that do so. However, pre-election surveys are an important exception to this rule.

It is common for survey firms, often with media partners, to conduct polls shortly before elections are held and use the survey results to predict the outcome. But the actual election outcome—the population parameters—will shortly be known; therefore, inaccurate predictions will be apparent to all. In short, it is possible to be shown to be wrong in this situation. Such was the case with the 2013 British Columbia provincial election; as discussed in Chapter 6, survey firms and analysts widely predicted a victory for the NDP, and were left surprised by the success of the incumbent Liberals, who returned with a majority government. As Angus Reid (2013), one of Canada's best-known pollsters, summarized, "The British Columbia election in 2013 was historic because never have so many public opinion firms missed the mark so badly with their final election projections. The average 'miss' was in the vicinity of twelve points." These projection errors followed on the heels of incorrect projections for the 2012 Alberta election, raising numerous public questions about the accuracy and value of pre-election surveys.

A number of reasons have been given to account for the mistaken projections in the British Columbia case. Reid attributed at least some of this error to how younger and older respondents are weighted in survey samples and suggested that there may be a need to "[adjust] the weight of younger voters not to their proportion of the general population, but to that of actual voters." Allan Gregg, another well-known pollster, argued that the use of online polls and question wording were contributing factors (Canadian Press 2013). What is clear is that the reputation of pre-election polling—and, for some, of survey research more broadly—has been diminished in the eyes of some Canadians.

significance is a statement about the correspondence between the sample and the population and cannot be used to draw conclusions about the relative importance of variables. You must be clear about this distinction.

Selecting Confidence Levels

Deciding whether or not a relationship exists in the population, whether the covariance between two variables in the data is significant, is by no means a straightforward process. How do we distinguish between random variation in the sample and evidence of a "real" relationship in the population? What standard of proof do we employ? If it were left to each researcher to determine the standards for rejecting the null hypothesis, there would be little consistency within or across the social sciences. When confronted with the same empirical evidence, one researcher could decide that the relationship was significant and another that it was not.

To avoid this situation, researchers use a set of probability-based norms to accept or reject null hypotheses. The question we ask is, "If no relationship exists between two variables in the population from which the sample was drawn, what is the probability that, by chance alone, we would observe a relationship in the sample data?" If the chances are pretty good that the observed relationship could have emerged this way, we tend to discount it and conclude that it is the product of sampling error or random variation. However, if the odds that we would have observed a relationship in the sample data solely by chance are remote, we tend to reject the null hypothesis, concluding instead that the best explanation for the sample finding is that a relationship exists within the larger population from which the sample was drawn.

But how do we operationalize "pretty good" or "remote"? To do so, we use confidence levels, also referred to as **alpha (α) levels**. A confidence level is the probability that a sample statistic is an accurate estimate of the population parameter. The scientific norms provide two primary standards. The first is the 95 per cent ($p < 0.05$) confidence level: we reject the null hypothesis if the probability of finding the observed relationship by chance alone is less than 5 per cent, or less than five chances in a hundred. With this standard, we are 95 per cent certain that the sample statistic is an accurate representation of the population parameter. The second standard is similar but more rigorous: we reject the null hypothesis at the 99 per cent ($p < 0.01$) confidence level if the probability of finding the observed relationship by chance alone is less than 1 per cent, or less than one chance in a hundred. In this case, we are 99 per cent certain that the sample statistic is an accurate representation of the population parameter. Very occasionally, you will encounter published research in which a 90 per cent ($p < 0.10$) confidence level is used. Because this test is more lenient, it tends to be employed only when sample sizes are small.

Regardless of which standard we use, if we reject the null hypothesis, we conclude that a significant relationship exists. Hence the term *tests of significance*. We never reject the null hypothesis with total certainty, for there is always the possibility, no matter how slight, that the observed relationship was the product of chance alone. We can only reject the null hypothesis with varying degrees of confidence; therefore, confidence levels are always specified when tests of significance are reported.

Keep in mind that researchers will use different language to describe the same thing. A 95 per cent confidence level and a 5 per cent confidence level ($p < 0.05$) both mean that the chances of having made an error in rejecting the null hypothesis are less than 5 per cent; a 99 per cent confidence level and a 1 per cent confidence level ($p < 0.01$) both mean that the chances of error are less than 1 per cent. The first approach (95 or 99 per cent) expresses the probability of not making an error by incorrectly rejecting the null hypothesis; the second approach (5 or 1 per cent) expresses the probability of making such an error.

The question remains regarding which confidence level to adopt. The answer is by no means clear-cut and depends, in part, on the quality of the data and the consequences of making a mistake. When psychologists work in an experimental setting with precise and tightly controlled measurements of the dependent and independent variables, they are prone to adopt the more stringent test. They want compelling evidence before rejecting the null hypothesis and will therefore employ the 99 per cent confidence level or even a 99.9 per cent level, refusing in the latter case to reject the null hypothesis unless the chances of being wrong are less than one in a thousand. Political scientists often work with less robust data and confront greater measurement noise and subject variability, particularly in survey research. As a consequence, they may adopt a less rigorous test and reject the null hypothesis at the 95 per cent confidence level. As we suggested, sample size also influences the confidence level chosen: researchers with large samples generally employ more stringent significance tests than do researchers with smaller samples. Finally, exploratory studies in which the researcher is looking for suggestive findings rather than ironclad results may employ lower levels of confidence, perhaps even the 90 per cent confidence level.

No golden rule for choosing a confidence level exists. Two researchers could look at the same empirical results with one rejecting the null hypothesis at the 95 per cent confidence level and the other failing to do so at 99 per cent.[3] What is essential is that the researcher decides on the level of confidence to use before looking at the empirical results. This practice will reduce the temptation of changing confidence levels in midstream in order to convert insignificant relationships into significant ones; we set our standards before the data analysis and maintain them when interpreting the data.

You might assume that social scientists would do everything possible to minimize the probability of error by using the most rigorous significance tests. However, there are two different types of errors that can be made—by minimizing the probability of one, we increase the probability of the other. A **Type I error**, or false positive, is made when the null hypothesis is incorrectly rejected; on the basis of sample results, we conclude that a relationship exists in the population when in fact it does not. Type I errors are more likely if we adopt a 95 per cent confidence level, making it relatively easy to reject the null hypothesis, than if we adopt a 99 per cent confidence level. A **Type II error**, or false negative, is made when we incorrectly fail to reject the null hypothesis; we conclude that a relationship does not exist in the population when in fact it does. Type II errors are more likely to be made if we adopt a 99 per cent confidence level than if we adopt a 95 per cent level. The distinction between Type I and Type II errors is expressed in Table 15.1.

Table 15.1 Type I and Type II Errors

		Reality	
		No Relationship	Relationship
Researcher's Conclusion	Relationship	**Type I Error**	Correct Conclusion
	No Relationship	Correct Conclusion	**Type II Error**

Expand Your Knowledge

Statistical Power, Sample Size, and Type II Error

Inferential statistics are influenced by sample size. This cuts two ways: in large samples it is easier for relationships between variables to meet the conventional standards for statistical significance, whereas in small samples it is difficult to meet these standards. In other words, in large samples it is easier to detect that variable A has an effect on variable B and reject the null hypothesis, while in small samples the risk of failing to detect relationships (effects) is much greater. Simply put, Type II errors are more likely with small samples.

The **power** of a statistic refers to the probability that its result will allow researchers to correctly identify relationships and correctly reject a false null hypothesis. Statistical power is influenced by three things: effect sizes, confidence levels, and sample sizes. Effect size is the amount of change in variable B that is caused by variable A. Large effects are easier to detect than small effects; hence, statistical power is greater when effect sizes are large. Statistical power is also greater with a lower confidence level, such as 90 per cent, than with a higher confidence level, such as 95 or 99 per cent. Finally, as sample sizes increase, statistical power is increased.

Because the effect size is outside the researcher's control and because the use of 95 or 99 per cent confidence levels are conventional practice in most disciplines, researchers must give consideration to what sample sizes are required to identify an effect while using a more stringent confidence level. While one might be tempted to simply have large sample sizes in all instances, doing so would be costly and time-consuming and would increase the risk of Type I error. Researchers can use statistical power analysis in advance of designing a study to help determine optimal sample sizes.

Unfortunately, there is no strategy that minimizes the probability of both Type I and Type II errors. We have to choose, and the choice hinges upon a number of factors, including the risks associated with either type of error and perhaps even the personality of the researcher (some people are naturally more cautious than others). The best illustration of the stakes involved comes from medical research. Suppose that a new drug appears to offer a promising treatment for a particular form of cancer. Before the company that developed the drug can release it for general use, it must undergo clinical trials to see if there are dangerous side effects. The null hypothesis is that there are no side effects. The question is, "What standard should be employed to accept or reject the null hypothesis?" If the researchers conducting the clinical trials make a Type I error, concluding that there are dangerous side effects when in fact there are not, the opportunity for a promising drug treatment would be missed. If the researchers make a Type II error, concluding that there are no side effects when there are, a dangerous drug could be unleashed on unsuspecting patients and their physicians. As you can imagine, the company that developed the drug, the researchers conducting the clinical trials, public health officials, insurance firms, patients, and physicians may have quite different views over whether a Type I or Type II error would be more problematic.

Along with determining a relationship between two variables, confidence levels can also be established for a range of scores. A polling organization may report that 45 per cent of respondents support the government of the day and that the poll findings are accurate within ±3 per cent, 19 times out of 20. In effect, the polling organization has established a confidence interval and has concluded that there is a 95 per cent probability that the percentage of the population (in this case, the electorate) supporting the government lies between 42 per cent (45 per cent – 3 per cent) and 48 per cent (45 per cent + 3 per cent). If the polling organization wanted to be even more confident that its result fell within population parameters by establishing a 99 per cent confidence interval, the interval would have to be larger. Hence the trade-off: a small confidence interval provides

APPLY YOUR UNDERSTANDING

Choosing between False Positives and False Negatives

Say that you are trying to decide between two home pregnancy tests. The box for one promises that the risk of a false positive is only 1 in 100, but the risk of a false negative is 5 in 100. The second kit promises that the risk of a false negative is only 1 in 100, but the risk of a false positive is 5 in 100. Which kit would you choose, and why? If you had to make the same choice with respect to tests for breast cancer or AIDS, would your choice change? If so, why? What factors might lead you to prefer the risk of a false positive to a false negative or the reverse?

APPLY YOUR UNDERSTANDING

Calculating Confidence Intervals

Calculate the confidence intervals for the following statistics. What is the probability that the population parameter falls within the confidence interval?

- 52 per cent agree, ±3 per cent, 19 times out of 20
- 67 per cent disagree, ±5 per cent, 99 per cent confidence level
- 33 per cent plan to vote Conservative, ±2.5 per cent, 95 per cent confidence level
- 28 per cent plan to vote Liberal, ±3 per cent, 99 times out of 100

greater precision but less confidence, while a large confidence interval provides less precision but more confidence.

The norm among commercial pollsters is the 95 per cent confidence interval, or "19 times out of 20." This standard means, incidentally, that 1 poll in 20 will be "rogue," with results that are not as close to the population mean as the polling organization might suggest. Unfortunately, because population parameters are estimated rather than known, it can never be determined which is the rogue poll and which are the 19 out of 20. This is why replication is essential to scientific research; when repeated studies are completed, it is easier to identify the atypical results.

Selecting Inferential Statistics

Once the confidence level has been established, an inferential statistic must be selected and calculated. How one chooses the appropriate inferential statistic depends on the assumptions underlying the statistic. **Parametric statistics** have built-in assumptions about the data distribution that must be met if the statistic is to be used, whereas **non-parametric statistics** do not have such assumptions. For inferential statistics, only interval-level variables are able to meet the distribution assumptions of the parametric tests; thus, to use these tests, one of the variables must be interval-level. That said, not all interval-level variables meet the distribution requirements of the parametric tests.[4] A chart for selecting inferential statistics is presented in Table 15.2. Please note, however, that there are always exceptions to such guidelines and that space does not permit the inclusion of all possible significance tests in this table or chapter.

We will look in turn at the chi-square, the t-test for differences between means, and the Mann-Whitney *U*-test; *F*-ratios, which are used with interval-level data only, are discussed in Chapter 17. In each case, we will calculate the test statistic, compare this statistic with the critical value, and, using this comparison, decide whether or not to reject the null hypothesis.

Table 15.2 Suggestions for Selecting Inferential Statistics

Variables in Correlation	Suggested Statistic(s)
Nominal-nominal	Chi-square
Ordinal-nominal	Chi-square, Mann-Whitney *U*
Ordinal-ordinal	Chi-square, Mann-Whitney *U*
Interval*-nominal	Difference of means
Interval*-ordinal	Difference of means
Interval*-interval*	*t*-test, *F*-test
Interval**-nominal	Mann-Whitney *U*
Interval**-ordinal	Mann-Whitney *U*
Interval**-interval*/**	Mann-Whitney *U*

*Normal distribution of cases
**Non-normal distribution of cases

Expand Your Knowledge

The Debate over Significance Tests

There is a methodological debate over the use (and misuse) of significance tests. As Christopher Shea (1996) writes, the critics of significance tests "point out that decisions about whether something is due to chance are based on a sliding scale of probability. Therefore, dividing research findings into two categories—significant and not significant—is a gross oversimplification." Gill (1999, 669) argues,

> The basic problem with the null hypothesis significance test in political science is that it often does not tell political scientists what they think it is telling them . . . it is very easy to confuse statistical significance with theoretical or substantive importance. It is also possible to have data which tells us something about an important political question, but which does not pass an arbitrary significance level threshold.

Part of the reaction to significance tests is manifest in the increased use of meta-analysis. This approach pulls together large sets of studies done over the years on particular research questions and seeks patterns that run through them. These patterns may not be statistically significant in each study but are nonetheless pronounced when the various studies are pooled. In this manner, meta-analysis gets around the problems associated with small samples and reveals studies that were insignificant in themselves but that give added weight to general patterns of research findings.

Chi-Square

Chi-square tests the independence of two variables by assessing the likelihood that the relationship observed in the sample is due to chance. In other words, the test asks, "What is the probability that the relationship does not exist in the population?" As a non-parametric statistic, chi-square lacks the power of the other significance tests. However, its lack of parameters makes it the only test statistic available when we look at relationships among nominal- and ordinal-level variables. (Nominal variables require non-parametric tests because the variable values—1, 2, 3, 4—refer to differences in kind, not in degree; ordinal variables do not have a standard unit difference between numerical values.) Chi-square has the distinct advantage, as we will see, of being a highly stable measure, one based on a cell-by-cell comparison of the observed relationship and the expected relationship under the null hypothesis. We can state the null and alternative hypotheses of chi-square as follows:

$$H_0: f_o = f_e$$

$$H_a: f_o \neq f_e$$

where f_O is observed frequencies and f_e is expected frequencies.

Before calculating chi-square, we must construct a **contingency table** (also referred to as a cross-tabulation table or a crosstab table). To create this table, we first need to identify the two variables under question and the number of categories, or values, within each variable. Let's say that our variables are age and support for conservatism and that both have three categories. Age is divided into young (18–30 years), middle (31–50 years), and old (51+ years). Support for conservatism is separated into low, moderate, and high. We place one variable across the top of the table, being certain to place the categories in order (low to high) if the variable is ordinal rather than nominal and to label the variable as well as all categories. We then place the second variable on the left-hand side of the table, again paying attention to ordering and labelling. The result is presented in Figure 15.1.

Our next step is to place individual cases in the table's cells. In a contingency table, the location of a particular case is contingent on its values for each of the two variables. Robert is 20 years old and ranks low on conservatism. To include Robert in the table, we first find his location on the age variable. Because he is 20 years old, he will be placed in the "young" category, which is the first column of the contingency table. We then need to place Robert according to the second variable. Robert is located in the "low" category of conservatism, which is the first row of the table. Thus, we place Robert in the cell where "young" intersects with "low conservatism," in this case, in row 1, column 1. Looking at the table, where would you place someone who is 58 years old and moderately conservative? Someone who is 31 years old and highly conservative? To create a contingency table, we must place each case in its appropriate cell. We then total the number of cases in each cell; for example, if the old, moderate conservatism cell (row 2, column 3) has a total of six cases, we place the number 6 in that cell.

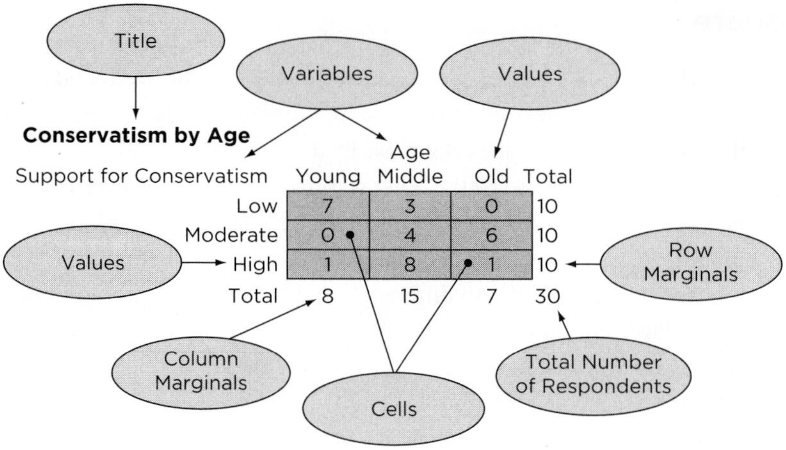

Figure 15.1 A Contingency Table

Our final step is to total the numbers in each row and column. These totals are known as **marginals**. To find row marginals, we add across the cells for each row. In our example, the row marginals provide the frequency distribution for support for conservatism. To find column marginals and hence the frequency distribution for age, we add down the cells for each column. The total number of cases in the data set (identified as *N*) is designated outside the lower right-hand corner of the table. The sum of the row marginals should be equal to *N*, as should the sum of the column marginals. If they are not, an error has occurred. Be sure to double-check your numbers!

Once the contingency table is constructed, we can use chi-square to test our hypothesis. The independence of the two variables is assessed by comparing the observed frequencies in a bivariate relationship with the expected frequencies that would occur if perfect independence existed. How many cases would we expect in each cell of our contingency table if the variables were independent? We calculate the expected frequencies for each cell of the table and then calculate chi-square by using the following formula:

$$\chi^2 = \frac{\Sigma(O - E)^2}{E}$$

where *E* is the expected frequency for a given cell and *O* is the observed frequency for the same cell.[5] For each cell in the contingency table, we subtract the expected frequency from the observed value to find the difference between the two frequencies. This value must be squared because we are summing variation: if we fail to do so, the deviations total zero.

Table 15.3 provides an opportunity to work through the chi-square calculations. The table presents the observed values for 100 respondents, categorized by both their sex and support for a hypothetical policy. The question asked in this analysis was, "Does an individual's sex impact attitudes toward this policy among the population as a whole?" We

Table 15.3 Support for Policy X by Sex (Observed Values)

	Female	Male	Total
Low support	15	5	20
Medium support	15	15	30
High support	25	25	50
Total	55	45	100

don't know the answer with certainty because the entire population has not been asked about this policy issue. Instead, we have (hypothetical) data from 100 people. Therefore, a more refined question is, "How likely is it that we would find a relationship of the strength observed in Table 15.3 in a sample of this size if there was no relationship between these variables in the population?" We wish to compare the number of respondents in each cell (the observed frequency) with the number of people we would expect to find under the null hypothesis (the expected cell frequency) if the two variables were unrelated.

The data in Table 15.3 present the observed cell frequencies. The upper left cell, for instance, shows that 15 of the respondents were women who registered a low level of support for the policy in question. The first step in computing the chi-square is to calculate the expected frequencies for every cell. For example, we wish to know how many women and how many men would have a low level of support for this policy if sex was not a factor. To answer this question, assume that the marginals of the table do not change; there are always 55 females and 45 males and 20 people with low support, 30 with medium support, and 50 with high support. But the numbers within the cells can change to reflect the null hypothesis.

One way of thinking about this matter is to ask what percentage of the total sample population has low support. In this example, it is 20 out of 100 cases, or 20 per cent. If sex does not affect attitudes toward the policy, 20 per cent of women and 20 per cent of men should have low support. How many women and men should have low support depends upon the number of each in the sample (55 and 45, respectively). To calculate the expected cell frequencies, we use the following general formula:

$$E = \frac{\text{(row marginal)(column marginal)}}{N}$$

For the low-support, female cell, our expected frequency is 11:

$$E = \frac{\text{(row marginal)(column marginal)}}{N} = \frac{20 \times 55}{100} = 11$$

In other words, if sex and support for policy X are independent, we would expect 11 women to support it.

The same calculation is used to determine the expected frequency for all other cells. Thus, for the low-support, male cell, the expected frequency is 20 (row marginal) multiplied by 45 (column marginal) divided by 100, which equals 9. The expected frequency for the medium-support, female cell is 16.5 (30 × 55, divided by 100); the expected frequency for the medium-support, male cell is 13.5 (30 × 45, divided by 100); and so on. We continue calculating expected frequencies until we have completed the expected frequencies table, shown in Table 15.4. Try calculating the last two expected frequencies on your own.

The next step is to calculate chi-square, which compares the observed frequencies (Table 15.3) with the expected frequencies (Table 15.4). Recall that the formula for chi-square is as follows:

$$\chi^2 = \frac{\Sigma(O - E)^2}{E}$$

We need to square the difference between the observed and expected frequencies and then divide that figure by the expected frequencies. This step must be undertaken for each cell. For the low-support, female cell we get the following:

$$\frac{(O - E)^2}{E} = \frac{(15 - 11)^2}{11} = \frac{16}{11} = 1.45$$

For the low-support, male cell we have

$$\frac{(O - E)^2}{E} = \frac{(5 - 9)^2}{9} = \frac{16}{9} = 1.78$$

The results for all the cells are shown in Table 15.5.

We next need to add all the resultant figures:

$$1.45 + 1.78 + 0.14 + 0.17 + 0.23 + 0.28 = 4.05$$

This final number is chi-square. We can now use chi-square to determine whether we should accept or reject the null hypothesis. Before doing so, however, we need to calculate the degrees of freedom (*d.f.*) for our contingency table, using the following formula:

$$d.f. = (r - 1)(c - 1)$$

where r is the number of rows and c is the number of columns. In our example, we are using a 3 × 2 table; thus, $d.f. = (3 - 1)(2 - 1) = 2 \times 1 = 2$. Degrees of freedom are important when we look at the chi-square table (an excerpt is presented in Table 15.6).

In the chi-square table, we find our **critical value**. Note that we look down the rows to find the degrees of freedom and across the columns to find our confidence level. Each cell contains the critical value for the given degrees of freedom and confidence level. This value is the number that the calculated chi-square must meet or exceed if we are to reject the null hypothesis. For a 5 *d.f.* table and 99 per cent confidence level, our calculated chi-square must meet or exceed the critical value 15.086. For a 1 *d.f.* table and 95 per cent confidence, our critical value is 3.841.

Table 15.4 Support for Policy X by Sex (Expected Frequencies)

	Female	Male	Total
Low support	11	9	20
Medium support	16.5	13.5	30
High support	27.5	22.5	50
Total	55	45	100

Table 15.5 Observed and Expected Frequencies

	Female	Male
Low support	Cell 1	Cell 2
Medium support	Cell 3	Cell 4
High support	Cell 5	Cell 6

Cell	Observed	Expected	*O* - *E*	(*O* - *E*)²	$\frac{(O-E)^2}{E}$
1	15	11	4	16	1.45
2	5	9	-4	16	1.78
3	15	16.5	-1.5	2.25	0.14
4	15	13.5	1.5	2.25	0.17
5	25	27.5	-2.5	6.25	0.23
6	25	22.5	2.5	6.25	0.28

Let's return to our example. We had a 2 *d.f.* table, and we will assume that we are using a 95 per cent confidence level (used most commonly in political science research). Our critical value is 5.991. How does this figure compare with our calculated chi-square value of 4.05? Our calculated value does not meet or exceed the critical value; therefore, we must conclude that there is a high probability that the sample relationship occurred by chance. We fail to reject the null hypothesis, which stated that the two variables are independent (H_0: $f_O = f_e$). In other words, the relationship has been found to be statistically insignificant. The conclusion is that, in the population as a whole, the sex of individuals has no significant

Table 15.6 Critical Values for Chi-Square

d.f.	$p = 0.05$	$p = 0.01$
1	3.841	6.635
2	5.991	9.210
3	7.815	11.341
4	9.488	13.277
5	11.070	15.086

Source: Adapted from Pedhazer (1982, 792).

impact on attitudes toward this policy question. If our calculated value had met or exceeded the critical value, we would have concluded that the relationship was, in fact, statistically significant and rejected the null hypothesis.

Chi-square tests are commonly used non-parametric tests for nominal- and ordinal-level relationships. However, chi-square values reflect not only independence but also sample size. As our sample size increases, so too do our calculated chi-square values, making it easy to use chi-square to reject the null hypothesis. Hence, the chi-square test can deem extremely weak and substantively insignificant relationships found in large samples statistically significant. Researchers should keep this limitation of chi-square in mind when interpreting their data. On the other hand, large samples are often used precisely because we wish to have small margins of error and high levels of statistical significance. The key point to remember is not to confuse statistical significance with a strong relationship (substantive significance).

Summary: Using Chi-Square

1. Calculate the expected frequencies table.
2. Calculate chi-square.
3. Determine the degrees of freedom.
4. Find the critical value on the chi-square table.
5. Compare the critical value and the calculated chi-square to draw a conclusion about the null hypothesis.

APPLY YOUR UNDERSTANDING

Calculating Chi-Square

A survey firm has collected data on public opinion toward tobacco advertising. Eleven hundred respondents were asked if they favoured a complete ban on tobacco advertising, a partial ban, or no restrictions whatsoever. The pattern of response for young (ages 18–30) respondents and not-so-young (ages 31+) respondents was as follows:

Opinion toward Tobacco Advertising	Ages 18–30 Years	Ages 31+ Years	Total
Complete ban	110	450	560
Partial ban	145	280	425
No restrictions	45	70	115
Total	300	800	1,100

Calculate the chi-square for this table. Does the evidence support the conclusion that age differences are present? Why or why not?

t-Tests for Differences between Means

One way to look for relationships between two variables is to subdivide, based on one variable's categories, the entire sample and then to look for differences in univariate statistics (measures of central tendency or variation) between the subsamples. (An example of this process was presented at the end of Chapter 14.) This approach allows us to look at relationships between nominal-/ordinal-level variables and interval-level variables. We use the category of a nominal- or ordinal-level variable to subdivide; we might divide our sample into two subsamples based on sex (men and women) or into three subsamples based on age (young, middle, and older).

Having divided our sample, we consider the univariate statistics of the interval-level variable within each subsample; most commonly, we look to the mean. Are the mean scores for the subsamples similar or different? This step is known as comparing the **difference of means**. Significantly different means suggest a relationship between the interval-level variable and the nominal-/ordinal-level variable that the subsamples are based on. Thus, our null hypothesis is that the subsamples are the same—there is no difference between the samples and no relationship between the two variables. Our alternative hypothesis is that the difference of means is statistically significant and that there is a relationship between the two variables in question. These hypotheses can be stated as follows:

$$H_0: \mu_1 = \mu_2$$

$$H_a: \mu_1 \neq \mu_2$$

where μ_1 designates the population mean of sample 1, and μ_2 designates the population mean of sample 2. (Recall that we are always interested in parameters rather than the statistics. Our hypotheses are always about the populations rather than the samples.)

One of the most common significance tests for differences of mean scores is the *t*-test. This test is parametric; consequently, the researcher must ensure that both samples are normally distributed. To understand the conceptual architecture of this test, imagine drawing a series of samples from the same population. If you were to calculate the sample means for this series, you would expect them to be similar but not identical; random variation would preclude identical means. (The larger the samples, the closer the means would be to one another.) Now, suppose you were to draw a sample of men and a sample of women and compare the mean mathematical abilities of the two samples. The null hypothesis would be that the two samples were drawn from the same population, which is to assume that there is no difference in math ability between men and women in the population at large. The question, then, is whether the observed difference in math ability between the two sample means is small enough to be attributed to chance alone (the null hypothesis is accepted) or large enough to suggest that the two samples were drawn from populations that differ in their math ability (the null hypothesis is rejected). To make this choice, we need a measure that takes into account the difference in sample means and the dispersion of scores about the two means.

The *t*-test provides just such a measure. It is based on the null hypothesis that the samples being compared are drawn from the same population and, therefore, that any observed difference in sample means can be attributed to chance alone. To apply the *t*-test to a difference in mean scores, we need to know the size, mean, and variance (see Chapter 14) for each of the two samples. The formula for the two-sample *t*-ratio, assuming that the samples are approximately the same size, is

$$t = \frac{\bar{X}_1 - \bar{X}_2}{\sqrt{\frac{S_1^2}{N_1} + \frac{S_2^2}{N_2}}}$$

$\bar{X}_1$ is the mean of the first sample, S_1^2 is the variance of the first sample, and N_1 is the size of the first sample; similarly, $\bar{X}_2$ is the mean of the second sample, S_2^2 is the variance of the second sample, and N_2 is the size of the second sample. Take two samples with statistics as follows:

Sample 1: $\bar{X} = 8$; $S^2 = 1.6$; $N = 30$

Sample 2: $\bar{X} = 5$; $S^2 = 2.1$; $N = 43$

The *t*-ratio for these samples would be

$$t = \frac{\bar{X}_1 - \bar{X}_2}{\sqrt{\frac{S_1^2}{N_1} + \frac{S_2^2}{N_2}}}$$

$$= \frac{8 - 5}{\sqrt{\frac{1.6}{30} + \frac{2.1}{43}}}$$

$$= \frac{3}{\sqrt{0.053 + 0.049}}$$

$$= \frac{3}{\sqrt{0.102}}$$

$$= \frac{3}{0.32} = 9.38$$

Table 15.7 Abbreviated Distribution of *t*

	One-tailed	0.05	0.025	0.01	0.005
d.f.	Two-tailed	0.10	0.05	0.02	0.01
40		1.684	2.021	2.423	2.704
60		1.671	2.000	2.390	2.660
120		1.658	1.980	2.358	2.617

Once the t-ratio has been found, it must be compared with the critical value found in the table of t-values, an excerpt of which is presented in Table 15.7. The formula for calculating the degrees of freedom for difference of means tests is

$$d.f. = N - k$$

where N is the total sample size ($N_1 + N_2 + \ldots$) and k is the number of samples. In our example, *d.f.* equals 71 (73 – 2).

You will notice on the t-table a distinction between one-tailed and two-tailed tests. If the direction of difference is not important to us, we use a **two-tailed test**. If we are not interested in whether men or women are better at math but in whether any sex difference exists, we would use the two-tailed test. If the direction of difference does matter to our theory—if, for example, we are testing the hypothesis that men have greater math ability—we use a **one-tailed test**. Marija J. Norusis (1990, 156) explains the distinction between the two tests:

> The procedure [for the one-tailed test] is the same as for the two-tailed test, but the resulting probability value is divided by 2, adjusting for the fact that the equality hypothesis is rejected only when the difference between the two means is sufficiently large and in the direction of interest. In the two-tailed test, the equality hypothesis is rejected for large positive or negative values of the statistic.

If we have theoretical justification for using the one-tailed test, it is preferred.

Let's return to our example. We have a t-ratio of 9.38 and 71 degrees of freedom. We will use the 95 per cent confidence level and a two-tailed test. Looking at the table, we find that the closest critical value is 2.000. Our calculated value exceeds this critical value, allowing us to reject the null hypothesis (H_0: $\mu_1 = \mu_2$) and support the alternative hypothesis (H_a: $\mu_1 \neq \mu_2$). The results suggest a significant difference between categories of the independent variable (e.g. males and females), leading to the conclusion that the relationship did not occur by chance.

Log on to our website to watch a tutorial on comparing means.

APPLY YOUR UNDERSTANDING

Using the *t*-Test

Imagine that a university decides to generate empirical data showing what a university education pays with respect to personal income. To this end, a survey of 500 respondents from the local community, of whom 150 have a university degree and 350 do not, is commissioned. The mean annual income for those respondents with a university degree is $66,000, and the standard deviation is $7,000. The mean annual income for those without a university degree is $61,000, and the standard deviation is $5,000. (Recall from Chapter 14 that the standard deviation is the square root of the variance; to calculate the variance, you must square the standard deviation.) Calculate a *t*-test to determine if the survey evidence supports the argument that a university education pays.

Mann-Whitney *U*-Test

An alternative method for looking at the significance of relationships between ordinal- and interval-level variables or between interval-level variables with non-normal data distributions is the Mann-Whitney *U* rank-order test. This test is based on the ranking of cases and can therefore be used for relationships in which one or both variables are ordinal- or interval-level. Like the chi-square test, it is non-parametric and is useful when we wish to test relationships in which the interval-level variables do not meet the normal distribution requirements of the parametric tests. Of course, like all other non-parametric tests, the Mann-Whitney *U*-test does not provide as much information as would a parametric statistic. Thus, if the researcher can use parametric tests, it is usually advised that he or she do so. The trade-off is between a less informative, non-parametric statistic that does not introduce important assumptions about the distribution of the data (such as a normal distribution or a linear relationship) and a parametric statistic that provides more information but that may also have assumptions (normality, linearity) that are not met by the data.

The logic of the Mann-Whitney *U*-test resembles that of the difference of means test: we compare two subsamples on a particular characteristic and determine if the populations are significantly different. If they are, we conclude that the bivariate relationship is significant. But where the difference of means test compares means, the Mann-Whitney *U*-test compares rankings. The latter test works as follows: we combine the two subsamples into a single sample (being certain to remember which case belongs to which sample); we rank each case from high to low, according to its score on the variable; and, finally, we again subdivide the two samples and total the rankings, comparing the totalled rankings of each subsample.

Why would the rankings within the different subsamples matter? Logically, "[i]f the groups have the same distribution, their sample distribution of ranks should be similar. If one of the groups has more than its share of small or large ranks, there is reason to suspect that the two underlying distributions are different" (Norusis 1990, 226). The rankings are summarized into the Mann-Whitney *U*-statistic, the significance of which is tested with the *z*-test statistic. The null hypothesis states that the populations will have equal rankings, whereas the alternative hypothesis says that the rankings will differ. These hypotheses can be shown as follows:

$$H_0: R_1 = R_2$$

$$H_a: R_1 \neq R_2$$

where R_1 is the ranking in population 1 and R_2 is the ranking in population 2.

We will demonstrate the Mann-Whitney *U*-test with the nominal-interval relationship we considered in the previous section—gender and math performance—by looking at the final grades of the students in a rather small section of a university math course. To select the Mann-Whitney *U*-test over the more powerful differences of means test, we have reason to assume that the math scores in one sample are not normally distributed; in this case, the men's sample has a few "geniuses" who skew the distribution.

Men		Women	
Case	Score	Case	Score
1	98	6	82
2	99	7	72
3	56	8	70
4	64	9	90
5	72	10	78

The first step is to look at the two samples as a single sample and assign ranks. Tied cases are averaged between the two ranks that they share. For this sample, case 2 is highest and therefore gets the highest ranking; case 1 is ranked second; case 9 is ranked third; and so on. Note that cases 5 and 7 are tied and are ranked at 6.5 ((6 + 7)/2).

Men			Women		
Case	Score	Rank	Case	Score	Rank
1	98	2	6	82	4
2	99	1	7	72	6.5
3	56	10	8	70	8
4	64	9	9	90	3
5	72	6.5	10	78	5

The next step is to sum the ranks of each sample. For the men, the sum is 28.5 (2 + 1 + 10 + 9 + 6.5); for women, it is 26.5 (4 + 6.5 + 8 + 3 + 5). We then calculate Mann-Whitney *U*, using the formula

$$U = N_1 N_2 + \frac{N_1 (N_1 + 1)}{2} - \Sigma R_1$$

where N_1 is the sample size of sample 1, N_2 is the sample size of sample 2, and ΣR_1 is the summed rankings of group 1. Calculating *U* for this sample, we get

$$5(5) + \frac{5(5 + 1)}{2} - 28.5$$

$$= 25 + 15 - 28.5$$

$$= 11.5$$

We then need to determine if this value is statistically significant. To do so, we calculate a *z*-value,[6] using the formula

$$Z = \frac{U - \frac{N_1 N_2}{2}}{\sqrt{\frac{N_1 N_2 (N_1 + N_2 + 1)}{12}}}$$

For this example,

$$Z = \frac{\frac{11.5 - 5(5)}{2}}{\sqrt{\frac{5(5)(5 + 5 + 1)}{12}}}$$

$$= \frac{-1}{\sqrt{22.92}} = \frac{-1}{4.79} = -0.209$$

This calculated *z*-value is compared to the charted critical value. For *z*-scores, our critical values are constant: at the 95 per cent confidence level, the critical value is $z = \pm 1.96$, and at the 99 per cent confidence level, the critical value is $z = \pm 2.58$. As we have learned, if the calculated score meets or exceeds the critical value, we can reject the null hypothesis. Clearly, we fail to reject the null hypothesis in this example: our calculated value of –0.209 falls short of the 95 per cent confidence critical value of ±1.96.

On the basis of this analysis, we would conclude that sex has no significant impact on math performance. Looking back at the data, we realize that this conclusion could probably also be reached by "eyeballing" the data. For example, although two of the males scored very high on the math test (99 and 98) and were ranked 1 and 2, two other males performed quite poorly (scores of 56 and 64) and ranked 9 and 10 out of 10. In this instance, the wide discrepancy in the performance of the males meant that they performed neither consistently higher nor lower than the women. However, these two groups did have different patterns of performance: the women as a group performed more consistently near the middle of the range; the men were more likely to be high or low. These differences did not register with the Mann-Whitney *U*-statistic. This serves as an important reminder: whenever possible, look closely at the data as well as at the summary statistic.

Although the Mann-Whitney *U*-test is useful for all ordinal-level relationships, its use with interval-level variables should be limited to those cases where they fail to meet parametric tests' normal distribution requirements. If a normal distribution exists, the researcher should use the difference of means *t*-test (for relationships with ordinal- and nominal-level variables) or the *t*-test and *F*-ratio (for relationships with other normally distributed interval-level variables), which we will examine in Chapter 17 when we discuss regression analysis.

Overall, we have seen that inferential statistics play a central role in hypothesis-testing. But after we have rejected the null hypothesis, we still need to find substantive support for our alternative hypotheses in order to advance our theories. This subject will be addressed in Chapters 16 and 17.

Working as a Team

1. Your group has been hired to determine if high-school students who have been exposed to educational material on the dangers of smoking are less likely to smoke than students who have not been exposed to such material. You have to decide whether to employ a 0.01 or 0.05 confidence level for the test of significance. What would you recommend, and why? What are the policy implications of your choice? What are the arguments for erring on the side of a Type I or Type II error? What are the ethical issues that come into play?

Self-Study

1. Calculate the chi-square for the following table, which looks at the (hypothetical) relationship between partisanship and support for carbon tax. Would you accept or reject H_0? What critical value would you use, and why?

	Conservative	Liberal	NDP	Green	Total
Oppose carbon tax	100	12	2	0	112
Support carbon tax	20	30	38	25	113
Total	120	42	40	25	227

2. A (hypothetical) study has examined whether individuals born in Canada have significantly different annual incomes than individuals born outside the country but now living in Canada do. The study included 500 respondents in each category. The mean annual income for those born in Canada was $64,000, with a standard deviation of $6,500. The mean annual income for those born outside the country was $59,000, with a standard deviation of $5,500. Using this data, construct a one-tailed and a two-tailed *t*-test. Which would be more appropriate? Would you use a 0.01 or 0.05 test of significance? What would you conclude about the difference in annual income between those born inside and outside Canada? Give reasons to support your answers.

Notes

1. Adapted from Norusis (1990, 159).
2. Readers with access to data analysis programs such as IBM SPSS, SAS, Stata, or R should note that the programs will calculate test statistics automatically and compare those statistics with the critical values. Thus, for many, the exercises in this chapter will be more pedagogical than practical.
3. In journal articles, political scientists often select a 0.05 confidence level but also distinguish higher levels ($p > 0.01$, $p > 0.001$) in the tables. This practice allows the reader to make his or her own assessment about confidence levels.
4. To test for the normal distributions required for parametric tests, researchers should examine the data with a diagnostics test such as SPSS's EXAMINE or with histograms and box plots.
5. Some texts use the symbols f_e and f_o to designate frequencies expected and frequencies observed, respectively.
6. For small sample sizes of the kind seldom encountered in survey research, *z*-scores may not be appropriate. For an alternative interpretive table, see Gibbons (1976, 409–16).

CHAPTER 16

Explaining the Political World
Nominal and Ordinal Data

Destination

By the end of this chapter, you should be able to

- construct and interpret contingency tables;
- summarize the use of measures of association;
- select appropriate measures of association;
- calculate and interpret measures of association; and
- control for a third variable.

Explanatory research is the means by which political scientists explore questions of cause and effect. We know from descriptive research that there is variation within political phenomena, and our goal is to identify the major causes of such variation. For example, people differ in their federal party support: some support the Liberal Party, others the Conservative, New Democratic, and Green parties. How can we explain these differences? Are there particular factors that predict the party affiliation of given individuals and help explain why others lack any affiliation?

One assumption of the scientific method is that there is order to the universe; for instance, people do not randomly adopt party affiliations. It is assumed that specific factors—variables—influence this choice. There is no supposition, however, that any single variable determines party affiliation. In social research, we know that there are no perfect correlations in the real world; it is rare that we can explain even most of the variation in the dependent variable by one external cause. This situation means that, in addition to discovering that a relationship exists between the dependent variable and a particular independent variable, social researchers need to measure and assess the strength of that relationship. How much of the variation in the dependent variable is caused by a given independent variable? We can measure the strength of a bivariate relationship with **measures of association.**

When conducting bivariate research, the political scientist needs to address four questions:

1. Is there a relationship?
2. What is the direction of the relationship?
3. What is the strength of the relationship?
4. Is the relationship statistically significant?

The final question was addressed in Chapter 15, where different tests of significance were introduced. This chapter will address the first three questions for nominal- and ordinal-level data. Chapter 17 will examine interval-level data.

Is There a Relationship? If So, What Is the Direction of the Relationship?

To look at a relationship between two variables, we need to arrange them in a way that will allow us to identify patterns. One way to do so is to use contingency tables, introduced in Chapter 15. When reading a contingency table, we are looking for a patterned relationship or correlation. A **perfect correlation** exists when knowing the value on one variable always lets us know the value on the other. In Table 16.1a, we see that there is a perfect relationship between age and support for conservatism: all young people show low support, all middle-aged people show moderate support, and all older people show high support. Under these circumstances, if asked to guess the conservatism of a stranger, we would be able to guess correctly 100 per cent of the time as soon as we discovered his or her age. A 22-year-old, for instance, would display low support for conservatism.

If even one case deviates from this pattern, we do not have a perfect relationship. Table 16.1b represents a **moderate relationship**: most young people show low support, most middle-aged people show moderate support, and most older people show high support. Under these circumstances, knowing a stranger's age would improve our ability to guess his or her conservatism, but we would not be certain. There is a good chance that a 22-year-old will display low support (that is our best prediction), but he or she might display moderate or high support. Moderate relationships, of course, will vary in strength; the second half of this chapter provides a number of techniques that can specify the precise strength of the relationship. Table 16.1c displays **no relationship**: there is no discernible

Table 16.1 Looking for Correlations in Contingency Tables

a) Perfect Correlation

		Age: Young	Age: Middle	Age: Old	
Support for Conservatism	Low	8	0	0	8
	Moderate	0	15	0	15
	High	0	0	7	7
	Total	8	15	7	30

b) Moderate Correlation

		Age: Young	Age: Middle	Age: Old	
Support for Conservatism	Low	5	1	2	8
	Moderate	2	12	1	15
	High	1	2	4	7
	Total	8	15	7	30

c) No Correlation

		Age: Young	Age: Middle	Age: Old	
Support for Conservatism	Low	2	4	2	8
	Moderate	4	8	3	15
	High	2	3	2	7
	Total	8	15	7	30

pattern between age and support for conservatism. Thus, knowing a stranger's age gives us no clue whatsoever as to his or her conservative views.

If we find a moderate or perfect relationship and if we have variables that can be ordered (i.e. ordinal- or interval-level variables), we want to consider the direction of the relationship. Tables 16.1a and 16.2b represent a positive relationship: as age increases, support for conservatism increases. (Recall that nominal variables cannot be ordered and therefore direction does not apply to relationships involving them.)

Contingency tables allow us to detect correlations for nominal- and original-level data visually. For interval-level data, correlations can be visually detected in **scatter plots**, or scatter diagrams. Figure 16.1 presents the hypothetical distribution of individuals according to their height (vertical axis) and weight (horizontal axis). Each dot on the diagram

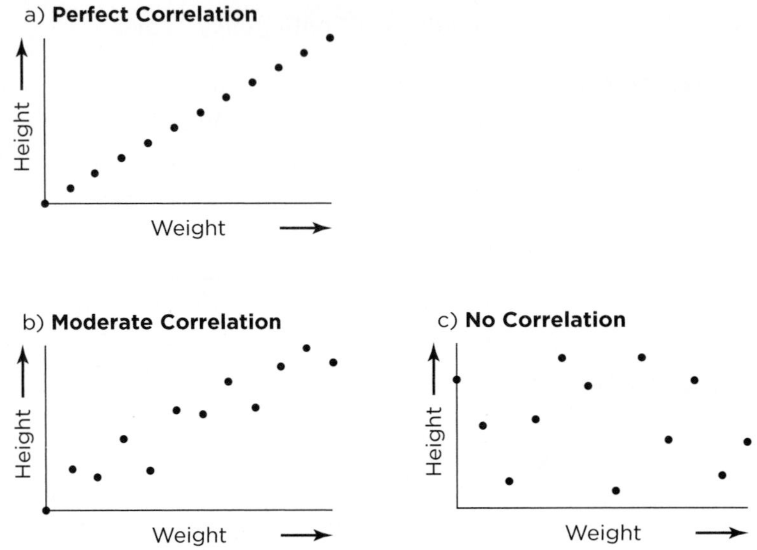

Figure 16.1 Looking for Correlations in Scatter Plots

represents one individual or case. Figure 16.1a shows a perfect correlation; for every increase in height, there is an equivalent increase in weight. (We assume that height drives weight rather than weight driving height!) The relationship is positive in that an increase in one variable (height) corresponds to an increase in the other (weight), which is represented by the scatter-plot line rising as one looks left to right. (For a negative relationship the scatter-plot line would fall as one looks left to right.) Figure 16.1b shows a positive but less than perfect correlation; the taller people are, the more they tend to weigh, but a person's height does not allow us to predict his or her weight perfectly. In Figure 16.1c, the scatter plot suggests no relationship between height and weight.

Having visually established that there is a relationship between two variables and having determined (for ordinal- and interval-level variables) the direction of the relationship, we next need to consider relationship strength.

How Strong Is the Relationship?

Most social and political events have multiple causes and influencing factors; indeed, it would be impossible to isolate every single influential factor for such dependent events as political partisanship, attitudes toward environmentalism, or political efficacy. Given that impossibility, social science research aims to identify the most important explanatory variables. What independent events have the most influence on the dependent event? Ultimately, the objective is to increase our predictive accuracy; just as the medical researcher wishes to predict the effect of drug A on a patient's health, we wish to predict the impact of independent variable A on a citizen's partisanship or public policy attitudes. And just as the medical researcher is not dealing with absolutes—there will always be some people for whom drug A has a different effect than clinical trials would suggest—so too must social researchers deal with variations and partial relationships. If we find that 75 per cent of women vote Liberal, we cannot state with certainty that Tanya will vote that way. However, we can state with confidence that, given no information other than gender, Liberal is the best prediction for Tanya's vote.

By measuring the strength of a relationship between an independent and a dependent variable, we are measuring the confidence we can place in our predictions. The strength of the relationship between two variables is gauged with measures of association, which condense the patterns in a contingency table or scatter plot into a single numerical value. When we visually assess the data, we may fail to notice certain patterns because of inexperience or bias in favour of our hypotheses. Similarly, we sometimes see stronger relationships than actually exist. Measures of association minimize such problems by providing a numerical check on our perceptions. (On the other hand, visual examination of the data can provide a useful check of the interpretation of summary statistics!) In addition, measures of association provide a standardized and compact way to convey relationship information to others; they are much easier to report and compare across studies than are complex contingency tables.

A number of measures of association are available, and the appropriate selection depends on the coefficients' technical limitations and the variables' level of measurement. As noted in Chapter 15, parametric statistics have assumptions that must be met if they are to be used and interpreted correctly. Less stringent, and hence more widely available, tests are referred to as non-parametric statistics. While parametric tests often have the advantages of being more robust (less subject to fluctuations) and more powerful, it is sometimes difficult to meet their many rigorous assumptions. For this reason, political scientists often select non-parametric statistics.

The second factor in selecting a correlation measure is the level of data measurement. As we have seen, political scientists are concerned with three levels: nominal, ordinal, and interval. We always use the measure of association that is most appropriate for the lowest level of measurement. If we have a bivariate relationship between a nominal-level variable and an ordinal-level variable, we select a measure of association appropriate for nominal-level data. If we have an ordinal-level and an interval-level variable, we use ordinal-level measures. Clearly, to use interval-level measures, we need to have only interval-level variables. (We will explore exceptions to this rule in Chapter 17.) When interval-level variables are used with nominal- or ordinal-level variables, the interval-level data are often grouped; age (in years) might be grouped into young (under 35), middle (35–64), and old (65 and over). This practice makes the contingency tables that accompany the measure of association easier to read.

Measures of association at the nominal level typically range from 0 to 1, while at the ordinal and interval levels the typical range is from −1 to +1. (Interval-level measures will be addressed in the following chapter.) For both nominal- and ordinal-level measures, 0 signifies no relationship (perfect independence): change in the independent variable is not correlated or associated with change in the dependent variable. The closer the coefficient is to 0, the weaker the relationship. For nominal-level measures, 1 indicates a perfect relationship: change in the independent variable is always and systematically correlated with change in the dependent variable. The closer the coefficient is to 1, the stronger the relationship.

The same principle holds for ordinal- and interval-level measures, with the addition of direction. For these measures, the coefficient can be either positive or negative. A positive coefficient indicates a positive relationship: as the value of the independent variable increases, the value of the dependent variable also increases. A negative coefficient indicates a negative relationship: as values of the independent variable increase, values of the dependent variable decrease and vice versa. Thus, the ± signification indicates direction rather than strength. As with nominal-level measures, we judge strength in ordinal- and interval-level relationships according to how close the coefficient is to 0 or ±1. If the coefficient is near 0, the relationship is very weak. If it is near ±1, the relationship is very strong.

Table 16.2 presents some general guidelines for interpreting measures of association, which are intended as a starting point rather than a final, definitive interpretation of relationship strength. For a number of reasons, the strength of a relationship is relative; in other words, coefficients of 0.5 do not always indicate relationships of the same strength. First, and as we will see, some measures of association are relatively more conservative or stringent, while others tend to inflate the strength of the relationship and therefore may be less robust. Second, research design impacts the strength of measures of association.

APPLY YOUR UNDERSTANDING

Selecting Measures of Association

For the following bivariate relationships, identify the level of measurement of each variable (nominal, ordinal, interval) and the appropriate level of measure of association (assume all distribution assumptions are met):

1. age (in years) and support for environmentalism (strong support-strong opposition)
2. sex and ideological position (left-centre-right)
3. party affiliation and level of education (number of years completed)
4. union membership and social class (working-lower middle-upper middle-upper)
5. religion and attendance of religious services (daily-weekly-monthly-annually-never)

Table 16.2 Starting Point Guidelines for Interpreting Measures of Association

0.00	No relationship
± 0.01–0.09	Extremely weak relationship
± 0.10–0.20	Weak relationship
± 0.21–0.30	Moderate relationship
± 0.31–0.49	Moderately strong relationship
± 0.50–0.99	Strong or very strong relationship
± 1.00	Perfect relationship

Experimental research has the greatest ability to control outside influences and tends to generate relatively strong measures of association. Survey research, on the other hand, is subject to greater amounts of "noise" and measurement error and generates smaller measures of association. A measure of association of 0.5 might be seen as moderate in experimental research but strong in survey research. Finally, we need to keep in mind the context of our study. The goal is to identify the best predictors of a given dependent event. For some situations, the predictors of a dependent event tend to be so weak that even a rather low coefficient may actually be our best known predictor. For this reason, it is always important to keep the hypotheses in mind.

A special class of measures of association is the **proportional reduction in error (PRE) measures**. A PRE measure is basically a ratio of errors (Norusis 1990, 121): we compare the amount of error we have without knowing the independent variable with the amount of remaining error after knowledge about the independent variable is taken into account. In other words, to what degree does knowledge about the independent variable reduce our error in predicting values of the dependent variable? The meaning of a PRE measure is best illustrated with an example.[1] Imagine that we have 100 people whose party affiliations are as follows:

Liberal	60
Conservative	30
NDP	10

If one of these individuals were to walk into the room and the preceding distribution was the only information we had, our best guess about the individual's party affiliation would be Liberal; this choice would ensure that we were right 60 times out of 100 and wrong 40 times out of 100. Not great odds, but the mode (the most frequently occurring category) is the best predictive option available with nominal-level variables such as these.

Now suppose that we obtain a second piece of information, the region in which respondents live. Given that regional residence may influence party affiliation, we construct a contingency table—party affiliation by region—and get the distributions shown in Table 16.3.

How do these new data affect our predicting abilities? Let's say we need to guess the party affiliation of a respondent from the West. If we guess Conservative, we will be correct 20 times out of 30. What if the individual is from central Canada? Here, our best guess is Liberal because we will be correct 25 times out of 40. Finally, for Atlantic Canadian respondents, guessing Liberal will make us correct 25 times out of 30. When we combine the results, we find that, by using the knowledge provided by the independent variable (region), we are correct 70 times (20 + 25 + 25) and incorrect 30 times (10 + 15 + 5). Our guessing abilities have been improved by adding the knowledge about the independent variable: we have decreased the errors from 40 to 30.

To find the proportionate reduction of error, we can use a basic ratio formula:

$$\text{PRE} = \frac{\text{error without IV} - \text{error with IV}}{\text{error without IV}}$$

where IV is the independent variable. In this example,

$$\text{PRE} = \frac{40 - 30}{40} = 0.25$$

The PRE coefficients can be expressed as a percentage; in this case, knowledge about the respondent's region of residence allowed us to improve our guessing by approximately 25 per cent.

This logic is seen in all PRE measures, but there are two caveats. First, the PRE formula is provided for illustrative purposes only. Although it explains the logic of the measures, it is not actually used to calculate lambda, gamma, and tau-b (the measures considered in this chapter). Second, only PRE measures can be expressed as a percentage reduction of error. Other measures—such as Cramer's V and tau-c—can be identified only in terms of strength and, occasionally, direction. With all measures of association, be they PRE or not, we need

Table 16.3 Party Affiliation by Region (PRE Example, Hypothetical Data)

	Region			
Party	**West**	**Central**	**Atlantic**	**Total**
Liberal	10	25	25	60
Conservative	20	5	5	30
NDP	0	10	0	10
Total	30	40	30	100

to note the strength of the relationship and, for ordinal-level measures, the direction of the relationship.

Having looked at the commonalties between measures of association, we can now turn to the various measures. You might find some of the statistical calculations in the next sections complex and detailed. Follow each step carefully and ensure that each aspect of the calculation is clear before you continue. You will find that calculating the formulas for yourself on paper or with a calculator will help you to better appreciate and interpret computer-generated statistics. The difference is profound, similar to the distinction between visiting a foreign country with a working knowledge of the language and with nothing more than a guidebook of common phrases.

Measures for Nominal-Level Data

Nominal-level measures of strength are used whenever one of the variables in the bivariate relationship is a categorical variable; we may have nominal–nominal, nominal–ordinal, or nominal–interval relationships (as previously stated, interval-level data in such cases are typically grouped). Non-parametric nominal-level measures are also used when our data fail to meet the requirements of the parametric tests. Remember that nominal-level measures have no direction and vary from 0.0 (perfect independence) to 1.0 (perfect correlation). We will look at two measures for nominal-level data: **lambda** and **Cramer's V**. Lambda is a PRE measure; Cramer's V is chi-square-based (we must calculate the chi-square statistic first). Although lambda is a more robust measure than Cramer's V and generally easier to calculate, there are instances in which the use of lambda is not advised.

Log on to our website to watch a tutorial on measures of association for nominal variables.

Lambda uses the mode to make predictions. Recall from Chapter 14 that the mode is the only measure of central tendency available for nominal-level data. The PRE example presented in the previous section illustrates lambda: both variables (party affiliation and region) were nominal level and the mode was used as the best predictor of party affiliation. However, we can calculate lambda in a less involved manner by using the following formula:

$$\lambda = \frac{\Sigma(f_i) - F_d}{N - F_d}$$

where f_i designates the mode in each category of the independent variable, F_d is the mode of the marginal totals of the dependent variable (that is, the largest of the row marginals), and N is the total number of cases.

Return to Table 16.3. To calculate lambda, we need to first find the mode for each category of the independent variable. The mode value for the West is 20 and 25 for both central and Atlantic Canada. Together, the modes total 70: $\Sigma(f_i) = 70$. The second value we need is the largest row marginal. Quick examination reveals that $F_d = 60$. Finally, we need to know the total number of cases: $N = 100$. Having gathered the necessary numbers, we are now ready to plug them into the formula:

$$\lambda = \frac{\Sigma(f_i) - F_d}{N - F_d}$$

$$= \frac{70 - 60}{100 - 60} = \frac{10}{40} = 0.25$$

Because this is a PRE measure, we can state that knowledge of the respondent's region improved our prediction ability by 25 per cent. The relationship is of moderate strength.

There are two limitations to lambda. Because of the formulation, the value that lambda takes will vary according to which variable is designated independent. Consequently, researchers must be clear in their theory (and table construction) regarding which variable is dependent. The other limitation is mathematical: if significantly more cases are grouped in one category of the dependent variable (that is, one row marginal is much larger than the others), lambda will approximate zero. This does not mean that perfect independence exists between the variables—it is simply a mathematical result. (Hence the need to look at both contingency tables and summary statistics!)

Table 16.4 presents a relatively modest adjustment to Table 16.3, namely an additional 10 respondents who are Liberal and from the West. The data in this new table appear to indicate that region affects party affiliation. For example, half the respondents in the West identify with the Conservatives, whereas only 5 of 40 (12.5 per cent) in central Canada and 5 of 30 (16.7 per cent) in Atlantic Canada identify with the party. In addition, 10 of 40 (25 per cent) central respondents, but none from the other regions, identify with the New Democrats.

Let's confirm this observation with lambda:

$$\frac{70 - 70}{110 - 70} = \frac{0}{40} = 0.0$$

In this case, a lambda of zero suggests that adding information about the independent variable has not reduced the errors in predicting the dependent variable. But visual inspection of the table clearly shows that there is a relationship. What is going on? The answer lies in the distribution of data in the dependent variable. Notice that, in a total sample size of 110, 70 cases (63.6 per cent) are in the Liberal category. Furthermore, as we read across columns of the independent variable, we find that the Liberals are the largest group in each category of the independent variable. Therefore, there were 70 correct predictions before knowing the independent variable and 70 correct predictions after knowing it, for no net improvement. In short, there is a relationship between region and party in Table 16.4, but this relationship is not captured by lambda.

Table 16.4 Party Affiliation by Region

	Region			
Party	**West**	**Central**	**Atlantic**	**Total**
Liberal	20	25	25	70
Conservative	20	5	5	30
NDP	0	10	0	10
Total	40	40	30	110

Lambda often underestimates the strength of the relationship between two variables when there is an unequal distribution among categories of the dependent variable. Always look at the table when using lambda to confirm that this undervaluing does not occur. It is also a good idea to run a second measure of association for nominal data, such as Cramer's V, as a check on lambda's robustness.

As we mentioned at the beginning of this section, Cramer's V is based on the test statistic chi-square. Recall from Chapter 15 that chi-square compares the observed frequencies in a bivariate relationship with the frequencies that would be expected if perfect independence existed. The steps for calculating Cramer's V are as follows:

1. Create an expected frequencies table.
2. Using the expected and observed frequencies, calculate chi-square.
3. Using chi-square, calculate Cramer's V.

Let's work through the steps by using the data in Table 16.3. How many cases could we expect in the Liberal–West cell if party affiliation and region are independent of each other? How many cases could we expect in the Conservative–Atlantic cell? Our first step in calculating Cramer's V is to calculate the expected frequencies for every cell of the contingency table. To do so, we take the row marginal for the cell, multiply it by the column marginal for the cell, and divide by the total number of cases:

$$E = \frac{\text{(row marginal)(column marginal)}}{N}$$

Thus, for the Liberal–West cell, the expected frequency is

$$E = \frac{60 \times 30}{100} = 18$$

If region and party affiliation are independent, we expect 18 westerners to be Liberals. We use the same calculation to determine the expected frequencies for all other cells (try the calculations yourself for practice) and thereby produce the expected frequencies in Table 16.5.

Table 16.5 Party Affiliation by Region (Expected Frequencies)

	Region			
Party	**West**	**Central**	**Atlantic**	**Total**
Liberal	18	24	18	60
Conservative	9	12	9	30
NDP	3	4	3	10
Total	30	40	30	100

Our next step is to calculate chi-square. The formula is

$$\chi^2 = \frac{\Sigma(O - E)^2}{E}$$

Using this formula, we calculate each individual $(O - E)^2/E$ and then sum the results (see Table 16.6). In doing so, we find that chi-square for our example is 40.62.

Having calculated chi-square, we come to our last step: calculate our measure of association, Cramer's V. The formula for Cramer's V is

$$V = \sqrt{\frac{\chi^2}{N(k - 1)}}$$

where k is the minimum number of rows or columns (if the number of rows is smaller, we use rows; if the number of columns is smaller, we use columns).

For a 4×3 table, $k = 3$. For a 2×3 table, $k = 2$. In this example, we have a 3×3 table, so $k = 3$, and $k - 1 = 2$. We know already that $N = 100$ and chi-square = 40.62, so we can put all these numbers into the formula to get our coefficient:

$$= \sqrt{\frac{40.62}{200}} = \sqrt{0.203} = 0.45$$

We can interpret this coefficient as indicating that there is a moderately strong relationship between party affiliation and region of residence. Cramer's V is not a PRE measure, so we cannot make statements about improvements in predictive accuracy.

You probably noticed that the Cramer's V coefficient ($V = 0.45$) suggested a much stronger relationship than did the lambda coefficient ($\lambda = 0.25$). It is not uncommon for two summary statistics calculated on the same table to yield different results, although the difference in this case seems especially large. In general, because lambda is based on a proportional reduction in error interpretation, it is often preferable to Cramer's V. If the two statistics yield similar results, lambda would be the reported statistic. When the two statistics diverge, as they do in this instance, we would ask why. The answer seems to lie in the distribution of the dependent variable. We showed that lambda was reduced to 0 by adding another 10 cases to the dependent variable. That suggests that the present distribution

Table 16.6 Calculating Chi-Square

Observed	Expected	O - E	(O - E)^2	(O - E)^2/E
10	18	-8	64	3.56
25	24	1	1	0.04
25	18	7	49	2.72
20	9	11	121	13.44
5	12	-7	49	4.08
5	9	-4	16	1.78
0	3	-3	9	3
10	4	6	36	9
0	3	-3	9	3
			Total	**40.62**

APPLY YOUR UNDERSTANDING

Calculating Lambda and Cramer's V

For the following table, calculate and interpret both lambda and Cramer's V.

Support for Social Welfare Policy by Gender

	Female	Male	Total
Low support	5	10	15
Moderate support	15	15	30
High support	20	5	25
Total	40	30	70

probably underestimates the strength of the relationship. And since lambda appears to do so, Cramer's V would be the preferred statistic. But we lose a bit in interpretive power, as Cramer's V is not based on a proportionate reduction in error. (A *V* of 0.45 is larger than a *V* of 0.225, but it is not twice as large.) We would conclude that there is a moderately strong effect of region on voting ($V = 0.45$) in this case.

Measures for Ordinal-Level Data

When we have either two ordinal-level variables or an ordinal- and an interval-level variable, we can use ordinal-level measures of association. However, because ordinal-level tests can understate the strength of non-linear relationships, researchers should ensure that the relationship between the variables is linear before using these measures. Both positive and negative relationships are examples of linear relationships and could be depicted by a straight line (moving up and to the right in the former, down and to the right in the latter). If our relationship is not linear (e.g. a curvilinear relationship), we should use the non-parametric, nominal-level measures. To discover if our bivariate relationship is linear, we need to look at our contingency tables carefully. Does the relationship appear positive at some points and negative (or non-existent) at others? Pattern inconsistencies in the data suggest a non-linear relationship. Tables 16.7a to 16.7d illustrate linear and curvilinear relationships.

Log on to our website to watch a tutorial on measures of association for ordinal variables.

The ordinal-level measures of strength explored here are **gamma**, **tau-b**, and **tau-c**. Gamma and tau-b are both PRE measures and can be interpreted in terms of percentage reduction of error; tau-c is not a PRE measure. Recall that, when interpreting ordinal-level coefficients, we need to consider not just strength but also direction. A negative number indicates a negative relationship, whereas a positive coefficient indicates a positive relationship. Finally, it is essential that we ensure that our tables are properly constructed before we begin the calculations. In each description in this section, we will assume that contingency tables are constructed with the independent variable running horizontally and the dependent variable vertically and that both variables are ordered from low to high. Before calculating the ordinal-level statistics, our first step is to check the table construction. If you are presented with a table that is ordered differently, you will need to reconstruct the table before you can begin your calculations.

Gamma and tau-b consider ordered pairs of observations. We look at two individual cases and ask how they compare on their rankings for both the independent and dependent variables.[2] Remember that our correlations can be either positive or negative. If we have a positive relationship, an increase in the independent variable will be accompanied by an increase in the dependent variable. When we evaluate pairs of cases, positive relationships are seen in **concordant pairs**: they exhibit similar ordering on the independent and dependent variables. If we have a negative relationship, an increase in the independent variable is accompanied by a decrease in the dependent variable. Negative relationships are seen in **discordant pairs** that exhibit dissimilar ordering of the independent and dependent variables.

Table 16.8 examines the relationship between appreciation for political science and number of years in university. Sally is ranked above Harry on both the independent and the dependent variables. Judging from this pair alone, we would believe that appreciation of political science increases the longer a student is in university. Harry and Sally are an example of a concordant pair. The relationship between time in university and appreciation is positive: as time increases, appreciation increases. Harry and Matteo are another example of a concordant pair: Matteo is ranked above Harry on both variables. Similarly, Harry and Trey are a concordant pair. Now look at the pairing of Sally and Sue. Sue ranks above Sally on the independent variable yet below her on the dependent variable. Judging from this pair alone, we would believe that appreciation of political science decreases the longer a

Table 16.7a Contingency Table Showing a Positive Relationship

	Low	Medium	High	Total
Low	20	10	0	30
Medium	10	10	10	30
High	0	10	30	40
Total	30	30	40	100

Table 16.7b Contingency Table Showing No Relationship

	Low	Medium	High	Total
Low	10	10	10	30
Medium	10	10	10	30
High	10	10	20	40
Total	30	30	40	100

Table 16.7c Contingency Table Showing a Negative Relationship

	Low	Medium	High	Total
Low	0	0	30	30
Medium	10	10	10	30
High	20	20	0	40
Total	30	30	40	100

Table 16.7d Contingency Table Showing a Curvilinear Relationship

	Low	Medium	High	Total
Low	0	30	0	30
Medium	10	0	20	30
High	20	0	20	40
Total	30	30	40	100

Table 16.8 Appreciation by Years of Undergraduate Study (Concordant and Discordant Pairs)

	Two years	Three years	Four years
Low appreciation	Harry		Sue
Medium appreciation		Sally	Matteo
High appreciation		Trey	

student is in university. The pair is discordant. The relationship between time in university and appreciation is negative: as time increases, appreciation decreases. Trey and Sue and Trey and Matteo are further examples of discordant pairs.

If our tables are constructed properly, we can find concordant pairs by looking down and to the right of any given cell. The cells in Table 16.9 have been labelled to make this point more clearly. Start in the upper-left-hand corner cell, cell *a*, and look down and to the right. For cell *a*, concordant pairs can be found in cells *e*, *f*, *h*, and *i*. For cell *b*, concordant pairs are in cells *f* and *i*. What are the concordant pairs for cell *c*? For this cell, we cannot move both down and to the right; therefore, cell *c* does not have any concordant pairs. For cell *d*, the concordant pairs are found in cells *h* and *i*; concordant pairs for cell *e* are limited to cell *i*. For cells *f*, *g*, *h*, and *i*, there are no cells that are both down and to the right, and these cells have no concordant pairs.

We use a similar process to find discordant pairs, moving up and to the right of any given cell. Here, we will start in the lower-left-hand corner, cell *g*, and work up. For cell *g*, the discordant pairs are found in cells *b*, *c*, *e*, and *f*. For cell *h*, discordant pairs are located in cells *c* and *f*. There are no cells up and to the right of cell *i*; thus, it does not have any discordant pairs. For cell *d*, discordant pairs are found in cells *b* and *c*; for cell *e*, the discordant pair is in cell *c*. And what of cells *f*, *a*, *b*, and *c*? If you said that these cells do not have any discordant pairs because of the absence of cells above and to the right, you are correct.

In summary, concordant pairs are found down and to the right on our tables and reflect positive relationships; discordant pairs are found up and to the right on the same tables and reflect negative relationships. Gamma, the measure of association to which we will turn shortly, looks at only concordant and discordant pairs, comparing the number of the former with the number of the latter. But this comparison does not exhaust all possible pairings. As Table 16.8 shows, there are also a number of **ties**, pairs of cases that differ on one variable but are tied on the other. Sue and Harry differ on the independent variable (she has four years of university education, while he has only two) yet are tied on the dependent variable (low appreciation of political science). Sally and Matteo are tied on the dependent variable as well. Notice that we look across the row for ties on the dependent variable. Trey and Sally are an example of a tie on the independent variable: both have three years of university education, although they differ in their appreciation scores. A second example of a tie on the independent variable is the Sue–Matteo pairing. For ties on the independent variable, we look down the column. Tau-b considers ties, including both the independent variable and dependent variable types.

Table 16.9 Finding Ordinal Pairs

	Two years	**Three years**	**Four years**
Low appreciation	*a*	*b*	*c*
Medium appreciation	*d*	*e*	*f*
High appreciation	*g*	*h*	*i*

We will now look at how to calculate the coefficients, beginning with gamma. Gamma is calculated by the following formula:

$$\gamma = \frac{N_s - N_d}{N_s + N_d}$$

where N_s designates the number of similar (concordant) pairs and N_d the number of dissimilar (discordant) pairs. To find N_s, we multiply each cell frequency by the sum of the frequencies of the cells below and to the right and add these products. To find N_d, we multiply each cell frequency by the sum of the frequencies of the cells above and to the right, and add these products. This process is best illustrated by the example in Table 16.10 (the cells have been labelled to make the steps clearer).

To calculate N_s for this table, we multiply down and to the right and then add the products:

$$\begin{aligned} N_s &= a(e + f + h + i) + b(f + i) + d(h + i) + e(i) \\ &= 0(30 + 5 + 5 + 5) + 10(5 + 5) + 5(5 + 5) + 30(5) \\ &= 0(45) + 10(10) + 5(10) + 30(5) \\ &= 0 + 100 + 50 + 150 \\ &= 300 \end{aligned}$$

To calculate N_d, we multiply up and to the right and then add the products:

$$\begin{aligned} N_d &= g(b + c + e + f) + h(c + f) + d(b + c) + e(c) \\ &= 15(10 + 5 + 30 + 5) + 5(5 + 5) + 5(10 + 5) + 30(5) \\ &= 15(50) + 5(10) + 5(15) + 30(5) \\ &= 750 + 50 + 75 + 150 \\ &= 1{,}025 \end{aligned}$$

Table 16.10 Ideological Position by Income

	Income			
Ideology	**Low**	**Middle**	**High**	**Total**
Left	0 *a*	10 *b*	5 *c*	15
Centre	5 *d*	30 *e*	5 *f*	40
Right	15 *g*	5 *h*	5 *i*	25
Total	20	45	15	80

To calculate gamma, we insert these figures into the following formula:

$$\gamma = \frac{N_s - N_d}{N_s + N_d}$$

$$= \frac{300 - 1{,}025}{300 + 1{,}025} = \frac{-725}{1{,}325} = -0.55$$

To interpret gamma, we need to keep in mind strength, direction, and the fact that gamma is a PRE measure. Hence, we can interpret this gamma value of –0.55 as indicating a negative and strong relationship: as income increases, support for the "right-wing" ideology decreases. Knowledge of the independent variable increased our predictive accuracy by approximately 55 per cent.

Tau-b is a PRE measure, but (unlike gamma) it includes ties. It is important to note that tau-b requires square tables, that is, 2 × 2, 3 × 3, 4 × 4, and so on. If the independent and dependent variables differ in the number of categories available, this measure cannot be used. The formula for tau-b is

$$\text{tau-b} = \frac{N_s - N_d}{\sqrt{(N_s + N_d + T_x)(N_s + N_d + T_y)}}$$

where T_x designates ties on the independent variable and T_y ties on the dependent variable.

To find ties on the independent variable, we remain within the column and move down; to find ties on the dependent variable, we remain within the row and move across. To find T_x, we multiply each cell frequency by the sum of the frequencies of the cells below and add these products. To find T_y, we multiply each cell frequency by the sum of the frequencies of the cells to the right and add these products.

Let's return to the data in Table 16.10. To calculate T_x, we multiply down in each column and then add the products:

$$\begin{aligned} T_x &= a(d + g) + d(g) + b(e + h) + e(h) + c(f + i) + f(i) \\ &= 0(5 + 15) + 5(15) + 10(30 + 5) + 30(5) + 5(5 + 5) + 5(5) \\ &= 0(20) + 5(15) + 10(35) + 30(5) + 5(10) + 5(5) \\ &= 0 + 75 + 350 + 150 + 50 + 25 \\ &= 650 \end{aligned}$$

To calculate T_y, we multiply across in each row and then add the products:

$$\begin{aligned} T_y &= a(b + c) + b(c) + d(e + f) + e(f) + g(h + i) + h(i) \\ &= 0(10 + 5) + 10(5) + 5(30 + 5) + 30(5) + 15(5 + 5) + 5(5) \\ &= 0(15) + 10(5) + 5(35) + 30(5) + 15(10) + 5(5) \\ &= 0 + 50 + 175 + 150 + 150 + 25 \\ &= 550 \end{aligned}$$

To calculate tau-b, we insert these figures into the formula (we already calculated N_s and N_d for Table 16.10 when we calculated gamma):

$$\text{tau-b} = \frac{N_s - N_d}{\sqrt{(N_s + N_d + T_x)(N_s + N_d + T_y)}}$$

$$= \frac{300 - 1{,}025}{\sqrt{(300 + 1{,}025 + 650)(300 + 1{,}025 + 550)}}$$

$$= \frac{-725}{\sqrt{(1{,}975)(1{,}875)}}$$

$$= \frac{-725}{\sqrt{(3{,}703{,}125)}}$$

$$= \frac{-725}{1{,}924.35}$$

$$= -0.38$$

We can interpret this tau-b value of –0.38 as indicating a negative and moderately strong relationship: as income increases, support for the right moderately decreases. Knowledge of the independent variable increased our predictive accuracy by approximately 38 per cent. The tau-b value suggests a weaker relationship than does the gamma value (–0.55); because tau-b includes information on the number of ties, it tends to be more conservative and less likely to inflate relationship strength. As a result, tau-b is often favoured over gamma.

For non-square tables, we can use tau-c. Like tau-b, tau-c is more conservative than gamma. However, tau-c is not a PRE measure, so we must be careful with the interpretation. The formula for tau-c is

$$\text{tau-c} = (N_s - N_d) \times [2m/(n^2(m-1))]$$

where m is the smaller of the number of columns or rows (that is, for a 2×3 table, $m = 2$) and n is the sample size. Consider the example in Table 16.11.

First, we calculate N_s:

$$N_s = a(d + f) + c(f)$$

$$= 5(30 + 10) + 10(10)$$

$$= 5(40) + 10(10)$$

$$= 200 + 100$$

$$= 300$$

Table 16.11 Ideological Position by Income

Ideology	Low	High	Total
Left	5	10	15
	a	*b*	
Centre	10	30	40
	c	*d*	
Right	15	10	25
	e	*f*	
Total	30	50	80

Next, we calculate N_d:

$$\begin{aligned} N_d &= e(b + d) + c(b) \\ &= 15(10 + 30) + 10(10) \\ &= 15(40) + 10(10) \\ &= 600 + 100 \\ &= 700 \end{aligned}$$

The sample size (n) is 80, and m is equal to 2 (the lesser of the number of rows and the number of columns). Thus, tau-c is

$$\begin{aligned} \text{tau-c} &= (N_s - N_d) \times [2m/(n^2(m - 1))] \\ &= (300 - 700) \times [2(2)/(80^2(2 - 1))] \\ &= -400 \times [4/(6{,}400(1))] \\ &= -400 \times [4/6{,}400] \\ &= -400 \times 0.000625 \\ &= -0.25 \end{aligned}$$

Compare this value to gamma for the same table:

$$\begin{aligned} \gamma &= \frac{N_s - N_d}{N_s + N_d} \\ &= \frac{300 - 700}{300 + 700} \\ &= -400/1000 \\ &= -0.40 \end{aligned}$$

APPLY YOUR UNDERSTANDING

Calculating Gamma and Tau

For the following table, calculate and interpret gamma and, depending on table dimensions, either tau-b or tau-c.

Support for Social Welfare Policy by Ideological Position

	Left	Centre	Right	Total
Low support	0	5	20	25
Moderate support	5	15	5	25
High support	15	10	0	25
Total	20	30	25	75

APPLY YOUR UNDERSTANDING

Interpreting the Lambda, Cramer's V, Gamma, Tau-b, and Tau-c

Interpret the following measures of association in sentence form. Be certain to note strength, direction (where relevant), and PRE (where relevant). Briefly explain why you interpreted strength as you did.

1. gamma = −0.02
2. Cramer's V = 0.40
3. lambda = 0.15
4. tau-b = 0.60
5. tau-c = −0.35

In summary, three measures of strength for ordinal-level variables have been discussed. Tau-b and gamma can be used for square tables, while tau-c and gamma can be used for non-square tables. The tau measures are less likely to inflate strength and are therefore preferred. However, if your analysis includes tables of different sizes, you may wish to report both gamma and the appropriate tau statistic to facilitate comparisons across tables.

Measures for Interval-Level Data

When we have two interval-level variables, we can use interval-level measures of association. The most commonly used is **Pearson's *r***, which measures the linear relationship between an independent and a dependent variable. Like ordinal measures of association, Pearson's *r*

Log on to our website to watch a tutorial on measures of association for interval variables.

varies between –1 and +1. Pearson's *r* assumes a linear relationship between the two variables. If the relationship is not linear (for example, if the scatter plot suggests a curvilinear relationship), the non-parametric test Spearman's rho is used. Spearman's rho converts numbers into ranks and then uses the Pearson's R formula (presented in Chapter 17).

Summary: Bivariate Relationships

As you will recall from the start of the chapter, we ask four questions when we consider the relationship between two variables:

1. Is there a relationship?
2. What is the direction of the relationship (ordinal- and interval-level variables only)?
3. What is the strength of the relationship?
4. Is the relationship statistically significant?

We determine the existence of a relationship and its direction by looking at the data itself, either in the form of a contingency table or a scatter plot. We determine the strength of a relationship by examining the appropriate measure of association. And, as explained in Chapter 15, we determine statistical significance by exploring the appropriate inferential statistic.

These principles are also used for multivariate relationships. The next section of this chapter looks at nominal- and ordinal-level multivariate relationships; multivariate relationships among interval-level variables are discussed in Chapter 17.

Adding a Third Variable to the Bivariate Relationship

In Chapter 3, we discussed the modelling of a simple bivariate relationship in which a single independent variable is hypothesized to affect a single dependent variable. This relationship takes the form of Figure 16.2.

In this type of analysis, we isolate these two variables from the complex interplay of social life and test empirically whether A has a discernible effect on B. Now we would like to remove the condition of isolation that we imposed and ask whether a true causal relationship exists between these two variables when taking other factors into account. These

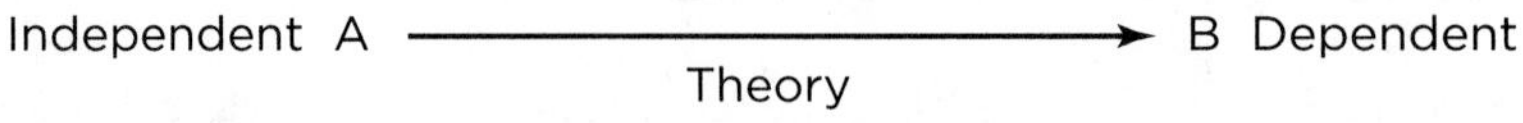

Figure 16.2 A Bivariate Causal Relationship

other factors can affect either the independent or dependent variables separately or the relationship between the independent and dependent variables in several ways. It is up to you as a researcher to model the relationship between the variables in your study and then to conduct an appropriate empirical examination of that model.

To contemplate the effects of a third variable, we must control for that variable. In other words, we must look at the relationship between our independent variable A and our dependent variable B while holding constant values of our control variable C. If we are controlling for sex, we would be interested in the relationship between A and B for men only and for women only. To do so, we would create separate contingency tables, calculate separate measures of association for men and women, and then decide if the relationship between A and B is similar between men and women.

When we control for variable C, there may be a number of outcomes, summarized in Table 16.12. First, we may see that the relationship between A and B holds constant—the measure of association retains its relative level of strength and the relationship remains statistically significant for all values of control variable C. If this is the case, we have greater confidence in our conclusion that A influences B. In the table, there is a moderately strong, positive relationship between the dependent and independent variables before gender is controlled; after controlling for gender, we continue to see a moderately strong, positive relationship across both categories (men and women) of our control variable. Thus, we can state that A influences B even after controlling for gender.

Second, the relationship between A and B may strengthen for all values of control variable C, as evidenced by an increase in the measure of association. If this is the case, we suspect that variable C is a reinforcing variable. As defined in Chapter 3, a reinforcing variable is one that can strengthen and magnify the relationship between an independent and a dependent variable. In Table 16.12, we see the relationship between A and B strengthen for both categories of our control variable (gender), suggesting that this variable magnifies the effects of the independent variable on the dependent variable.

Third, the relationship between A and B may weaken for all values of control variable C and may fail to achieve statistical significance. In the table, we see that the gamma value for each control variable category (men gamma = 0.210, women gamma = 0.028) is significantly lower than was seen before controls were introduced (gamma = 0.450) and that the relationship fails to achieve conventional statistical significance levels for one of the two control variable categories (women $p = 0.051$). When a relationship weakens after the introduction of a control variable, we suspect either that variable C is a confounding variable and the relationship between A and B is spurious or that variable C is an intervening variable.

As discussed in Chapter 3, a spurious relationship occurs when a relationship between two variables can be accounted for by a third variable. An intervening variable is one that comes between an independent and a dependent variable, but the direction of causality flows from the independent variable to the intervening variable to the dependent variable. How do we know the difference? Here we must consider temporal order. If variable

Table 16.12 Possible Outcomes When Using Control Variables

Outcome	Example	Interpretation
Relationship between dependent and independent variable holds constant	Relationship without gender control: gamma = 0.450, p = 0.000 Relationship controlling for gender: Men: gamma = 0.438, p = 0.000 Women: gamma = 0.456, p = 0.000	The control variable does not affect the relationship between the dependent and independent variable
Relationship between dependent and independent variable gets stronger	Relationship without gender control: gamma = 0.450, p = 0.000 Relationship controlling for gender: Men: gamma = 0.488, p = 0.000 Women: gamma = 0.548, p = 0.000	Suspect that the control variable reinforces the influence of the independent variable on the dependent variable
Relationship between dependent and independent variable gets weaker or disappears	Relationship without gender control: gamma = 0.450, p = 0.000 Relationship controlling for gender: Men: gamma = 0.210, p = 0.000 Women: gamma = 0.028, p = 0.051	Suspect that the control variable is a confounding variable (i.e. the control variable causes variation in both the dependent and independent variables and the relationship between them is spurious), or suspect that the control variable is an intervening variable; use temporal order and theory to decide between spurious or intervening interpretation
Relationship between dependent and independent variable varies across categories of the control variable	Relationship without gender control: gamma = 0.450, p = 0.000 Relationship controlling for gender: Men: gamma = 0.012, p = 0.068 Women: gamma = 0.542, p = 0.000	Suspect that the relationship between the dependent and independent variables differs between the control variable subgroups

C comes before our independent variable A, we suspect that C causes variation in both A and B and that the relationship between A and B is spurious. If variable C comes after independent variable A, we suspect that C is an intervening variable. To return to the example in Table 16.11, the control variable is gender and thus exists prior to independent variable A; given this information, we would suspect that gender causes variation in both independent variable A and dependent variable B and that the relationship between them is spurious.

Finally, the relationship between A and B may vary between values of control variable C. In our example, the relationship between A and B is strong and statistically significant for women (gamma = 0.542, $p = 0.000$) but weak and statistically insignificant for men (gamma = 0.012, $p = 0.068$). Stated another way, the relationship between A and B exists only in a subgroup (women) and does not exist within the entire population.

Contingency Tables with Control Variables

When beginning an analysis, it is always useful to map the relationship you wish to examine. Doing so will help you establish the direction of causality you are hypothesizing and identify the role of each variable (which are the independent and dependent variables and what is the hypothesized impact of the third variable).

For the current example, we will assume that the initial hypothesis is as shown in Figure 16.3. The initial bivariate relationship is between age and political interest, and the hypothesis is that as age increases, so too does political interest. The multivariate model then suggests that education acts to reinforce the relationship between age and political interest. An analysis of this model includes an examination of the following relationships: (1) age and political interest; (2) education and political interest; (3) age and education; and (4) age and political interest, controlling for education.

Our dependent variable, general political interest, is coded into a three-point measure ranging from low to high.[3] Our independent variables are age and education. The age variable is coded into four categories (18–34, 35–49, 50–64, and 65 and over). The education variable has three categories (less than completed high school, completed high school and/or attended technical college, and completed college and/or attended or completed university).

Table 16.13 shows the effect of age on level of political interest. Notice that this relationship is between two ordinal-level variables; therefore, we anticipate a linear relationship. The data conform to this expectation and also reveal a moderate, positive relationship between the variables. Since these are ordinal data and the table is non-square, the gamma and tau-c statistics are appropriate. A gamma of 0.234 and a tau-c of 0.173 indicates a relationship of weak to moderate strength. We conclude that age has a weak to moderate effect on level of political interest. The p value ($p = 0.000$) indicates that that relationship is statistically significant.

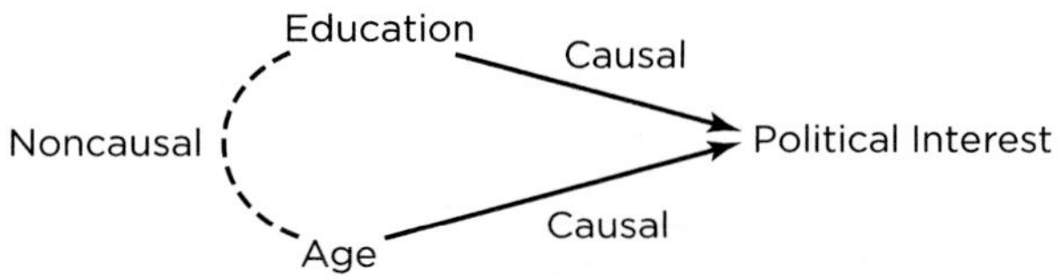

Figure 16.3 Hypothesized Impact of Age on Political Interest, Controlling for Education as a Reinforcing Variable

Table 16.13 The Effect of Age on Political Interest

	Age				
Political Interest	**18–34**	**35–49**	**50–64**	**65+**	**Total**
Low	336 (40.3%)	390 (30.3%)	262 (21.9%)	174 (18.9%)	1,162 (27.4%)
Moderate	261 (31.3%)	440 (34.2%)	407 (33.9%)	278 (30.3%)	1,386 (32.7%)
High	237 (28.4%)	456 (35.5%)	530 (44.2%)	467 (50.8%)	1,690 (39.9%)
Total	834 (100%)	1,286 (100%)	1,199 (100%)	919 (100%)	4,238 (100%)

Note: Percentages may not add to 100 due to rounding.
Gamma = 0.234
Tau-c = 0.173
p = 0.000

The effect of education on political interest is shown in Table 16.14. Since education is measured with three categories, we produce a 3 × 3 table, allowing us to use tau-b. Once again, we find a linear relationship of weak to moderate strength. The effect of education on political interest (gamma = 0.277) is stronger than age on interest (gamma = 0.234). This relationship is statistically significant as well.

Table 16.15 shows the effect of age on education level. Note that these two variables are related but that the relationship is negative: as age increases, level of education decreases. For example, among those aged 18–34 and 35–49, only 8.5 per cent and 11.2

Table 16.14 The Effect of Education on Political Interest

	Education			
Political Interest	**Less Than Completed High School**	**High School-Technical College**	**Post-Secondary**	**Total**
Low	280 (37.2%)	710 (30.2%)	157 (15.4%)	1,147 (22.3%)
Moderate	238 (31.6%)	801 (34.1%)	306 (30.0%)	1,345 (32.6%)
High	234 (31.1%)	840 (35.7%)	556 (54.6%)	1,630 (47.8%)
Total	752 (100%)	2,351 (100%)	1,019 (100%)	4,122 (100%)

Note: Percentages may not add to 100 due to rounding.
Gamma = 0.277
Tau-b = 0.173
p = 0.000

Table 16.15 The Effect of Age on Education

	Age				
Education	**18–34**	**35–49**	**50–64**	**65+**	**Total**
Less than completed high school	69 (8.5%)	140 (11.2%)	191 (16.6%)	355 (39.8%)	755 (18.4%)
High school–technical college	549 (67.4%)	738 (59.0%)	638 (55.3%)	421 (47.1%)	2,346 (57.1%)
Post-secondary	197 (24.2%)	372 (29.8%)	325 (28.2%)	117 (13.1%)	1,011 (24.6%)
Total	815 (100%)	1,250 (100%)	1,154 (100%)	893 (100%)	4,112 (100%)

Note: Percentages may not add to 100 due to rounding.
Gamma = −0.272
Tau-c = −0.178
p = 0.000

per cent, respectively, had less than high-school education, compared with 39.8 per cent for those aged 65 and over. In addition, only 13.1 per cent of those aged 65 and over have a post-secondary education, compared with more than 24 per cent for the other age cohorts. In short, the youngest segments of the population have the highest levels of education, a finding that is consistent with the rapid expansion in the post-secondary education system that occurred in Canada beginning in the early 1960s. Once again, the relationship is statistically significant.

What impact does a negative association between age and education have on the relationship between age and political interest? To obtain an answer, we can rerun the analysis of age's effect on political interest, controlling for level of education. To control for education means to hold education constant. We do this by running separate analyses and producing separate contingency tables for each category of education. In other words, we ask, "What is the impact of age on political interest among those with a low level of education? What is the impact among those with a moderate and a high level of education?" With a three-category control variable, the analysis produces three separate tables, included here as Tables 16.16a to 16.16c.

Table 16.16a examines the effect of age on political interest among those with a low level of education. Once again, the relationship is statistically significant and linear: as age increases, the likelihood of having a high level of political interest increases as well. The strength of the relationship has also increased, from a tau-c of 0.173 for the population as a whole to a tau-c of 0.222 among those with a low level of education. We are more interested in the latter finding: a stronger impact of age on political interest among those with a low level of education suggests that education intervened in the relationship between age and interest in a negatively reinforcing manner.

A similar finding follows from an analysis of Tables 16.16b and 16.16c. Among those with a moderate level of education, the effect of age on political interest is given by a tau-c statistic of 0.203, well above the original tau-c of 0.173. For those with a high level of education, tau-c remains strong at 0.199. Thus, among each educational group, the relationship between age and political interest is higher than among the population as a whole. This finding indicates that the effect of age on political interest is negatively reinforced by level of education. Put another way, there is a relationship between age and interest that is somewhat offset by the negative effect of age on education. This is due to the significant

Table 16.16a The Effect of Age on Political Interest, Controlling for Education (Low Education)

	Age				
Political Interest	**18–34**	**35–49**	**50–64**	**65+**	**Total**
Low	36 (52.2%)	74 (52.9%)	75 (39.5%)	92 (26.8%)	277 (37.3%)
Moderate	22 (31.9%)	38 (27.1%)	66 (34.7%)	109 (31.8%)	235 (31.7%)
High	11 (15.9%)	28 (20.0%)	49 (25.8%)	142 (41.4%)	230 (31.0%)
Total	69 (100%)	140 (100%)	190 (100%)	343 (100%)	742 (100%)

Note: Percentages may not add to 100 due to rounding.
Gamma = 0.326
Tau-c = 0.222
p = 0.000

Table 16.16b The Effect of Age on Political Interest, Controlling for Education (Moderate Education)

	Age				
Political Interest	**18–34**	**35–49**	**50–64**	**65+**	**Total**
Low	239 (43.6%)	247 (33.6%)	150 (23.7%)	71 (17.1%)	707 (30.3%)
Moderate	167 (30.5%)	264 (35.9%)	232 (36.6%)	131 (31.6%)	794 (34.0%)
High	142 (25.9%)	225 (30.6%)	252 (39.7%)	213 (51.3%)	832 (35.7%)
Total	548 (100%)	736 (100%)	634 (100%)	415 (100%)	2,333 (100%)

Note: Percentages may not add to 100 due to rounding.
Gamma = 0.272
Tau-c = 0.203
p = 0.000

Table 16.16c The Effect of Age on Political Interest, Controlling for Education (High Education)

	Age				
Political Interest	**18–34**	**35–49**	**50–64**	**65+**	**Total**
Low	51 (25.9%)	67 (18.0%)	33 (10.2%)	5 (4.3%)	156 (15.5%)
Moderate	66 (33.5%)	125 (33.6%)	88 (27.2%)	26 (22.6%)	305 (30.3%)
High	80 (40.6%)	180 (48.4%)	203 (62.7%)	84 (73.0%)	547 (54.3%)
Total	197 (100%)	372 (100%)	324 (100%)	115 (100%)	1,008 (100%)

Note: Percentages may not add to 100 due to rounding.
Gamma = 0.315
Tau-c = 0.199
p = 0.000

increase in the availability of post-secondary education during the 1960s, an increase that has led to significant differences in educational attainment between younger and older Canadians. Over time, as the level of education among all age groups becomes more common, we would expect the effect of age on political interest to strengthen.

Working as a Team

1. A common notion in political science is that of the left–right spectrum, with the left representing support for a more interventionist government and the right representing support for minimal government. Survey respondents are often asked to locate themselves along this spectrum. In your study of support for the political "right," you hypothesize that two factors, family income and age, influence self-placement on the spectrum; more specifically, you believe that, as each of these two variables increases, support for the right increases. (You also assume that age and family income are not correlated.) You conduct a survey to test your theory, asking respondents to locate themselves on a six-point left–right scale, with 1 representing the extreme left and 6 representing the extreme right:

   Left - Right
   1 2 3 4 5 6

   Thus, a respondent who identifies herself as a 5 considers herself to be right wing, whereas a respondent who identifies himself as a 4 considers himself to be politically moderate, or centre–right, in orientation.

Your survey work provides the following data:

Case	Age	Income ($)	Left–Right Placement
1	42	65,000	5
2	36	28,000	3
3	55	58,000	4
4	19	15,000	2
5	56	45,000	6
6	25	29,000	6
7	31	50,000	2
8	65	90,000	3
9	23	31,000	1
10	47	70,000	5
11	39	10,000	1
12	50	35,000	2
13	28	45,000	4
14	26	34,000	3
15	49	58,000	5
16	63	90,000	5
17	60	67,000	6
18	38	39,000	4
19	30	18,000	1
20	61	40,000	3

a. State your null and alternative hypotheses for each possible relationship.
b. Draw the causal model for your theory. Identify the dependent and independent variables.
c. Create two bivariate tables (spectrum by age, spectrum by income), classifying the data as follows:
   age: young = 18–30; middle = 31–49; old = 50+
   income: low = $0–$35,000; middle = $36,000–$59,000; high = $60,000+
   spectrum: left = 1–2; centre = 3–4; right = 5–6
d. As a group, decide if the tables allow you to reject your null hypothesis. Is there support for your alternative hypothesis? Explain your reasoning.

Self-Study

1. For each of the following tables and data sets, calculate and interpret the stated measure of association. Which would you choose to report in your final write-up? For ordinal-level statistics, indicate how you determined linearity.

Opinion on Issue X by Religious Affiliation

	Catholic	Protestant	Jewish	Total
Support X	20	10	0	30
Oppose X	0	10	20	30
Total	20	20	20	60

Compute lambda and Cramer's V. Use inferential statistics to test statistical significance.

Support for Issue X by Level of Political Activity

	Low Activity	Moderate Activity	High Activity	Total
Low support	5	9	9	23
Moderate support	9	10	9	28
High support	11	6	7	24
Total	25	25	25	75

Compute gamma and tau-b. Use inferential statistics to test statistical significance.

2. Interpret each of the following in sentence form:
   a. gamma = –0.02
   b. lambda = 0.70
   c. Cramer's V = 0.12
   d. tau-b = 0.30
   e. tau-c = –0.42

Notes

1. Adapted from Manheim and Rich (1981, 284–6).
2. Example adapted from White (1994, 318–19).
3. The data used to test this model are from the 2006 CES. Original CES data were grouped for this demonstration. The principal co-investigators of the 2006 CES are André Blais, Joanna Everitt, Patrick Fournier, Elisabeth Gidengil, and Neil Nevitte. The CES surveys can be found at http://ces-eec.org/.

CHAPTER 17

Multivariate Analysis

An Introduction to the Deep End of the Pool

Destination

By the end of this chapter, you should be able to

- understand the use of scatter plots for examining the relationship between interval data;
- explain the assumptions underlying ordinary least squares regression techniques;
- describe the relationship between regression coefficients (the slope) and the standard error;
- interpret a regression analysis table that includes the regression coefficients and standard errors for each of the independent variables, together with the intercept and the value of R^2; and
- explain the use of dummy variables in regression analysis.

This chapter begins with a discussion of measures of association for interval-level data. We will introduce regression analysis, focusing on ordinary least squares regression. Using a step-by-step approach, we demonstrate how to calculate the regression coefficient and the standard error. The chapter then examines tests of statistical significance, followed by multiple regression. These techniques can reveal much about the strength of relationships in the complex world of political science research. However, because they are based on strong assumptions about the underlying data and can be misinterpreted, they must be used with care.

Measures for Interval-Level Data

Recall that interval-level measures of association are parametric tests and, as such, assume the relationship to be linear. In fact, the most common interval-level statistical technique is known as **basic linear regression**. Almost all advanced statistical techniques follow a logic similar to that of basic linear regression; thus, it is an important technique to understand. Our first step prior to beginning basic linear regression is to test for linearity.[1] We used a contingency table to look for linearity in ordinal-level variables, but to do so with interval-level variables would require the creation of an unmanageable table that is difficult to interpret. Instead, we use a scatter plot. We set up a graph, with the dependent variable along the *y*-axis (vertical) and the independent variable along the *x*-axis (horizontal), and locate each case according to its position on both axes. We then look at the pattern among the data: Does it suggest a linear, curvilinear, or no relationship? A pattern that could have a straight line drawn through it indicates a linear relationship. Figure 17.1 shows the scatter plot for the following data set:

	X	Y
Case 1	2	8
Case 2	3	5
Case 3	1	4
Case 4	6	9
Case 5	4	7

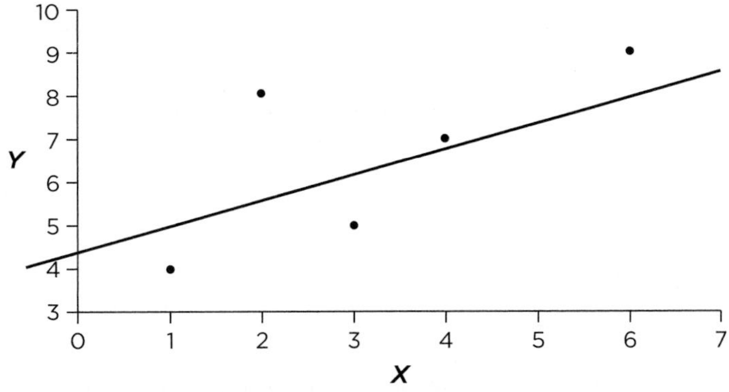

Figure 17.1 A Scatter Plot with Regression Line

When using real data in the social sciences, we rarely have a line that perfectly fits, that is, a line on which all cases fall exactly. Instead, we seek to find the line that best fits the data, known as the **regression line**. The regression line is essentially a line of prediction and is conceptually similar to the proportional reduction in error (PRE) measures. We ask ourselves, "Without knowledge of the independent variable, what is our best prediction of the value of the dependent variable for any particular case?" Given that the dependent variable is measured at the interval level, our best prediction would be the mean. The regression line provides a best prediction of dependent variable scores for any given independent variable score. To do so, however, the line must be calculated according to the **ordinary least squares (OLS)** method.

The OLS method places the regression line in a way that minimizes the squared deviations between the observed and predicted values. This process is analogous to the mean as a predictor of values on a single variable; the mean is the value that reduces the error in predicting scores on an interval variable. Any other predicted value produces more errors (larger squared deviations) than the mean. Likewise, the OLS regression line minimizes the errors (squared deviations) in predicting the values on an interval-level dependent variable for any given value on the independent variable. The OLS formula is used to determine the position of the regression line. It is stated as

$$Y' = a + bX$$

where Y' is the predicted value of the dependent variable, X is the value of the independent variable, a is the **intercept**, and b is the **slope**.

Y' is understood to be a linear function of X; it changes only when X changes (see Figure 17.2). The intercept, which is the value of Y' when X is equal to zero, is a constant and tells us the position of Y' on our graph where the regression line crosses the y-axis. The slope

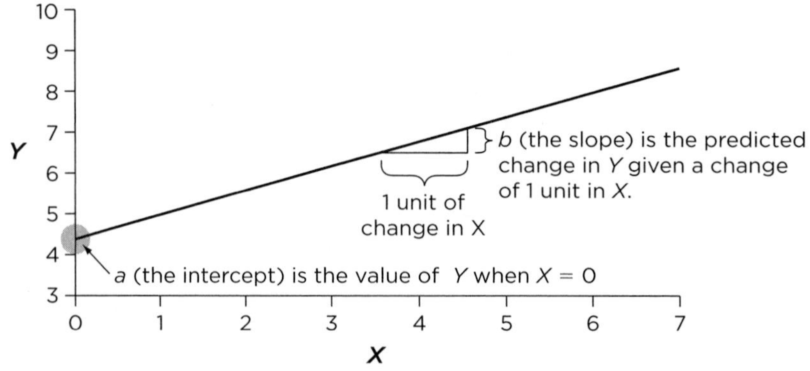

Figure 17.2 The Intercept (a) and Slope (b) of a Regression Line

represents the unit change in Y' for every unit increase in X. We have said that the dependent variable varies with the independent variable, but by how much? The slope tells us the unit change and, in doing so, indicates the angle that the regression line should take on the graph. The slope also indicates the direction of the relationship: a slope upward and to the right indicates a positive relationship and a slope downward and to the right a negative relationship.

Let's say that the dependent variable is weekly income (measured in dollars) and the independent variable is university education (measured in years). It is hypothesized that income varies positively with university education. The data collected and assessed reveal the following regression formula:

$$Y' = 200 + 100X$$

This formula tells us two things. First, we can see that, with no university education ($X = 0$), predicted weekly income (Y') is equal to \$200. We know this because the intercept (a) is equal to \$200. Second, the slope (b) is equal to 100, which means that we have a \$100 increase in weekly income for every one-year increase in university education (X). The slope also shows that the relationship between weekly income and university education is positive: as university education increases, weekly income increases (see Figure 17.3).

Let's try another example (Figure 17.4). The dependent variable is "total fine due on speeding ticket" (measured in dollars), and the independent variable is "kilometres over speed limit" (measured in kilometres). Interpret the following regression formula in writing:

$$Y' = 5 + 0.8X$$

Hopefully, you came to the following explanations: with no kilometres over the speed limit, the predicted speeding ticket total is \$5 and, for every one-kilometre increase in

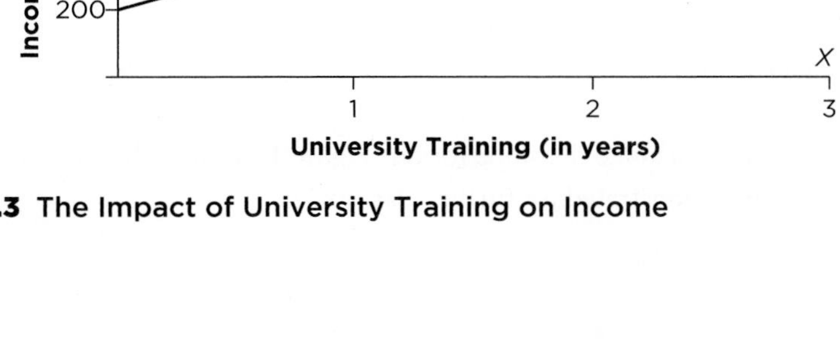

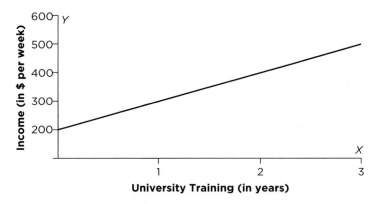

Figure 17.3 The Impact of University Training on Income

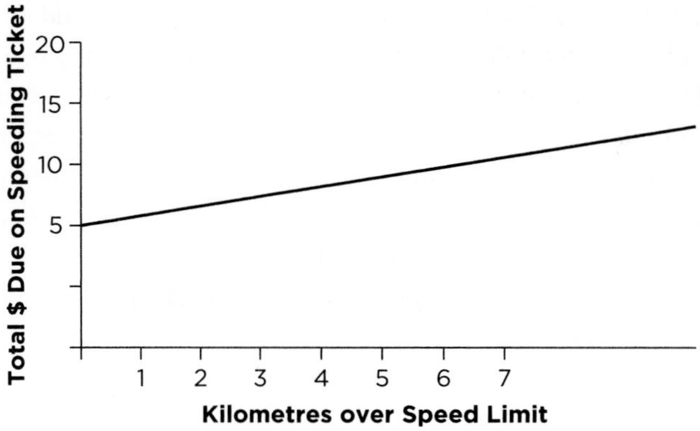

Figure 17.4 The Impact of Rate of Speed on the Size of Speeding Ticket

speed above the limit, there is an \$0.80 increase in the cost of the ticket. Now, you may be saying to yourself, that does not make sense. How can I get a speeding ticket when I have not exceeded the speed limit? Assuming that you live in an area where police are honest, this situation is clearly not possible. What the illustration shows, therefore, is that the intercept of the regression line can at times be substantively meaningless, serving more to help us position the regression line than to accurately predict the values of Y' when X equals zero.

How do we calculate the intercept and the slope? There are specific OLS formulas to determine each. We begin with the slope:

$$b = \frac{\text{sum of products}}{\text{sum of squares}} = \frac{\Sigma(x_i - \bar{x})(y_i - \bar{y})}{\Sigma(x_i - \bar{x})^2}$$

We calculate the slope in a series of steps:

1. Find the means of both x and y.
2. From each individual case, subtract the mean.
3. Calculate the products $(x_i - \bar{x})(y_i - \bar{y})$.
4. Calculate the sum of the products.
5. Calculate the squares $(x_i - \bar{x})^2$.
6. Calculate the sum of the squares.
7. Calculate the slope.

Let's use these steps to calculate the slope for our Figure 17.1 data (the first calculations of each step have been demonstrated for further clarity):

X	Y	$\bar{X}$	$\bar{Y}$	$(Y_i - \bar{Y})$	$(X_i - \bar{X})$	$(X_i - \bar{X})(Y_i - \bar{Y})$	$(X_i - \bar{X})^2$
2	8	3.2	6.6	(8 − 6.6 = 1.4)	(2 − 3.2 = −1.2)	(1.4 × −1.2 = −1.68)	((−1.2)² = 1.44)
3	5	3.2	6.6	−1.6	−0.2	0.32	0.04
1	4	3.2	6.6	−2.6	−2.2	5.72	4.84
6	9	3.2	6.6	2.4	2.8	6.72	7.84
4	7	3.2	6.6	0.4	0.8	0.32	0.64
						$\Sigma = 11.4$	$\Sigma = 14.8$

$$\bar{y} = \frac{(8 + 5 + 4 + 9 + 7)}{5} = 6.6$$

$$\bar{x} = \frac{(2 + 3 + 1 + 6 + 4)}{5} = 3.2$$

$$b = \frac{\text{sum of products}}{\text{sum of squares}} = \frac{\Sigma(x_i - \bar{x})(y_i - \bar{y})}{\Sigma(x_i - \bar{x})^2}$$

$$= \frac{11.4}{14.8} = 0.77$$

The slope is 0.77; for every 1-unit increase in X, there is a 0.77-unit increase in Y.

The OLS formula for the intercept is much less involved:

$$a = \bar{y} - b\bar{x}$$

After calculating the slope, we have the numbers needed to find the intercept:

$$a = 6.6 - 0.77\ (3.2)$$

$$= 6.6 - 2.46$$

$$= 4.14$$

The intercept is 4.14; this result tells us that, when X is equal to 0, the predicted value of Y is 4.14.

We now know how to calculate the regression line. But how does any of this fit with correlation coefficients? What do regression lines have to do with measures of strength in bivariate relationships? Recall that the regression line is a prediction line: it states what the value of Y is predicted to be at any given value of X. However, the line does not tell us how close the individual cases are to the line or how good our predictions are. The same OLS equation—identical intercepts and slopes—can represent two very different data sets.

Figure 17.5 shows a relatively weak relationship and Figure 17.6 a relatively strong relationship, even though both have the same slope and *Y* intercept.

To measure the strength of the linear interval-level relationship, we ask, "How well does the regression line fit the data?" We are assessing "goodness of fit." If there were a perfect bivariate relationship, all the variation in *Y* could be explained by *X* and all our cases would line up on the regression line. When we have cases that deviate from the regression line, we have an **unexplained variance**, a variation in *Y* that is not explained by the value of *X*. If the total squared deviations from the regression line are relatively large, this means that *X* does not explain a lot of the variation in *Y* and we have a weak relationship. If the total squared deviations from the regression line are relatively small, this means that *X* captures much of the variation in *Y* and we have a strong relationship.

The Standard Error of the Estimate

Figures 17.5 and 17.6 illustrate the goodness of fit of the regression line for the two sets of data, illustrating a much better fit (and hence a stronger relationship) in Figure 17.6.

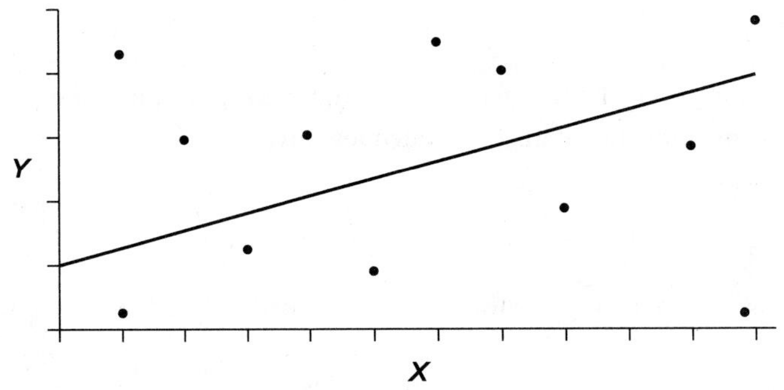

Figure 17.5 Weak Relationship

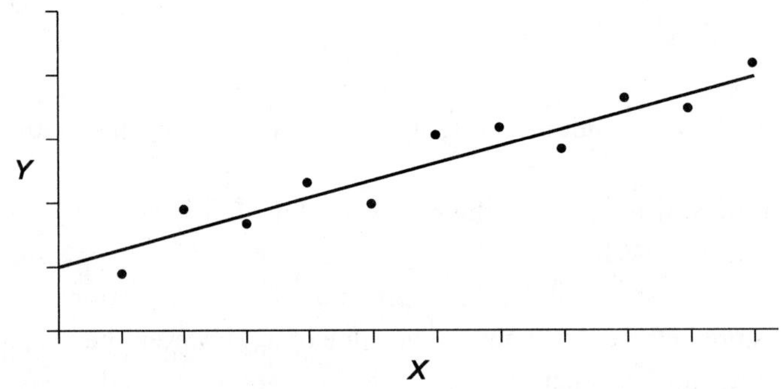

Figure 17.6 Strong Relationship

A statistic used to calculate the regression line's goodness of fit is the standard error of estimate, which is analogous to the standard deviation of the mean. That is, the smaller the standard error of estimate, the smaller the error in predicting the dependent variable on the basis of the independent variable.

The identification of the standard error of estimate can be seen in Figure 17.7. The three panels present the same data and illustrate three types of variation. In Figure 17.7a, the comparison is between the observed Y values and the mean of Y ($\bar{Y}$). This panel shows the error in predicting the Y value without knowledge of X; we indicated previously that the mean would be the best predictor as it would minimize the errors of predicting Y. Figure 17.7b compares the mean value of Y (the prediction before knowing the X value) with the predicted value of Y after knowing the X value (Y'). It is labelled "explained variation" because it is the amount of variation in Y that is accounted for by the X value. Figure 17.7c compares the observed values of Y with the predicted values of Y and is labelled the "unexplained variation," or sometimes the "residual variation"—the amount of variation in Y that exists after knowing the X values. Notice that the total variation is a sum of the explained and unexplained variations. The latter is used in computing the standard error of estimate, which has the following formula:

$$se = \sqrt{\frac{\Sigma(Y - Y')^2}{N - 2}}$$

where se is the standard error, Y is the observed value of Y, Y' is the predicted value of Y, and N is the number of cases.

Continuing with the example from Figure 17.1, we compute the standard error of estimate by first calculating the predicted value of Y':

$$\begin{aligned} Y' &= a + bX \\ &= 4.14 + 0.77X \end{aligned}$$

Using this formula for each value of X, we find Y', as shown in the following table:

X	Y	Y' = 4.14 + 0.77X	Y'	(Y - Y')	(Y - Y')²
2	8	Y' = 4.14 + 0.77(2)	5.68	2.32	5.38
3	5	Y' = 4.14 + 0.77(3)	6.45	-1.45	2.10
1	4	Y' = 4.14 + 0.77(1)	4.91	-0.91	0.83
6	9	Y' = 4.14 + 0.77(6)	8.76	0.24	0.06
4	7	Y' = 4.14 + 0.77(4)	7.22	-0.22	0.05
					$\Sigma = 8.42$

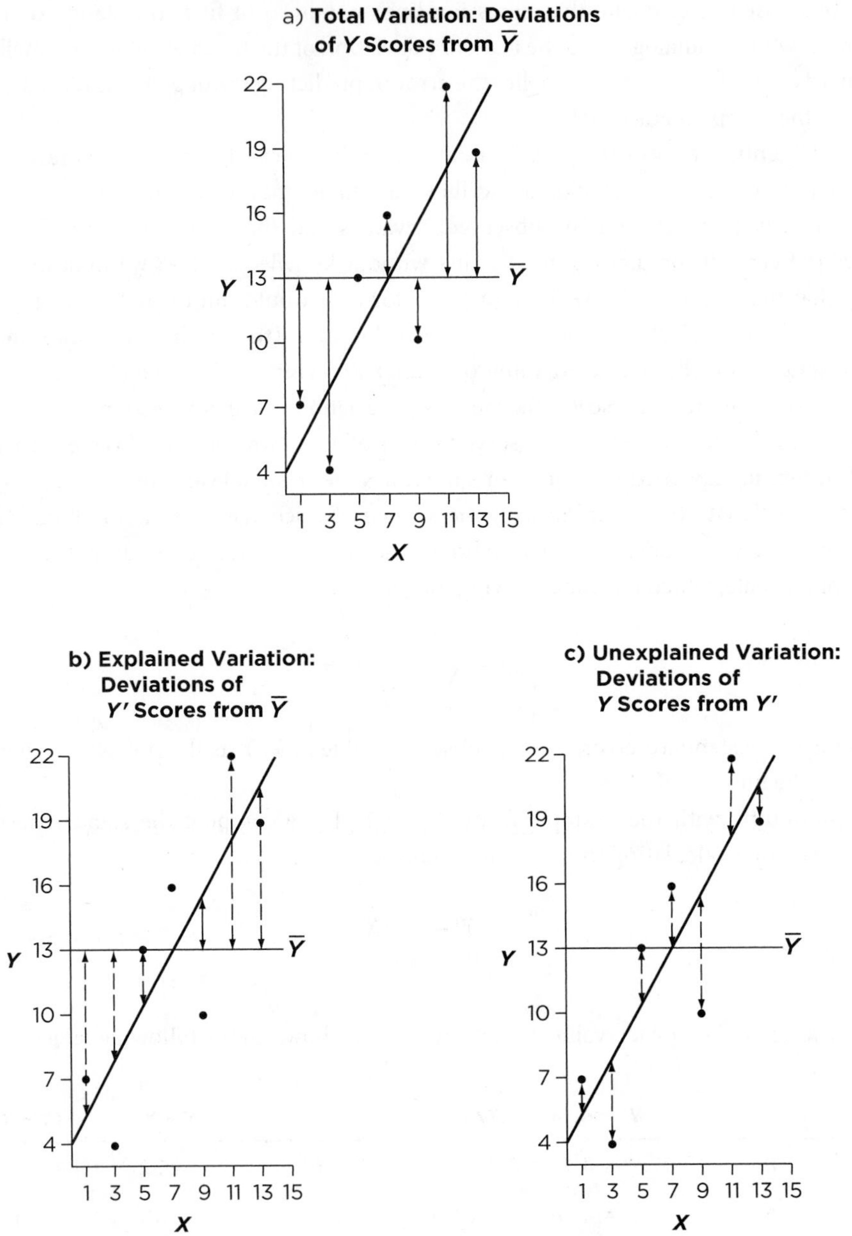

Figure 17.7 A Comparison of Total, Explained, and Unexplained Variations in Regression Analysis

Source: Adapted from Elifson et al. (1990).

Using this calculation of the unexplained variation, we can work out the standard error of estimate:

$$se = \sqrt{\frac{\Sigma(Y-Y')^2}{N-2}}$$

$$= \sqrt{\frac{8.42}{5-2}}$$

$$= \sqrt{\frac{8.42}{3}}$$

$$= \sqrt{2.81}$$

$$= 1.68$$

Figures 17.5 and 17.6 illustrated that a common slope and intercept can represent relationships of vastly different strength. It is always useful to evaluate the slope (or the regression coefficient) relative to the standard error. In the present example, the regression coefficient is 0.77 and the standard error is 1.68. These results suggest that, for each time the value of *X* increases by one unit, *Y* increases by 0.77 units. However, on average, we still "misplace" the values of *Y* by 1.68 units. The obvious question is, "Is the new predicted value of *Y* a good predictor or a bad predictor?" Or, alternatively, "Is a standard error of 1.68 large or small relative to the regression coefficient of 0.77?"

We can answer these questions by using either an inferential statistic and asking how likely this result would occur by chance alone or a summary descriptive statistic, which measures the strength of association. The appropriate statistics—and the ones generated by most of the popular computerized statistics packages—are the *t*-statistic for statistical inference and R^2 as a measure of the strength of relationship. Before calculating the former and testing for the level of statistical significance in the current example, it is worthwhile to examine the calculation of *t*-tests and *F*-ratios for interval-level data.

t-Tests and *F*-Ratios for Interval-Level Relationships

The test of R^2 is a test of the bivariate linear relationship. As previously discussed, the null hypothesis states that a relationship does not exist in the population, whereas the alternative hypothesis states that a relationship does exist. Stated in proper form, this is

$$H_0: R^2 = 0$$

$$H_a: R^2 \neq 0$$

To test the R^2 value, we use the F-ratio, which is calculated with the formula

$$F = \frac{\frac{R^2}{k}}{(1-R^2)/(N-k-1)}$$

where k is the number of independent variables. For bivariate regression, $k = 1$. Once we calculate the F-statistic, we compare it to the appropriate critical value (derived from a table of critical values of F) to decide whether to accept or reject the null hypothesis.

Imagine that a regression run between two interval-level, normally distributed variables from a sample of 50 cases produces an R^2 value of 0.30. To test whether this sample statistic is representative of a relationship in the population, we calculate F:

$$F = \frac{\frac{R^2}{k}}{(1-R^2)/(N-k-1)}$$

$$= \frac{\frac{0.30}{1}}{(1-0.30)/(50-1-1)}$$

$$= \frac{0.30}{(0.70)/(48)}$$

$$= \frac{0.30}{0.015}$$

$$= 20$$

We now need to look up the critical value on the F-distribution table, presented in abbreviated form in Table 17.1. Notice that the table requires two different degrees of freedom values. The formulas for these are as follows:

$$d.f.\ 1 = k,\ d.f.\ 2 = N - k - 1$$

Table 17.1 Abbreviated *F*-Table at the 95 Per Cent Confidence Level

***d.f.* 1**	**1**	**2**	**3**
d.f. 2			
46	4.05	3.20	2.81
48	4.04	3.19	2.80
50	4.03	3.18	2.79

For this example, *d.f.* 1 equals 1 and *d.f.* 2 equals 48 (50 – 1 – 1). Looking at the table, we can see that the appropriate critical value is 4.04. Our calculated *F*-value exceeds the critical value; therefore, we reject the null hypothesis. The relationship has been found to be statistically significant.

When we test the slope of the regression line, our null hypothesis is that the population slope equals zero; in other words, changes in one variable are not associated with changes in the other. Thus,

$$H_0: \beta = 0$$

$$H_a: \beta \neq 0$$

where beta (β) is the population slope. To test the significance of our slope, we use a *t*-test. Here, *t* is calculated with the formula

$$t = \frac{b}{S_b}$$

where S_b is the standard error of *b*.[2] (An alternative method of finding t for bivariate relationships is to take the square root of the *F*-score.) As with the *t*-test for differences of means, we compare the calculated value to the critical value found in the *t*-test. Degrees of freedom are equal to $N - k - 1$.

Calculating the *t*-Statistic and Conducting a Significance Test with Our Five-Case Example

In the present example, we calculate *t* as

$$t = \frac{b}{S_b}$$

$$= \frac{0.77}{1.68}$$

$$= 0.46$$

The degrees of freedom for this example, which has five cases and two variables, is given by

$$d.f. = N - k - 1$$

$$= 5 - 2 - 1$$

$$= 2$$

Referring to a table of critical values of Student's *t*, the inclusion of a two-tailed significance test at the 0.05 confidence level, we find that the significant value of *t* is 4.303. The observed value of *t* in our example is 0.46, which is well short of the critical value required for statistical significance. With this minute sample, we would conclude that the amount of error gives us little confidence that the relationship did not occur by chance. Therefore, we would not reject the null hypothesis.

To test for strength of relationships in the regression model, we use a correlation coefficient known as Pearson's *r*. In the OLS method, as we have seen, the total squared distances from the regression line should be less than the total squared distances from the mean (also known as the sum of squares or the **total variance**). Pearson's *r* asks if this is in fact the case by comparing the **explained variance** in *y* (that is, the variance that can be attributed to variation in *x*) with the total variance:

$$\text{total variance} = \text{explained variance} + \text{unexplained variance}$$

$$\text{Pearson's } r = \frac{\text{explained variance}}{\text{total variance}}$$

Unfortunately, Pearson's *r* on its own can be difficult to interpret. However, by squaring Pearson's *r*, we can obtain a better elaboration of its meaning. The result, known as r^2, indicates the proportion of *y* that can be explained by *x* and can be read as a percentage. Using the regression line, we can reduce our prediction errors by the value of r^2. As such, r^2 is similar in interpretation to PRE measures. We can calculate Pearson's *r* with the formula

$$r^2 = \frac{\Sigma\,(xy)^2}{\Sigma x^2\,\Sigma y^2}$$

As with calculating the slope, r^2 requires a series of steps:

1. Multiply individual *x* and *y* scores.
2. Square the products of *x* and *y*.
3. Sum the squared products.
4. Square individual *x* scores.
5. Sum the squared *x* scores.
6. Square the individual *y* scores.
7. Sum the squared *y* scores.
8. Solve for r^2.

In the table that follows, we have worked through our example data set, showing all calculations for the first case.

X	Y	(xy)	$(xy)^2$	x^2	y^2
2	8	(2 × 8 = 16)	(16 × 16 = 256)	(2 × 2 = 4)	(8 × 8 = 64)
3	5	15	225	9	25
1	4	4	16	1	16
6	9	54	2,916	36	81
4	7	28	784	16	49
			$\Sigma = 4{,}197$	$\Sigma = 66$	$\Sigma = 235$

$$r^2 = \frac{\Sigma\,(xy)^2}{\Sigma x^2\,\Sigma y^2}$$

$$= \frac{4{,}197}{(66)(235)}$$

$$= \frac{4{,}197}{15{,}510} = 0.27$$

In this data set, 27 per cent of the variation in y can be explained by x, leaving 73 per cent unexplained. The r^2 value does not tell you the unit change in y for every unit change in x or the direction of change. For this information, we need to look at the slope. The lowercase r signifies a simple linear regression; only one independent variable is included in the model. When we look at **multiple regression** (multivariate linear models; explained later in this chapter), an uppercase R is used.

In summary, when using simple linear regression, we take four steps:

1. Construct a scatter plot to ensure linearity.
2. Calculate the slope and intercept.
3. Calculate the standard error of estimate.
4. Calculate and interpret r^2.

Regarding the first step, researchers often find that, after scatter-plotting the variables, the relationship is not linear. However, they may wish to use the regression model in the testing because of the technique's power and accuracy advantages. To overcome this problem of non-linearity, the researcher may transform the variables by, for example, using the logarithm of the variable or the cosine and so forth. Various power transformations for variables have been found by statisticians to transform non-linear relationships into linear. The important thing to remember here is that we are no longer working with the original variables. For example, we would be looking at the relationship between level of education and the log of income. Consequently, we must state our interpretations in this form. You should expect to encounter such advanced statistics in the academic literature.

Another noteworthy technique seen in the literature is the use of **dummy variables**, which allows the researcher to use nominal- and ordinal-level variables in the linear model. A dummy variable is one in which a nominal or ordinal variable is transformed into one or more variables with or without a quality or character. For example, to create a set of dummy variables from the nominal variable of region of Canadian residence (assuming four regions of Atlantic, Quebec, Ontario, and the West), one could create three dummy variables (number of categories minus 1; in this example, 4 – 1). One of the categories must be suppressed, which means that no variable is created for it and it becomes the referent or comparison category. There could be the variables Atlantic, Quebec, and West, and, in each instance, a person is scored 1 if he or she lives in that region, and 0 if he or she does not. The resulting dummy variable coefficients would be interpreted as the effect of living in that region compared with the suppressed category, in this case to those living in Ontario. In other words, do people in Atlantic Canada, Quebec, or the West think or behave differently from people who live in Ontario? Although region of residence is a nominal-level variable, it can be used in a regression equation by creating a set of dummy variables. A second method of exploring the relationships between nominal- or ordinal-level variables and interval-level variables is the analysis of variance. Another option is to group the interval-level variable and use nominal- or ordinal-level correlation coefficients.

In voting behaviour research, one of the variables of greatest interest to researchers is to explain why people vote for one party or another. It is apparent, though, that the "direction of vote" variable is not measured at the interval level but is usually thought of as a nominal variable. If the vote choice is between Conservative, Liberal, NDP, Bloc Québécois, and Green Party (as well as several other minor parties), the assignment of numerical values to vote direction is arbitrary. It doesn't matter whether Conservative is 1, 2, or 3, as long as a Conservative voter can be distinguished from a voter for a different party.

Since this variable is of such great interest to voting behaviour specialists and OLS regression requires interval-level data, another solution is commonly used. Instead of using a straight line to estimate the relationship between variables (as in OLS), researchers use a statistical technique that approximates the strength of relationship with a line that curves. A statistical solution called **logistic regression** is a form of regression analysis used when the dependent variable is a dichotomous variable (i.e. it has two categories, which typically are scored as 0 to indicate the absence of a characteristic and 1 to show the presence of the characteristic).

Logistic regression analysis, or logit analysis, uses a logistic function to estimate the relationship between a variable measured as a 0 and 1 dichotomy (such as 0 for not voting Conservative and 1 for voting Conservative). The logistic function resembles an S-shaped curve over the range of 0 to 1, which means that the left side of the line lags near 0 as the independent variable increases, rises sharply near the mid-point, and lags again near the upper level of 1. The result with logistic regression is that there is not a uniform change in the dependent variable with a unit change in the independent variable, which stands to

APPLY YOUR UNDERSTANDING

Calculating and Interpreting OLS Equations and Coefficients

Complete the following steps for the data set provided in the following table:

1. Test for linearity.
2. Calculate and interpret the slope.
3. Calculate and interpret the intercept.
4. Calculate and interpret r^2.

Case	Age (years)	Monthly Volunteer Service (hours)
1	18	4
2	63	12
3	47	8
4	56	9
5	36	6
6	42	7

reason since the dependent variable in reality is not continuous but has only two categories. The end result is a method of estimating the strength of the relationship that is more true to the actual distribution of data but, at the same time, is less intuitively understandable than simple linear regression using OLS estimation.

Logistic regression is one of a family of more advanced regression analysis techniques and is beyond the scope of this textbook to review in detail. That said, the multiple regression analysis example on page 357 uses logit analysis, allowing you to see this technique in action (and possibly whetting your appetite for the study of more advanced regression techniques).

Multiple Regression Analysis

The simple regression model, using a single independent variable to predict a single dependent variable, can be extended through multiple regression analysis to include additional independent variables. Indeed, one of the most notable advantages of regression analysis is that it enables the simultaneous analysis of multiple predictors in a single equation. This ability contrasts sharply with contingency table analysis using nominal or ordinal variables. In the latter instances, the inclusion of additional control variables produces a growing number of tables with decreasing cases. For example, we might wish to examine how attitudes of alienation toward the federal government affected voting in the 2011 Canadian federal election. The hypothesis may be that those with higher levels of alienation were less likely to vote Conservative (that is, for the government) than those with lower alienation were. Assuming this analysis was conducted on a large sample of 3,000 Canadians, we should be able to examine the impact of alienation with a high level of confidence.

Now imagine that we wish to complicate the analysis by examining whether the relationship varies by province of residence; there is good reason to believe that province may influence the level of alienation and party supported in the election. Using the standard five-region categorization (Atlantic, Quebec, Ontario, Prairies, British Columbia), this single control variable would result in the initial table being broken down into five separate tables, with an average sample size of 600 each (the exact number, of course, would depend on the number of interviews conducted in each province). We might also expect that voting and level of alienation are influenced by feelings toward the prime minister. If we assume that these feelings are measured on a three-point scale (positive, neutral, negative), the inclusion of the second control variable would produce 3 additional tables for each region, for a total of 15 tables with an average table size of 200 cases. If we further assume that alienation is measured on a three-point scale and vote has six categories (Conservative, New Democrat, Liberal, Bloc Québécois, Green, and other), each of the 15 tables would have up to 18 cells. Thus, it can be seen that contingency table analysis, with as few as two control variables, can easily produce a table with too few cases in the cells for meaningful analysis.

Yet the point was made earlier that a characteristic feature of the social sciences generally and political science in particular is that the world we wish to examine and explain is highly complex, and multiple independent variables may affect any given dependent variable. We often wish to model this complexity into our analysis. Multiple regression analysis is an extremely useful statistical technique because of its ability to examine simultaneously the effects of multiple independent variables on a dependent variable. The number of independent variables included in multiple regression must be no greater than $N - 1$. When the analysis is based on several thousand cases (*N*s), as regularly happens with survey research, the number of independent variables that could be included greatly exceeds the limit of what one might wish to use.

In view of this feature, it is apparent why political scientists may wish to use multiple regression analysis. However, this approach should be used with considerable caution due to the key assumptions that underlie it. One is that the independent variables are independent of one another. When this assumption is violated, the analysis suffers from **multicollinearity** and the coefficients become less robust. A second assumption is that the regression line exhibits a constant error across the values of the independent variables. When this assumption holds, the error is referred to as **homoskedastic**; when the assumption is violated, the error is called **heteroskedastic**. Once again, heteroskedasticity produces less robust regression coefficients.

One of the causes of heteroskedasticity is that the relationship between the independent and dependent variables may be non-linear, as where Y' may be a logarithmic function of X.

In such instances, one may wish to transform the data to more clearly approximate linearity. More generally, though, it is worth noting that the issues of multicollinearity and heteroskedasticity provide significant challenges to the assumptions of multiple regression analysis.

A third major assumption of multiple regression analysis, and another possible limitation on its use, is the fact that it assumes that the data are measured at the interval level. We suggested in Chapter 3 that few variables in the social sciences meet the rigorous assumption of interval data: that increases across the values of a variable are characterized by a constant unit. Think of the 100-point feeling thermometer used in much public opinion and voting research. Respondents are presented with a 100-point thermometer and asked to state their feelings about some political object, such as Canada or the prime minister. Such measures are frequently interpreted as interval data. But if we take the topic further, is it reasonable to expect that all voters mean the same thing by the rating of, for example, 65 on such a scale? Does 65 represent "warmth" toward that political object, since it is above the mid-point of 50, or does it suggest "coolness," since it is a full 35 points from 100? Such interpretation differences speak to the difficulty of assigning an interval category to social data. Despite such difficulties, many analysts are prepared to accept the conceptual ambiguity in exchange for the more powerful statistical technique available through multiple regression.

With simple regression, we examine the effect of a single independent variable on a single dependent variable. With multiple regression, we can examine the impact of several independent variables by extending the simple regression equation to

$$Y' = a + b_1X_1 + b_2X_2 + b_3X_3 + \ldots + b_iX_i$$

The slope (b) of the regression line for each independent variable represents the amount of change in the Y variable for each unit change in X, controlling for (that is, holding constant) the effects of the other independent variables. Remember, though, that the variance within the dependent variable can be explained only once. (Think of the explained variance as a pie. When a part of the pie is eaten by one person, it is no longer available for others to eat. Once the explained variance of a dependent variable has been accounted for by one variable, it is not available for the others.) As additional independent variables are brought into the equation, they can account for only unexplained or residual variance.

There are a number of procedures available for specifying the order in which independent variables enter a regression equation, so the effect can vary in an equation depending on which procedure is used. Nonetheless, the general point remains and suggests the potential problems that can emerge when independent variables are highly correlated. The effect of two independent variables that have much common explanatory power will show more of the effect attributed to one and less to the other. Thus, it is important to look out for high levels of correlation among the independent variables.

The simplified model of the multiple regression equation presented earlier in this chapter does not include two different estimates of error. There is error associated with each of the independent variables and error associated with the equation as a whole. Both types of error enable us to assess the model's goodness of fit. The standard error of estimate is the error associated with each regression coefficient (that is, with each *b*) and is usually reported along with the regression coefficient. The error associated with the entire equation is the residual variance. It normally is not reported directly but can be inferred from its opposite, the explained variance (R^2) of the model, which is normally presented.

When conducting a multiple regression analysis, it is often helpful to begin by generating a correlation matrix to examine the relationship between the independent and dependent variables and among the independent variables. This practice will enable an initial test of the assumption of independence among the independent variables. Since we have already discussed the computation of correlation coefficients, regression coefficients, and standard errors in the section on simple regression, we will not repeat the calculations here. Instead, we will use examples of printed output that one would obtain from SPSS. Our model predicts attitudes toward Stephen Harper in the 2011 election.

Predicting Attitudes toward Party Leaders: Assessments of Stephen Harper

Many analyses of Canadian voting behaviour have revealed that attitudes toward party leaders are significant in Canadians' voting decisions. (Note the use of attitudes toward party leaders as an independent variable in the preceding statement.) Therefore, it is useful to develop a model to try to account for or to explain attitudes toward the leaders (in this model, attitudes toward party leaders is a dependent variable). Based on a reading of previous studies of this topic in the political science literature, together with extrapolation from some reading you have done in economics and sociology, you might hypothesize the model in Figure 17.8.

Your research design, of course, would provide the rationale for hypothesizing that each of these independent variables affects attitudes toward Harper. For example, with the variable "age," you may be testing the theory that voters become more conservative as they age,

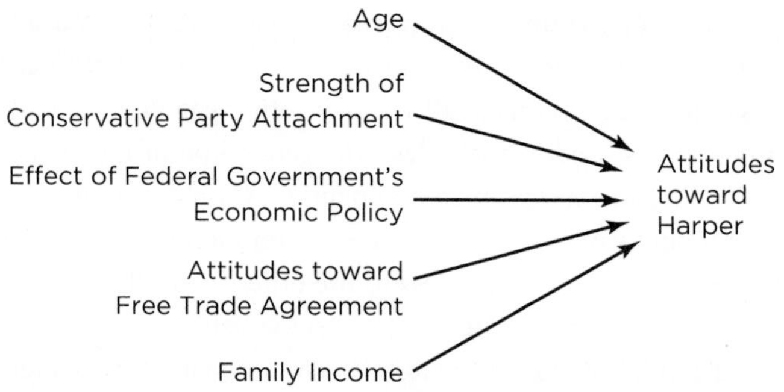

Figure 17.8 A Model of Determinants of Attitudes toward Stephen Harper

which leads to the hypothesis that older voters have more positive assessments of Harper than do their younger counterparts. Similarly, you might hypothesize that party identification influences attitudes toward party leaders by colouring one's view of the political world; Conservatives are more likely than Liberals to view Harper through rose-coloured lenses. For the variable examining the impact of the federal government's economic policies, you might be testing the theory that voters are self-interested utility maximizers and support the government because they find it in their self-interest to do so.

In addition to the expectation that voters can be influenced by attitudes toward a specific set of economic policies, you may believe that voters are influenced by general political or ideological orientations. One such orientation that may be tested is that those who believe in market liberalism are more likely to support Stephen Harper; a market liberalism variable could be added to the model. Similarly, you would want to provide a theoretical justification for the inclusion of other independent variables. You are then able to assess the utility and accuracy of the competing theories through their simultaneous inclusion in the model, which would take the following form:

$$\text{Harper} = a + b_1(\text{age}) + b_2(\text{partyid}) + b_3(\text{econpol}) + b_4(\text{marketlib}) + b_5(\text{income})$$

The following analysis of this equation uses hypothetical data. You may wish to replicate the analysis using data from the CES series. The correlation matrix for the hypothetical data for these six variables (that is, the single dependent variable and five independent variables) is shown in Table 17.2.

The correlation matrix shows that three of the five independent variables are at least moderately related to attitudes toward Harper and that two are very weakly correlated, if at all. It also reveals that two of the independent variables—party identification and attitudes toward market liberalism—are moderately related (r = 0.37). In the context of the 2011 federal election, when the NDP emerged as the official opposition for the first time in Canadian history, it might be expected that general ideological orientations (between right and left) were more important than the more typical election outcome of the Liberals being

Table 17.2 Correlation Matrix of the Determinants of Attitudes toward Stephen Harper

	Harper	Age	Partyid	Econpol	Marketlib
Harper	1.000				
Age	0.002	1.000			
Partyid	0.360	0.056	1.000		
Econpol	0.341	-0.001	0.228	1.000	
Marketlib	0.507	0.035	0.372	0.221	1.000
Income	0.050	-0.098	0.067	0.039	0.172

the Conservatives' principal opponent. Although these independent variables are related, the strength of relationship is not such to suggest that they are measuring the same underlying concept. Yet the strength of the correlation is sufficiently large that we need be mindful of possible multicollinearity problems.

After examining the correlation matrix, we can turn to the multiple regression table. The table provides a regression coefficient for each independent variable and for the constant (that is, the point of intersection of the y-axis) and a standard error for each coefficient (printed in parentheses). Normally, we are looking for the regression coefficient to be twice the size of the standard error in order that the finding can be said to be statistically significant. Table 17.3 represents statistical significance with an asterisk (*) at the 0.05 level of significance and two asterisks (**) at the 0.01 level of significance. A regression table usually presents the R^2 value as well.

The table shows that three of the five independent variables are extremely strong and significant predictors of attitudes toward Harper, two others are much weaker, and one lacks statistical significance altogether. Regression coefficients should always be interpreted relative to the size of the standard error: the larger the regression coefficient relative to the standard error, the stronger the effect of the variable. In this example, the strongest predictor of attitudes toward Harper is the respondent's position on market liberalism. The second most important predictor is the perception that the federal government's economic policies have benefited the respondent. Those who felt this way were much more likely to rate Harper positively than those who did not. Moreover, the strength of Conservative attachment impacted attitudes toward Harper. Each step up the strength of partisanship measure—from non-Conservatives (0) to weak (1), moderate (2), and strong (3) Conservatives—resulted in a 5-point increase in the 100-point feeling thermometer ratings

Table 17.3 The Determinants of Attitudes toward Stephen Harper in 2011

	Dependent Variable	
	Attitudes toward Harper	
Independent Variables	***b***	***se***
Age	-0.04	(0.03)
Partyid	4.99**	(0.61)
Econpol	9.24**	(0.81)
Marketlib	10.32**	(0.51)
Income	-0.45*	(0.20)
Intercept	14.26**	(2.30)

R^2 = 0.34
* $p < 0.05$
** $p < 0.01$.

of Harper, other things being equal. Income had a weak negative impact on Harper ratings; the wealthiest respondents felt less positively toward Harper, on average, than their less affluent counterparts did. However, the standard error was quite large relative to the regression coefficient, and the relationship barely achieved statistical significance. Finally, the age variable did not achieve statistical significance at all, allowing us to conclude that age does not influence attitudes toward Harper, other things being equal.

The model enables a fuller comparison of the relative impact of the five independent variables than would have been possible by using a series of contingency tables. It also provides an overall assessment of the importance of these five variables in explaining attitudes toward Harper. Using hypothetical data, we found that the five independent variables explained 34 per cent of the variance in these attitudes. We might be led to ask what variables could help explain this residual variance. One alternative that has been examined in the political science literature is attitudes toward the personal characteristics of the party leader. Note that, in our example, none of the independent variables relate to Harper's personal characteristics. Might perceptions of Harper's competence or personality influence a person's overall assessment of him? The answer, of course, is yes. And so the analysis could continue with some variables, such as age and income, being dropped and others, such as opinions of Harper's personal characteristics, being added (see Johnston et al. 1992 for a fuller discussion of character and competence as key indicators of leader assessment).

Log on to our website to watch a tutorial on multiple regression.

Block Recursive Models of Voting Behaviour

In addition to providing the ability to examine the impact of a number of independent variables simultaneously, regression analysis gives the researcher control over other elements of the analytical procedure. One such area that has become popular in analyses of voting in Canada is specifying the order in which variables are entered into the equation. For example, one can specify a model with the assumption that certain factors arise relatively early in the decision process and other factors occur later, or closer to the actual decision. A block recursive model enables the researcher to specify the order of entry of each variable into the equation so that its inclusion corresponds to the causal sequence of each variable's effect. The term *block recursive* refers to the fact that each variable that reflects an analytical concept is entered simultaneously. If there are four questions measuring attitudes to enduring political beliefs, this group of variables is entered together, as a block. In their use of the block recursive model to explain voting choice in the 2011 election, Fournier et al. (2013, 878) describe the model:

> In line with the tradition of bloc-recursive models of voting behavior . . . we estimate all models in a step-wise fashion, starting with the demographics and adding each subsequent block . . . in turn. All estimations rely on multinomial

> logit, appropriate for a categorical variable such as vote choice. . . . So the effects of demographic variables come from a model which includes demographics only; the effects of general orientation variables originate from a model that contains general orientations as well as the preceding demographic block; partisanship's effects take into account controls for general orientations and demographics; and so on. We do this based on the assumption that the ordering of blocks is linked to causal precedence and the stability of variables.

The model, then, enables the researcher to include a wide range of factors that can affect the voting decision and to "stage" the analysis such that each factor is entered sequentially according to the researcher's theoretical assumptions. In the case of Fournier and colleagues' analysis, the model includes six blocks of independent variables that are used to explain vote choice. The blocks' order of inclusion is demographic characteristics, general orientations, partisanship, issue positions, and leader evaluations (Fournier et al. 2013, Table 3). The logic of the model is such that the variables entered early in the analysis can affect the vote directly and the factors that enter the model later. Therefore, demographic characteristics such as the respondents' region of residence, age, religion, ethnicity, education, and union household can affect the vote directly or do so indirectly by affecting factors entered later, such as a person's general orientations (attitudes toward accommodating Quebec's demands in the federal system, market liberalism, attitudes toward Canada–US relations). A recursive model assumes one-way causality. In this instance, the block recursive model assumes that demographic characteristics can affect beliefs and values but that the relationship is not reversed.

In a block recursive analysis, the data analysis proceeds by entering each block of independent variables sequentially and assessing the relative impact of variables, along with the model's overall goodness of fit after each set of variables is included. The situation is somewhat more complicated in Fournier et al.'s analysis by the fact that the dependent variable is not continuous (as is assumed with OLS regression) but dichotomous. The researchers wish to explain vote choice in the election but cannot use OLS regression on a variable that includes categories such as (1) Conservative, (2) Liberal, (3) NDP, (4) BQ, etc. Instead, Fournier et al. conducted separate analyses using multinomial logit (MNL) estimations for each of the first three parties. Because they believed that vote choice was significantly different in and outside Quebec in view of the fact that the BQ contested elections only in Quebec, they also conducted separate analyses among Quebec voters and non-Quebec voters (see Table 17.4 for the latter). MNL may be used when the dependent variable is dichotomous and there is no rank ordering among the two categories. The resulting outcome is a regression coefficient and standard error for each of the independent variables and a measure of the model's overall goodness of fit.

This single table conveys a great deal of information. (You may be interested in reviewing Fournier et al.'s interpretation of the findings in more detail.) There is considerable consistency in the determinants of voting in Canada from one election to the next, even

Table 17.4 The Determinants of Vote Choice in the Rest of Canada

	Conservative				Liberal				NDP			
	2008	2011	Year Δ	Cam Δ	2008	2011	Year Δ	Cam Δ	2008	2011	Year Δ	Cam Δ
Demographics												
Atlantic	-0.14**	-0.05	*		0.06*	0.04			0.08**	0.01	*	
West	0.10**	0.11**			-0.16**	-0.16**		*	0.06**	0.04*		
Women	-0.06**	-0.03			0.01	0.00		**	0.05**	0.03		
Under 35 years old	-0.03	-0.04			-0.05	0.03			0.09**	0.02		
Over 54 years old	0.01	-0.05**			0.02	0.07**			-0.03	-0.01		
Catholic	-0.02	-0.01		*	0.04*	0.00		*	-0.02	0.00		
Visible minority	-0.22**	-0.24**		**	0.27**	0.15**		**	-0.05	0.09	*	
High-school dropout	-0.05	0.03			-0.05	-0.04			0.10**	0.00	**	**
University graduate	-0.12**	-0.14**			0.13**	0.11**			-0.01	0.03		
Union household	-0.09**	-0.11**			-0.04	-0.02			0.12**	0.13**		
General Orientations												
Accommodate Quebec	-0.23**	-0.22**			0.17**	0.17**		*	0.06**	0.05		
Continentalism	0.30**	0.26**			-0.16**	-0.15**			-0.13**	-0.12**		
Market liberalism	0.25**	0.26**			-0.07**	0.02	**		-0.19**	-0.28**		
Moral traditionalism	0.22**	0.22**			-0.10**	-0.07**			-0.12**	-0.15**		
Political disaffection	-0.22**	-0.25**			0.06*	0.13**	*		0.17**	0.12**	*	
Regional alienation	-0.07**	-0.04*			0.05**	0.02			0.03*	0.01		
Partisanship												
Conservative	0.36**	0.33**		**	-0.22**	-0.17**		**	-0.14**	-0.16**		
Liberal	-0.23**	-0.24**			0.31**	0.29**			-0.09**	-0.05**		
NDP	-0.26**	-0.41**	**		-0.13**	-0.15**			0.38**	0.56**		**
Economic perceptions												
Personal retrospect.	0.01	0.02		**	-0.01	0.01		**	0.00	-0.03**	*	
National retrospect.	0.02*	0.02*			-0.02*	0.01	*		0.00	-0.03**		
Issue positions												
Personal taxes	-0.04**	-0.03**			0.04**	0.01		*	0.00	0.02		
Corporate taxes	-0.01	-0.05**	**		-0.01	0.00			0.02	0.05**		
Health spending	0.02	-0.01	*		-0.06**	0.01	**	**	0.04*	-0.01		**
Defence spending	0.04**	0.03**		**	-0.04**	-0.02			0.00	-0.01		
Environment spending	-0.04**	-0.04**			0.06**	-0.02	**		-0.02	0.06**	**	*
More immigration	-0.01	-0.01			0.01	0.01			-0.01	0.00		
Leader evaluations												
Stephen Harper	.26**	0.19**	**		-0.16**	-0.07**	**		-0.10**	-0.12**		
Stéphane Dion/ Michael Ignatieff	-0.09**	-0.09**			0.13**	0.18**	*	**	-0.04**	-0.09**		
Jack Layton	-0.15**	-0.10**	*		-0.01	-0.09**	**		0.16**	0.19**		
Year				2008						2011		
Number of cases				1835						1725		
Pseudo R-squared				0.56						0.55		

1. In the first two columns, entries are marginal effects of multinomial logit estimations and the dependent variable is the post-election reported vote. Marginal effects represent the average change in the probability of the dependent variable for all one-point movements of the independent variable. Contrary to MNL coefficients, they do not imply a reference category. The third column shows the significance of the difference between the first two columns (Year Δ). The fourth column shows the significance of the difference between the variable's impact on vote intentions during the first two weeks of the 2011 campaign and its impact during the last two weeks (Campaign Δ).

Statistical significance: * < 0.10; ** < 0.05

Source: Fournier et al. (2013)

when the election outcomes are substantially different. Regarding the Conservatives, demographic variables had quite similar impacts in both elections, with support being stronger in the West and lower in the Atlantic region amongst women, visible minorities, university graduates, and those in union households. The effects of general political and ideological orientations were consistent between elections as well.

One change worth noting is on attitudes toward market liberalism. Such opinions had the same impact on Conservative supporters in 2011 as they did in 2008. However, there appears to have been some polarization among Liberal and NDP supporters. Market liberalism attitudes were statistically significant and negative predictors of Liberal vote in 2008 but had no impact in 2011. These views had an even stronger negative impact on support for the NDP in 2011 compared to 2008. Similarly, where partisanship had a strong impact on Conservative and Liberal support in both elections, partisanship was even more strongly related to backing of the NDP in 2011, with the data showing that this relationship strengthened in the second half of the campaign as support for the party grew.

Another striking characteristic of Table 17.4 is the complexity and depth of analysis that is made possible by multiple regression techniques—which, in this instance, involve a clear ordering of the sequence in which variables are entered into the model—and the comparison of the impact of a large number of independent variables. The overall explanatory power of the model is quite high, with a pseudo R^2 of 0.56 using the data from 2008 and 0.55 for the 2011 data.

Multiple regression analysis provides substantial analytical advantages. By including a large number of independent variables, we can more accurately map the complex reality of social relations and directly examine the relative impact of variables. In many ways, the logic underlying multiple regression analysis serves as a gateway to other more complex statistical techniques. Analysis of variance, logistic analysis, path analysis, factor analysis, and LISREL are but a few of the more advanced techniques that are used for quantitative analysis in political science. Once you have mastered the material in this text, you will be prepared to begin exploring these more complex models. In all instances, though, your decision of what statistical technique to employ should be guided by a desire to provide greater insight and understanding of our political world.

Working as a Team

1. Using data from a recent CES (available at queensu.ca/cora/ces.html), conduct a regression analysis of age, family income, and strength of partisan identification (independent variables) on political interest (dependent variable). Develop measures of each concept at the interval (or at least the ordinal) level. Briefly review the distribution of each variable. Enter the dependent variable and the three independent variables

into the SPSS regression procedure, selecting the STEPWISE selection method. Using the output generated by SPSS, construct a table that presents the results, including the intercept, regression coefficients, and standard errors for each independent variable and the R^2 value for the full equation. On the basis of the table, discuss the determinants of political interest in Canadian politics.

Self-Study

1. For the following data set, (1) test for linearity, (2) calculate and interpret the slope, (3) calculate and interpret the intercept, and (4) calculate and interpret r^2.

Case	Age (years)	Job Satisfaction (units)
1	25	8
2	63	2
3	47	4
4	50	3
5	36	5
6	42	4

2. Interpret the following simple regression equations:
   a. political interest (in units) = 18 + 2 age (in years)
   b. final grade (in points) = 75 – 4 skipped lectures
3. Describe and assess the assumptions of regression analysis.
4. Obtain a copy of a machine-readable data set and statistical software such as SPSS. Identify a dependent variable and a set of independent variables. Compute a correlation matrix and discuss. Run a simple regression analysis with one of the independent variables, then include a second independent variable and repeat. Note the differences in the regression coefficient and the standard errors of the variable that initially had been used for the simple regression analysis. Interpret the differences in findings. Now add a third independent variable to the analysis. Repeat the steps for the first two independent variables.

Notes

1. There are a number of other assumptions that must be met before using linear regression techniques; see, for example, Berry (1993).
2. To calculate the standard error of *b*, use the formula $S_b = \sqrt{\text{variance/sum of squares}}$.

CHAPTER 18

Writing the Report

Destination

By the end of this chapter, you should be able to

- outline the strategic considerations in writing a research report;
- identify the components of a research report; and
- explain the different elements and formats that can be used to convey research findings.

To this point in the book, we have discussed a variety of qualitative and quantitative tools for conducting empirical research in political science. In the vast majority of research projects, we are interested in conveying the findings to an external audience; research is seldom done for personal edification alone, although it may be a motivation behind many scholars' larger research agendas. It is through the research report that we convey our findings to others, such as course instructors, fellow students, research colleagues, sponsors of a particular piece of research, readers of an academic journal, government departments, or members of a community association or an interest group. The report, then, is the capstone rather than an incidental stage in the research enterprise. It distills, presents, explains, and defends a complex empirical investigation in a format appropriate to its intended audience.

The research report brings together existing knowledge in the field, new data and information generated by the research project, and the expertise and insights of the author(s) into a document designed for a particular audience (see Figure 18.1). In these respects, therefore, the research report is an interactive document. The emphasis is not simply on *presenting* one's research findings; it is on *communicating* those findings to an

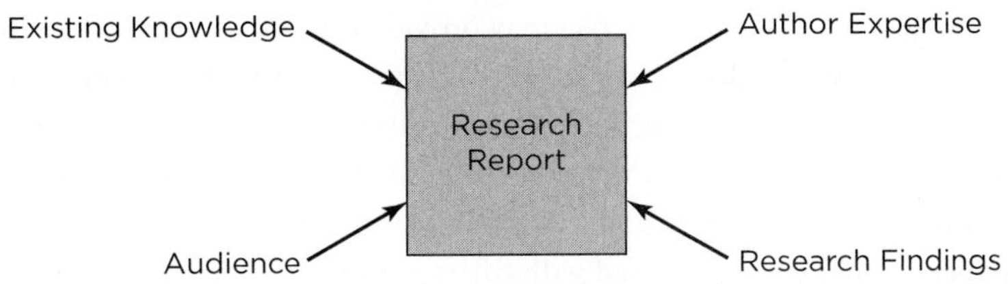

Figure 18.1 The Research Report

audience. In this chapter, we will explore the interactive nature of the research report by looking first at audience considerations and then at various components of the report.

The Audience

Because audiences differ in many respects, there is no single, generic format that can be used across all situations. For example, audiences will vary in their methodological sophistication. What you might present to your course instructor or the assessors for a scholarly journal could be quite different than what you might present to a community group. The former will understand quantitative measures of association, whereas the latter might be best served by a more general discussion of association. It would not be enough, and perhaps not even appropriate, to present correlation coefficients to the group; the meaning of covariance must be described in a more accessible format. Matters such as tests of significance may be readily understood by one audience but require detailed explanation for another. Audiences will also differ in the extent to which they are interested in how your research findings fit into the established literature in the field. Your instructor might be very interested in how you have managed to locate your findings within established disciplinary knowledge, but a community group may want to know only the specific results in the case.

Remembering your audience's level of sophistication and particular research interests does not imply that you should "dumb down" the analysis. It simply means that effective communication entails knowing one's audience and writing to it in a way that clearly transmits the material. Of course, this imperative becomes more difficult if you are writing the same research report for more than one audience. In this case, appendices and footnotes can be used to convey the detail and complexity required by one audience but not another. Keep in mind that statistical or theoretical jargon is not necessarily bad; the issue is whether the vocabulary you are using is appropriate for your target audience.

Research reports will frequently have secondary audiences that may play an important role in the dissemination of research findings. Research reports are seldom written explicitly for media outlets; when they are, they convey only a fraction of the information discussed in this chapter. However, reports written for other audiences regularly find their way into the media and through the media into broader dissemination. Off-the-cuff comments or humour directed at a specific audience may provide unfortunate grist for editorial comment or news coverage. Pleading that you were misquoted or that the comment was taken out of context will not get you off the hook. It makes sense, then, to keep the potential public audience in mind, even if it is not the primary or intended audience. Before finishing the final draft of the research report, read it as if you were encountering your comments in your local newspaper. Would you be pleased with the reporting?

For academic research, there is normally an opportunity to provide an oral presentation in addition to the written report. The oral presentation usually occurs at an academic conference, in which presenters are required to summarize the research they have been working on for months or years into a 15- to 20-minute time slot. Such a framework puts a premium on clarity, brevity, and organization. The presentation includes the principal elements that comprise the research report and often is enhanced by presentation software, such as PowerPoint. When using such software, applying the following rules will make for a better learning experience for presenter and audience alike:

- *Less is more.* Avoid the temptation to fill the slide with text and read it to the audience. Use text sparsely and provide your extrapolation in the oral presentation.
- *A picture is worth a thousand words.* Many arguments can be illustrated and summarized with a graphic representation. This approach provides a creative queue to the audience and keeps them more engaged with your material.
- *Simplify tables and charts.* Remember that the presentation is used to highlight key features of a longer and much more detailed research paper. In the oral presentation, the audience will benefit from material in digestible form. Those who are more interested in pursuing the detail will do so later through reading the full paper.
- *Keep it simple.* You will find that, as a researcher, you have had to make a remarkably large number of decisions about how the concepts will be defined and measured in your study, and the details, while important, may be distracting. A simple presentation of a complex topic may lead to many questions that can be followed up.

Constructing an Argument

A good research report is more than a collection of findings; it presents a coherent, well-structured, and thoughtful argument. The report is not only addressed to an audience, but it also tells a story. As such, it must set the stage, provide some context, move coherently from step to step, follow a consistent story line or plot, and reach a conclusion. Thinking of the research report in this manner is a good way to keep your specific audience in mind. Moreover, it helps you keep to the golden rule of storytelling: don't put your audience to sleep! (Even small children will not be amused if you try to put them to sleep by reading dull political science research reports.) Although you may sometimes find it difficult to write up quantitative research in a lively and engaging fashion, it can be done.

Expand Your Knowledge

The Legal Analogue

The components of a good research report are analogous to the components of a good case in a court of law. A lawyer must be aware of legal precedence, just as a scholar must be aware of the existing literature in the field. The lawyer should use his or her opening statement to capture the interest and attention of the judge and jury. A systematic and solid argument must be developed, one that draws from the facts of the case. While the lawyer is clearly an advocate, he or she cannot ignore contrary evidence and soft spots in the case. A good argument brings all the evidence into play while emphasizing the most important bits. Ignoring opposing arguments is a poor strategy in court, and ignoring inconvenient or theoretically inconsistent evidence is a poor strategy in the social sciences. A successful lawyer is also attentive to the particular features of the judge and jury, just as the successful research report is crafted with a specific audience in mind. Finally, there must be a strong closing argument; the facts cannot be left to speak for themselves. Neither the lawyer nor the social scientist simply reports the facts—both use their expertise to weave facts into a coherent and compelling argument.

The analogy between a well-crafted story and the research report should not be overstated, for the two differ in some key respects. The report is theory-driven, or at least reflects theory-driven research, whereas the story sets out to entertain (and perhaps to convey a moral rather than theoretical message). The research report has an explicit thesis statement and employs explicit evidence; the underlying "thesis" of a good story is generally implicit, when it exists at all. The report builds directly and explicitly from the data, and the data analysis is linked back to guiding hypotheses and the literature foundation. Perhaps the primary difference is that the research report is held together by a logical argument, yet the storyteller can draw from a wider range of integrative techniques including imagery, tone, and metaphor.

An author's expertise comes most clearly into play in the construction of the argument. The research report should be seen as a creative document, not in the sense of inventing information but in using language to its fullest extent. It is the creative ability of the author that makes data stand up and jump through hoops.

Components of the Research Report

As we noted earlier in this chapter, there is no generic research report. However, there are a number of report components that should be included in most cases, even though they will be addressed by various methods and in different sequences according to the report's audience.

The Abstract or Executive Summary

No matter how brief your report might be or how concise your writing and data presentation, some people will not want to read the entire report, at least not right away. As a consequence, virtually all publications in scholarly journals include an **abstract** for readers who want to cut to the bottom line, perhaps to determine if the entire report is worth reading in the context of their immediate research interests. Abstracts are particularly useful for readers whose first language is not that in which the report is written; they provide brief overviews that can be digested with minimal effort devoted to translation. For similar reasons of economy, political leaders are notorious for wanting brief **executive summaries**; their days are simply too full to digest more than a page or two of a document. A research study that cannot be summarized on a page, maybe even on a 3 × 5 card, may never be read, much less digested. Therefore, most reports prepared for public consumption, including those for government departments and interest groups, include executive summaries.

It is excellent practice to prepare an abstract or executive summary for writing projects such as term papers. Think of the exercise as similar to a chance encounter at a party, where someone you are attracted to asks you to describe your thesis or current work interests. You have a very limited amount of time to make your pitch; if you are too long-winded or too boring, your audience will drift away in pursuit of livelier fare. Thus, you need to present the main findings, and the principal theoretical hooks they are hung on, in a concise and interesting fashion. A well-written abstract or executive summary does more than describe; it engages and entices the reader. If you find yourself "alone at the party," you know that your executive summary needs more work.

The utility of this writing exercise goes beyond the convenience of busy or lazy readers. It forces you to describe your findings and their significance in a precise, interesting fashion. Writing an abstract or executive summary makes you come to grips with the essential

APPLY YOUR UNDERSTANDING

Writing an Abstract

Find a research report of some reasonable length that does not have an abstract or executive summary attached. You might, for example, use an article in a magazine such as *The Atlantic* or *Alberta Views*. Once you have located an article, prepare an abstract of no more than 150 words. Were you able to capture the report's major points, findings, and arguments? What kinds of material did you have to set aside? Given your abstract, would there be any need for most readers to read the entire article? What does the article have to offer beyond the information contained in the abstract? Sometimes the answer to this question can be a depressing "very little."

core of your research project. As you will discover, it can often be more difficult to "write short" than to "write long." Preparing the abstract or executive summary could be the most difficult writing assignment in the entire report!

Introduction

The primary objective of the introduction is to capture the reader's interest. The introduction should explain the research topic and its relevance, present the basic research question or thesis statement, sketch in briefly the line of argument to be pursued, and explain the architecture of the report. A clear and emphatic thesis statement is particularly important. The intent is to introduce the reader to the research project, thereby establishing a context for what is to come and an enticement to read the entire report.

Although the introduction to the research report will resemble the abstract or executive summary in many respects, it will generally not provide an overview of the research findings. The similarity between the two will be less disconcerting to you, the author, if you keep in mind that the abstract or executive summary is meant to stand alone; it should be intelligible even if the report itself is never read. The introduction, however, is a part of the research report. It sets the stage for the larger project and is not meant to stand alone.

Literature Review

The importance of this component is a function of the report's audience. Reports written as course assignments or submissions to academic journals must include a **literature review**, although not necessarily labelled as such. The literature review serves a number of central functions. First, readers will expect to see how your research project grew out of the existing literature. What are the holes, lacunae, or contradictions it was designed to address? Are you replicating previous research in a different setting or at a different time? If so, are you incorporating significant innovations in your research design beyond the spatial or temporal change? In short, you must demonstrate how your research fits into the larger body of literature but is still unique.

Second, the literature review may provide the foundation for many of the empirical measures embedded in your report. For example, if you are exploring the relationship between globalization and support for neo-liberalism, you must explain the literature roots of your measures of these terms. As was observed in Chapters 4 and 5, there are many alternative conceptualizations and operationalizations for any given term. You should acknowledge if your measure fits with the existing body of literature or differs from conventional practice.

Third, readers will want to know how your findings fit into the established knowledge in the field. Have you confirmed, reinforced, challenged, expanded, or contradicted existing knowledge? Have you pushed the boundaries of knowledge or altered what we thought we knew? All these questions are important and interesting, and none of them can be addressed unless a literature review has been put into place.

A good literature review is more than a description of what has come before. It should present a critical overview of the existing literature, including an identification of problems, omissions, and contradictions. After all, if the existing literature has "said everything," the value of your own report will be thrown into question. The literature review helps establish the rationale for your research project and shows how you are improving, rather than re-inventing, the wheel.

Nonetheless, literature reviews tend to be quite abbreviated in reports that are not targeted at an academic or a scholarly audience. For example, a report prepared for the Ontario Liberal Party on gender differences in partisan support would be unlikely to include an extensive literature review. The client commissioning the report will be more interested in the current landscape than in what came before. Even here, however, a brief summary of existing knowledge could be useful. If nothing else, it provides some handle on change over time.

Early in their research career, students often are uncertain about what level of detail is included in a literature review and how to start preparing such a review. It may help by asking the following questions: What do we know about the topic you are studying? What contribution to this understanding do you expect to result from your research?

Suppose you are interested in studying the decline of youth voting in Canadian elections. You might begin the literature review by examining what we know about turnout among youth, in Canada and elsewhere. Are you the first person who has ever observed and written about this topic or have others already examined it or some aspect of it? For just about any question you can imagine, the answer will be the latter—others have already observed it and perhaps tried to explain it.

Therefore, you can seek books and articles in which youth turnout has been examined. You will find that one of the best sources for information about other studies on the topic will be the references listed in the academic studies you read. In reviewing this material, you may find that the results are quite nuanced. Some researchers might focus on youth participation in a broad range of political activities—such as protesting, demonstrating, voting, becoming a candidate for office—whereas others will focus exclusively on voting. Part of the literature review might involve an examination of different definitions of the dependent variable, either youth political engagement or youth electoral engagement. The literature review typically highlights significant trends in the dependent variable and any differences in conceptual or operational definitions.

Your literature review will also need to examine different theories regarding a decline in youth engagement. What theories have other researchers used to examine this question, and how successful have they been in explaining the decline in youth voting? This part of the literature review may look at differences in the definition or measurement of independent variables. For example, there may be studies that point to a growth in political cynicism among youth. If so, how is cynicism defined and measured in these studies? Are there differences across the studies in the definition and measurement of cynicism and in the impact that cynicism has on voting?

Expand Your Knowledge

Reading Critically

Although students are urged to "read critically," it may not be clear what this exhortation means in practice. By asking the following questions, your skill as a critical reader may be improved:

- Is the methodology adequately explained? Would you be able to replicate the research if you had the resources and inclination to do so?
- Is there a clear thesis statement? Does the author provide a road map for the analysis to come?
- Is there a literature review? Is the research project given a context within social science research on the same or similar topics conducted to date?
- Does the argument proceed logically? Is there a connection between the evidence provided and the conclusions drawn?
- Are the conclusions overstated?
- Is the analysis balanced? Does the author deal with contradictory evidence and/or alternative explanations?

The more you read about previous work in your research area, the more likely you are to find that there is a group of scholars working on this topic and, furthermore, that they may either be reinforcing or challenging one another's methods and findings. This analysis among the research community can be thought of as a scholarly dialogue, in which argument and evidence are frequently followed by counter-argument and more evidence. Over time, this exchange leads to a storyline about our knowledge in this area. Your literature review helps to place your research into this ongoing storyline, positioning it as a contribution to this body of knowledge.

Research Design

In our earlier discussion of the scientific method, we stressed that good science must be capable of replication. If Professor Perrault finds X through method Y, it should be possible for Professor Santini to come to the same conclusions if she follows the same method. This duplication means that the research method must be clearly identified in the research report, which is done through a detailed explication of the project's research design.

Theory-building research typically begins with stated research questions, such as "How and why does B (the dependent variable) vary? Under what conditions does B vary?" The answers to these questions lead to causal arguments that help to explain variation in B. Theory-testing, on the other hand, usually begins with a thesis statement that takes the following form: A causes B because of X. In this schemata, A is the independent variable, B is the dependent variable, and X is the theory that explains why A causes B to vary. If you cannot map your research design in a graphic way using this formulation, you do not have a sufficiently clear theory-testing research project.

When considered in this way, one can observe that the thesis statement is clear, simple, indicates a causal relationship, is directional (that is, A and B not only are correlated, but A also causes B), and falsifiable. This last condition is important because it highlights the fact that the project's data will be used to test the thesis that A causes B. If we find that A and B are not related, the thesis cannot be correct. In a more formal sense, we do not test the thesis statement directly but state it as a null hypothesis—that there is no relationship between the independent and dependent variable. If our thesis is correct, and A causes B, the data should show this relationship, enabling a rejection of the null hypothesis.

But what exactly should be covered in the research design, or methodology component, of the report? If the research project included the collection of new data, the collection procedures should be described in detail. What ethical issues were encountered, and how were they addressed? Was sampling used? If so, what were the population, sampling frame, respondent selection procedures, possible sources of bias, and response rate? Were empirical measures constructed for theoretical concepts? If so, how were they constructed? What reliability and validity checks were used? It is not enough, for example, to say that levels of political apathy were higher among native-born British Columbians than they were among recent migrants to the province unless you indicate how political apathy was measured and how recent was defined.

The research design component should cover the study's theoretical points of departure, the hypotheses used to frame the study, and the operationalization of key concepts. It may also provide an explanation for the types of data analysis employed. Perhaps the key thing to remember is that the research design is more than a description of what you did. It is an *explanation* and a *justification* as well. If readers are to have confidence in your findings and conclusions, they must first have confidence in your research design.

Presentation of Findings

This section is the core of the research report. It is here that your contribution to the existing knowledge in the field is made. Given the importance of this component, there are a number of strategic choices to be made:

- Because all the possible findings cannot be presented, which should you choose and emphasize? Remember, if you try to present everything, the reader may be overwhelmed or lose interest. You must be selective.
- Which findings are important enough to warrant detailed presentation in the form of detailed quotations, tables, graphs, and/or figures? Which findings might be mentioned more in passing?

- What level of methodological sophistication is best for your target audience? Will your audience expect the use of advanced techniques or would the use of such techniques lose the readers?

Graphical elements can be a significant part of a well-designed research report. However, you must remember that figures do not always speak for themselves; they generally require explanatory text. Graphs and figures can be presented in a variety of ways, but only some ways are appropriate for certain kinds of data. For example, pie charts and bar graphs are appropriate for nominal data, whereas line graphs are not. Complex tables can be difficult for many readers to understand. If they are included, it is essential that you provide an interpretative guide. Tables are even less likely than charts or graphs to speak for themselves.

Given that quantitative research reports are often "number rich," you must be careful to use the appropriate numbers. Do not overstate the precision of your data; if the average age of your respondents is 46.253 years, round it to 46 years. If a Pearson correlation coefficient is +0.3763, round to +0.38. Be sure to use the appropriate correlation coefficients and to report tests of significance in a consistent manner. Do not, for instance, reject one finding as insignificant at the 0.01 confidence level while accepting another as significant at the 0.05 confidence level.

Keep in mind the potential importance of negative findings, instances where the null hypothesis was not rejected. Sometimes students and scholars are inclined to stress only positive correlations, the relationships that are found to exist rather than the ones that do not. It may seem uninteresting to report what did not happen, to note expectations that were not met. Yet, in many cases, negative findings—the absence of a relationship—can be theoretically significant. Imagine that you were testing for the existence of class differences in partisan support within the Atlantic provinces and you found there were no statistically significant differences. Such findings could be vital in a substantive sense for our understanding of the contemporary political scene. You should be no quicker to reject negative findings as uninteresting than you should be to accept positive findings as interesting. It may all depend on your theoretical point of departure and the hypotheses that frame your research.

Discussion

Research reports are commonly constructed so that the data findings are first presented or described and then discussed. In the discussion section, the author steps back from the details of the data presentation and tries to explore, usually in more general language, just what the empirical findings might suggest. In many respects, the discussion section involves stepping back from the trees and examining the forest.

In the discussion section, you have the opportunity, indeed the obligation, to tie your findings back to the literature review and back to the study's guiding hypotheses. As a general rule, the discussion section should be accessible even to those readers who may not be able to follow the details of your statistical or qualitative analysis. Many readers will rely upon you to make sense of the data analysis for them; they may read the literature review and research design and then skip to the discussion.

Conclusions

The conclusions should take the reader back to the report's introduction. Recap the research problem and the thesis statement. Remind the reader what you set out to do and then discuss to what extent those objectives have been accomplished. Remember, data seldom speak for themselves. You cannot assume that the reader will draw the same conclusions from the data analysis that you have drawn. Hence, you need to provide some interpretation of the findings.

Some readers will read only your conclusions. As a consequence, your conclusions should be strongly and clearly stated. At the same time, you should not ignore nuances that may have emerged in the data analysis or discussion sections. If some readers are to carry away only the concluding paragraph(s) of your report, you want to be sure that they do not have a distorted impression of your findings.

The concluding section of the research report frequently contains recommendations for action, for the next steps that should be taken. If the report is aimed at the scholarly community, such recommendations might be suggestions for future research. If you could do the research again, what might you do differently, and why? Has your research closed off some doors for future research while opening others? If the report is aimed more at a non-academic audience, the recommendations are more likely to be policy recommendations than suggestions for future research, such as "In light of the findings of this report, we recommend that your organization take the following steps if it wants to accomplish X." In both instances, the same question applies: "Are your findings actionable?"

References

The list of references at the end of the research report serves two primary functions. First, it provides specific bibliographical details for any theoretical or empirical citations in your report. It therefore allows your reader, should he or she be inclined to do so, to backtrack through the literature foundation for your research. Second, it provides readers with leads they can follow if your findings spark interest. Thus, the reference section is an essential complement to the literature review.

Sometimes authors will inflate the reference section by including works that played, at best, a peripheral role in the research project. While it is essential to include full bibliographic references for any works directly cited in the research report, avoid excess padding. Research reports are seldom judged by the number of references; thoughtful readers expect you to be as selective in your references as you were in the presentation of your findings.

The Final Polish

We live in a time when personal computers and sophisticated printers mean that even the shoddiest piece of research can be presented in a very impressive way. Although we would never suggest that style can substitute for content, it is essential to pay close attention to the manner in which research findings are presented. Is the layout of the research report as attractive as possible? Does it have an attractive cover, a useful table of contents? Have you carefully checked for spelling and grammatical mistakes? If you get the small things wrong, if the report is poorly written or presented, the reader may assume that you have the big picture wrong as well. Packaging is critically important, for it conveys a sense of how careful you have been and how seriously you take the report. Sloppy work is quickly dismissed.

Remember, the report is where it all comes together. A great deal of painstaking work can be discounted if it is poorly presented. The theoretical import of your work can be lost, along with the implications of your empirical evidence. You owe it to yourself, and to others who may be involved in the research enterprise, to put as much effort into the presentation of your research as you did into gathering the empirical evidence.

Working as a Team

1. If you are preparing draft research reports as course assignments, try exchanging drafts and writing an abstract of no more than 100 words. Read the abstract to the original author. Does he or she accept the abstract as a reasonable distillation? Could you reduce the abstract to 75 words and still be successful? To 50 words?
2. Have your group pull together a variety of research reports prepared in different formats and for different audiences. You might, for example, use royal commission reports, stories in news magazines, articles in academic journals, and reports in trade books. How do these different research reports compare with respect to format and components? Do they do the same things in different ways or do they have little in common?

Self-Study

1. Take one or more of your old term papers and prepare an abstract of 150 words. Were you successful in capturing the core of the paper? What important elements, if any, were lost? What do you feel needed to be said but was squeezed out? Now see if you can trim this abstract to only 100 words. Can you trim it to 75 words? How low can you go before the abstract becomes useless?
2. Select two articles from a recent volume of the *Canadian Journal of Political Science* or *Canadian Public Policy*. What similarities and differences exist between the two? Do they present their findings in a similar way? Do they use abstracts in a similar fashion? Do they both include explicit research designs and thesis statements?

Glossary

abstract a brief summary of an article or research paper that helps the reader quickly understand the purpose and findings of the research.

accidental sample a non-probability sample technique in which researchers gather data from individuals whom they "accidentally" encounter or who are convenient; also known as a sample of convenience or haphazard sample.

action (or advocacy) research a reflective and iterative process of research focused on solving specific "real world" problems; typically practised by individuals who are deeply committed to an issue, often with a goal of marshalling evidence to heighten public debate and discussion of the issue and to influence the policy process.

aggregate data grouped data for a specified geographic area.

agree/disagree questions questions that present a statement and ask respondents to rate their agreement on a continuum of agree/disagree responses.

alpha (α) level see *confidence level.*

alternative hypothesis the statement of a possible causal relationship in contrast to another statement, often the research hypothesis; can be helpful in assessing the relative magnitude of the relationship in the research hypothesis.

ambiguous questions survey questions that are unclear and/or are misunderstood by the respondents, making their responses unreliable (e.g. questions with multiple stimuli).

analysis of variance (ANOVA) a statistical technique in which the observed variance is partitioned into components (within-group and between-group variances); in political science, often used when the dependent variable is measured at the nominal or ordinal level (particularly the former) and the independent variables are measured at the interval level.

anonymity an aspect of research that keeps a person's identity and identifying features unknown; respondents must be informed whether their identity will be revealed or whether they will remain anonymous.

applied research a term that is often used in contrast to pure research or basic research to indicate that the research addresses a topic or problem in the real world.

audit trail a record of decisions made when gathering and analyzing data.

authenticity the extent to which the analysis of a phenomenon corresponds with reality.

axial coding the second stage of qualitative data analysis, during which specific passages are labelled as belonging under certain themes; see *tagging.*

bandwagon effect a phenomenon in which a number of people hold a certain belief or act a certain way because many others think or act that way; a type of group normality.

basic linear regression see *ordinary least squares regression.*

basic research research conducted to increase understanding of the world, whether or not the results of the research have immediate or obvious applications; often used in contrast to applied research.

behavioural revolution period from the 1940s to the 1960s, in which political scientists developed a more positivist approach to studying political behaviour.

between-subjects design an experimental design in which different subjects are randomly assigned to various treatment and control groups; causality is inferred based on post-treatment differences observed between these groups.

bivariate involving two variables.

Canadian Election Studies (CES) a series of academic surveys conducted on a sample of the Canadian electorate at the time of federal elections from 1965 to the present-day (with the exception of the 1972 election); provide a rich source of data on political beliefs and voting behaviour.

case a single unit of analysis.

case identification a number or combination of numbers and letters used to identify the case.

case study a method of analysis that involves an in-depth investigation of a single individual, group, or event; in political science, generally used with the intent of identifying general causal principles.

categorical (or nominal) measurement a level of measurement in which variables are given numerical values (1, 2, 3, etc.) that represent a difference in kind rather than in degree (e.g. 2 is not higher than 1 but simply different).

causal effect the difference between the value of an outcome when a subject receives a treatment and when a subject does not receive the treatment.

causality the relationship between two events, in which one is a consequence of the other (i.e. a cause-and-effect relationship).

census an enumeration or a record of the full population.

central tendency the centre of a data distribution; measures include the mode, median, and mean.

central value the numeric representation of the centre of a data distribution; also known as measure of central tendency.

chunks passages of text that serve as indicators of a given theme.

closed coding coding of each case based on a specific list of values.

closed (or close-ended) questions questions that include a full set of acceptable responses for participants to choose from.

cluster sampling a probability sampling technique in which the researcher divides the population into a number of subgroups (i.e. clusters) and then randomly selects clusters within which to randomly sample.

codebook developed to guide coding, an instrument that lists the elements of the text that will be observed (variables) and itemizes how they will be categorized (values).

coding the systematic categorization of different aspects of communication.

coding sheet a sheet on which coders can record the values for each case.

comparative research a research design that seeks to compare phenomena across different political systems or cultures.

complex multiple indicator a combination of variables, such as the aspects of a person's political participation, into an index or scale; used to provide a more complete description or measurement of a concept.

computer-assisted qualitative data analysis software (CAQDAS) computer programs designed to assist researchers in coding, retrieving, storing, and analyzing qualitative data.

concept an abstract idea that represents or symbolizes a quality.

concordant pairs pairs of cases that exhibit similar ordering on the independent and dependent variables.

confidence interval the estimated range of values within which the population parameter is likely to fall.

confidence level the probability that the sample statistic is an accurate estimate of the population parameter; also known as alpha level.

confidentiality an aspect of research in which information is available only to those who are authorized to access it; in political science research, subjects typically are provided with a guarantee of confidentiality and, to ensure this, respondents' names and other identifying features are excluded from the data set used for analysis.

confirmability the extent to which a study's results may be verified by an independent researcher.

confounding the presence of some unobserved difference between groups that is correlated both with the outcome and the independent variable of interest, thereby making causal inference impossible.

content any message that can be communicated, including words, meanings, symbols, and themes.

content analysis quantitative research technique used to analyze the message characteristics in any form of communication (Neuendorf 2002, 1; Neuman 2007, 227).

contingency table a table that presents data for two variables, with the location of a particular case being contingent on its values for each variable; also known as a cross-tabulation or cross-tab table.

continuous variable a variable whose responses can be arrayed along the entire range of the measure, with no gaps or breaks in the distribution.

continuum a continuous series or event whose parts are indistinguishable from each other.

control condition see *control group*.

control group a group of subjects randomly assigned not to receive the treatment in an experiment; identical to the treatment group in all other respects.

control variable a variable that is kept constant (e.g. a study that examines the effect of variable A on variable B among men and then examines the effect among women holds gender constant).

convergent validity the assessment of a measure in which the indicators reveal the same or similar qualities; the opposite of discriminant validity.

correlation the measurement or observation of a common variation among multiple concepts or measures; can exist without a causal relation.

counter-intuitive a condition that occurs when a situation, event, or outcome differs from dominant theoretical expectations or common sense.

coverage bias type of bias that occurs when a research sampling frame excludes particular groups.

Cramer's V a chi-square-based measure of association for nominal-level data.

credibility the extent to which the results of an analysis "fit" with the reality being depicted.

critical discourse analysis (**CDA**) an investigation of how discourses reflect, reproduce, and reinforce relationships of dominance.

critical value the number that the calculated inferential statistic must meet or exceed if the null hypothesis is to be rejected.

cross-sectional data data collected from individuals at one point in time.

cross-sectional studies a type of research design intended to gather empirical evidence on an entire population or a representative sample of the population at a particular point in time.

data saturation the point at which interviews no longer provide a researcher with new relevant information.

deductive reasoning a type of reasoning that shows or attempts to show that a conclusion necessarily flows from a set of premises; in political science, often used in rational choice analysis, where individuals are assumed to be utility maximizers and their actions are assessed in relation to what they would be if this premise was true.

dependability the extent to which a researcher has produced accurate results, based on precise methods.

dependent variable the outcome event or the event to be explained in a research project; the research hypothesis is that an independent variable or variables act on or affect the dependent variable.

descriptive case study a study that aims to chronicle or describe some aspect of reality; involves questions of who, what, where, and when.

determinism the view that a certain outcome is inevitable.

difference of means a statistical test to determine if the difference in mean scores for two subgroups from the sample population is statistically significant.

direction placement of a message along a continuum or classification scheme in order to identify its type.

discordant pairs pairs of cases that exhibit dissimilar ordering of the independent and dependent variables.

discourse analysis a qualitative approach to analyzing texts that focuses on the meanings reflected in and created by discourses.

discourse fragment the discourses or portions of discourses to be analyzed with discourse analysis.

discourse plane the societal places from which discourses emerge, such as politics, media, science, business, or everyday life (Jäger 2001, 49).

discourses sets of ideas, images, symbols, and messages that, taken together, articulate a particular version of events.

discourse strand the coalescing of various discourse fragments into a uniform theme, such as racism, sexism, and neo-liberalism (Jäger 2001, 49).

discriminant (or divergent) validity the assessment of a measure in which those elements or factors that are expected to differ from the measure are shown to be different; the opposite of convergent validity.

double-blind design a research design in which both the subjects and the research team are unaware of who receives the treatment and who receives a placebo; intended to reduce the risk of the researchers providing subjects with cues about how they should react and to control for bias in the data collection.

dummy variable a measure in which a quality is dichotomous and is represented by the presence and the absence of the quality, usually using the values of 0 and 1 (e.g. 0 = not female, 1 = female).

ecological fallacy the assumption that group-level patterns imply individual-level patterns.

empirical research the reliance on observation of the real world to test theories and gain knowledge.

endogenous a set of variables that are included within the model being assessed.

epistemology the study of knowledge (or "how we know what we know").

equivalent measures indicators that measure the same concept across different countries, political systems, or cultures.

equivocal having the possibility of several different meanings; ambiguous.

executive summary a short document that identifies the key elements from a longer report or set of reports so that the reader can become familiar with them without reading the full report(s).

exhaustive inclusion of all the possible causal factors in an explanatory model; inclusion of all possible response options in a measure.

exogenous a set of variables that are excluded from the model being assessed.

experimental (or treatment) group a group of subjects exposed to the intervention of interest in an experiment; identical to the control group is all respects except that the control does not receive the treatment.

experimental research research that involves the researcher intervening in some way to randomly assign some subjects to a treatment group and others to a control group before an event takes place.

explained variance the amount of variation in the dependent variable that is accounted for by the independent variables.

explanatory research research that aims to account for or explain some aspect of reality; involves questions of why or how.

exploratory research research that aims to discover factors relating to a largely unknown subject.

external validity the extent to which the findings drawn from the cases under examination may be used to make generalizations about phenomena outside the original study.

face validity a validity test based on the fact that the outcome "looks" how it is expected to look.

failed most-likely case a case that is expected to confirm the operating assumptions of a particular theory but in practice refutes them.

falsifiable the idea that a hypothesis is not true by definition and is stated in such a way that empirical data could demonstrate that it is false.

feasibility the extent to which a study is capable of being completed, given the researcher's skills and resources.

feeling thermometer a type of measure in which the metaphor of a thermometer is used to assist respondents to identify their beliefs, feelings, or thoughts as relatively "warm" or relatively "cold"; often used with a 100-point scale.

field experiment an experiment in which a researcher's intervention is implemented in a subject's natural environment.

field notes detailed descriptions of events observed during observation research.

forced choice question a question that asks respondents to select between a limited number of statements.

frames patterns of selection, emphasis, and presentation that draw on familiar myths, themes, or cultural values to organize discourses.

frequency a measurement of whether something occurs and, if it does, how often.

frequency distribution a list of the number of cases for all possible values of a variable.

fundamental problem of causal inference a situation referring to the fact that causal effects cannot be observed in the real world and that causal inferences are therefore required.

gamma a proportional reduction of error (PRE) measure of association for ordinal-level data.

hard-to-reach population a population that is difficult for researchers to identify and/or that is less likely to participate in research studies than others.

Hawthorne effect a phenomenon that occurs when subjects under observation alter their behaviour because of the researcher's presence.

heterogeneity how dissimilar a population is with respect to the variable of interest.

heteroskedastic a term that indicates that the error in predicting the dependent variable is inconsistent along the full range of the dependent variable.

homogeneity how similar a population is with respect to the variable of interest.

homoskedastic a term that indicates that the error in predicting the dependent variable is consistent along the full range of the dependent variable.

hypothesis a statement of a proposed causal relationship between two concepts.

hypothesis-testing a method used in statistics to test the validity of a statement by comparing expected results with empirical or observed results; typically involves testing the null hypothesis and, based on the results, deciding whether to accept or reject it.

idea the issue or message being communicated.

ideal type concept formulation based on a notion of its "true form" rather than in relation to how it operates in the real world.

ideological assertions messages that strongly emphasize a particular ideological position.

impartiality the extent to which a study offers findings based on observation and evidence, as opposed to opinion or conjecture.

independent variable the measure used as the proposed causal influence in a relationship between two measures.

index a complex measure that combines responses from more than one question in the creation of a new measure.

indicator a variable that is used to represent the presence of a quality.

inductive reasoning a type of reasoning that bases conclusions on the presence of empirical evidence; evidence is used for theory development.

inferential statistics statistics used to determine if sample statistics are representative of population parameters.

informed consent the idea that respondents in a research project fully understand the nature of the project and the extent of their participation and agree to participate based on these understandings.

intensity the strength of a message.

intercept in regression analysis, the point at which the regression line crosses the *Y*-axis.

intercoder reliability the extent to which different coders reach the same conclusions (i.e. assign the same values when coding); a high level of agreement indicates that the coding instrument is reliable.

internal validity the extent to which the researcher has produced results reflective of reality, as measured within the confines of the study.

interpretivism also referred to as anti-positivism, the view that reality does not exist independent of individuals and that all knowledge is socially constructed; argues that there is no such thing as objective reality that can be understood by all observers and measured through techniques such as survey research; methodologically, associated with more qualitative approaches.

intersubjectivity a situation in which a phenomenon is experienced by more than one person (i.e. two people, acting independently, perceive the same thing).

interval measurement a level of measurement in which all values have a numerical category, the categories are ranked and there is a consistent range between each value.

intervening variable a situation in which a third variable comes between an independent and dependent variable; the independent variable influences the intervening variable, which in turn influences the dependent variable.

interviewer effect a situation in which a respondent provides the answer that he or she thinks the interviewer wants.

interview framework a written list of questions that the interviewer intends to ask the respondent.

investigator triangulation the use of multiple researchers in a single research study as a means of ensuring the trustworthiness of the examination.

knowledge mobilization a term used to describe the practical social application of research.

laboratory experiment an experiment in which subjects are recruited to a common location where the researcher exerts a relatively large degree of control over the experimental setting.

lambda the proportional reduction of error (PRE) measure of association for nominal-level data.

large-*N* study research involving a large number of cases.

latent content the underlying or implied meaning of a message.

levels of measurement the precision used in interpreting the numerical values of the measures used in the research project; distinction is made among nominal, ordinal, and interval measures.

linear regression a statistical technique used to assess the strength of the relationship between two or more variables measured at the interval level, in which the model assumes a consistent (linear) relationship across all values of the dependent variable.

literature review a text that attempts to identify the current state of knowledge in a given subject area, with a particular focus on the main substantive understandings and theoretical approaches.

logistic regression analysis that uses a logistic function to estimate the relationship between a variable measured as a 0 and 1 dichotomy (e.g. 0 = not voting Conservative and 1 = voting Conservative).

longitudinal data data collected from the same individuals over time.

longitudinal (or panel) studies studies that interview the same respondents at different points in time in order to study change.

manifest content the literal, or surface, meaning of the message.

marginals the total number of cases in a row (row marginal) or column (column marginal) of a table.

margin of error a range around the estimate, expressed in percentage terms (e.g. ±5 per cent), that likely contains the population parameter; used by researchers to state their sample statistics as a confidence interval.

mean the arithmetic average, calculated by adding all scores in a distribution and dividing by the total number of cases.

measurement validity the extent to which the measurement of a particular concept matches its operational definition.

measures the ways concepts are measured; for example, the importance of a political actor within a news story could be measured by whether he or she is named in the headline of the news story, by the frequency with which he or she is referred to in the story, or by the length of any direct quotes attributed to this actor within the story.

measures of association statistical measures of the strength of a relationship between two variables; also known as coefficients of association or relationship measures.

measures of variation statistical measures for the dispersion of scores around the central tendency.

median the value above which and below which 50 per cent of the cases fall.

member checks the process of verifying study results in consultation with its subjects.

memoing the process of writing notes about the coding process.

metadata the technical documentation that accompanies secondary data.

microdata non-aggregated data that allows the researcher to consider individual units of analysis (such as individuals or households).

minimal risk a term used in the research ethics review process to indicate that the risks associated with participating in a research project are no greater than the risks encountered in everyday life.

mixed methods research research that uses a variety of qualitative and quantitative methodologies in the confines of a single study.

mode the most frequently occurring value in a distribution of scores.

moderate relationship a relationship in which a change in the independent variable is to some degree correlated with change in the dependent variable.

most-different-systems design a comparative research design in which the researcher compares very different systems in an attempt to explain similarities between them.

most-similar-systems design a comparative research design in which the researcher compares very similar systems in an attempt to explain differences between them.

multicollinearity the existence of a relationship between a study's independent variables, which generally violates the linear regression assumption that independent variables should be unrelated to one another; leads to unstable estimates of the relationship's effect.

multidimensional a concept that comprises different elements or dimensions, each of which must be captured in the definition and measurement.

multiple regression a regression model that includes more than one independent variable.

multivariate involving three or more variables.

mutually exclusive the idea that two elements cannot coexist.

narrative structures standard storylines or narrative devices used to create tension and keep an audience's attention.

natural (or naturally occurring) experiment a course of naturally occurring events in which different conditions appear to be randomly assigned to subjects without the planned intervention of the researcher (e.g. a lottery); to qualify as a natural experiment, assignment to experimental and control groups must be allocated as if by random assignment.

negative correlation a relationship between two variables in which increases in one are associated with decreases in the other.

nominal measurement see *categorical measurement.*

non-parametric statistics statistics whose use is not contingent on the parameters of the data distribution.

non-probability sampling sampling techniques that are not based on probability theory; sample selection is not random and some cases in the population are more likely than others to be selected for participation.

non-random error systematic error that, for example, occurs because people lie; voter turnout is often affected by this error, as many people say they voted even though they did not.

non-response bias the sampling error that occurs when survey respondents and non-respondents differ in an important way.

non-singular a model that is open to different possible interpretations.

no relationship perfect independence between two variables; change in the independent variable is not correlated with change in the dependent variable.

normal curve a curve that represents the normal distribution.

normal distribution a bilaterally symmetrical curve in which the mean, median, and mode are all equal and that meets other mathematical conditions; a mathematical distribution of cases.

normative analysis a type of analysis that is value-laden, in which indications of ought or should are often used.

null hypothesis the inverse of the research hypothesis; the claim that there is no relationship between the independent and dependent variables; empirically tested in political science research.

objectivity the extent to which a study's results are unbiased by the researcher's predispositions.

observational design a research design in which researchers have not intervened to randomly assign a treatment but observe an event and analyze the data after the event has taken place.

observation research a research design in which the researcher observes actual behaviour; also known as field research or ethnography.

observation schedule a checklist for recording behaviour in observation research.

obtrusive observation research observation research in which the subjects are aware that they are being observed.

official statistics statistics that governments and international organizations release to the public.

omnibus surveys surveys that are not dedicated to examining one specific issue or to focusing on the concerns of only one sponsor but are more general in character and often involve multiple sponsors.

one-tailed test an inferential statistical test used when the direction of difference is relevant to the hypothesis-testing.

open coding the first stage of qualitative data analysis, during which general patterns or themes are identified.

open (or open-ended) questions questions that are framed in such a way that respondents can state their position without any cueing from the researcher.

operational definition a researcher's description of a variable for a particular study; often involves very specific issues, such as how to deal with non-responses, "don't knows," and the like; provides a way to measure an abstract concept for all cases in a study.

operationalization the process of moving from a conceptual definition (an abstraction) to a measure or a set of measures (concrete) that enables a researcher to empirically observe the construct in his or her particular research project.

optical character recognition (OCR) software designed to translate non-electronic text into machine-readable format.

ordinal measurement a level of measurement in which values represent differences and can be ranked from lowest to highest (e.g. level of agree on an agree/disagree question); unlike interval variables, there is not a consistent unit across the range of values.

ordinary least squares (OLS) regression a form of regression analysis in which the slope (or regression coefficient) is estimated on the basis of a technique that minimizes the squared variations between the dependent variable's observed and predicted values.

paradigm a theoretical framework that includes general agreement on the laws, theories, conceptual definitions, and manner of measuring variables.

parametric statistics statistics with assumptions about the data's distribution that must be met if they are to be used and interpreted correctly.

participant observation an unobtrusive observation research design in which the researcher becomes part of the community under observation.

passages parts of a study that are labelled as belonging under certain themes; see *tagging*.

Pearson's *r* the Pearson product moment correlation coefficient that examines the strength of the relationship between two variables, ranging from –1 to +1.

peer evaluation process a very common practice within the scholarly community that subjects new research findings to a double-blind review by experts; used by major academic journals to assess whether an article merits publication.

perfect correlation a relationship between two variables in which a change in the independent variable is always and systematically correlated with change in the dependent variable.

pilot study a preliminary investigation intended to test and refine the methodology employed in the main study.

placebo a form of stimuli that does not contain the precise treatment the researcher is testing; often takes a form similar to the experimental treatment without exposing subjects to the specific ingredient that is hypothesized to have a causal effect (e.g. a sugar pill); a type of control group in that it offers the experimenter a point of reference to estimate the treatment's effect.

planned intervention a situation in which an experimenter purposefully manipulates one or several aspects of subjects' conditions according to a predefined scheme.

plausibility when compared with alternative accounts, the extent to which a study's results offer a reasonable, believable account of reality.

policy analysis the analysis of public policy processes or outcomes.

population in research, the group that a researcher wishes to generalize about (e.g. Canadian citizens in 2015); in content analysis, the texts most appropriate for answering the research question.

population parameter population characteristics, expressed in numeric terms when the responses of each member (or case) of the population are measured.

portability the extent to which a study's results may be used to draw conclusions about other cases not immediately under investigation.

positive correlation a relationship between two variables in which an increase in one is associated with an increase in the other.

positivism a philosophical position that states that the scientific approach is the best way to gain knowledge.

postmaterialism a social theory developed by Ronald Inglehart in the 1970s that postulated that advanced industrial societies were moving from a division based on material wealth and physical security to one based on individual autonomy, concern for the environment, and self-expression.

postmodernism a philosophical position that states that it is impossible to identify objective knowledge because all knowledge is embedded within the power, class, gender, and racial structure of society.

postulates propositions that are viewed as self-evident.

power see *statistical power*.

precision the extent to which a study offers an accurate account of reality, based on the ability of other researchers to reach similar conclusions under similar circumstances.

predictive validity a condition in which a concept measurement is affirmed, in part because it consistently leads to accurate predictions.

prior conditions the nature or status of a situation before the inclusion of an independent effect.

probability the mathematical likelihood that the results of a study apply beyond the cases under examination to other cases under the same general category.

probability sampling sampling techniques that are based on probability theory; sample selection is random and each case in the population has an equal chance to be selected for participation.

process tracing a research method that generates causal pathways between the independent and dependent variables of a case by connecting a series of observations.

prominence the placement and importance of a message in a text.

proportional reduction in error (PRE) measures a special class of measures of association that compare the amount of error that exists without knowing the independent variable with the amount of remaining error after knowledge about the independent variable is taken into account.

proposition a statement expressing the truth or falseness of a situation.

purposive sampling a non-probability sampling technique in which researchers use their judgment to select cases that will provide the greatest amount of information; also known as judgmental sampling.

qualitative research the non-numerical examination of reality; typically conducted through the use of verbal depiction.

qualitative tradition an analytic approach involving the use of non-numerical techniques, including theming.

qualitize the process of supplementing quantitative data with non-numerical evidence.

quantitative research the numerical examination of reality; typically conducted through the use of statistical analysis.

quantitative tradition an analytic approach involving the use of numbers, counting, and mathematics.

quantize the process of supplementing qualitative data with numerical evidence.

quasi-experiments a course of events in a subject's environment that implies neither "as if" random assignment nor any planned intervention by the researcher.

question order the order in which questions are posed in a survey questionnaire.

quota sampling a non-probability sampling technique in which the researcher combines purposive or accidental sampling with stratification; the researcher identifies a number of target groups (strata) and then sets a quota number that must be met for each group.

random assignment the process of assigning some members of a population to a treatment group and others to a control group; random assignment ensures that the two groups are identical in all respects aside from the receipt of treatment.

random errors inaccuracies caused by factors that are not systematic and/or intentional; found in all samples because the full range of possible respondents cannot be included; amount of random error can be estimated in a probability sample.

random selection a selection technique in which all cases in a population have an equal opportunity for inclusion in the sample.

range the difference between the lowest and highest values in a distribution of scores.

regression line the line that corresponds to the slope in a regression model, adjusted by the intercept; in ordinary least squares regression, it minimizes the errors in predicting the dependent variable.

reinforcing variable a variable that strengthens or magnifies the relationship between the two other variables.

reliability the extent to which the measurement of a particular variable yields consistent results.

replicability the extent to which a study is repeatable or duplicable.

replication the repetition of a study in an attempt to duplicate and confirm results from a previous study.

representative sample a sample that accurately reflects the larger population from which it was drawn.

research design the manner in which the research question has been structured in light of the literature review of the topic, including how data are to be gathered and analyzed to test the major hypothesis or hypotheses of the study; often presented in a written document before the data are analyzed.

residual the amount that is left over or unexplained.

response set the group of response categories that comprise all responses to a particular question.

rhetorical devices semantic techniques of persuasion, including irony, hyperbole, and metaphor.

right to withdraw the condition in a study that respondents must be able to exit a study at any time they want and must be informed of this right; required in order for research on humans to be deemed ethical.

rigour the validity and reliability of the research.

sample a record of a subset of a population.

sampling choosing a number of cases or available texts from a larger population rather than analyzing the entire population.

sampling distribution the theoretical distribution of a sample statistic (e.g. the mean) for a given sample size.

sampling error the difference between the sample statistic and the population parameter.

sampling frame a list of all the units in the target population.

scatter plot a graphical presentation of the relationship between all cases on a dependent and independent variable, typically where these variables are measured at the interval level.

science a systematic approach to gaining knowledge and understanding based on a method of formulating hypotheses and testing them with empirical data.

scientific analysis analysis that uses the scientific method, in whichever discipline the study is taking place.

scientific approach to politics the application of the scientific method to the study of political phenomena.

scope conditions the limits to which particular research can make valid claims.

secondary data data that are not collected directly by the researcher (e.g. official statistics and data gathered by other research teams).

selective coding the third and final stage of qualitative data analysis, during which the researcher verifies the accuracy of earlier coding decisions.

self-selection a process in which individuals select themselves for participation in a sample (e.g. radio call-in programs).

silences and omissions the exclusion of discussion regarding certain groups or topics.

simple random sampling the process by which every case in the population is listed and the sample is selected randomly from this list.

single-blind design an experimental design in which subjects remain unaware of various types of information—such as whether they are part of the treatment, placebo, or control group—in order to reduce the possible bias that this information could induce.

size the amount of space or time a message takes up within the text.

skew the opinion an uneven distribution of opinion on a topic, in which a disproportionate percentage of the respondents hold an opinion on one side of the issue.

slope sometimes described as the rise over the run, the amount of change in the dependent variable for a one-unit change in the independent variable.

small-*n* studies research involving a small number of cases.

small population a population with relatively few members (e.g. cabinet ministers).

snowball (or network) sampling a non-probability sampling technique in which the researcher begins by identifying a few cases and, from these, gets referrals for other cases and continues to branch out.

spurious the relationship between the independent and dependent variables that, while initially thought to be causal, is non-causal and is a function of the presence of a third variable, which causes the variation in both variables.

standard deviation a number that represents the average of how cases vary from the mean.

standardized scores scores expressed in terms of the number of standard deviations they fall from the mean of the total distribution of scores; also known as *z*-scores.

statistic a numeric estimate of the population parameter.

statistical power the ability of a research design to detect effects should such effects exist; a power analysis can give researchers an idea of what sample sizes will make an experiment sensitive enough to detect effects of certain sizes.

stimulus/stimuli the treatment(s)—often involving exposure to different forms of information—to which subjects in an experimental group are exposed.

stratified sampling a probability sampling technique in which the researcher breaks the population into mutually exclusive subgroups, or strata, and then randomly samples from each group.

structural features elements used to convey a message within a text; structural features of a newspaper story include the headline, lead paragraph, author, length, type of story, etc.

substantive features the substantive meanings communicated by a text.

successful least-likely case a case that is expected to refute the operating assumptions of a particular theory but in practice confirms them.

sum of squares the sum of the squared deviations from the mean.

surface structures elements such as the form, format, structure, and layout of the text.

survey experiment an experiment implemented in the context of a survey involving the random manipulation of a part (or parts) of the survey instrument.

syntactical structures the arrangements of words, symbols, or images in the text.

systematic selection a probability sampling technique in which the researcher calculates a selection interval and uses it to select cases from the sampling frame.

tagging the process of labelling specific passages as belonging under a given theme.

tau-b a proportional reduction of error measure of association for ordinal-level data; requires square tables.

tau-c a measure of association for ordinal-level data; requires non-square tables.

temporal order the sequencing of events based on the order in which they occur.

text any form of communication (written, visual, spoken, etc.).

textual analysis the systematic examination of the messages and meanings conveyed by texts.

theories statements that attempt to explain the causal relationship between two variables.

theory testing case study research that seeks to modify an existing theory or generate a new theory.

ties pairs of cases that differ on one variable but are tied on the other.

total variance the full amount by which the observed occurrences of the dependent variable differ from the estimated or predicted value based on the independent variable.

transferability the extent to which researchers can export the lessons drawn from one investigation to develop conclusions about another set of cases.

treatment the intervention of interest; also known as stimulus.

triangulation the use of multiple approaches to data collection and analysis as a means of drawing trustworthy conclusions about reality.

trustworthiness the extent to which a study produces legitimate knowledge.

two-tailed test an inferential statistical test used when the direction of difference is not relevant to the hypothesis-testing.

Type I error the error made when the null hypothesis is incorrectly rejected; also known as a false positive.

Type II error the error made when the null hypothesis is incorrectly retained; also known as a false negative.

typology the classification of things on the basis of their characteristics (e.g. a typology of political party systems based on the number of competitive parties in the system).

underdog effect a phenomenon in which respondents hold views or perspectives based on the perception that a group or individual is trailing a leader, as in a party or candidate getting additional support because of sympathy toward his or her position.

unexplained variance the total amount of deviation between the observed and predicted values of the dependent variable that is not due to the presence of the independent variable.

unit of analysis the portion of text that will be coded (e.g. the headline of a news story).

univariate involving a single variable.

universe synonymous with *population*.

univocal having one meaning; unambiguous.

unobtrusive observation research observation research in which the subjects are unaware that they are being observed.

validity the extent to which the results of a study reflect reality.

values categories that capture the variance between observable characteristics of phenomena; for effective coding to be effective, values should be collectively exhaustive and mutually exclusive.

variables the observable characteristics of phenomena that can take on more than one value; specific and concrete measurements of a concept.

variance the sum of the squared deviations from the mean, divided by the number of cases.

variation ratio the number of cases that are not in the modal category.

within-subject design an experimental design in which researchers evaluate subjects before and after exposure to a given treatment; may also involve comparisons made to the before and after observations of the control group; causality is inferred based on any differences observed between comparisons.

***z*-scores** see *standardized scores*.

References

Abu-Laban, Yasmeen, and Linda Trimble. 2010. "Covering Muslim Canadians and Politics in Canada: The Print Media and the 2000, 2004 and 2006 Federal Elections." In *Mediating Canadian Politics*, edited by Shannon Sampert and Linda Trimble, 129–50. Toronto: Pearson.

Albrow, Martin. 1970. *Bureaucracy*. London: Pall Mall Press.

Allison, Graham T., and Zelikow, Philip. 1999. *Essence of Decision: Explaining the Cuban Missile Crisis*, 2nd edn. New York and Harlow, UK: Longman.

Altheide, David L. 1996. *Qualitative Media Analysis*. Thousand Oaks, CA: Sage.

Angus Reid Public Opinion. 2013. *Conservatives Stable, NDP Drops and Liberals Gain in Canada*. http://www.angusreidglobal.com/polls/48586/conservatives-stable-ndp-drops-and-liberals-gain-in-canada/ (accessed 16 October 2013).

Angus Reid Strategies. 2008. *Conservatives Close Campaign Ten Points Ahead of Liberals*. http://angus-reidstrategies.com/uploads/pages/pdfs/2008.10.13_Final.pdf (accessed 17 November 2009).

Anker, Elisabeth. 2005. "Villains, Victims and Heroes: Melodrama, Media and September 11." *Journal of Communication* 55 (1): 22–37.

Archer, Keith, and Roger Gibbins. 1997. "What Do Albertans Think? The Klein Agenda on the Public Opinion Landscape." In *A Government Reinvented: A Study of Alberta's Deficit Elimination Program*, edited by Christopher J. Bruce, Ronald Kneebone, and Kenneth McKenzie, 462–85. Toronto: Oxford University Press.

———, ———, Rainer Knopff, and Les Pal. 1995. *Parameters of Power: Canada's Political Institutions*. Toronto: Nelson Canada.

Babbie, Earl, and Lucia Benaquisto. 2002. *Fundamentals of Social Research*, Canadian edn. Scarborough: Thomson Nelson.

Bahry, Donna L. 1991. "Crossing Borders: The Practice of Comparative Research." In *Empirical Political Analysis: Research Methods in Political Science*, 3rd edn, Jarol B. Manheim and Richard C. Rich, 213–26. Englewood Cliffs, NJ: Prentice-Hall.

Bailey, Kenneth D. 1978. *Methods of Social Research*. New York: The Free Press.

Baker, Sarah Elsie, and Rosalind Edwards. 2012. *How Many Qualitative Interviews Is Enough? Expert Voices and Early Career Reflections on Sampling and Cases in Qualitative Research*. National Centre for Research Methods Review Paper. Southampton, UK: Economic and Social Research Council.

Bakvis, Herman, and Laura G. Macpherson. 1995. "Quebec Block Voting and the Canadian Electoral System." *Canadian Journal of Political Science* 28 (December): 659–92.

Barabas, Jason, and Jennifer Jerit. 2010. "Are Survey Experiments Externally Valid?" *American Political Science Review* 104 (2): 226–42.

Barbolet, Herb, Vijay Cuddeford, Fern Jeffries, Holly Korstad, Susan Kurbis, Sandra Mark, Christiana Miewald, and Frank Moreland. 2005. *Vancouver Food System Assessment*. http://www.sfu.ca/cscd/publications/documents/final_draft_compress.pdf (accessed 7 January 2010).

Bardach, Eugene. 2009. *A Practical Guide for Policy Analysis: The Eightfold Path to More Effective Problem Solving*, 3rd edn. Washington, DC: CQ Press.

Barnett, Michael, and Martha Finnemore. 2004. *Rules for the World: International Organizations in Global Politics*. London: Cornell University Press.

Baxter-Moore, Nicolas, Terrance Carroll, and Roderick Church. 1994. *Studying Politics: An Introduction to Argument and Analysis*. Toronto: Copp Clark Longman.

Becker, Howard S. 1998. *Tricks of the Trade: How to Think About Your Research While You're Doing It*. Chicago: University of Chicago Press.

Bedford, David. 2003. "Aboriginal Voter Participation in Nova Scotia and New Brunswick." *Electoral Insight*. www.elections.ca.

———, and Sidney Pobihushchy. 1995. "On-Reserve Status Indian Voter Participation in the Maritimes." *Canadian Journal of Native Studies* 15 (2): 255–78.

Behringer, Ronald M. 2005. "Middle Power Leadership on the Human Security Agenda." *Cooperation and Conflict: Journal of the Nordic International Studies Association* 40 (3): 305–42.

Bell, Edward, Harold Jansen, and Lisa Young. 2007. "Sustaining A Dynasty in Alberta: The 2004 Provincial Election." *Canadian Political Science Review* 1 (2): 27–49.

Bennett, Andrew, and Colin Elman. 2007. "Case Study Methods in International Relations Subfield." *Comparative Political Studies* 40 (2): 170–95.

Berdahl, Loleen, Christopher Adams, and Greg Poelzer. 2009. "Aboriginal Provincial Party Support in Manitoba." Paper prepared for the 2009 Canadian Political Science Association Annual Meetings, Ottawa, 27 May 2009.

Berg, Bruce L. 1989. *Qualitative Research Methods in the Social Sciences*. Boston: Allyn & Bacon.

———. 2004. *Qualitative Research Methods for the Social Sciences*, 5th edn. Toronto: Pearson.

Berger, Eva, and Dorit Naaman. 2011. "Combat Cuties: Photographs of Israeli Women Soldiers in the Press Since the 2006 Lebanon War." *Media, War & Conflict* 4 (3): 269–86.

Berry, William D. 1993. *Understanding Regression Assumptions*. Newbury Park, CA: Sage.

Bertrand, Marianne, Simeon Djankov, Rema Hanna, and Sendhil Mullainathan. 2007. "Obtaining a Driver's License in India: An Experimental Approach to Studying Corruption." *The Quarterly Journal of Economics* 122 (4): 1639–76.

Bethlehem, Jelke. 2009. "Can We Make Official Statistics with Self-Selection Web Surveys?" *Symposium 2008: Data Collection: Challenges, Achievements and New Directions*. Ottawa: Statistics Canada.

Blais, André, Pierre Martin, and Richard Nadeau. 1995. "Attentes économiques et linguistiques et appui à la souverainete du Québec: Une analyse prospective et comparative." *Canadian Journal of Political Science* 28 (December): 637–57.

———, Elisabeth Gidengil, Richard Nadeau, and Neil Nevitte. 2001. "Measuring Party Identification: Canada, Britain and the United States." *Political Behavior* 23: 5–22.

———, Simon Labbé-St-Vincent, Laslier Jean-François, Nicolas Sauger, and Karine Van der Straeten. 2011. "Strategic Vote Choice in One-Round and Two-Round Elections An Experimental Study." *Political Research Quarterly* 64 (3): 637–45.

Blalock, Hubert M. 1964. *Causal Inferences in Nonexperimental Research*. Chapel Hill: University of North Carolina Press.

Bond, Robert M., Christopher J. Fariss, Jason J. Jones, Adam D. I. Kramer, Cameron Marlow, Jaime E. Settle, and James H. Fowler. 2012. "A 61-Million-Person Experiment in Social Influence and Political Mobilization." *Nature* 489: 295–8.

Boyatzis, Richard E. 1998. *Transforming Qualitative Information: Thematic Analysis and Code Development*. Thousand Oaks, CA: Sage.

Boyd, Paul C. 2006. "By the Numbers: A Sample Size Table." *Quirk's Marking Research Review* (December): 30.

Brady, Henry E., David Collier, and Jason Seawright. 2004. "Refocusing the Discussion of Methodology." In *Rethinking Social Inquiry: Diverse Tools, Shared Standards*, edited by D. Collier and H. E. Brady, 15–32. Boulder, CO: Rowman & Littlefield.

Broadhead, Robert S. 1984. "Human Rights and Human Subjects: Ethics and Strategies in Social Science Research." *Sociological Inquiry* 54: 107–23.

Brodie, Ian, and Neil Nevitte. 1993. "Evaluating the Citizens' Constitution Theory." *Canadian Journal of Political Science* 26 (June): 235–59.

Brodie, M. Janine, and Jane Jenson. 1980. *Crisis, Challenge and Change: Party and Class in Canada*. Toronto: Methuen.

Bryman, Alan. 2001. *Social Research Methods*. Toronto: Oxford University Press.

———. 2004. *Social Research Methods*, 2nd edn. Toronto: Oxford University Press.

Budge, Ian, and Judith Bara. 2001. "Introduction: Content Analysis and Political Texts." In *Mapping Policy Preferences: Estimates for Parties, Electors and Governments 1945–1998*, edited by I. Budge, H.-D. Klingermann, A. Volkens, J. Bara, and E. Tanenbaum, 1–18. New York: Oxford University Press.

Bullock, John G., Donald P. Green, and Shang E. Ha. 2010. "Yes, but What's the Mechanism? (Don't Expect an Easy Answer)." *Journal of Personality and Social Psychology* 98 (4): 550.

Burr, Vivien. 1995. *An Introduction to Social Constructionism*. London: Routledge.

Cairns, Alan C. 1975. "Political Science in Canada and the Americanization Issue." *Canadian Journal of Political Science* 8 (June): 191–234.

———. 1993. "A Defence of the Citizens' Constitution Theory: A Response to Ian Brodie and Neil Nevitte." *Canadian Journal of Political Science* 26 (June): 261–7.

———. 2001. *Citizens Plus: Aboriginal Peoples and the Canadian State*. Vancouver: University of British Columbia Press.

Campbell, Angus, Philip E. Converse, Warren E. Miller, and Donald E. Stokes. 1960. *The American Voter*. New York: Wiley.

Campbell, Donald T., and H. Laurence Ross. 1968. "The Connecticut Crackdown on Speeding: Time-Series Data in Quasi-Experimental Analysis." *Law and Society Review*: 33–53.

Campus, Donatella. 2013. *Women Political Leaders and the Media*. Hampshire: Palgrave MacMillan.

Canadian Press. 2013. "Pollsters Scramble to Explain How Polls Could Be So Wrong in Three Provinces." *Maclean's*, 16 May. http://www2.macleans.ca/2013/

05/16/pollsters-scramble-to-explain-how-polls-could-be-so-wrong-in-three-provinces/ (accessed 3 December 2013).

Carbert, Louise. 2006. *Rural Women's Leadership in Atlantic Canada: First-Hand Perspectives on Public Life and Participation in Electoral Politics*. Toronto: University of Toronto Press.

Carey, Martha Ann, and Jo-Ellen Asbury. 2012. *Focus Group Research*. Walnut Creek, CA: Left Coast Press.

Carroll, Lewis. 1990. *Alice's Adventures in Wonderland and Through the Looking Glass*. Notes by Martin Gardner. New York: Random House.

Carter, Chris. 1996. "Herrenvolk," *The X-Files*, season 4, episode 1, directed by R. W. Goodwin, aired 4 October. Los Angeles: Twentieth Century Fox.

Carty, R. Kenneth, and Munroe Eagles. 2006. *Politics Is Local: National Politics at the Grassroots*. Toronto: Oxford University Press.

Cash, Heather. 2006. "Security Council Resolution 1593 and Conflicting Principles of International Law: How the Future of the International Criminal Court is at Stake." *Brandeis Law Journal* 45 (2).

CBC News. 2010a. "Calgary Chooses Nenshi as New Mayor." 19 October. http://www.cbc.ca/news/canada/calgary/calgary-chooses-nenshi-as-new-mayor-1.867664 (accessed 13 October 2013).

———. 2010b. "StatsCan Head Quits over Census Dispute." 21 July. http://www.cbc.ca/news/canada/statscan-head-quits-over-census-dispute-1.866937 (accessed 28 July 2014).

———. 2010c. "StatsCan Warned of Poor Census Response Rate." 10 August. http://www.cbc.ca/news/politics/statscan-warned-of-poor-census-response-rate-1.894958 (accessed 28 July 2014).

Chadwick, Bruce A., Howard M. Bahr, and Stan L. Albrecht. 1984. *Social Science Research Methods*. Englewood Cliffs, NJ: Prentice-Hall.

Chong, Dennis, and James N. Druckman. 2007a. "Framing Public Opinion in Competitive Democracies." *American Political Science Review* 101 (4): 637–55.

———, and ———. 2007b. "Framing Theory." *Annual Review of Political Science* 10: 103–26.

———, and ———. 2013. "Counterframing Effects." *The Journal of Politics* 75 (1): 1–16.

CIHR, NSERC, and SSHRC. 2010. *Tri-Council Policy Statement: Ethical Conduct for Research Involving Humans*. http://www.pre.ethics.gc.ca/pdf/eng/tcps2/TCPS_2_FINAL_Web.pdf (accessed 19 June 2014).

———, ———, and ———. 2011. *The Tri-Agency Framework: Responsible Conduct of Research*. http://www.rcr.ethics.gc.ca/eng/policy-politique/framework-cadre/.

Clarke, Harold D., Jane Jenson, Lawrence LeDuc, and Jon Pammett. 1979. *Political Choice in Canada*. Toronto: McGraw-Hill Ryerson.

Coe, Kevin, and Rico Neumann. 2011. "The Major Addresses of Modern Presidents: Parameters of a Data Set." *Presidential Studies Quarterly* 41 (4): 727–51.

Copsey, Nathaniel. 2008. *Focus Groups and the Political Scientist*. European Research Working Paper Series, Number 22. http://www.eri.bham.ac.uk/documents/research/wp22-copsey.pdf (accessed 7 January 2010).

Creswell, John W. 1998. *Qualitative Inquiry and Research Design: Choosing Among Five Traditions*. Thousand Oaks, CA: Sage.

———. 2003. *Research Design: Qualitative, Quantitative, and Mixed Methods Approaches*. Thousand Oaks, CA: Sage.

———, and Vicki L. Plano Clark. 2007. *Designing and Conducting Mixed Methods Research*. Thousand Oaks, CA: Sage.

Dahl, Robert. 1961. *Who Governs? Democracy and Power in an American City*. New Haven, CT: Yale University Press.

———. 1989. *Democracy and Its Critics*. New Haven, CT: Yale University Press.

Davis, James A. 1985. *The Logic of Causal Order*. Newbury Park, CA: Sage.

DeKeseredy, Walter. 1994. "Addressing the Complexities of Woman Abuse in Dating: A Response to Gartner and Fox." *Canadian Journal of Sociology* 19 (1): 75–80.

———, and Katherine Kelly. 1993. "The Incidence and Prevalence of Woman Abuse in Canadian University and College Dating Relationships." *Canadian Journal of Sociology* 18 (2): 137–59.

Denzin, Norman K., and Yvonna S. Lincoln. 1994. "Entering the Field of Qualitative Research." In *Handbook of Qualitative Research*, edited by N. K. Denzin and Y. S. Lincoln, 1–17. Thousand Oaks, CA: Sage.

de Tocqueville, Alexis. 1863. *Democracy in America*. New York: Amereon House.

Dolence, Michael G., and Donald M. Norris. 1995. *Transforming Higher Education: A Vision for Learning in the 21st Century*. Ann Arbor, MI: Society for College and University Planning.

Downs, Anthony. 1957. *An Economic Theory of Democracy*. New York: Harper & Row.

Driscoll, Kathleen, and Joan McFarland. 1989. "The Impact of a Feminist Perspective on Research

Methodologies: Social Sciences." In *The Effects of Feminist Approaches on Research Methodologies*, edited by Winne Tomm, 185–203. Waterloo, ON: Wilfrid Laurier University Press.

Druckman, James N. 2001. "On the Limits of Framing Effects: Who Can Frame?" *Journal of Politics* 63 (4): 1041–66.

———, Donald P. Green, James H. Kuklinski, and Arthur Lupia. 2006. "The Growth and Development of Experimental Research in Political Science." *American Political Science Review* 100 (4): 627–35.

Dunning, Thad. 2012. *Natural Experiments in the Social Sciences: A Design-Based Approach*. New York: Cambridge University Press.

———, and Lauren Harrison. 2010. "Cross-Cutting Cleavages and Ethnic Voting: An Experimental Study of Cousinage in Mali." *American Political Science Review* 104 (1): 21–39.

———, and Janhavi Nilekani. 2013. "Ethnic Quotas and Political Mobilization: Caste, Parties, and Distribution in Indian Village Councils." *American Political Science Review* 107 (1): 35–56.

Eckstein, Harry. 1975. "Case Study and Theory in Political Science." In *Handbook of Political Science*, vol. 7, edited by Fred L. Greenstein and Nelson W. Polsby, 79–138. Reading: Addison-Wesley Publishing Company.

Edwards, Allen L. 1969. *Statistical Analysis*. New York: Holt, Rinehart and Winston.

———. 1990. *Statistical Analysis*, 3rd edn. New York: Holt, Rinehart and Winston and McGraw-Hill.

Elifson, Kirk W., Richard P. Runyon, and Audrey Haber. 1990. *Fundamentals of Social Statistics*, 2nd edn. New York: McGraw-Hill.

Elkins, David J. 1978. "Party Identification: A Conceptual Analysis." *Canadian Journal of Political Science* 11 (June): 419–21.

Elman, Miriam Fendius. 1997. *Paths to Peace: Is Democracy the Answer?* Cambridge, MA, and London: MIT Press.

Ember, Carol R., Melvin Ember, and Bruce Russett. 1992. "Peace between Participatory Polities: A Cross-Cultural Test of the 'Democracies Rarely Fight Each Other' Hypothesis." *World Politics* 44 (4): 573–99.

Entman, Robert M. 1993. "Framing: Toward Clarification of a Fractured Paradigm." *Journal of Communication* 43 (4): 51–8.

Environics Institute. 2010. *Urban Aboriginal Peoples Study: Main Report*. Toronto: Environics Institute.

Esterberg, Kristin G. 2002. *Qualitative Methods in Social Research*. Boston: McGraw-Hill.

Fairclough, Norman. 2001. *Language and Power*. London: Longman.

Falk, Erika. 2010. *Women for President: Media Bias in Eight Campaigns*, 2nd edn. Urbana, IL: University of Illinois Press.

———. 2013. "Clinton and the Playing-the-Gender-Card Metaphor in Campaign News." *Feminist Media Studies* 13 (2): 192–207.

Feis, Herbert. 1961. *Japan Subdued: The Atomic Bomb and the End of the War in the Pacific*. Princeton, NJ: Princeton University Press.

Finch, Janet. 1984. "'It's Great to Have Someone to Talk To': The Ethics and Politics of Interviewing Women." In *Social Researching: Politics, Problems, Practice*, edited by Colin Bell and Helen Roberts, 70–87. London: Routledge & Kegan Paul.

Flanagan, Tom. 1995. *Waiting for the Wave: The Reform Party and Preston Manning*. Toronto: Stoddart.

Forum Research Inc. 2013. "Liberals on Track for Majority in Nova Scotia." News release, 7 October. http://www.forumresearch.com.

Fournier, Patrick, Fred Cutler, Stuart Soroka, Dietlind Stolle, and Eric Belanger. 2013. "Riding the Orange Wave: Leadership, Values, Issues and the 2011 Canadian Election." *Canadian Journal of Political Science* 46 (December): 863–98.

Fowler, James H. 2006. "Altruism and Turnout." *Journal of Politics* 68: 647–83.

Fox, Bonnie J. 1993. "On Violent Men and Female Victims: A Comment on DeKeseredy and Kelly." *Canadian Journal of Sociology* 18 (3): 321–4.

Franklin, Bob, ed. 2008. *Pulling Newspapers Apart: Analyzing Print Journalism*. London and New York: Routledge.

Fraser Institute. n.d. "Alberta." http://alberta.compareschoolrankings.org/high/SchoolsByRankLocationName.aspx (accessed 26 June 2014).

———. n.d. "School Performance: Rating Your Child's School." http://www.fraserinstitute.org/report-cards/school-performance/overview.aspx (accessed 26 June 2014).

Gaines, Brian J., James H. Kuklinski, and Paul J. Quirk. 2007. "The Logic of the Survey Experiment Reexamined." *Political Analysis* 15 (1): 1–20.

Gartner, Rosemary. 1993. "Studying Woman Abuse: A Comment on DeKeseredy and Kelly." *Canadian Journal of Sociology* 18 (3): 313–20.

George, Alexander L. 2006. "Quantitative and Qualitative Approaches to Content Analysis." In *Documentary Research*, vol. 1, edited by J. Scott. Thousand Oaks, CA: Sage.

———, and Andrew Bennett. 2005. *Case Studies and Theory Development in the Social Sciences*. Cambridge, MA, and London: MIT.

Gerber, Alan S., and Donald P. Green. 2000. "The Effects of Canvassing, Direct Mail, and Telephone Contact on Voter Turnout: A Field Experiment." *American Political Science Review* 94 (3): 653–63.

Gerber, Linda M. 2006. "Urban Diversity: Riding Composition and Party Support in the Canadian Federal Election of 2004." *Canadian Journal of Urban Research* 15 (2): 105–18.

Gerring, John. 1998. *Party Ideologies in America, 1828–1996*. Cambridge: Cambridge University Press.

———. 2004. "What is a Case Study and What Is It Good for?" *American Political Science Review* 98 (2): 341–54.

———. 2012. *Social Science Methodology: A Unified Framework*, 2nd edn. Cambridge: Cambridge University Press.

Gibbons, Jean Dickinson. 1976. *Nonparametric Methods for Quantitative Analysis*. New York: Holt, Rinehart and Winston.

Gill, Jeff. 1999. "The Insignificance of Null Hypothesis Significance Testing." *Political Research Quarterly* 52 (3): 647–74.

Gill, Rosalind. 2000. "Discourse Analysis." In *Qualitative Researching with Text,*

Image and Sound, edited by Martin W. Bauer and George Gaskell, 172–90. London: Sage.

Gitlin, Todd. 1980. *The Whole World is Watching: Mass Media in the Making and Unmaking of the New Left*. Berkeley, CA: University of California Press.

Goertz, Gary. 2006. *Social Science Concepts: A User's Guide*. Princeton, NJ, and Woodstock, UK: Princeton University Press.

Goldberg, Michael A., and Maurice D. Levi. 1994. "Growing Together or Apart: The Risks and Returns of Alternative Constitutions of Canada." *Canadian Public Policy* 20 (December): 341–52.

Gomez, Brad T., Thomas G. Hansford, and George A. Krause. 2007. "The Republicans Should Pray for Rain: Weather, Turnout, and Voting in US Presidential Elections." *Journal of Politics* 69 (3): 649–63.

Grant, Tavia. 2013. "Canadian Income Data 'Is Garbage' without Census, Experts Say." *The Globe and Mail*, 4 October. http://www.theglobeandmail.com/report-on-business/economy/without-census-data-on-canadian-income-garbage-experts/article14701515/#dashboard/follows/ (accessed 11 October 2013).

Green, Donald P. 2004. "Experimental Design." In *The Sage Encyclopedia of Social Science Research Methods*, edited by M. Lewis-Beck, A. E. Bryman, and T. F. Liao. Thousand Oaks, CA: Sage.

———, Alan S. Gerber, and David W. Nickerson. 2003. "Getting Out the Vote in Local Elections: Results from Six Door-to-Door Canvassing Experiments." *Journal of Politics* 65 (4): 1083–96.

Griffin, John Howard. 1977. *Black Like Me*, 2nd edn. Boston: Houghton Mifflin.

Guba, Egon G., and Yvonna S. Lincoln. 1985. *Naturalistic Inquiry*. Thousand Oaks, CA: Sage Publications.

———, and ———. 1994. "Competing Paradigms in Qualitative Research." In *Handbook of Qualitative Research*, edited by N. K. Denzin and Y. S. Lincoln, 105–17. Thousand Oaks, CA: Sage Publications.

Guérin, Daniel. 2003. "Aboriginal Participation in Canadian Federal Elections: Trends and Implications." *Electoral Insight*. www.elections.ca.

Gupta, Dipak K. 2001. *Analyzing Public Policy: Concepts, Tools, and Techniques*. Thousand Oaks, CA: CQ Press.

Hackett, Robert A., William O. Gilsdorf, and Philip Savage. 1992. "News Balance Rhetoric: The Fraser Institute's Political Appropriation of Content Analysis." *Canadian Journal of Communication* 17 (1). (Online version accessed 8 December 2009).

Hairston, Thomas W. 2013. "Continuing Inequity through Neoliberalism: The Conveyance of White Dominance in the Educational Policy Speeches of President Barack Obama." *Interchange: A Quarterly Review of Education* 43 (3): 229–44.

Halperin, Sandra, and Oliver Heath. 2012. *Political Research: Methods and Practical Skills*. Oxford: Oxford University Press.

Hartz, Louis. 1964. *The Founding of New Societies: Studies in the History of the U.S., Latin America, South Africa, Canada and Australia*. New York: Harcourt, Brace, and World.

Hayslett, H. T., Jr. 1968. *Statistics Made Simple*. New York: Doubleday.

Healy, Andrew J., Neil Malhotra, and Cecilia Hyunjung Mo. 2010. "Irrelevant Events Affect Voters' Evaluations of Government Performance." *Proceedings of the National Academy of Sciences* 107 (29): 12804–9.

Henrich, Joseph, Steven J. Heine, and Ara Norenzayan. 2010. "The Weirdest People in the World." *Behavioral and Brain Sciences* 33 (2–3): 61–83.

Hesse-Biber, Sharlene Nagy, and Patricia Leavy. 2006. *The Practice of Qualitative Research*. Thousand Oaks, CA: Sage.

Hibberts, Mary, R. Burke Johnson, and Kenneth Hudson. 2012. "Common Survey Sampling

Techniques." In *Handbook of Survey Methodology for the Social Sciences*, edited by L. Gideon, 53–74. New York: Springer.

Hite, Shere. 1976. *The Hite Report: A Nationwide Study of Female Sexuality*. New York: Macmillan.

———. 1981. *The Hite Report on Male Sexuality*. New York: Ballantine Books.

Hodder, Ian. 1994. "The Interpretation of Documents and Material Culture." In *Handbook of Qualitative Research*, edited by N. K. Denzin and Y. S. Lincoln, 393–402. Thousand Oaks, CA: Sage.

Holland, Paul W. 1986. "Statistics and Causal Inference." *Journal of the American Statistical Association* 81 (396): 945–60.

Holliday, Adrian. 2007. *Doing and Writing Qualitative Research*, 2nd edn. Thousand Oaks, CA: Sage.

Horowitz, Gad. 1966. "Conservatism, Liberalism and Socialism in Canada: An Interpretation." *Canadian Journal of Political Science and Economics* 32 (June): 143–71.

Imai, Kosuke, Luke Keele, Dustin Tingley, and Teppei Yamamoto. 2011. "Unpacking the Black Box of Causality: Learning about Causal Mechanisms from Experimental and Observational Studies." *American Political Science Review* 105 (4): 765–89.

Inglehart, Ronald. 1977. *The Silent Revolution: Changing Values and Political Styles among Western Publics*. Princeton, NJ: Princeton University Press.

Iyengar, Shanto. 1996. "Framing Responsibility for Political Issues." *Annals of the American Academy of Political and Social Science* 546 (July): 59–70.

———. 2002. "Experimental Designs for Political Communication Research: From Shopping Malls to the Internet." Paper read at Workshop in Mass Media Economics, Department of Political Science, London School of Economics.

———, and Donald R. Kinder. 1989. *News That Matters: Television and American Opinion*. Chicago: University of Chicago Press.

Jäger, Sigfried. 2001. "Discourse and Knowledge: Theoretical and Methodological Aspects of a Critical Discourse and Dispositive Analysis." In *Methods of Critical Discourse Analysis*, edited by Ruth Wodak and Michael Meyer, 32–62. London: Sage.

Jenson, Jane. 1975. "Party Loyalty in Canada: The Question of Party Identification." *Canadian Journal of Political Science* 8 (December): 543–53.

———. 1978. "Comment: The Filling of Wine Bottles Is Not Easy." *Canadian Journal of Political Science* 11 (June): 437–8.

Johnson-Cartee, Karen S. 2005. *News Narratives and News Framing*. Lanham, MD: Rowman & Littlefield.

Johnston, Richard, André Blais, Henry E. Brady, and Jean Crete. 1992. *Letting the People Decide: Dynamics of a Canadian Election*. Montreal: McGill-Queen's University Press.

Jones, Susan R., and Marylu K. McEwen. 2002. "A Conceptual Model of Multiple Dimensions of Identity." In *Qualitative Research in Practice*, edited by S. B. Merriam, 163–74. San Francisco: Jossey-Bass.

Kelly, Katherine D. 1994. "The Politics of Data." *Canadian Journal of Sociology* 19 (1): 81–5.

Kern, Thomas, and Sang-Hui Nam. 2013. "From 'Corruption' to 'Democracy': Cultural Values, Mobilization, and the Collective Identity of the Occupy Movement." *Journal of Civil Society* 9 (2): 196–211.

Key, V. O. 1966. *The Responsible Electorate*. Cambridge, MA: Harvard University Press.

King, Gary, Robert Keohane, and Sidney Verba. 1993. *Designing Social Inquiry: Scientific Inference in Qualitative Research*. Princeton, NJ: Princeton University Press.

———, ———, and ———. 1994. *Designing Social Inquiry: Scientific Inference in Qualitative Research*. Princeton, NJ, and Chichester, UK: Princeton University Press.

Kinnear, Michael. 2003. "The Effect of Expansion of the Franchise on Turnout." *Electoral Insight*. www.elections.ca.

Krippendorff, Klaus. 2004. *Content Analysis: An Introduction to Its Methodology*, 2nd edn. Thousand Oaks, CA: Sage.

Kuhn, Thomas. 1962. *The Structure of Scientific Revolutions*. Chicago: University of Chicago.

———. 1970. *The Structure of Scientific Revolutions*, 2nd edn, rev. Chicago: University of Chicago Press.

Lachapelle, Erick, Éric Montpetit, and Jean-Philippe Gauvin. Forthcoming. "Public Perceptions of Expert Credibility on Policy Issues: The Role of Expert Framing and Political Worldviews." *Policy Studies Journal*.

Lane, Robert E. 1962. *Political Ideology: Why the American Common Man Believes What He Does*. New York: The Free Press.

Lather, Patti. 1988. "Feminist Perspectives on Empowering Research Methodologies." *Women's Studies International Forum* 11: 569–81.

Laver, Michael. 2001. "Why Should We Estimate the Policy Position of Political Actors?" In *Estimating the Policy Positions of Political Actors*, edited by M. Laver, 3–9. London: Routledge.

Lazerwitz, Bernard. 1968. "Sampling Theory and Procedures." In *Methodology in Social Research*, edited by Hubert M. Blalock, Jr., and Ann B. Blalock, 278–328. New York: McGraw-Hill.

LeDuc, Lawrence, Harold Clarke, Jane Jenson, and Jon Pammett. 1984. "Partisan Instability in Canada: Evidence from a New Panel Study." *American Political Science Review* 78: 470–83.

Lee, Raymond M. 1993. *Doing Research on Sensitive Topics*. London: Sage Publications.

———, and Claire M. Renzetti. 1990. "The Problems of Researching Sensitive Topics." *American Behavioral Scientist* 1 (May–June): 510–28.

Levy, Jack S. 2008. "Case Studies: Types, Designs, and Logics of Inference." *Conflict Management and Peace Science* 25 (1): 1–18.

Lewis, Jane, and Jane Ritchie. 2006. "Generalising from Qualitative Research." In *Qualitative Research Practice: A Guide for Social Science Students and Researchers*, edited by J. Ritchie and J. Lewis, 263–86. Thousand Oaks, CA: Sage.

Lipset, Seymour Martin. 1990. *Continental Divide: The Values and Institutions of the United States and Canada*. New York: Routledge.

Loewen, Peter John, Royce Koop, Jaime Settle, and James H Fowler. 2014. "A Natural Experiment in Proposal Power and Electoral Success." *American Journal of Political Science* 58 (1): 189–96.

Lublin, David, and D. Stephen Voss. 2002. "Context and Francophone Support for the Sovereignty of Québec: An Ecological Analysis." *Canadian Journal of Political Science* 35 (March): 75–101.

Luntz, Frank. 1994. "Focus Group Research in American Politics." *The Polling Report*. http://www.pollingreport.com/focus.htm (accessed 7 January 2010).

Lupia, Arthur. 1994. "Shortcuts versus Encyclopedias: Information and Voting Behavior in California Insurance Reform Elections." *American Political Science Review* 88: 63–76.

McDermott, Rose. 2002a. "Experimental Methodology in Political Science." *Political Analysis* 10 (4): 325–42.

———. 2002b. "Experimental Methods in Political Science." *Annual Review of Political Science* 5 (1): 31–61.

Manheim, Jarol B., and Richard C. Rich. 1981. *Empirical Political Analysis: Research Methods in Political Science*. Englewood Cliffs, NJ: Prentice-Hall.

———, ———, and Lars Willnat. 2002. *Empirical Political Analysis: Research Methods in Political Science*, 5th edn. Toronto: Longman.

———, ———, ———, and Craig Leonard Brians. 2008. *Empirical Political Analysis: Quantitative and Qualitative Research Methods*, 7th edn. New York: Pearson Education.

Marshall, Catherine, and Gretchen B. Rossman. 1989. *Designing Qualitative Research*. Thousand Oaks, CA: Sage.

——— and ———. 2006. *Designing Qualitative Research*, 4th edn. Thousand Oaks, CA: Sage.

Merriam, Sharan B. 2002a. "Assessing and Evaluating Qualitative Research." In *Qualitative Research in Practice*, edited by S. B. Merriam, 18–36. San Francisco: Jossey-Bass.

———. 2002b. "Introduction to Qualitative Research." In *Qualitative Research in Practice*, edited by S. B. Merriam, 3–17. San Francisco: Jossey-Bass.

Michels, Robert. 1962. *Political Parties: A Sociological Study of the Oligarchical Tendencies of Modern Democracy*. New York: The Free Press.

Milbrath, Lester. 1965. *Political Participation*. New York: Rand McNally.

Milgram, Stanley. 1963. "Behavioral Study of Obedience." *Journal of Abnormal and Social Psychology* 67: 371–8.

———. 1974. *Obedience to Authority: An Experimental View*. London: Tavistock.

Montpetit, Éric, André Blais, and Martial Foucault. 2008. "What Does it Take for a Canadian Political Scientist to be Cited?" *Social Science Quarterly* 89 (3): 802–16.

Monroe, Kristen Renwick, ed. 2005. *Perestroika!: The Raucous Rebellion in Political Science*. Princeton, NJ: Yale University Press.

Morin-Chassé, Alexandre. 2010. "Response Order Effects in Dichotomous Voting Intention Questions: Evidence from the 2008 US Presidential Election." MA thesis, Political Science, Université Laval.

Morse, Janice M., and Lyn Richards. 2002. *Read Me First for a User's Guide to Qualitative Methods*. Thousand Oaks, CA: Sage.

Morton, Rebecca B., and Kenneth C. Williams. 2010. *Experimental Political Science and the Study of Causality: From Nature to the Lab*. Cambridge: Cambridge University Press.

Mutz, Diana C. 2011. *Population-Based Survey Experiments*. Princeton, NJ: Princeton University Press.

———, and Robin Pemantle. n.d. "The Perils of Randomization Checks in the Analysis of Experiments." Unpublished manuscript.

Nachmias, David, and Chaua Nachmias. 1987. *Research Methods in the Social Sciences*, 3rd edn. New York: St. Martin's Press.

Nelson, Thomas E., Rosalee A. Clawson, and Zoe M. Oxley. 1997. "Media Framing of a Civil Liberties Conflict and Its Effect on Tolerance." *American Political Science Review*: 567–83.

Neuendorf, Kimberly A. 2002. *The Content Analysis Guidebook*. Thousand Oaks, CA: Sage.

Neuman, W. Lawrence. 1994. *Social Research Methods: Qualitative and Quantitative Approaches*, 2nd edn. Boston: Allyn & Bacon.

———, and Karen Robson. 2007. *Basics of Social Research: Qualitative and Quantitative Approaches*, Canadian edn. Toronto: Pearson Education.

———, and ———. 2009. *Basics of Social Research: Qualitative and Quantitative Approaches*, 2nd Canadian edn. Toronto: Pearson.

Nevitte, Neil, and Roger Gibbins. 1990. *New Elites in Old States: Ideologies in the Anglo-American Democracies*. Toronto: Oxford University Press.

Nie, Norman, Sidney Verba, and John Petrocik. 1976. *The Changing American Voter*. Cambridge, MA: Harvard University Press.

Nock, Steven L., and Thomas M. Guterbock. 2010. "Survey Experiments." In *Handbook of Survey Research*, edited by P. V. Marsden and J. D. Wright, 837–64. Bingley, UK: Emerald Group.

Norusis, Marija J. 1990. *SPSS Introductory Statistics Student Guide*. Chicago: SPSS Inc.

Ollivier, Michele, and Manon Tremblay. 2000. *Questionnements feministes et methodologie de la recherché*. Montreal and Paris: L'Harmattan.

Onwuegbuzie, Anthony J., Wendy B. Dickinson, Nancy L. Leech, and Annmarie G. Zoran. 2009. "A Qualitative Framework for Collecting and Analyzing Data in Focus Group Research." *International Journal of Qualitative Methods* 8 (3): 1–21.

Oren, Michael B. 1992. "Faith and Fair-Mindedness: Lester B. Pearson and the Suez-Crisis." *Diplomacy and Statecraft* 3 (1): 48–73.

Palfrey, Thomas R. 1991. *Laboratory Research in Political Economy*. Ann Arbor: University of Michigan Press.

Palys, Ted. 2008. "Purposive Sampling." In *The Sage Encyclopedia of Qualitative Research Methods*, edited by Lisa M. Givens, 697–8. Thousand Oaks, CA: Sage.

Patton, Carl V., and David S. Sawicki. 1993. *Basic Methods of Policy Analysis and Planning*, 2nd edn. Englewood Cliffs, NJ: Prentice-Hall.

Pedhazur, Elazar J. 1982. *Multiple Regression in Behavioural Research*, 2nd edn. Orlando: Harcourt Brace.

Pickup, Mark, and Richard Johnston. 2008. "Campaign Trial Heats as Election Forecasts: Measurement Error and Bias in 2004 Presidential Campaign Polls." *International Journal of Forecasting* 24: 270–82.

Pierce, Roger. 2008. *Research Methods in Politics*. London: Sage.

Pitsula, James M. 2001. "First Nations and Saskatchewan Politics." In *Saskatchewan Politics: Into the Twenty-First Century*, edited by Howard A. Leeson, 349–66. Regina: Canadian Plains Research Centre.

Platt, Jennifer. 2006. "Evidence and Proof in Documentary Research: Part II, Some Shared Problems of Documentary Research." In *Documentary Research*, vol. 1, edited by J. Scott. Thousand Oaks, CA: Sage.

Press, Daryl G., Scott D. Sagan, and Benjamin A. Valentino. 2013. "Atomic Aversion: Experimental Evidence on Taboos, Traditions, and the Non-Use of Nuclear Weapons." *American Political Science Review* 107 (1): 188–206.

Punch, Keith F. 2005. *Introduction to Social Research: Quantitative and Qualitative Approaches*, 2nd edn. Thousand Oaks, CA: Sage.

Putnam, Robert. 1993. *Making Democracy Work: Civic Traditions in Modern Italy*. Princeton, NJ: Princeton University Press.

Putt, Allen D., and J. Fred Springer. 1989. *Policy Research: Concepts, Methods, and Applications*. Englewood Cliffs, NJ: Prentice-Hall.

Ragin, Charles C. 1994. *Constructing Social Research: The Unity and Diversity of Method*. Thousand Oaks, CA, and London: Pine Forge.

Reid, Angus. 2013. "What Went Wrong with the Polls in British Columbia?" *Maclean's*, 8 July. http://www2.macleans.ca/2013/07/08/angus-reid-what-went-wrong-with-the-polls-in-british-columbia/ (accessed 3 December 2013).

Reinharz, Shulamit. 1992. *Feminist Methods in Social Research*. New York: Oxford University Press.

Remler, Dahlia K., and Gregg Gerard Van Ryzin. 2011. *Research Methods in Practice: Strategies for Description and Causation*. Thousand Oaks, CA: Sage.

Richards, Lyn. 2005. *Handling Qualitative Data: A Practical Guide*. Thousand Oaks, CA: Sage.

Richerson, Peter J., and Robert Boyd. 2004. *The Origin and Evolution of Cultures*. London: Oxford University Press.

Riffe, Daniel, Stephen Lacy, and Frederick G. Fico. 2005. *Analyzing Media Messages: Using Content Analysis in Research*. Mahwah, NJ: Lawrence Erlbaum Associates.

Ritchie, Jane, Jane Lewis, and Gillian Elam. 2003. "Designing and Selecting Samples." In *Qualitative Research Practice: A Guide for Social Science Students and Researchers*, edited by Jane Ritchie and Jane Lewis, 77–108. London: Sage.

Roberts, Chris. 2013. "A Functional Analysis Comparison of Web-Only Advertisements and Traditional Television Advertisements from the 2004 and 2008 Presidential Campaigns." *Journalism & Mass Communication Quarterly* 90 (1): 23–38.

Rothenberg, Stuart. 2007. "For the Thousandth Time: Don't Call Them 'Push Polls.'" *Roll Call* (8 March). http://www.rollcall.com/issues/52_90/-17368-1.html (accessed 16 December 2013).

Ryan, Gery W., and H. Russell Bernard. 2003. "Data Management and Analysis Methods." In *Collecting and Interpreting Qualitative Materials*, 2nd edn, edited by N. K. Denzin and Y. S. Lincoln, 259–309. Thousand Oaks, CA: Sage.

Sampert, Shannon, and Linda Trimble. 2010. "Putting It into Practice: A Primer on Content and Discourse Analysis." In *Mediating Canadian Politics*, edited by Shannon Sampert and Linda Trimble, 326–37. Toronto: Pearson Education.

———, ———, Angelia Wagner, and Bailey Gerrits. 2014. "Jumping the Shark: Mediatization of Canadian Party Leadership Contests, 1975–2012." *Journalism Studies* (forthcoming).

Scheufele, Dietram A. 1999. "Framing as a Theory of Media Effects." *Journal of Communication* 49 (1): 103–22.

Schuman, Howard, and Stanley Presser. 1981. *Questions and Answers in Attitude Surveys: Experiments on Question Form, Wording, and Context*. Thousand Oaks, CA: Sage.

Scientific American. 2007. "The Genetics of Politics." http://www.scientificamerican.com/article/the-genetics-of-politics/ (accessed 12 January 2009).

Sekhon, Jasjeet S., and Rocio Titiunik. 2012. "When Natural Experiments are Neither Natural nor Experiments." *American Political Science Review* 106 (1): 35–57.

Shea, Christopher. 1996. "Psychologists Debate Accuracy of 'Significance Test.'" *The Chronicle of Higher Education*, 16 August, A12, A17.

Shipman, Matt. 2013. "The Challenge of Negative Results." *SciLogs* (28 May). http://www.scilogs.com/communication_breakdown/negative-results/.

Sieber, J. E., and B. Stanley. 1988. "Ethical and Professional Dimensions of Socially Sensitive Research." *American Psychologist* 43: 49–55.

Sigelman, Lee. 2006. "The Coevolution of American Political Science and the American Political Science Review." *American Political Science Review* 100 (4): 463–78.

Simon, Julian. 1995. "Earth's Doomsayers Are Wrong." *The Next City* 1 (2): 10–11.

Singleton, Royce, Jr., Bruce C. Straits, Margaret M. Straits, and Ronald J. McAllister. 1988. *Approaches to Social Research*. New York: Oxford University Press.

Skocpol, Theda. 1979. *States and Social Revolutions: A Comparative Analysis of France, Russia, and China*. Cambridge: Cambridge University Press.

Small, Tamara. 2012. "E-tack Politics: Negativity, the Internet, and Canadian Political Parties." In *How Canadians Communicate IV*, edited by David Taras and Christopher Waddell, 169–88. Edmonton: Athabasca University Press.

Smithson, Janet. 2000. "Using and Analyzing Focus Groups: Limitations and Possibilities." *International Journal of Social Research Methodology* 3 (2): 103–19.

Soroka, Stuart, and Blake Andrew. 2010. "Media Coverage of Canadian Elections: Horse-Race Coverage and Negativity in Election Campaigns." In *Mediating Canadian Politics*, edited by Shannon Sampert and Linda Trimble, 113–28. Toronto: Pearson Education.

Stake, Robert E. 1995. *The Art of Case Study Research: Perspectives on Practice*. Thousand Oaks, CA, and London: Sage.

Statistics Canada. 1989. *The Labour Force* 71-001 (December).

———. 2009a. *Data Liberation Initiative: DLI Survival Guide*. Section 4: Data. www.statcan.gc.ca/dli-ild/guide-trousse/guide-trousse/toc-tdm/3000276-eng.htm (accessed 5 January 2010).

———. 2009b. *Overview of the Census: A Brief History*. www12.statcan.ca/census-recensement/2006/ref/dict/overview-apercu/pop1-eng.cfm (accessed 5 January 2010).

———. 2009c. *2006 Census Reference Materials, Aboriginal Peoples Technical Report, Concepts and Variables*. www12.statcan.ca/census-recensement/2006/ref/rp- guides/rp/ap-pa/p1-eng.cfm (accessed 5 January 2010).

———. 2013a. *Median After-Tax Income, Families of Two Persons or More, Provinces and Targeted Census Metropolitan Areas, 2010*. http://www.statcan.gc.ca/pub/75-202-x/2010000/c-g/ct002-eng.htm.

———. 2013b. *Statistics: Power From Data!* Ottawa: Statistics Canada. http://www.statcan.gc.ca/edu/power-pouvoir/toc-tdm/5214718-eng.htm (accessed 7 October 2013).

———. 2014a. *Aboriginal Peoples in Canada: First Nations People, Métis and Inuit*. http://www12.statcan.gc.ca/nhs-enm/2011/as-sa/99-011-x/99-011-x2011001-eng.cfm.

———. 2014b. *Aboriginal Peoples Technical Report: National Household Survey 2011*. Ottawa: Statistics Canada. http://www12.statcan.gc.ca/

nhs-enm/2011/ref/reports-rapports/ap-pa/99-011-x2011002-eng.pdf.

Steinem, Gloria. 1983. *Outrageous Acts and Everyday Rebellions*. New York: Holt, Rinehart and Winston.

Stoop, Ineke. 2012. "Unit Non-Response Due to Refusal." In *Handbook of Survey Methodology for the Social Sciences*, edited by L. Gideon, 121–48. New York: Springer.

Strauss, Anselm, and Juliet Corbin. 1994. "Grounded Theory Methodology: An Overview." In *Handbook of Qualitative Research*, edited by N. K. Denzin and Y. S. Lincoln, 273–85. Thousand Oaks, CA: Sage.

St-Vincent, Simon Labbé. 2013. "An Experimental Test of the Pivotal Voter Model under Plurality and PR Elections." *Electoral Studies* 32 (4), 795–806.

Sumser, John. 2001. *A Guide to Empirical Research in Communication: Rules for Looking*. Thousand Oaks, CA: Sage.

Suri, Jeremi. 2002. "Explaining the End of the Cold War: A New Historical Consensus?" *Journal of Cold War Studies* 4 (4): 60–92.

Taras, David. 2012. "The Past and Future of Political Communication in Canada." In *How Canadians Communicate IV*, edited by David Taras and Christopher Waddell, 1–25. Edmonton: Athabasca University Press.

Tashakkori, Abbas, and Charles Teddlie, eds. 2003. *Handbook of Mixed Methods in Social and Behavioural Research*. Thousand Oaks, CA: Sage.

Thomas, Gary. 2011. "A Typology for the Case Study in Social Science Following a Review of Definition, Discourse, and Structure" *Qualitative Inquiry* 17 (6): 511–21.

Tingley, Dustin H., and Barbara F. Walter. 2011. "The Effect of Repeated Play on Reputation Building: An Experimental Approach." *International Organization* 65 (2): 343–65.

Trimble, Linda. 1997. "Feminist Politics in the Alberta Legislature, 1972–1994." In *In the Presence of Women: Representation in Canadian Governments*, edited by Jane Arscott and Linda Trimble, 128–53. Toronto: Harcourt.

———, and Shannon Sampert. 2004. "Who's in the Game? Framing of the Canadian Election 2000 by the *Globe and Mail* and the *National Post*." *Canadian Journal of Political Science* 37 (March): 51–71.

———, Laura Way, and Shannon Sampert. 2010. "Drawn to the Polls? Representations of Canadian Voters in Editorial Cartoons." *Journal of Canadian Studies* 44 (2): 70–94.

Turcotte, André. 2007. "'What Do You Mean I Can't Have a Say?' Young Canadians and Their Government: Charting the Course for Youth Civic and Political Participation." Ottawa: Canadian Policy Research Networks.

Tversky, Amos, and Daniel Kahneman. 1974. "Judgment under Uncertainty: Heuristics and Biases." *Science* 185 (4157): 1124–31.

van Dijk, Teun A. 1991. *Racism and the Press*. London: Routledge.

———. 2008. *Discourse and Power*. Hampshire and New York: Palgrave Macmillan.

Vehovar, Vasja, Ana Slavec, and Nejc Berzelak. 2012. "Costs and Errors in Fixed and Mobile Phone Surveys." In *Handbook of Survey Methodology for the Social Sciences*, edited by L. Gideon, 277–95. New York: Springer.

Verba, Sidney, and Norman Nie. 1972. *Participation in America: Political Democracy and Social Equality*. New York: Harper & Row.

Wesley, Jared J. 2011. *Code Politics: Campaigns and Cultures on the Canadian Prairies*. Vancouver: University of British Columbia Press.

Wetstein, Matthew E., and C. L. Ostberg. 2003. "Strategic Leadership and Political Change on the Canadian Supreme Court: Analyzing the Transition to Chief Justice." *Canadian Journal of Political Science* 38 (September): 653–73.

White, Louise G. 1994. *Political Analysis*, 3rd edn. Belmont, CA: Wadsworth.

Woliver, Laura R. 2002. "Ethical Dilemmas in Personal Interviewing." *PS: Political Science & Politics* 35 (4): 677–8.

Wright, R. L. D. 1976. *Understanding Statistics*. New York: Harcourt Brace Jovanovich.

Yin, Robert K. 2012. *Applications of Case Study Research*, 3rd edn. London: Sage.

Index